ON THE WINGS OF WAR AND PEACE

ON THE WINGS OF WAR AND PEACE

THE RCAF DURING THE EARLY COLD WAR

EDITED BY RANDALL WAKELAM, WILLIAM MARCH, AND PETER RAYLS

UNIVERSITY OF TORONTO PRESS
Toronto Buffalo London

© University of Toronto Press 2023
Toronto Buffalo London
utorontopress.com

ISBN 978-1-4875-2675-7 (cloth)   ISBN 978-1-4875-2678-8 (EPUB)
ISBN 978-1-4875-2676-4 (paper)   ISBN 978-1-4875-2677-1 (PDF)

Library and Archives Canada Cataloguing in Publication

Title: On the wings of war and peace : the RCAF during the early Cold War / edited by Randall Wakelam, William March, and Peter Rayls.
Names: Wakelam, Randall T. (Randall Thomas), 1953– editor. | March, William, editor. | Rayls, Peter, editor.
Description: Includes bibliographical references and index.
Identifiers: Canadiana (print) 20230487459 | Canadiana (ebook) 20230487548 | ISBN 9781487526757 (cloth) | ISBN 9781487526764 (paper) | ISBN 9781487526771 (PDF) | ISBN 9781487526788 (EPUB)
Subjects: LCSH: Canada. Royal Canadian Air Force — History – 20th century. | LCSH: Aeronautics, Military – Canada – History – 20th century. | LCSH: Cold War.
Classification: LCC UG635.C2 O27 2023 | DDC 358.40097109/045–dc23

Cover design: Liz Harasymczuk
Cover images: Photo of three jet aircraft courtesy of the Department of National Defence Canada; RCAF roundel, 1946–1965, courtesy of WikiCommons

Unless otherwise indicated, all images appear courtesy of the Department of National Defence Canada.

We wish to acknowledge the land on which the University of Toronto Press operates. This land is the traditional territory of the Wendat, the Anishnaabeg, the Haudenosaunee, the Métis, and the Mississaugas of the Credit First Nation.

University of Toronto Press acknowledges the financial support of the Government of Canada, the Canada Council for the Arts, and the Ontario Arts Council, an agency of the Government of Ontario, for its publishing activities.

 Canada Council for the Arts / Conseil des Arts du Canada

 ONTARIO ARTS COUNCIL / CONSEIL DES ARTS DE L'ONTARIO
an Ontario government agency
un organisme du gouvernement de l'Ontario

 Funded by the Government of Canada / Financé par le gouvernement du Canada

CONTENTS

Foreword   ix
    GEN (RETD) PAUL MANSON

Preface   xiii

Glossary   xvii

Introduction   1
    RANDALL WAKELAM

Section 1 Introduction   5
    PETER RAYLS

1 The Expansion and Contraction of Canada's First Line of Defence: The RCAF in the Cold War, 1945–1968   9
    BERTRAM FRANDSEN AND PETER RAYLS

2 No. 1 Air Division, Royal Canadian Air Force   38
    RAYMOND STOUFFER

3 The RCAF, USAF, and Continental Air Defence, 1945–1957   60
    RICHARD GOETTE

4 NORAD Peaks, 1957–1964   82
    JOSEPH T. JOCKEL

Section 2 Introduction   103
    RANDALL WAKELAM

5 Hubris: The CF-105 Avro Arrow Program and the End of the Golden Age of the Royal Canadian Air Force   107
    RUSSELL ISINGER AND DONALD C. STORY

6 Educating Air Power Practitioners   128
    RANDALL WAKELAM

7 Training the Flyers: The Legacy of Canada's International Air Training Schemes and the NATO Air Training Plan   152
    RACHEL LEA HEIDE

8 RCAF Air Maintenance   181
    TERRY LEVERSEDGE

9 The Forgotten Decade: Women and the RCAF, 1952–1962   205
    ALLAN ENGLISH

10 The Air Reserves: A Functional Second Line of Defence?   228
    MATHIAS JOOST

Section 3 Introduction   251
    WILLIAM MARCH

11 The RCAF at the Dawn of the Space Age, 1958–1965   255
    ANDREW GODEFROY

12 The Search for Rescue Leadership   278
    JAMES PIEROTTI

13 On Wings of Hope and Peace: The RCAF and Humanitarian and Peacekeeping Operations, 1946–1967   299
    WILLIAM MARCH

14 Maritime Air   325
    ERNEST CABLE

15 From Army Co-operation to Army Co-optation: Canada's Struggles with Aviation Support to the Land Forces   349
    DEAN BLACK

16 Air Transport Command: Versatile and Ready in Cold War and Hot War   371
   BERTRAM FRANDSEN

Annex A: Budget, Personnel, and Organization   393

Annex B: Chiefs of the Air Staff   411

Notes on Contributors   427

Index   431

FOREWORD

History is the story of change in human society. Given the dynamic nature of warfare since the earliest days, military history is a prominent part of the story with its endless accounts of this all-too-often disastrous aspect of civilization. Its telling has value that goes beyond academic achievement and entertainment, and this has never been truer than today, when the destructive consequences of modern war demand avoidance of armed conflict. In this, past experience and lessons need to be studied and applied.

On the Wings of War and Peace is a modest but important part of the process, presenting the history of the Royal Canadian Air Force from 1945 to the mid-1960s. The broader history of the RCAF falls into a series of distinct eras, ranging from the First World War, the interwar years, the Second World War, the early Cold War period, unification of the Canadian Forces and its immediate consequences, and the gradual recovery of the RCAF from unification's impact from 1975 through to the present. Much has been written about each of these phases; in particular, there exists a massive body of excellent writings about the early Cold War period that is the subject of this volume. These accounts, however, focus mainly on the day-to-day activities and personal experiences of the RCAF during those years; there is a shortage of higher-level coverage telling the story from what might be called the strategic level. This book is a significant step in that direction.

When we consider this period of RCAF history, we are right to think of it as the Service's halcyon years, as it signifies a time that was both a happy and rewarding era for the RCAF. In the wake of its magnificent performance in the Second World War across a broad range of operations, Canada's air force emerged from that conflict well prepared for the move into a very different strategic environment, marked by the rapid evolution of the Soviet Union as an existential threat to Canada and its allies. That the RCAF conducted itself so well throughout the immediate postwar era was a source of great pride and satisfaction to those who wore the light blue and who provided essential support through to the advent of unification.

Unfortunately, however, this superb achievement was not fully known or understood by the Canadian public, for reasons that are to some extent understandable. As eminent Canadian historian Tim Cook pointed out in his recent book *The Fight for History*, Canadians were burdened by a heavy war fatigue into the 1950s, shared in large measure by the returning veterans themselves, who wanted to get on with their interrupted personal lives. Meanwhile, Canada's postwar military posture was directed primarily towards Europe where, as an active participant in NATO's response to the expanding Soviet threat on that continent, our forces were geographically removed from the detailed media coverage back home that became the norm in later years. RCAF flying fatalities in NATO Europe, of which there were many in the fifties and sixties, received scant media coverage.

Back in North America meanwhile, military activity during those years was likewise not in the forefront of Canadians' minds, even though there was a substantial amount going on, in the form of flying training, air defence, air transport, peacekeeping, search and rescue, air reserves, maritime surveillance, humanitarian efforts, army tactical support, and other operations. And backing all of this were the usually unheralded but vital support services.

These factors, and much more, contributed to the shortage of a comprehensive, overall historical narrative of the RCAF's 1945–68 halcyon years. The authors of this book have filled the void in expert and compelling style.

Allow me to introduce their detailed chapters with some personal thoughts, influenced by my own experience over the entire era that is the subject of this book, including four periods of air force duty in NATO Europe and numerous postings in Canada.

First and foremost, I have always seen RCAF history as being dominantly a story of two vital elements – namely, people and aircraft. The abiding influence of both is eloquently shown in the authors' accounts to be the foundation of the service's success throughout the postwar era.

In the 1950s and 1960s it was the superb quality and performance of the RCAF's serving men and women, whether as leaders, aircrew, maintainers, staff, or support personnel, that brought great honour to Canada through our Air Division in Europe, in NORAD operations, by our magnificent aerobatic teams, and indeed in all RCAF activities. In this, I would be remiss not to mention – in the same context – the equally impressive accomplishments of those who served in Army and Naval aviation; they are very much part of the greater story.

One vital component of the RCAF's success was the inheritance of the outstanding training system that was developed in Canada in the course of the Second World War, primarily in the form of the British Commonwealth Air Training Plan. When I underwent pilot training in the early fifties almost all my instructors had wartime ribbons, as did all senior officers. As a measure of Canada's world class leadership in air training skills, numerous flight cadets from allied European air forces came to Canada in those days to undergo flying training. One consequence was the high regard in which the RCAF's Air Division was held as we worked with our NATO allies in Europe later on.

Concerning the airplanes that are so central to the history of the postwar era, here is one aspect that was of critical importance: the emergence of the turbine engine. By the 1950s jet engines and turboprops were in common use. Of necessity, this introduced great changes in the RCAF's equipment, strategy, tactics, and doctrine as it girded itself for a very different operational world. It was an exciting time, and the many challenges were met in remarkable ways. Our F-86 Sabres were said to dominate the skies of Western Europe, as evidenced by the winning of numerous competitive awards in NATO competitions. In the sixties Canadian CF-104 Starfighters contributed significantly to NATO's deterrent posture with their nuclear strike and photo reconnaissance capabilities. (It is worth noting that in 1969 Canada's two CF-104 reconnaissance squadrons came first and second in NATO's Royal Flush recce competition.)

The jet engine also brought the Canadian military into the changing world of air transport, notably with the introduction of the Comet in the 1950s and the Boeing 707 a decade later, the latter replacing the venerable Yukon and North Star aircraft as the workhorses of Air Transport Command. Smaller turboprop transports like the Dash-7 gave yeoman service and a sense of pride as these Canadian-designed and -built aircraft found a worldwide market.

Another wartime invention that became common in almost all military operations during the early postwar years was radar, especially in its application to aviation.

Meanwhile, an entirely new field of technology entered the scene: space. The shock wave created in the West by Soviet Russia's Sputnik and Gagarin events raised vital questions about military applications of the new technology in what quickly became a fourth domain of warfare, and the RCAF was compelled to pursue these challenges. The combination of nuclear weapons and space systems introduced a whole new strategic dimension to warfare. Deterrence was the only rational response, and the RCAF played an important part in it.

Another emerging technology that was eventually to have profound importance was the application of computers to defence. My own early experience in the fifties was with primitive airborne analogue devices, but by the sixties the RCAF was employing digital technology – still very basic, but it was a good beginning. The Starfighter, for example, had an impressive second-generation inertial navigation system. These were merely first steps, but they led to the enormously improved computer-based systems that were common in later years.

So much more could be said about the influences that contributed to the RCAF's working environment in the era covered by this book, but it is the detail, so well presented by the authors of the following chapters, that bring out the depth of this marvellous story in a fascinating and eminently readable way.

As you examine the achievements of outstanding people and the performance of great aircraft during the RCAF's halcyon years, you will be treated to an account of that time in its full magnificent scope. In a style that is analytic and comprehensive, yet not boringly academic, the story told on these pages will allow you to come away with a greater appreciation for a part of Canada's military history that needed a better telling.

General (retd) Paul Manson (1934–2023)

PREFACE

Between 1980 and 1993 the Directorate of History of the Department of National Defence published three volumes of official history that examined the record of Canadian air services and aviators between 1914 and 1945. By comparison to the official histories of other major air forces, these volumes were prepared long after the events they described, but happily aviation scholars generally agreed that this lateness allowed the authors an opportunity to deal with issues that had become relevant and to tap sources that might not otherwise have been available.

Coming out in relatively quick succession, the volumes created a swell of interest among a disparate group who wanted to know more about a variety of issues that were only partly addressed in the broad sweep of the official documents, and this interest soon manifested itself in a number of air power projects at various universities in the research plans of a number of academics and their graduate students. These in turn led to many papers, articles, and volumes dealing with important topics that did not fit the typical mandate of official histories. Among them were matters of personnel selection, aircraft procurement, interallied decision-making, and civil military relations to name just a few.

Some of this research looked at the RCAF's experiences during the period of the official histories, but a significant number of projects focused on the post-1945 air force. Indeed, the three official volumes had whetted the collective appetite for explorations of the RCAF during the first decades of the Cold War, covering the roughly 20 years from 1945 until the air force was disbanded when the unified Canadian Forces came into being between 1964 and 1968. Two aspects of these new inquiries are of note. First, while researchers had ready access to the archival material and advice of the staff of the Directorate of History (what has since become the Directorate of History and Heritage) the historians on staff did not have the resources or mandate to themselves begin work on a postwar history. Second, many of the students looking at postwar questions were either serving officers or had close connections to the military and thus had some fairly well-formulated research topics and questions based on their own experiences. Their work led to a number of insightful studies that have since become the basis for other research.

In 2015, the incoming commander of the RCAF, Lieutenant General Michael Hood, made the production of a fourth volume of official history, covering the decades in question in this volume, a priority within a group of activities intended to capture the RCAF's experiences of the post-1945 era. These efforts were envisioned to prepare the RCAF for its centenary in 2024. Work on the fourth volume has started, but as with the previous three publications the official historians are working slowly and carefully, and as a result the completion of an official volume before 2024 seems unlikely. Thus was born the raison d'être behind this book.

This volume provides a compendium of several of the research efforts described above. The editors have approached the authors of many of the major academic works dealing with the period and asked for a chapter that either captures the main themes, events, and findings of their earlier work or, where possible given the limitations of research during the COVID-19 pandemic, a study of a closely related theme.

Not all the various and important facets of the RCAF will be found in the following pages, and as we go towards publication it is apparent to us that there is room for either an expanded edition or perhaps even a second volume. More work needs to be done on matters of people. Here we mean both the leaders and the rank and file. Who were the leaders and how were they recruited and developed to lead the air force? What sorts of policies and plans existed to recruit and train the thousands of technicians needed to keep the flyers airborne? How were families supported in remote locations like the Pinetree radar stations and the sometimes lonely overseas stations? What was the place of minorities and, in particular, Francophones. And so the chapters that follow do not cover all the issues that the nation and the RCAF lived through and with, but we hope that readers, both those who have served in the RCAF in those days or since and those coming to these stories for the first time, will find this material interesting and perhaps even compelling.

We want to acknowledge the contributions of many people and organizations. We must first recognize the financial contributions of the RCAF Historical Fund and the RCAF Association Trust Fund, without which the actual publication of the volume would not have been possible. We would also like to thank Len Husband, Christine Robertson, and everyone who assisted them at University of Toronto Press for taking our words and images and putting them together in this pleasing and, we believe, valuable book. Ms Catherine Murphy, Head of the Information Resource Centre at the Canadian Forces College in Toronto, a college that emerged from the RCAF Staff College described in these pages, assisted in many ways. Chief among these was the indexing of the volume, but she also offered her time in the preparation of the glossary. Equally important, her assistance to researchers on matters of air force history has been essential to the work of many of the contributors and a huge number of researchers and students in the 35 years that she has led the college's library and information services. Equally key to the research and products of the volume is the assistance and guidance of Dr Stephen Harris and his team at the Directorate of History and Heritage. These women and men are little known to Canadians, but their work on air force and other service histories is essential to telling the stories of those who serve Canada. Finally, we would like to thank the authors of the individual chapters for taking on the challenge during the COVID-19 pandemic and at the same time acknowledge the unique contribution of the late General Paul Manson who first donned an RCAF uniform during the halcyon years.

GLOSSARY

Air Chief Marshal   A/C/M
Air Commodore   A/C
Air Defence Command   ADC
Air Defence Control Centre   ADCC
Air Defence Group   ADG
Air Force Headquarters   AFHQ
Air Interceptor and Air Warning annex to the Basic Security Plan   AIAW Plan
Air Marshal   A/M
Air Materiel Command   AMC
Air Member for Personnel   AMP
Air Member for Support and Organization   AMSO
Air Member for Technical Services   AMTS
Air Officer Commanding   AOC
Air Officer Commanding-in-Chief   AOC-in-C
Air Transport Command   ATC
Air Vice Marshal   A/V/M
Aircraftsman First Class   AC1
Aircraftsman Second Class   AC2
Allied Air Forces Central Europe   AAFCE
Allied Command Atlantic (within NATO)   ACLANT
Allied Tactical Air Force   ATAF
Anti-submarine warfare   ASW
Cabinet Defence Committee   CDC

Canada-US Basic Security Plan   BSP
Canada-US Military Cooperation Committee   MCC
Canadian Armament Research and Development Establishment   CARDE
Canadian Atlantic Area   CANLANT
Canadian Chiefs of Staff Committee   COSC
Canadian Forces College (formerly the RCAF Staff College 1943–65)   CFC
Canadian Joint Air Training Centre   CJATC
Chief of the Air Staff   CAS
Chief of the General Staff   CGS
Commander in Chief   CinC
Continental Air Defense Command (USAF)   CONAD
Continental Air Defense Integration-North program   CADIN
Defence Research Board   DRB
Deputy Chief of the Air Staff   D/CAS
Development and Associated Research Policy Group (Canadian Forces)   DARPG
Directorate of History and Heritage   DHH
Flight Lieutenant   F/L
Flight Sergeant   F/Sgt
Ground Controlled Intercept or Interception   GCI
Group Captain   G/C
Home War Establishment   HWE
Leading Aircraftsman   LAC
Library and Archives Canada   LAC
Maintenance Command   MC
Maintenance Command Headquarters   MCHQ
North American Air Defence Command   NORAD
Royal Air Force   RAF
Royal Canadian Air Force   RCAF
Royal Canadian Navy   RCN
Satellite Identification Tracking Unit (RCAF)   SITU
Semi-Automatic Ground Environment   SAGE
Sergeant   Sgt
Space Defence Center (USAF)   SDC
Space Defence Program (RCAF)   SDP
Space Detection and Tracking System   SPADATS
Space Detection and Tracking System (USAF)   SPADATS
Space Indoctrination Program   SIP

Squadron Leader   S/L
Strategic Air Command (USAF)   SAC
Strike/Reconnaissance   S/R
Supreme Allied Commander Atlantic (within NATO)   SACLANT
Supreme Allied Commander Europe   SACEUR
Supreme Headquarters Allied Powers Europe   SHAPE
US Continental Air Defense Command   CONAD
US Northeast Command   USNEC
Vice Chief of the Air Staff   V/CAS
Warrant Officer Class 1   WO1
Warrant Officers Class 2   WO2
Wing Commander   W/C
Women's Division (including women serving in)   WD

INTRODUCTION

RANDALL WAKELAM

In 1945 the Royal Canadian Air Force (RCAF) looked nothing like it had six years earlier when war began, or indeed as it had just 21 years earlier when the Royal Canadian Air Force was created in 1924. Nor would the 1945 version of the RCAF look anything like what it would 20 years later, and it is the stories of those two postwar decades that are the heart of this volume.

These two decades came to be known by many as the "halcyon years." This was a period of unimaginable expansion for the RCAF, fuelled by the emerging and expanding threats of the Cold War and the memories of Canadians of the terrible costs of the two world wars. To draw from the meanings of the word "halcyon," this was a period generally of growth, prosperity, and happiness when the air force was seen by its members, and generally by Canadians, as a central element of national defence and was accorded the mandates and resources to do its job. But it was also a story of how a military service must respond to the needs of the democracy that it serves, and thus of the slow waning of the air force beginning in the late 1950s.

Before continuing, we should explain a bit about why we consider this work a celebration. First, the volume is due to be published in time for the centenary of the Royal Canadian Air Force and thus is part, if not officially, of that celebration. Over the longer life of the volume, we believe that when a reader comes to understand how a service that had seen many ups and downs in the preceding quarter century grew in responsibility, capability, and size, even for only for less than 20 years, that reader will see cause for celebration, or at least admiration.

Many of the events that precede these years would influence certain decisions and events during the halcyon years, and so before taking up the story of the RCAF at the close of the Second World War a brief review of Canadian air power prior to 1945 is appropriate to set the scene.

Before and even during the First World War, attempts to create a Canadian air service were unsuccessful. Even though Alexander Graham Bell's Silver Dart was the first aeroplane to take to the air in the British Empire, and Bell and his colleagues attempted to sell a flying machine to the Canadian Department of Militia, there was no interest in engaging in this seemingly experimental technology, even if the European powers and Britain were making such experiments. When war was declared the minister of militia, the ill-famed Sam Hughes, did authorize the creation of a Canadian Aviation Corps, consisting of one aircraft and three personnel. But when the remains of the aircraft reached England, it having been shipped to Britain on the open deck of a steamer, the idea died. This did not mean that Canadians were dispassionate about serving in the Empire's flying services; hundreds of young men either joined the Royal Flying Corps or the Royal Naval Air Service, having first paid for their own flying training at the Curtiss School in Toronto. Others transferred to these two services from ground or sea appointments in Canadian and British units.

Canadians joined the flying services through a wide variety of plans and suffered losses equally as grave as subalterns in the infantry, so it has been hard to identify precisely how many Canadians flew for Britain and the Empire, but the estimates are that about 25 per cent of RFC flyers were Canadian and that the figure in the RNAS was closer to 35 per cent at one point. With this level of participation there was some thought at the midpoint of the war to create a Canadian flying corps, much as the Australians had done, but again there was no appetite in Ottawa. There was interest in contributing to the flying effort, however, by hosting a Royal Flying Corps training scheme (known simply as RFC Canada), in 1917 and 1918, with the creation of a number of schools in southern Ontario, including at Camp Borden. Only in the closing months of the war did the government decide that it would be a good idea to have Canadians in Canadian squadrons, both within the Royal Air Force (which replaced the British flying services in April 1918) and the Royal Canadian Naval Air Service. But as these Canadian organizations were formed late in the war, neither saw active service.

With the coming of peace, the question was again one of the necessity of having a Canadian air arm. War fighting capability was clearly unnecessary, and if Canada was to have a flying service, proponents realized that an air arm capable of paramilitary and non-military service would be most attractive to Canadians and their government. While a Canadian Air Force was established and given a Royal designation on 1 April 1924, those serving spent almost all of the first 15 years doing work in providing services to various government departments and programs that could benefit from air support. Fisheries patrols, forest-fire tracking, and anti-drug operations were just some of these activities. Meanwhile a very small cadre of professional officers served on the Air Staff in Ottawa, not as an independent headquarters but within the militia's general staff. Not until 1937 did the RCAF break away from the army with the appointment of the first chief of the air staff. The fact that these aviators were part of a military air service was not lost on them, and during these years Canadians attended many courses in the UK to maintain and improve their professional knowledge; in particular some 20 senior officers attended the RAF Staff College.

With international tensions rising in the late 1930s, Canadian politicians felt pressure both from Britain and from their constituents to indicate what Canada would be prepared to do if war came. Prime Minister Mackenzie King saw some merit in focussing on air force contributions, as these would surely be less costly in casualties than an equivalent commitment of soldiers. But he was not prepared to offer anything concrete until war was declared, at which point he was a key negotiator for the British Commonwealth Air Training Plan, which would, in theory, more or less limit Canada to the training of aircrew.

Part of the agreement involved establishing a block of squadrons – the "400" squadrons, with units accorded numerical designators from 400 to 449, for example 408 Squadron – that would be identifiable as RCAF units. Over time those squadrons were activated, as were dozens more for the defence of Canada and its coasts. The 400 squadrons were to be controlled, in theory, by an RCAF Overseas Headquarters, but because the squadrons were created and equipped largely based on RAF priorities they were, with the exception of No 6 (RCAF) Group of Bomber Command, never in effect commanded or controlled from the Overseas HQ, despite earnest and repeated efforts and demands from Ottawa.

Despite these political problems, the RCAF grew in numbers and competency to become the third largest Allied air force of the Western nations. The BCATP produced some 130,000 flyers of all trades, of which more than half were Canadians, and employed roughly 35,000 RCAF personnel and another 6,000 civilians. The Home War Establishment squadrons saw action, albeit limited, over the Atlantic and in the Aleutians campaign. The 400 series squadrons served in all theatres of operations alongside the RAF. When the European war ended the government and air force turned their attention to bringing veterans home and helping the refugees in Europe, but not without starting preparations to conduct operations against Japan in conjunction with US and Commonwealth air forces. These operations were not in the end needed, and by the end of August 1945 the RCAF and the nation were done with war.

The RCAF began a transition to a peacetime air force based on planning that had begun in late 1943. Those plans were centred on a desire to maintain a balanced air force of some 44 squadrons, which would be sufficient for most eventualities in a world that, while at peace, was now facing the threat of communist expansion. The Royal Canadian Navy and the Canadian Army had similar views and recommendations for the government. None of the three were accepted; while the politicians too were aware of the Soviet peril, they had also to deal with the economic fallout of six years of conflict spending. By the end of 1945 the RCAF's plan had been cut back to just eight regular squadrons and a slightly larger reserve force – on paper, that is.

It is at that point that the chapters of this volume pick up the story. The work includes three sections, each of which has an introduction to the specific chapters. In general terms, the four chapters of Section One looks at issues of national security policy and how these played out in the formation of air force policy, plans, and major national and international organizations. Section Two turns to matters of the people and resources needed to make those plans a reality, examining the technical backbone of the RCAF, officer education and aircrew training, the reserve air force, the place of women in the RCAF and in the broader RCAF community, and finally aircraft procurement, with a focus on the Avro Arrow. Section Three contains studies of specific functions including northern operations, search and rescue, and air transport, as well as the RCAF's service to peacekeeping. Included as well are two flying additional studies: maritime air and land aviation.

As a final bit of gen (an old RCAF term for information), readers should expect to find that the topics of the chapters are not discussed solely within those chapters. As can be imagined, the RCAF was a large and complex entity where the warp and weft of the institution meant that a "simple" issue in officer training, for instance, could have a ripple effect across policy and operations. And so, if you are interested in a particular matter, please do start with the related chapter but also consult the volume's index to find other threads that will give a more textured understanding.

SECTION 1

INTRODUCTION

PETER RAYLS

There is a tendency to think of air forces in terms of aircraft and their associated technologies. Choosing which aircraft to procure and how to employ them does not happen in a vacuum. Leaders select aircraft to support specific missions and capabilities, which allow air forces to enact the strategies and policies set forth by government leaders. This section examines the RCAF as an institution and its leaders within the context of how they supported government decisions and policies that were reacting to external global conditions and internal political realities. While procuring aircraft is an important part of the RCAF's history of this period, there is greater depth to the story. Whereas contributions in later sections of this edition illuminate specific aspects of the RCAF's Cold War operations, this section seeks to provide context and background to understand those more focused chapters.

The chapters in this section highlight the wax and wane of the RCAF during the two decades following the end of the Second World War. They stress the unique circumstances presented by the early Cold War that allowed the RCAF to expand during the 1950s, when political and military leaders, with memories of the Second World War, did not want to be caught flat-footed against the Soviet Union. Additionally, the spectre of nuclear warfare, especially after August 1949, contributed to the notion that a third world war would be a quick and calamitous affair for a side unprepared to swiftly spring into action. At the forefront of this thinking was the increasingly important role of air power as the primary bringer of and defender against nuclear warfare.

Much like the United States, Canada came out of the Second World War relatively unscathed. Its economy and industry were able to support the US and NATO in creating a force to deter the Soviets from expanding into Western Europe. This would lead to what were clearly the RCAF's most important missions during this period: continental air defence and No. 1 Air Division's support of NATO. The importance of those priorities to the RCAF is reflected in the chapters dedicated to those missions in this section. However, unlike the Second World War where the RCAF had contributed a balanced air force within the confines of the RAF, the RCAF of the Cold War contributed a fighter-focused force that acted in concert with (and often under the control of) the USAF. Chapters in this section highlight the shift from operating within the RAF sphere to working within the USAF sphere. Closer to home, key to the RCAF's "success" during this period was the alignment between the RCAF's institutional goals and culture with the national security goals of the Canadian government under Louis St. Laurent.

The arrival of the Diefenbaker government in June 1957 signalled a dramatic shift for the RCAF that was felt across all of its missions and commands. The immediacy of the Cold War in the early 1950s gave way to the relative stability and protracted nature of the Cold War in the 1960s. For Canada, this resulted in political policies that emphasized fiscal restraint and a reprioritization of national resources towards domestic concerns such as building up Canada's social welfare system (see annex A for budget and personnel numbers). This refocusing also led to a divergence between the RCAF's view of its missions and how Canada's political leaders viewed of the world and Canada's place in it. Furthermore, America's immersion into the Vietnam War led to the deprioritzation of the USAF's continental air defences, which hurt the RCAF's attempts to convince Ottawa to reinforce its air defence forces. This came as both American and Canadian political leaders were reconsidering the necessity of air defence in light of the emergence of the ICBM threat and expanding defence costs.

Another common theme throughout this section is the interaction between the RCAF and the USAF. It was typical during these years for the RCAF to place its units under the operational control of American-led forces. However, this was done for differing reasons and with differing results. In Europe, RCAF leaders fought hard to ensure that the Air Division would remain an intact, national unit. This contrasts with the RCAF's experience in North America where there was more openness to having RCAF squadrons controlled by USAF leaders when needed.

The first chapter in this section sets the stage not only for this section but for the book as a whole. Frandsen and I focus largely on the interplay between the global situation, Canada's political reaction to that situation, and the RCAF's attempts to operate within that situation and Canada's reaction. We have painted a general picture with the understanding that other chapters provide deeper discussion of the issues we touch on. However, we have worked to show how those various issues were connected to each other and how military activities were based on decisions made by Canada's political leaders, which they in turn based on their view of the Cold War and Canada's role within that war. One issue that some readers will see as fundamental to the existence of the RCAF, and the character of air operations subsequently, is the unification of the three services. We do not disagree with that view, but we have described and discussed unification as but one of a number of forces that saw both the expansion and reduction of the RCAF and of the place of air power over the decades.

Raymond Stouffer examines No. 1 Air Division, which fulfilled one of the RCAF's two primary remits during the early Cold War, and the role that the Division played in providing Canada with a significant contribution to NATO's forces in Western Europe, while also allowing the RCAF to realize some of its postwar dreams. His study reflects on how changes in NATO strategy and Canadian politics affected the aircraft, missions, and ultimately the existence of the Air Division. Furthermore, he balances his description of the operational and tactical level of the Air Division's operations while relating this to the strategic interplay between NATO, Ottawa, and the RCAF.

Richard Goette examines the rise of the RCAF's second primary mission: continental air defence. He focuses on how the air defence of North America set the RCAF's domestic priorities at the end of the Second World War, and how the pursuit of this mission fostered cooperation with the USAF. Goette traces the RCAF's deliberate path that culminated in the creation of NORAD in September 1957. Vital to this path were the RCAF's successful efforts to define its niche within its cooperative efforts with the USAF. These included not only procuring the necessary aircraft and radar but reaching agreements on how the RCAF would contribute to continental air defence.

Joseph Jockel continues the story of Canada's involvement in NORAD during its early years. Where Goette focuses on the expansion of the air defence mission, Jockel examines the highs and lows that accompanied the United States and Canada's efforts to cope with and define continental defence in a period where the idea of what constituted the threat to North America changed dramatically. The change away from the manned-bomber threat to ICBM and space threats would redefine NORAD and the nature of the bilateral relationship within the context of continental air defence.

The early Cold War was undoubtedly a golden age for the RCAF. However, it was an age that would last less than two decades. In examining these halcyon years for the RCAF, it is clear that a unique set of circumstances allowed RCAF leaders to build the service into Canada's main military contribution to what was a frightening time. However, as the fears changed, so too did the fortunes of the RCAF.

CHAPTER ONE

THE EXPANSION AND CONTRACTION OF CANADA'S FIRST LINE OF DEFENCE: THE RCAF IN THE COLD WAR, 1945–1968

BERTRAM FRANDSEN AND PETER RAYLS

Introduction

Canada's experience during the Second World War ensured that air power would be an essential part of Canadian defence policy in the post-1945 period. While planning at the end of the war called for an independent air force that was small but balanced, increasing Cold War tensions, climaxing with the Korean War, dashed this idea.[1] The outbreak of the war in 1950 was the impetus for the Cabinet to approve and fund a rapid expansion of the RCAF to meet the demands of collective defence in North America and Western Europe. The development of a small, balanced force gave way to a large fighter force based on specialized alliance roles.

During the St. Laurent years, air power became the "Canadian way of war," or at least the "Canadian way of deterrence." For a brief period, the RCAF was considered one of the best air forces in the world.[2] The St. Laurent government's "airmindedness" (the embrace of aviation as a key to the nation's future) created conditions for the RCAF to emerge as the "senior" military service, with the largest budget and personnel levels and as a leading influencer in the development of Canada's aviation industry.[3] This large air force enabled the government to make a critical and credible contribution to Western defence for a short period of time, reflecting a continuation of the earlier approach of "limited liability" based on air power and industry introduced by previous Liberal governments, an approach that provided the government with a viable alternative when discussions arose regarding increased military contributions to NATO or the UN. It was during these years that the RCAF reached the apex of its size and development; a period some have referred to as the "golden years of the RCAF."[4]

While the RCAF was able to achieve both quality and quantity, it was unable to sustain this level of effort in the longer term. Many of the difficulties and significant cutbacks that the air force endured under the Diefenbaker and Pearson governments were manifestations of lapses of judgment during the St. Laurent years. Declining defence budgets were a factor for both governments and resulted in an RCAF that became numerically smaller and less capable in some areas. However, it was not only budgetary matters that impacted the RCAF. With the election of the Diefenbaker government in June 1957, the RCAF was subjected to a half decade of constant turmoil resulting from cancelled aircraft projects, such as the Avro CF-105 Arrow, the adoption of the strike reconnaissance role for No. 1 Air Division, and the modernization of the Air Defence Command (ADC). These developments were accompanied by Diefenbaker's indecision in accepting the nuclear weapons needed to obtain the maximum effectiveness of selected weapons systems (e.g., the BOMARC and CF-104).

The arrival of the Pearson government in April 1963 and its reluctant willingness to allow the RCAF to field nuclear weapons suggested a return to the airmindedness of the St. Laurent years. However, the RCAF continued to contend with the decline started by Diefenbaker. This culminated in 1968 with the unification of the Canadian Armed Forces and the end of the RCAF as an independent military service. In retrospect, these changes were not so surprising; however, they demonstrated that the RCAF had lost its ability to shape policy, operations, and procurements as had occurred during the 1950s.

Canadian air power made an important contribution during a critical period of the nation's history. From 1948 to 1957, the RCAF became the leading air force among the middle powers. Along with the buildup of the RCAF, there had been the equally successful expansion of the Canadian aviation industry that was vital to sustaining a large air force. This expansion allowed the RCAF to enhance the strategic defence of Western Europe and North America during the 1950s. However, rapid strategic and technological transformations significantly weakened that role during the 1960s. These transformations, along with changing political and economic priorities, led to the decline of an RCAF that seemingly lost touch with its political masters and their vision for coping with the Cold War.

Planning and Re-establishing the Postwar Air Force

Planning for the postwar RCAF began while the Second World War was still in progress. In December 1943, A/C K. M. Guthrie, the Deputy Air Member Air Staff (Plans) completed the "Brief on Post-War Planning for the Royal Canadian Air

Force."[5] It outlined four principles that the RCAF should use as a guide for future planning. First, the RCAF should be capable of both offensive and defensive operations. Second, it should be organized to quickly mobilize from peace to a wartime footing. Third, the training system should also be capable of rapid expansion. Fourth, the RCAF should be capable of deploying and fighting in either North America or overseas.[6]

Based on requests from the multi-agency Post-Hostilities Problems Working Committees and the Chiefs of Staff Committee, the RCAF convened the Post War Organization Committee, headed by A/C Hugh Campbell. The committee focused primarily on formulating a plan for the RCAF's postwar composition. RCAF leaders wanted an air force that was balanced in its capabilities (i.e., fighter-interceptor, bomber, transport, and reconnaissance abilities), focused on a relatively small Regular Force capable of maintaining the abilities and readiness of the larger Auxiliary and Reserve Forces, and evenly distributed across Canada.[7] However, the committee received little guidance from Ottawa and seemed to pay little attention to the reality of the RCAF's situation in the face of impending cutbacks.[8] They eventually developed a plan for a postwar Regular RCAF consisting of 16 squadrons, including day-fighter, medium bomber, heavy bomber, general reconnaissance, long-range transport, troop transport, and photographic survey squadrons. In addition to the Regular squadrons, RCAF leaders wanted 28 Auxiliary squadrons with fighter, medium bomber, fighter-bomber, and photo-reconnaissance squadrons.[9] The RCAF would require 30,000 Regular Force personnel to operate these squadrons and to train the Auxiliary and Reserve Forces, all of this with an annual budget of $78 million.[10] This compared remarkably to the pre-war RCAF that had consisted of 4,000 members and a $10 million budget in Fiscal Year (FY) 1938/39.

Government limitations on spending considerably reduced the organization proposed by the committee. RCAF leaders continued to argue for Regular personnel strength of 20,000 with ten squadrons and an Auxiliary Force of 10,000 and nineteen squadrons. In early 1946, the RCAF presented the Cabinet with three options with decreasing costs and personnel numbers. These options also saw the RCAF drop its desire of maintaining a postwar bomber force. The Cabinet approved a plan that capped the RCAF Regular Force at eight squadrons with just over 16,000 members and a budget of $59 million. The goal of this air force now changed from being a small force capable of limited combat to one providing Canada with the nucleus of an air force that could rapidly mobilize in the event of a future war.[11]

Parallel to this planning was the rapid demobilization of the wartime air force. Unfortunately for the RCAF, the government's demobilization actions did not align with the postwar plans approved by the Cabinet. On VE-day (Victory in Europe),

Air Marshal Wilf Curtis. Curtis served as Chief of the Air Staff 1947–1953, and is considered to be the father of the postwar RCAF.

the RCAF had a strength of 70 squadrons; but within 10 months of VJ-day (Victory in Japan), the RCAF only had three squadrons assigned to non-combat missions. Additionally, the RCAF struggled with identifying, attracting, and retaining quality members during the fast and confusing days of demobilization. As Sandy Babcock states, "The postwar RCAF suddenly had less fighting capability than even the prewar force, which had been considered inadequate."[12]

It is an understatement to say that the period from 1945–8 represented a transition for the RCAF. On the one hand, the RCAF, like the Army and RCN, endured rapid demobilization along with massive cuts in budget and personnel. On the other hand, key RCAF leaders, such as Wilfred Curtis, C.R. Dunlap, Hugh Campbell, C. Roy Slemon, Claire Annis, and Keith Hodson, began to lay the groundwork for a resurgence in the RCAF. Collaboration with the US Army Air Force (USAAF, the USAF's predecessor) through transnational groups, like the Permanent Joint Board on Defence (PJBD) and Military Cooperation Committee (MCC), developed plans, such as the Basic Security Plan, that the RCAF used as a basis to create its own plans to revitalize and expand the air force to fit its new role as a partner to the US flying service in the emerging Cold War. The RCAF expressed this new vision through a series of plans that contained multi-year schemes to gradually expand and modernize the RCAF.[13]

The St. Laurent Government and Re-armament, 1948–1957

Prime Minister MacKenzie King's retirement in November 1948 coincided with the emergence of the Cold War between the United States and Soviet Union. Louis St. Laurent's elevation to the position of prime minister ushered in a period of expansion for the RCAF. The Cold War caused the St. Laurent government and the RCAF to begin taking steps to expand the air force.[14] The RCAF expressed its approach to this growth in its Plans F and G, which called for an expansion of the service and placed greater attention on its air defence mission. This focus included efforts to upgrade the RCAF's radar capabilities and the development and acquisition of new aircraft, such as the Avro CF-100 and F-86 Sabre.[15]

Under the leadership of the CAS, A/M Wilfred Curtis, the RCAF also began a process of reorganization. After the Second World War, the air force had continued to use geographic commands, which sought to efficiently manage a service that was small but spread out across the country. The creation of No. 1 Air Defence Group in December 1948 was part of the service's change to functional commands, which RCAF leaders felt would be a more effective way to manage its missions. These new organizations also facilitated greater partnership with allied air forces. This new co-operation was evident in the RCAF's collaboration with the RAF in gaining initial bases for Canadian NATO-bound squadrons and in combined training exercises held with US air defence forces.[16]

Although the increasing tensions in Europe, the formation of NATO, and the detonation of a Soviet atomic bomb in August 1949 provided an impetus for limited Canadian re-armament, the start of the Korean War on 25 June 1950, was the true catalyst for the creation of a large air force. The North Korean invasion revealed the RCAF's inability, with its fleet of P-51 Mustang and de Havilland Vampire jet fighters, to respond to the needs of collective security with a serious contribution of capable modern combat aircraft. Indeed, the air force's principal support to the Korean War consisted of No. 426 Squadron, which flew 599 transport missions between McChord Air Force Base in Washington state and Haneda Air Base in Japan under the operational control of the USAF's Military Air Transport Service between 1950 and 1954.[17] Additionally, 22 RCAF fighter pilots served on exchange tours with USAF Sabre squadrons in Korea, and 40 RCAF flight nurses served with the USAF on aero-medical evacuation flights.[18]

The start of the Korean War convinced the Cabinet to spend significantly more on defence in general and the RCAF specifically. In July 1950, the Cabinet approved a $40–$50 million increase in the defence budget for FY 1950/51 and an increase in the size of the military by 5,000 to 6,000 personnel.[19] The Cabinet also approved the construction of three new radar sites in eastern Canada and the purchase of 100

The three built-in-Canada jet aircraft that were the backbone of the RCAF, from top to bottom, F-86 Sabre, T-33 Silver Star, and CF-100 Canuck. Between 1950 and 1958, over 3,000 of these aircraft equipped the RCAF and allied air forces.

surplus USAF Mustangs to help the RCAF fill its gap in aircraft until new jets were available.[20] In August, the Cabinet also allowed the RCAF to expand the Regular force to nine interceptor squadrons, increase its Air Control & Warning (AC&W) units to nine squadrons, and grow the overall strength of the air force to just under 25,000 members (across the Regular, Auxiliary, and Reserve forces). The Cabinet also approved increases in the production of F-86s and CF-100s.[21] In October, the Cabinet accepted the RCAF's request to have the Defence Research Board begin developing a guided air-to-air missile.[22] Finally, in January 1951, the Cabinet approved a further expansion of the RCAF to create 11 fighter squadrons for service in NATO. This was in addition to the nine squadrons destined for air defence duty in North America.[23]

The expansions in funds and personnel were significant because they allowed the RCAF to address the perception that Canada's air defence capabilities had fallen behind those of the USAF.[24] The increased resources helped the RCAF gain the trust of the USAF by showing that it was a committed partner in continental air defence. The growth in squadrons also allowed the RCAF to treat its air defence and NATO missions equally, with fewer concerns about having to prioritize one mission over the other.[25] In announcing the expansion in February 1951, Defence Minister Brooke Claxton highlighted the leading role that the government expected the RCAF to take in Canada's defence policy:

> Canada's most substantial contribution to the planned force in being will be our air force participation. … Because of the large requirements of the RCAF not only in building up to its total of 40 regular and auxiliary squadrons, but also in the training services, the RCAF will, we expect, have more men than the army has today and will be spending as much as the other two services put together.[26]

The Cabinet's actions set in motion the development of the RCAF into a large air force for the next decade.

Following the rearmament announcement on 5 February 1951, RCAF expansion began in earnest. While RCAF leaders saw the air defence and NATO missions as equally important, the establishment of No. 1 Air Division was their immediate priority. This should come as no surprise given Canada's leading role in creating NATO.[27] The initial deployment of No. 1 (Fighter) Wing to RAF Station Luffenham commenced in November 1951, followed by three additional wings deployed to France and West Germany between 1952 and 1953, with No. 1 Wing relocating to France in 1954 (see chapter 2). Important to the RCAF was its successful effort to place the Air Division under the operational control of the USAF-led 4th Allied Tactical Air Force (4 ATAF) instead of the RAF-led 2 ATAF.[28] The RCAF's frustrations with the RAF during the Second World War and its deepening ties with the USAF's air defence community drove this desire to operate in 4 ATAF to the discontent of leaders in the Army and the Department of External Affairs, who favoured locating Canada's entire NATO contingent in the same area, under UK control.[29] At its peak in December 1954, the Air Division consisted of 6.000 members (including 500 fighter pilots) and 300 Sabre jets. In 1954, the Air Staff agreed to re-equip one squadron in each of the four wings with CF-100s, a process completed in 1957. This decision increased the Air Division's capabilities to fight Soviet bombers while allowing RCAF leaders to delay their final decision to eventually replace the Sabres.[30]

Although the RCAF prioritized the buildup of the Air Division, it also proceeded with the expansion of forces at home. This activity coincided with RCAF's

Minister of National Defence Brooke Claxton addressing personnel of 3 (Fighter) Wing, Zweibrucken, Germany. Equipped with F-86 Sabres, the Wing was one of four belonging to the RCAF's 1 Air Division, part of NATO. As defence minister, Claxton was astute in appreciating the importance of Canadian air power.

reorganization from geographic to functional commands. Air force leaders clearly viewed ADC and its role as the service's most important domestic mission. The period from 1950 to 1957 saw the ADC expand and modernize both its interceptor fleet (moving from Mustangs and Vampires to Sabres and CF-100s) and early warning radar networks. By 1956, ADC had nine Regular and 10 Auxiliary fighter squadrons along with an elaborate aircraft control and warning system, including radar stations across the country, supplemented by the civilian members of the Ground Observer Corps.[31] As part of these efforts, RCAF leaders also emphasized the need to collaborate with the USAF in creating an air defence system capable of protecting North America from nuclear-armed Soviet bombers. This collaboration was best demonstrated in successful efforts that shared the costs for constructing and staffing the Pinetree and Distant Early Warning radar lines. In these action, RCAF leaders agreed with their USAF counterparts that successful continental air defence should protect not only population and industrial centres, but more importantly, the USAF's Strategic Air Command's (SAC) nuclear bombing force, which acted as a deterrent to Soviet aggression.[32] RCAF leaders

Aerial view of RCAF Station Dana, SK, a Pinetree Radar site. This image is indicative of the isolation of the radar sites of both the Pinetree and Mid-Canada lines, but the Distant Early Warning (DEW) line sites were situated in even more isolated locations with very austere living conditions.

also agreed with USAF air defence leaders in the potential to integrate guided surface-to-air missiles into the existing interceptor force and the potential for nuclear-armed, air-to-air rockets to add significant capabilities to the interceptor force.[33]

By 1956, the RCAF considered 19 fighter squadrons insufficient to defend the entirety of Canadian airspace and requested the creation of six additional CF-100 squadrons, which it would spread across the country between 1957 and 1959.[34] RCAF leaders also came to view the Auxiliary squadrons as ineffective due to their aging aircraft and a perception that Auxiliary aircrews could not successfully transition to more modern jets. This thinking was part of a philosophy that discounted the role of reserve forces in air defence, where an emphasis was put on forces-in-being, ready to fight on short notice.[35] The plan would have thickened the air defences north of the principal industrial areas of Quebec and Ontario and provided air defences across the Prairies and the interior of British Columbia to assist in protecting SAC's bases. However, the Cabinet did not approve this proposal, as fiscal

An impressive line up of aircraft at RCAF Station Whitehorse, Yukon Territory, in support of a joint exercise involving the Mobile Strike Force.

worries in 1956 were starting to affect the government's willingness to sustain a large defence budget, and a reduction in the RCAF budget from $863 million to $814 million was already forecasted for FY 1956/57.[36]

The importance that RCAF leaders placed on the air defence and NATO missions often came at the expense of other commands within the service. This was especially true of the Maritime Air Command (MAC) and Tactical Air Command (TAC). The lesser priority given to these commands provides insight into the RCAF's interactions with the RCN and the Army. In the case of MAC, not only was its mission of supporting SACLANT and NATO's anti-submarine role given a relatively low status, but this role also put the command in competition with the RCN's Aviation Branch, which also engaged in anti-submarine activities. This left MAC using obsolescent aircraft (the Lancaster M.R. Mk. 10) and facing difficulties during the 1950s in updating its fleet with the aircraft desired by the Air Staff: the Lockheed Neptune and the Canadair Argus.[37] Of even lower

Line up of Harvard training aircraft at RCAF Station Gimli, MB. This aircraft would be used to train thousands of RCAF and NATO pilots during the Cold War.

priority, TAC existed primarily to support the Mobile Striking Force (MSF), a Canadian Army airborne brigade group responsible for territorial defence. The RCAF's decision to assign two Auxiliary squadrons equipped with Second World War Mitchell light bombers demonstrates TAC's low priority. The Army often bemoaned the fact that TAC did not have the organic aircraft necessary to support the MSF. The demise of the MSF and the retirement of TAC's Mitchell bombers, in 1958, left little purpose or interest in Tactical Air Command, which the RCAF disbanded in 1959.[38]

The RCAF's Training Command also played an important role in the expansion of the air force during the first half of the 1950s. In addition to its role in training the pilots, ground crews, radar operators, and others needed for the RCAF's missions, Training Command also reprised a role played by the RCAF during the Second World War. Much like the BCATP, Training Command opened its flight training centres to trainees from various NATO nations and was another way for

Canada to demonstrate its support for its European allies. Additionally, Training Command, in coordination with the USAF, RAF, and US Navy, maintained plans to further ramp up aircrew training in North America in the event of another war in Europe. The NATO air training plan produced a total of 3,218 Canadian and 5,299 NATO graduates between 1950 and 1958 when the program ended.[39]

While RCAF leaders did not consider Air Transport Command (ATC) as vital as the Air Division or ADC, they always understood the importance of the command. It initially proved its worth in the postwar period with its support to UN operations during the Korean War. With the formation of the Air Division, RCAF leaders recognized ATC's critical role in the Division's buildup and sustainment. ATC took on new importance to the RCAF and Canada in 1956 when it provided aircraft to support the UN Emergency Force's efforts to end the Suez Crisis. While this was a new mission and new role for the RCAF, it was one that the service increasingly participated in during the next decade.[40] In light of ATC's importance to peacekeeping, air force leaders gained Cabinet support for maintaining a relatively modern fleet capable of strategic airlift. Considering this importance, the RCAF transitioned Auxiliary squadrons to transport roles as the TAC mission disappeared and the RCAF reconsidered the value of the Auxiliary in the air defence role.[41]

"The Defence Débâcle, 1957–1963"[42]

A convergence of strategic uncertainties and economic concerns greeted the government of John Diefenbaker when it came into office in June 1957. In many ways, the RCAF was at the height of its power in terms of its size, percentage of the budget, and status as Canada's premier strategic instrument when Diefenbaker assumed power. However, it was during this period, from June 1957 to April 1963, that the RCAF's power begin to wane. Diefenbaker became prime minister just as the RCAF was trying to begin an ambitious program to update its capabilities to meet the potential threats envisioned by air force leaders – a vision shared by its partners in the USAF and NATO. He also came to power just as Canada was experiencing its first significant recession in the postwar period.[43] Additionally, Diefenbaker's rise to power also heralded a period of Canadian nationalism that sometimes manifested itself as anti-Americanism (or at least resistance to American approaches, ideas, and proposals).[44]

The Diefenbaker government did not necessarily disagree with the RCAF's vision and desire to modernize. More often than not, Ottawa disagreed about the best way to counter the present and emerging threats with the resources that were available. Throughout Diefenbaker's tenure there was continual friction between politics and economics, strategy and technology, and their application to Canadian air power. Decision makers were unable to come to terms with profound changes in strategy and technology. This was compounded by political indecision and tighter fiscal constraints, which they introduced at a time when the defence costs were escalating. These frictions not only contributed to the downfall of the Diefenbaker government but also signalled the start of a decline in the RCAF's fortunes.

The wax and wane of the RCAF during this period is demonstrated organizationally in its air defence mission. One of Diefenbaker's first acts as prime minister was to approve the formation of NORAD in July 1957. The creation of the binational command served to reinforce the RCAF's strategic importance to Canada's security policy. RCAF leaders could be justifiably proud of the new roles that they gained in NORAD's headquarters in Colorado Springs; these, in turn, gave them new insight and influence regarding the air defence of North America.[45] However, the Cuban Missile Crisis of 1962 challenged this role when Diefenbaker, upset over differing ideas of what constituted "consultation," vacillated over how to respond when USAF General John Gerhart (CINCNORAD) requested that Ottawa increase ADC's readiness in anticipation of a potential Soviet attack on North America.[46] Furthermore, Ottawa's 1961 decisions to decrease the number of ADC squadrons in the wake of the Arrow's cancellation in February 1959 (along with the adoption of the CF-101 as the ADC's primary interceptor and the introduction of the BOMARC surface to air missile) weakened the stature of the RCAF.[47]

Changes also occurred in the Air Division during the period. Throughout the mid-1950s, NATO's air strategy underwent a transformation that increasingly stressed a desire to utilize nuclear weapons in anticipation of a Soviet nuclear strike on Western Europe.[48] In 1957, NATO's commander, USAF General Lauris Norstad, requested that the Canadian government refit the Air Division and allow it to assume NATO's "Strike/Reconnaissance" role as its primary mission, with the "strike" role being a euphemism for battlefield nuclear attack. In looking to fulfill this proposed new mission, Air Division and RCAF leaders examined several options. Among these were upgrading the Sabres to allow them to employ tactical nuclear weapons and the use of a modified form of the Arrow to fulfill the Strike/Recce role.[49] Ultimately, the Diefenbaker government decided to adopt the CF-104 as the Air Division's new fighter in June 1959.[50]

Diefenbaker's decisions to have the RCAF field the BOMARC, CF-101, and CF-104 created a new headache for his government and the RCAF. In all three cases, the RCAF assumed (as did their USAF and NATO partners) that it would arm these systems with nuclear weapons. A strong case can be made that Prime Minister Diefenbaker had also acknowledged this understanding, at least implicitly,

Two CF-101 Voodoos airborne over the Centennial Bridge, Chatham, NB, 1966.

in various statements. However, from 1959 until the end of its tenure, Diefenbaker's government was plagued by controversy and infighting regarding whether he would allow the RCAF (and the other services) to accept nuclear weapons. The conflicts often pitted the RCAF's leadership and minister for national defence (George Pearkes and subsequently Douglas Harkness) against the secretary of state for external affairs, Howard Green, with Diefenbaker in the middle and unwilling or unable to make a decision. Ultimately, Diefenbaker's vacillation contributed to his election defeat in April 1963.[51]

A decade prior to Diefenbaker's fall, the RCAF began laying the foundations for a program to modernize the capabilities of its two priority organizations: ADC and the Air Division. RCAF leaders including the CAS, A/M Roy Slemon, his two VCASs, A/V/Ms Frank Miller and Larry Dunlap, and key staff officers, such as A/Cs Clare Annis, William MacBrien, and Max Hendrick, developed a plan intended to meet several needs: the anticipated Soviet threats of the 1960s, factor in the expected lifespan of existing equipment, keep the service technologically up to date,

RCAF CF-104 Starfighter on takeoff.

and continue to support Canada's aviation industry.[52] For these officers, the RCAF needed these updates to meet the assumed changes to the threats to North America and Western Europe: the Soviets' transition from propellor-driven bombers to jet bombers capable of flying at high altitudes and ever-increasing speeds. RCAF leaders viewed the ADC's fleet of CF-100s and the Air Division's fleet of Sabres and CF-100s as being incapable of coping with the emerging threat.[53] Additionally, there were legitimate concerns about the service life of these aircraft, especially the Sabres. While RCAF leaders did not discount the emergence of ICBMs, their insistence on accounting for assumed changes to the Soviet bomber fleet (and their assumed continued use into the 1960s) put them at odds with Canada's civilian leaders, who became increasing fixated on the ICBM threat, especially after the launch of Sputnik on 4 October 1957 (coincidentally, the same day that Avro unveiled the Arrow to the public).[54] Finally, RCAF leaders were eager to support their USAF allies in the general trend towards the increased use of nuclear weapons in both continental air defence and NATO's air strategy.[55]

Test launch of an RCAF BOMARC surface-to-air missile (SAM). The RCAF fielded two SAM squadrons located at RCAF Stations North Bay, ON, and La Macaza, QC.

At the heart of the RCAF's plan was the program to develop the CF-105 Arrow. While designed principally for air defence as a replacement for the CF-100, RCAF leaders hoped, at certain points in its development, that Avro might be able to adapt the Arrow to make it a useful replacement for the Air Division's Sabres.[56] Throughout the life of the program, the Arrow's development costs and anticipated production costs continued to rise. These increases occurred because of a combination of unforeseen changes (e.g., the need to switch to Avro's Iroquois engine); attempts to utilize advanced technologies seen as vital to countering the Soviet threat (e.g., the Astra fire control system); and a failure, late in its development, to find a foreign air force interested in purchasing the Arrow.[57]

Parallel to the Arrow program were schemes to update the weaponry for the RCAF's fighter force with a shift from guns and rockets to guided air-to-air missiles, and the RCAF's devotion to the idea of integrating the air defence force to include a complementary mix of interceptors and surface-to-air missiles (SAMs), especially Boeing's BOMARC.[58] RCAF leaders were also keen on incorporating computer technology into the ADC's ground environment to increase the speed that radar data was transmitted to air defence control centres, thus allowing faster decision-making and simplifying the process of scrambling interceptor and SAMs. This planning for modernization coincided with the last years of the St. Laurent government as it was becoming clear that the intense defence effort that defined the first half of the decade was unsustainable. With the Diefenbaker government, there would be significant cuts to the RCAF budget.

The government reduced the RCAF budget by more than 30 perc cent between FY 1953/54 and 1964/65 (see annex A). In 1953, the RCAF's share of allocations for the three services was 56 per cent, and by 1965 it dropped to 47 per cent.[59] Throughout the years of the Diefenbaker government, the RCAF had to either cancel or reduce programs that were part of its modernization plan. These cuts were, in part, a response to Canada's first postwar recession in the late 1950s and the increasing public and political desire to strengthen Canada's social welfare system (a priority that continued into the Pearson government).[60] The most spectacular of these cancellations occurred on 20 February 1959, when Diefenbaker cancelled the CF-105 program, which had seen the estimated per unit cost mushroom from $2 million to $12 million, with a requirement for only 169 aircraft, compared to the original estimate of 600 aircraft. The subsequent introduction of the CF-101 and the CF-104 did not represent one-for-one substitutions for the aircraft they replaced. Maritime Air Command and ATC also witnessed similar reductions to their planned replacements. RCAF leaders were not oblivious to the need to think about the service's future. In June 1961, the CAS, A/M Hugh Campbell, named A/C Fred Carpenter, following the completion of his assignment as ATC's AOC, as chief of the Special Studies Group on Long Range Objectives for the RCAF. Campbell wanted Carpenter's team to develop long-range strategic guidance for the RCAF into the 1970s. The group submitted its report to Campbell on 29 June 1962, and it was promptly filed away in a classified filing cabinet.[61] Referred to as the "Carpenter Report," it identified the Soviet Union as being the main military threat, but the one least likely to result in total war. In contrast, the new threat of so-called "brushfire" conflicts required highly flexible and mobile conventionally armed military forces, including air forces, capable of a range of operations including monitoring truce agreements, counterinsurgency operations, and participation in limited wars. To respond to these types of conflict the report proposed a revised RCAF structure featuring conventionally armed, multi-role combat aircraft and a significant increase in tactical and strategic transport capabilities.

In bureaucratic terms, the submission of the Carpenter Report could not have come at a worse time. DND, including the RCAF, was going through further expenditures reductions for FY 1962/3. Overall government spending was to be reduced by $250 million, including $67 million for DND. Of that amount, the RCAF share was $29 million, representing a 4.1 per cent reduction in its already constrained budget.[62] In September 1962, Campbell retired and was replaced by A/M Larry Dunlap, the RCAF's last CAS prior to unification. Dunlap had to run an air force while also contending with ongoing crises that engulfed the government. The Cuban Missile Crisis and the fall of the Diefenbaker government overshadowed any interest in alternative RCAF force structures. However, many of the report's proposals influenced the defence policy of Lester Pearson's Liberal government.

The Twilight of Canadian Air Power, 1963–1968

The Pearson years could have represented a period of renewal and reappraisal for the RCAF, but other factors ultimately intervened. These included the confusion and chaos resulting from the integration and unification of the armed forces, and the continuing decline in defence expenditures exacerbated by the continuation of existing military commitments while introducing new military roles. Despite some small improvements to the RCAF (particularly for ATC), the overall result of the Liberal's defence policies between 1963 and 1968 made this period a continuation of the defence debacle of the Diefenbaker years. The Liberal government proved to be more politically decisive than its predecessor. However, it was constrained by fiscal realities that, when considering the existing strategic and technological factors, limited the Liberal government's freedom of action in undertaking a new policy direction.

Additionally, one should not discount how changes in American defence policy and thinking impacted Ottawa's consideration of the RCAF. The growing emphasis on ICBMs, the transition from Eisenhower's Massive Retaliation to Kennedy's Flexible Response, and the growing costs associated with air defence led to American leaders deemphasizing the importance of NORAD and ADC within the American military sphere. This coincided with the gradual escalation of America's commitment to fighting the Vietnam War. By the late 1960s, NORAD and the USAF ADC were seen as dead-end assignments by USAF officers.[63] This served as a signal to Ottawa that there would be little consequences to the bilateral relationship if it cut the RCAF's air defence forces.[64]

Pearson quickly fulfilled his campaign promise to equip the RCAF's nuclear weapon delivery systems with the warheads required to make them useful. Ironically though, this occurred as the Americans, under the Kennedy administration, had recognized the need for larger and better-equipped conventional armed forces to deal with limited wars. This led Kennedy and his successor, Lyndon Johnson, to de-emphasize the centrality of nuclear weapons in American defence policy. This resulted in NATO's change to the doctrine of Flexible Response in 1967, a doctrine that centred on maintaining sufficient conventional forces to act as a tripwire in the event of Soviet aggression. Only when the Soviets attacked would the US and NATO consider using nuclear weapons.[65] The Carpenter Report had sketched out a non-nuclear future for the RCAF, including strategic and tactical transport in support missions such as UN peacekeeping. Although these ideas had attracted little support from the Air Staff, they now resonated with approaches favoured by Paul Hellyer, the new defence minister. Though defence issues had been in the public spotlight throughout 1962 and 1963, they were not at the top of Pearson's agenda.[66] Under the new Liberal government, the defence budget accounted for less than 25 per cent of federal expenditures compared to 50 per cent during St. Laurent's tenure.[67]

As defence minister, Hellyer was a wilful individual with strong ideas. His appointment had dire consequences for the RCAF, though he is better remembered as the minister who initiated the unification of the armed forces. Hellyer's views on air power grew from his own lived experiences: time at the Northrop Aeronautical Institute, wartime RCAF service, post-war experience as Associate MND, and later as the defence critic for the Official Opposition.[68] Hellyer opposed the creation of a nuclear-armed air force and as Official Opposition defence critic had been a vociferous opponent of the CF-104 and the Air Division's strike-reconnaissance mission. He distrusted senior air force leaders, a perspective that influenced his approach to selecting new equipment for the RCAF.[69] Rather than accepting the RCAF leadership's desire to acquire new and expensive multi-role combat aircraft, such as the F-4 Phantom, Hellyer preferred spending DND's limited capital resources on an increased number of transport aircraft and a simpler ground support aircraft suitable for operations in Third World conflicts but not for fighting in NATO's Central Region.[70]

In March 1964, the Liberal government published its *White Paper on Defence*, which addressed a number of outstanding air power issues looking out to 1974.[71] The white paper confirmed that the government would not procure additional CF-104s to replace those lost through attrition. Over time, this led to a reduction in the number of CF-104s available for operations.[72] But at the same time, the white paper mentioned the acquisition of a "high performance aircraft" to conduct tasks ranging from "ground attack to air surveillance." This aircraft would be capable of rapid deployment, allowing units to be stationed in either Canada or Europe. There

At perhaps one of the last meetings between senior RCAF Officers and the Minister of National Defence prior to Unification, 14 April 1964. Left to right: Air Vice Marshal C. Annis, Air Materiel Command, Air Marshal Roy Slemon, Deputy Commander in Chief NORAD, MND Paul Hellyer, and Air Marshal C.R. Dunlap, Chief of the Air Staff.

was also a desire for the European-based squadrons to be more directly involved in the support of Canadian ground troops.[73] The paper suggested a decrease in resources for the North American air defence mission; however, the three CF-101 squadrons would continue their mission for the life of the aircraft while the RCAF would operate its two BOMARC squadrons "as long as they form an integral and essential part of the NORAD system."[74]

The centrepiece of the white paper was the creation of a mobile force, which would include land and tactical air forces. The organization would be supported by a significant enhancement of air transport capabilities, where "to have the flexibility in circumstances where improved air strips are not available … a considerable augmentation of the 'air truck' component of the air transport fleet is being undertaken."[75] Lessons learned from Canada's peacekeeping experiences during the Suez

Crisis in 1956 and in the Congo in 1960 provided further rationale for expanding ATC's capabilities.[76]

The white paper was vague regarding the future of MAC and the Air Reserves. In the area of anti-submarine forces, where MAC was making a substantial contribution, the white paper noted that ongoing studies were working on determining the most effective force mix, including maritime aircraft.[77] There was also the issue of a fundamental shift in the air force's anti-submarine role, from hunting and destroying Soviet submarine wolf packs to offensive operations against Soviet ballistic missile-launching submarines.[78] Equally uncertain was future facing the Air Reserves. They were mentioned in less than a single sentence: "… the Air Force Reserves have a role in support of ground forces in civil survival."[79] The number of Auxiliary squadrons would be reduced from ten to six and quipped with de Havilland Otter light transports.[80]

The eventual selection of a new tactical aircraft reflected a political rather than military choice and did not bode well for the RCAF's future. At Hellyer's direction, the government ruled out the McDonnell Douglass F-4 Phantom II (the choice of many RCAF leaders); and he limited the tactical aircraft competition to four aircraft.[81] The staff's recommendation, submitted on 15 February 1965, rated the A-7A Corsair II as the best option, with the A-4E Skyhawk second. The staff dropped the A-6A Intruder from consideration because of its cost and complexity, while it rated the F-5 as unsuitable.[82] The chief of the defence staff (CDS), A/C/M Frank Miller, noted that the CF-5 was ineffective for the air superiority role as it lacked radar, and it was equally unsuitable for the ground attack role because it lacked sufficient range when carrying a weapons load.[83] Ultimately, the government announced a contract for up to 125 licence-built Canadair CF-5s on 15 July 1965. Some suggested that Hellyer's vision of air power influenced the procurement of the CF-5 as much as Finance Minister Walter Gordon's fiscal constraint.[84]

The RCAF's further decline was evident during a Special Meeting of the Air Members, held on 12 June 1964 (shortly before the demise of the Air Staff, the decision-making body of the RCAF since the early days of the Second World War), which considered the RCAF program for FY 1965/66 and looked ahead to FY 1969/70. The overall RCAF budget was expected to remain constant at approximately $662 million. However, the service expected cuts from $541 to $498 million in the funding "envelopes" allocated to personnel, operations, and maintenance over the next five years.[85] A/C M.P. Martyn, the acting air member for personnel, anticipated a reduction of 4,000 members from the 1965 RCAF Regular Force strength of 51,135 by FY 1966/67, a number he subsequently expected to remain stable.[86] In fact, personnel ceilings would be considerably less than anticipated:

45,000 in 1966, 43,500 in January 1968, and 42,700 in 1969 prior to yet more personnel cuts enacted by the Pierre Trudeau government.[87]

Armed Forces Re-organization and the RCAF

The integration and then unification of the armed forces effectively broke up the air force and the other services as institutions, and thus greatly diminished the advocacy for a large air force within the defence establishment.[88] Furthermore, unification did not consider the cultural differences that existed between the three armed services.[89] The first change was Bill C-90, the 1964 "Act to Amend the National Defence Act," which restructured National Defence Headquarters, created the CDS position as the government's senior military advisor, and did away with the services' chiefs and their staffs. These changes resulted in an integrated Canadian Forces Headquarters (CFHQ), consisting of a single staff with senior officers from each service placed into various functional positions. Though there were RCAF officers who held various integrated appointments, there was no longer a professional head of the RCAF. Senior appointments of RCAF officers in the four integrated CFHQ staff branches included A/M Clare Annis as the chief of technical services, A/V/M F.W. Ball as deputy chief plans, A/V/M Edwin Reyno as deputy chief personnel, and A/C R.B. Whiting as deputy chief construction engineering. The new organization relegated the senior air force operations officer to the position of Director General Air Forces, at the rank of air commodore.[90]

The follow-on introduction of an integrated command structure for the Canadian Armed Forces in 1965 was another change that impacted the RCAF as an institution. The reorganization that replaced the existing command structure of the three services was based on a total of 11 functional and geographical commands, with six integrated functional commands consisting of: Mobile, Maritime, Air Defence, Air Transport, Training, and Materiel Command. ADC and ATC were continuations of the previous RCAF commands, while the RCN and RCAF had operated an integrated Maritime Command since 1959. No. 1 Air Division now reported directly to CFHQ rather than through a separate air force chain of command. In the field commands, the greatest change was the creation of Mobile Command, which consisted of mobile land and tactical air forces in Canada.[91] The commander of Mobile Command was an army officer, but there were two deputy commanders representing the Army and RCAF, this dual structure reflecting the initial importance assigned to tactical air support in the new command.

In May 1967, Parliament passed Bill C-243, the Canadian Forces Reorganization Act, which unified the three services into a single service, the Canadian Armed Forces, a structure that went into effect on 1 February 1968. Though the act did not directly change the conduct of daily operations on the flight line or in the cockpit, there was a significant impact on the institutional air force that many observers downplayed or ignored. The organizational restructuring at the strategic headquarters level and in the field commands violated the air force's cultural belief that centralized control of air power ensured that a single air force commander would provide the required "coherence, guidance and organization" in making the most effective use of air resources to accomplish objectives.[92] Unification's "penny packeting" of air force resources destroyed this tenet. The absence of a single authority that could speak on behalf of Canadian air power resulted in the emergence of various and insular air force communities: fighters, transport, maritime, and tactical aviation. These presented a fragmented, wasteful, and incoherent approach to air power and also signalled a further decline of a large air force voice and the cessation of any notion of independent air power in the Canadian context. Canada's air forces remained decentralized until the government reversed course and established the Air Command on 2 September 1975.[93]

Conclusion

Canadian air power played a vital role during a critical period of the nation's history. From 1948 to 1957, the RCAF became the leading air force among the middle powers. Along with the buildup of the RCAF, there had been the equally successful expansion of the Canadian aviation industry that was integral to sustaining a large air force. The RCAF contributed to the strategic defence of Western Europe and North America during the 1950s, but rapid technological advancements, strategic policy changes, and fiscal demands diminished that role by the early 1960s.

In their study, *Why Air Forces Fail: The Anatomy of Defeat,* Robin Higham and Stephen Harris postulate that "Service doctrine that is not in harmony with government policy is likely to produce circumstances in which air forces will fail; government policy made in isolation of service capabilities tends to do the same."[94] The RCAF found itself in this situation starting in June 1957. During its expansion after February 1951, the RCAF and the government maintained a synchronized policy that enabled the RCAF to emerge as Canada's dominant service, bringing about its "golden years." However, a synchronized policy could not exist in the absence of a coherent strategic vision.[95] For political and economic reasons, the government could not sustain the large air force that RCAF leaders envisioned, and the Diefenbaker and Pearson governments reduced the size of the RCAF. The demise of the large air force was evident both in the quantity and quality of its aircraft holdings. From a peak of 2,968 aircraft in 1956, the RCAF shrank to 1,300 aircraft by 1963.[96] In terms of quality, the RCAF of the 1950s was equipped with top-of-the-line fighters, such as the Sabre and the CF-100. The government selected their 1960s replacements, the CF-104 and the CF-101, primarily on political and fiscal grounds rather than as the best available equipment for the RCAF. The acquisition of the CF-5 represents a case of the dangers associated when there is inconsistency in the strategic visions of political and military leaders.

By the mid-1960s, the air force was caught in an unresolvable conflict between two concepts of air power. On the one hand, there was the institutional RCAF that had embraced the independent roles of the nuclear air force with its CF-104s, CF-101s, and BOMARCs. On the other, there was the development of a more balanced and flexible force designed to contend with the more likely forms of expected conflict. The RCAF had, as a result, to contend with the inflexibility of operating specialized aircraft designed for single roles that it could not use for other purposes. With its insistence on the nuclear air force, the RCAF failed to deliver flexible air power that would have provided the government with choices – the result was the imposition of strong political direction in what should have been essentially military decisions.

The expansion of the RCAF into one of the world's leading air forces during the St. Laurent years represented a considerable achievement for a nation of 14 million people. A dynamic political and military leadership acknowledged the need to allocate the required resources to counter the perceived Soviet threat. The existence of a strong aviation industry ensured the development and production of aircraft to meet not only the operational needs of the RCAF but also the requirements for the RCAF's greatly expanded training system that supported NATO needs and the provision of aircraft to Allied air forces. The development and realization of the large air force occurred at a unique time in the nation's history. "In 1945, it had been expected that the central government's preoccupation would be social security and domestic improvement. Instead, it was defence."[97] A large part of this preoccupation on defence was the attention devoted to air power. However, by the late 1950s, the quest for improved social and economic development became the priority for both political leaders and the public, challenging the rationale for the large air force. It was the existence of unique circumstances that enabled the RCAF to develop into a large air service, becoming Canada's first line of defence and representing the "Canadian way of war" during this vital period of the Cold War, circumstances that are not likely to be repeated.

NOTES

1. Alexander Angus Babcock, "The Making of a Cold War Air Force: Planning and Professionalism in the Postwar Royal Canadian Air Force, 1944–1950" (PhD diss., Carleton University, 2008).
2. Stephen J. Harris, "The Demand-Resource Dilemma: The Experience of 2nd and 3rd Tier Air Forces," Aerospace Power Forum 2005, Centre for Defence and Security Studies, University of Manitoba, Winnipeg, MB, November 22–3, 2005.
3. Bertram C. Frandsen, "The Rise and Fall of Canada's Cold War Air Force, 1948–1968" (PhD diss., Wilfrid Laurier University, 2015), 4, 7; Jonathan Vance, "The Royal Canadian Air Force and the Campaign for Air-Mindedness," in *Combat if Necessary, but Not Necessarily Combat*, ed. William March, vol. 3, *Sic Itur Ad Astra: Canadian Aerospace Power Studies* (Ottawa: Department of National Defence, 2011), 6.
4. Larry Milberry, *Sixty Years: The RCAF and CF Air Command 1924–1984* (Toronto: CANAV Books, 1984), 258; James Eayrs, *In Defence of Canada – Volume 4: Growing Up Allied* (Toronto: University of Toronto Press), 1980, 38.
5. James Eayrs, *In Defence of Canada – Volume 3: Peacemaking and Deterrence* (Toronto: University of Toronto Press, 1972), 79.
6. Eayrs, *In Defence of Canada – Volume 3*, 80.
7. Babcock, 38–56; Frandsen, 66–7.
8. Babcock, 37, 301.
9. Babcock, 44.
10. Eayrs, *In Defence of Canada – Volume 3*, 80.
11. Babcock, 73–6.
12. Babcock, 80–1, 87.
13. Babcock, 146–53; Frandsen, 99–100.
14. Frandsen, 80–1.
15. RCAF, "A Summary of Requirements and Estimates for Plan 'F' 1950–1951," 1949, 181.004 (D 46), DHH; RCAF, "Plan 'G' for the Royal Canadian Air Force 1 Sept. 1950 - Revision," September 1, 1950, 181.004 (D 47), DHH; Frandsen, 81, 100–1.
16. Group Headquarters, "Report on Exercise 'Drummer Boy' Held in the Puget Sound Area Nov 4th to 14th Inclusive 1949 Ex" (12 Group Headquarters, November 24, 1949), 181.003 (D40), DHH; Carl A. Christie, "Swords for Peace: RCAF Sabres with RAF Fighter Command," in *Combat If Necessary, but Not Necessarily Combat*, 16–18.
17. Lawrence Motiuk, *Thunderbirds for Peace: Diary of a Transport Squadron* (Ottawa: Larmot Associates, 2004).
18. Hugh Halliday, "In Korean Skies," *Canadian Aviation Historical Society Journal*, Vol. 24, No. 4, Winter 1986; Carl Mills, "Canadians in the Korean War," *Air Force Magazine*, Vol. 34, No. 4, April 2011.
19. Cabinet Defence Committee, "Extract from the Minutes of the 65th Meeting of Cabinet Defence Committee," July 19, 1950, 73/1223, Series 3, Subseries II, File 1324, DHH.
20. C. M. Drury to Chiefs of Staff Committee, "Acceleration of Defence Program," July 20, 1950, 73/1223, Series 3, Subseries II, File 1324, DHH.
21. RCAF, "Plan 'G.'"
22. F. H. Darragh, "Development of an Air to Air Guided Missile for the RCAF," October 30, 1950, 73/1223, Series 3, Subseries II, File 1324, DHH.
23. "Cabinet Conclusions of February 1st, 1951," February 19, 1951, 73/1223, Series 3, Subseries II, File 1325, DHH.

24 K.L.B. Hodson, "A Study of the Improvements Required in the Defence Measures to Be Taken in Canada in the Event of Sudden Attack or Threat of Attack Prior to Discussion with the US of Desirable Methods for Achieving Concerted Action in an Emergency of the Co-ordinated Defence Forces of the Two Nations," June 26, 1951, 96/24 AF HQ Fond, Box 4, File 6 [S-096-105 vol. 6], DHH; H. C. Lansdell, "Air Defence in Canada (Draft)" (Toronto: Human Resources Section, Defence Research Medical Laboratories, Defence Research Board, Department of National Defence, August 1951), 2003/32, File 48, DHH.

25 H.S. Rayner, "Chiefs of Staff Committee: Minutes of the 482nd Meeting," January 16, 1951, 3–6, 112.3M2 (D566), Box 1, File 2, DHH.

26 *House of Commons Debates*, 21st Parliament, 4th Session, February 5, 1951, 95–6.

27 Ray Stouffer, *Swords, Clunks and Widowmakers: The Tumultuous Life of the RCAF's Original 1 Canadian Air Division* (Trenton, ON: Royal Canadian Air Force, 2015), 24.

28 H.S. Rayner, "Minutes of the 503rd Meeting," August 14, 1951, 4, 112.3M2 (D566), Box 1, File 2, DHH; Stouffer, 76–7.

29 RCAF, "Air Council Minutes, 1951," 1951, 73/1223, Series 3, Subseries XIII, Box 90, File 1822, DHH; Secretary, Chiefs of Staff, National Defence Headquarters, "Chiefs of Staff Committee Minutes 1951," 1951, 112.3M2 (D566), Box 1, File 2, DHH.

30 RCAF, "Substitution of CF-100 Aircraft for some F86 Aircraft in 1 Air Division – Europe" in "Minutes of the 206th Meeting of the Air Members," 26 November 1954, 73/1223, Series 3, Box 91, DHH (All minutes for Air Members Meetings, referred to as the Air Council when the Minister was present, are located in this box. Here after cited as Air Member Minutes and either the date of the meeting or the meeting number); Stouffer, 93–6.

31 H.C.D. Upton, "The Ground Observer Corps," *The Roundel*, vol. 5, no. 8 (September 1953): 10–13.

32 The Canada – United States Military Study Group, "Interim Report," October 8, 1953, 73/1223, Series 1, File 92, DHH; C. Roy Slemon to Chairman, Chiefs of Staff, "Air Defence Planning Policy First Priority Target System for Air Defence," October 27, 1954, 73/1223, Series 1, Box 58, File 1105, DHH.

33 Hugh Campbell, "Brief by CAS to Cabinet Defence Committee," 1957, 73/1223, Series 5, Box 112, File 2500C, DHH. Air Council meetings between 1955 and 1957 regularly discussed the role of SAMs and nuclear rockets in air defence (e.g., see meetings held on July 6–7, 1955, December 22, 1955, May 6, 1957, and October 15, 1957).

34 Minister of National Defence to Cabinet Defence Committee, "Additional Regular Force Air Defence Squadrons and Bases," February 29, 1956, 73/1223, Box 20, File 356, DHH.

35 "Minutes of a Special Meeting of the Air Members," December 8, 1955.

36 A/V/M V.S.J. Millard, Chart 4 to Appendix C to Comptroller's Address to 1964 AOC Conference, April 14–16, 1964, 73/1223, File 2000, DHH. The growth and slow decline of the Auxiliary Air Force is described in more detail in Mathias Joost's chapter.

37 Plan "H" for the RCAF (August 1, 1952), 96/24, Box 4, File 9, DHH.

38 Frandsen, 179–83.

39 "Aircrew for NATO," *The Roundel* vol. 10, no. 5 (June–July 1958): 2–6. See chapter 8 for more on this important RCAF function.

40 William March, "A Most Abrupt Departure: The Royal Canadian Air Force and the United Nations Emergency Force," in *From Hot War to Cold War*, ed. Mike Bechtold and William March, Volume 6, *Sic Itur Ad Astra: Canadian Aerospace Power Studies* (Ottawa: Department of National Defence, 2017), 57–69.

41 Frandsen, 188–95.

42   While this is a summary of Granatstein's chapter, we acknowledge that his idea, chronology, and chapter title resonated with us as we prepared this chapter. J.L. Granatstein, "The Defence Débâcle, 1957–1963," in *Canada 1957–1967: The Years of Uncertainty and Innovation*, vol. 19, 19 vols., The Canadian Centenary Series: A History of Canada (Toronto: McClelland & Stewart LTD, 1986), 101–38.

43   Granatstein, *Canada 1957–1967: The Years of Uncertainty and Innovation*, 12, 62; Desmond Morton, *A Short History of Canada*, Sixth (Toronto: McClelland & Stewart LTD, 2006), 270, 275; J.L. Granatstein and Norman Hillmer, *For Better or For Worse: Canada and the United States to the 1990s* (Toronto: Copp Clark Pitman, 1991), 203.

44   Stouffer, *Swords, Clunks, and Widowmakers*, 113–14; Asa McKercher, "Dealing with Diefenbaker: Canada-US Relations in 1958," *International Journal* 66, no. 4 (Autumn 2011): 1043; Granatstein, *Canada 1957–1967: The Years of Uncertainty and Innovation*, 8–9; Granatstein and N. Hillmer, *For Better or For Worse*, 190–1.

45   C. Roy Slemon, Interview in Colorado Springs, interview by Dr. W.A.B. Douglas and Dr. W.J. McAndrew, Transcript, October 20, 1978, 79/128, DHH; Joel J. Sokolsky, "A Seat at the Table: Canada and Its Alliances," in *Canada's Defense: Perspectives on Policy in the Twentieth Century*, ed. B.D. Hunt and R.G. Haycock (Toronto: Copp Clark Pitman, 1993), 145–62.

46   Charles Foulkes, "The Complications of Continental Defence," in *Neighbours Taken for Granted*, ed. Livinston T. Merchant (New York: Praeger, 1966), 123; Peter T. Haydon, *The 1962 Cuban Missile Crisis: Canadian Involvement Reconsidered* (Toronto: Canadian Institute of Strategic Studies, 1993), 4, 8, 60–2.

47   Joseph T. Jockel, *Canada in NORAD, 1957–2007: A History* (Montreal & Kingston: McGill-Queen's University Press, 2007), 45–9.

48   Frandsen, 241, 248–50; Stouffer, *Swords, Clunks, and Widowmakers*, 98, 105–7.

49   Stouffer, *Swords, Clunks, and Widowmakers*, 107.

50   "Record of Cabinet Decision – Meeting of July 2nd, 1959," July 10, 1959, 73/1223, Series 1, Box 149, File 364, DHH; Raymond Stouffer, "Nuclear Virgin or Nuclear Strike?: John Diefenbaker and the Selection of the CF104 Starfighter," in *Combat If Necessary, but Not Necessarily Combat*, 29–40.

51   Foulkes, "Complications of Continental Defence," 103–5; Basil Robinson, *Diefenbaker's World: A Populist in Foreign Affairs* (Toronto: University of Toronto Press, 1989), 86, 91, 107, 114–15, 296; Michael D. Stevenson, "'Tossing a Match into Dry Hay': Nuclear Weapons and the Crisis in U.S.-Canadian Relations, 1962–1963," *Journal of Cold War Studies* 16, no. 4 (Fall 2014): 5–34.

52   Air Council minutes for July 7, 1953, July 9, 1953, and July 21, 1953.

53   Air Council minutes for 216th Meeting, April 13 and 15, 1955.

54   "Minutes of Special Meetings of the Air Members Sep 8, Sep 14, and Sep 5, 54;" P.F. Peter and C.R. Phripp, "A Study of the Canadian Air Defence Problem" (Directorate of Armament Engineering, Chief of Armament, RCAF, April 13, 1953), 2003/32, File 44, DHH.

55   Air Council minutes for June 4, 1954, July 2, 1954, October 4, 1954, December 22, 1956, and May 6, 1957.

56   Air Council minutes of November 26, 1954.

57   "CF-105 Aircraft – Appendix 'A' to "Report the Development of the CF-105 Aircraft and Associated Weapons System 1952–1958," 73/1223, Series 1, File 632, DHH. See Russell Isinger's chapter for more details on the Arrow.

58   Air Council minutes for October 15, 1957, October 19, 1957, and October 25, 1957.

59   John W. Warnock, *Partner to Behemoth: The Military Policy of a Satellite Canada* (Toronto: New Press, 1970), 324.

60 McKercher, "Dealing with Diefenbaker," 1046; Granatstein, *Canada 1957–1967: The Years of Uncertainty and Innovation*, 3, 12, 62, 193; Robert Bothwell, *Canada and the United States: The Politics of Partnership* (Toronto: University of Toronto Press, 1992), 89; Granatstein and Hillmer, *For Better or For Worse*, 203.

61 "Report of the Special Studies Group on Long Range Objectives for the RCAF," June 1962, 73/1223, Series 3, Subseries 13, Box 90, File 1819, DHH; Fred Carpenter, "The RCAF Report That Wasn't," *Canadian Military Journal*, Vol. 3, no. 2 (Summer 2002): 62–3; Paul Hellyer, *Damn the Torpedoes: My Fight to Unify Canada's Armed Forces* (Toronto: McClelland and Stewart, 1990), 109–10.

62 "Comptroller's Briefing to Members of Air Council and Visiting AOCs on 1962–63 Budget Reductions," July 11. 1962, 2, 73/1223, File 1863, DHH.

63 David A. Burchinal, U.S. Air Force Oral History Interview at Northrop Corporation Suite, Washington, DC, interview by Colonel John B. Schmidt and Lt Col Jack Straser, Transcript, April 11, 1975, 129, K239.0512-837, AFHRA; Dean C. Strother, U.S. Air Force Oral History Interview in Colorado Springs, CO., interview by Dr. James C. Hasdorff and Major Scottie S. Thompson, Transcript, August 21, 1978, 155, K239.0512-1095 C.1; IRIS #01043798, AFHRA; Arthur Agan, U.S. Air Force Oral History, interview by Lt Col Vaughn H. Gallacher, Transcript, April 19, 1976, 388, K239.0512-900, AFHRA; Gordon H. Austin, U. S. Air Force Oral History Interview in Alexandria, VA, interview by Hugh N. Ahmann, Transcript, May 18, 1982, 293–4, K239.0512-1325, AFHRA.

64 Robert A. Doughty et al., *Warfare in the Western World*, vol. II: Military Operations since 1871 (Lexington, MA: D.C. Heath and Company, 1996), 860–1; Kenneth Schaffel, *The Emerging Shield: The Air Force and the Evolution of Continental Air Defense, 1945–1960* (Washington, D.C.: Office of Air Force History, 1991), 260, 268; Schaffel, 106; Jockel, *Canada in NORAD*, 66–7.

65 Flexible Response was detailed in NATO MC 14/3 and MC 48/3. Jane E. Stromseth, *The Origins of Flexible Response: NATO's Debate over Strategy in the 1960s* (New York: St Martin's Press, 1988), chapters 2 and 9; Tom Keating and Larry Pratt, *Canada, NATO and the Bomb: The Western Alliance in Crisis* (Edmonton: Mel Hurtig Publishers, 1988), chapter 3.

66 Robert Bothwell, *Alliance and Illusion: Canada and the World, 1945–1984* (Vancouver: UBC Press, 2007), 180.

67 Ibid.; *Interim Report of the Special Committee of the House of Commons on Matters Relating to Defence* (Ottawa: House of Commons Canada, 20 December 1963), 12.

68 Raymond Stouffer, "Cold War Air Power Choices for the RCAF: Paul Hellyer and the Selection of the CF-5 Freedom Fighter," *Canadian Military Journal*, vol. 7, no. 3, Autumn 2006, 63–74.

69 Hellyer, 34.

70 Ibid.

71 Paul Hellyer, *White Paper on Defence*, Ottawa: Queen's Printer, 1964.

72 Ibid., 22.

73 Ibid.

74 Ibid.

75 Ibid.

76 See the chapter on peacekeeping in this edition.

77 Ibid.

78 Frandsen, 269–70.

79 Hellyer, *White Paper on Defence*, 22.

80 Ibid.

81 MND to CDS, "Equipment RCAF – Tactical Aircraft," January 7, 1965, Selection of a Tactical Aircraft, 73/1223, Series 1, File 214, DHH.

82 "Equipment RCAF – Tactical Aircraft, 8001-1500-(COPR)," February 15, 1965, Selection of a Tactical Aircraft DHH 73/1223, Series 1, File 214, DHH; Letter – comparison of A-4 and F-5, October 29, 1964, 981–100 (D/COPR), 73/1223, Series 1, File 215, DHH; "Equipment RCAF – Tactical Aircraft, 8001-1500 (ASec (COPR))," June 21, 1965, Tactical Aircraft – comparison of A-7A and F-5, 73/1223, Series 1, File 215, DHH.

83 Letter from CDS to the Minister, June 7, 1965, Tactical Aircraft, Equipment RCAF – Tactical Aircraft, 8001-1500 (CDS), 73/1223, Series 1, File 215, DHH.

84 W.H. Carsley, "History of Procurement CF-5 Aircraft and Tactical Aircraft Programs," 16 November 1971, CF5 History of Events 1964–1971, 73/1223, Series V, Box 113, File 2501, DHH; Ross Fetterly, "The Influence of the Environment of the 1964 Defence White Paper," *Canadian Military Journal*, vol. 5, no. 4, (Winter 2004–2005): 47–54.

85 "RCAF Defence Programme 65–66, A Special Meeting for Members," June 12, 1964, S000-115-65 (CAS) June 1, 1964, 73/1223, File 1965, DHH.

86 Ibid., 7.

87 *The Military Balance*, volumes 66, 68 and 69, Oxford University Press.

88 Vernon J. Kronenberg, *All Together Now: The Organization of the Department of National Defence in Canada 1964–1972*, Wellesley Paper 3/1973, (Toronto: Canadian Institute of International Affairs, 1973); Douglas L. Bland, *Chiefs of Defence: Government and the Unified Command of the Canadian Armed Forces*, (Toronto: Brown Book Company Limited, 1995).

89 Bland, 77–8; Allan D. English, *Understanding Military Culture: A Canadian Perspective*, (Montreal and Kingston: McGill-Queen's University Press, 2004); W.A. Curtis, "Testimony to Special Committee on Defence," June 9, 1964.

90 Kronenberg. More information for this reference? [FN not required – can delete]

91 Sean M. Maloney, "'Global Mobile': Flexible Response, Peacekeeping and the Origins of Forces Mobile Command, 1958–1964," *The Army Doctrine and Training Bulletin*, vol. 3. no. 3 (Fall 2000); "'Global Mobile II': The Development of Forces Mobile Command, 1965–1972," *The Army Doctrine and Training Bulletin* vol. 4, no. 2 (Summer 2001).

92 Canada. National Defence. *Canadian Forces Aerospace Doctrine*, B-GA-400-000/FP-000, Trenton: Canadian Forces Aerospace Warfare Centre Production Centre, 2007, 30.

93 W.K. Carr, "Canadian Forces Air Command: Evolution to Founding," *The Royal Canadian Air Force Journal* vol. 1, no. 1 (Winter 2012): 13–23.

94 Higham and Harris, 348.

95 Paul Dickson, *Strategic Visioning in Canada's Air Force*, DRDC CORA TR 2007–01, Ottawa: Defence R&D Canada, Centre for Operational Research and Analysis, January 2007. Scot Robertson, "What Direction? The Future of Aerospace Power and the Canadian Air Force – Part 1," *Canadian Military Journal* vol. 8, no. 4 (Winter 2007–2008): 5–13; Scot Robertson, "What Direction? The Future of Aerospace Power and the Canadian Air Force – Part 2," *Canadian Military Journal* vol. 9, no. 1 (Spring 2008): 30–8.

96 William Green and Dennis Punnett, *Macdonald World Air Power Guide*, (London: Macdonald & Co., 1963), 6.

97 Robert Bothwell, Ian Drummond, and John English, *Canada Since 1945: Power, Politics and Provincialism*, (Toronto: University of Toronto Press, 1981), 135.

CHAPTER TWO

NO. 1 AIR DIVISION, ROYAL CANADIAN AIR FORCE

RAYMOND STOUFFER

Introduction

No history of the RCAF during the Cold War would be complete without a chapter on the No. 1 Air Division. As Canada's primary air contribution to the North Atlantic Treaty Organization's (NATO's) forces in Europe for almost two decades, the Air Division satisfied a myriad of political and military goals at the national strategic, operational, and tactical levels. The story of the Air Division includes the aspirations, achievements, and frustrations of both airmen and politicians. These leaders were collectively responsible for the creation and operational sustainment of an overseas air force spread over four bases in eastern France and southwestern Germany. Ultimately, this civil-military effort made No.1 Air Division a successful symbol of Canada's contribution to the Alliance during the early Cold War. However, this collaborative journey was not always smooth. Not surprisingly, given the longevity of the Air Division, the expectations of Canadian airmen were not always satisfied as its later years were affected by the forces of change in Canadian defence policy. The RCAF could not escape reduced defence funding and the resulting re-evaluation of its institutional priorities. Consequently, the roles that the Air Division adopted, the aircraft it used, and its operational locations evolved over its lifespan.

Symbolic of the RCAF's "golden" years were the contrails of Air Division Sabres dogfighting over French and German skies. This impression, no doubt essential to the RCAF's public image, showcased the high-water mark of the air defence

Sabres conducting a flypast, No. 3 Fighter Wing, Zweibrucken, Germany.

role in the Air Division. Missing in this romantic image is the path that led to the RCAF's air power choices in support of NATO in Central Europe. This chapter will concentrate on the institutional, operational, and political compromises underpinning these choices. Two themes are noteworthy. First, while the air defence and later nuclear strike missions satisfied the RCAF's institutional and operational ambitions, Canadian airmen achieved these outcomes largely because they also fulfilled Canadian political and Alliance objectives. Second, if institutional security characterized the RCAF's air power choices for the Air Division, these decisions had national and operational implications. Eschewing the ground support role, and not wishing to operate under British command, Canadian airmen were not positioned to support the Canadian Army brigade in northern Germany. This decision pushed the RCAF operationally, culturally, and organizationally further into the orbit of the US Air Force. The Regular Force RCAF's skill in the air to ground role, acquired during the Second World War and retained in the early postwar years, was one that it would not regain until the later stages of the Air Division's life.

Sabres of No. 1 Fighter Wing, North Luffenham, England, conducting a flypast.

The Creation of NATO and the Birth of No.1 Air Division

Western European nations created NATO in April 1949 to counter the perceived growing postwar belligerence of the Soviet Union. The Alliance developed and deployed its military component, the NATO Integrated Forces, in July 1950. However, these forces were initially ill-equipped to meet the Soviet threat to Europe.[1] The catalyst for the much-needed defence spending by Canada and the Alliance was North Korea's attack on South Korea in June 1950. NATO leadership believed that the North Korean invasion was a Soviet-inspired diversion from its main goal, an attack on Western Europe.[2] On 30 October 1950, Defence Minister Brooke Claxton told the NATO Defence Committee that, "if the United States were to take part in an integrated force in Europe, Canadians would too, subject to parliamentary approval …"[3] On 28 December, the Cabinet Defence Committee (CDC) and Cabinet accepted NATO's request for one army brigade group (roughly one third of an army division) and 11 RCAF squadrons of aircraft. NATO initially wanted a composite air component of three air defence fighter squadrons, seven fighter bomber squadrons, and one fighter reconnaissance squadron. The Cabinet approved the request on 1 February 1951.[4]

The genesis of No.1 Air Division began months earlier. On 12 October 1950, the CDC authorized the deployment of three RCAF Sabre squadrons to RAF Station North Luffenham.[5] Originally sent to the UK as part of an RCAF training exercise, these squadrons formed the first of four fighter wings sent to Europe as mandated by the Canadian government. In July 1951, the RAF approved the transfer of RAF Station North Luffenham to the RCAF. No. 1 RCAF (Fighter) Wing Headquarters became operational on 1 October 1951, and flying operations at North Luffenham commenced on 15 November, with the arrival of 410 Squadron. The remaining two Sabre squadrons, 441 and 439, arrived the following spring. By the summer of 1952, No. 1 RCAF (Fighter) Wing was operational and integrated into the air defence of Great Britain.[6]

Building an Air Division

In several ways, establishing No. 1 Fighter Wing in the UK was opportune for the RCAF as it took three years to build its permanent base on the continent. In the interim, the RCAF learned important operational, logistical, and administrative lessons on how to run an air division overseas. The first wing commander, G/C Edward Hale, proved an excellent choice. Recognizing that he was commanding the first RCAF wing in the UK since 1946, Hale stressed discipline while maintaining a high degree of operational efficiency. His three Sabre squadrons gained much needed flying experience in the air defence role in Europe. But this was not just a training deployment. While in the UK, No. 1 Fighter Wing formed an integral part of the RAF's Fighter Command and was under the operational control of its commander-in-chief (CinC). However, wing administration and discipline remained under the control of the RCAF, a key national demand that would also be fundamental to the Air Division Headquarters in France.[7] Lastly, although the RCAF was welcomed by its British hosts, Canadian officials made it clear that the wing's stay in North Luffenham was temporary. Dana Wilgress, the Canadian high commissioner, reminded Britons that the RCAF was ultimately stationed in Europe for the defence of the whole Atlantic community, not just the UK.[8]

The UK experience aside, planning for the Air Division's presence on the continent was exceedingly challenging. There was a lack of guidance from Supreme Headquarters Allied Powers Europe (SHAPE), and Allied Air Forces Central

No. 1 Air Division Headquarters, Château de Mercy, Metz, France.

Europe (AAFCE) due to growing pains associated with being new organizations. This deficiency was exacerbated by a lack of RCAF staff at these headquarters. At a minimum, Air Force HQ (AFHQ) staff in Ottawa needed answers on air power roles, command and control (C2), and force structure. Without specific direction, AFHQ adopted the organization of the wartime RAF 2nd Tactical Air Force as a model. Consequently, the Air Staff chose a tactical air division of 11 squadrons, self-contained as to combat elements and ground services. The CAS, A/M Wilfred Curtis, informed General Charles Foulkes, Chairman of the Chiefs of Staff Committee (COSC), that "while it observed the principle of economy of force, this structure permitted the maximum utilization of the principles of concentration of force, mobility and flexibility."[9] In May 1951, a clearer picture on air power roles emerged after AFHQ staff conducted visits to SHAPE and AAFCE. USAF Lieutenant General Lauris Norstad, CinC AAFCE, placed priority on gaining air superiority. Given that the RCAF was equipped with the interceptor variant of the Sabre (F-86E or Sabre 2), Norstad wanted the RCAF to concentrate on that role. He needed the RCAF to protect USAF F-86 and F-84 bases. This guidance was good news for the RCAF. Limiting the Air Division to the air defence role was an extension of RCAF priorities in North America. Moreover, adding the attack version of the Sabre, the F-86F, would have required more expensive logistical support. Norstad also stated that the RCAF would come under the control of either an American or British tactical air force.[10]

In the end, General of the Army Dwight Eisenhower, Supreme Allied Commander Europe (SACEUR), made the decision in September 1951 to have the RCAF operate with the Americans and French in the 4th Allied Tactical Air Force (4 ATAF) and not the British-dominated 2 ATAF.[11] SACEUR's decision relieved Claxton of having to decide in favour of his pro-British chief of the general staff, Lieutenant General Guy Simonds, or the pro-American Foulkes. This decision also pleased the RCAF. First, there were operational and logistical commonalities between the USAF and the RCAF. Both used the F-86E in the air defence role in Europe and North America. Second, supporting the Canadian Army brigade for reasons of common nationality ignored the reality that the F-86E was not a tactical air support fighter. Third, the area of operations assigned to the RCAF in NATO's central region far exceeded the operational area of the Canadian Army brigade.[12] Fourth, and most significantly, the RCAF had institutional concerns about operating under RAF command. Postwar RCAF leaders felt that the British had hindered leadership opportunities for worthy Canadian airmen during the Second World War. A/M Curtis, who had been second in command of the RCAF in the UK in 1942 and 1943, resented the RAF's interference in the RCAF's attempts to increase national autonomy during the Second World War.[13] RCAF leaders raised similar concerns in connection to the RCAF operating in 2 ATAF. With the RCAF responsible for air defence and ground support of the Canadian Army, RCAF leaders feared that the RAF might break up these squadrons into more than one tactical air force. Reflecting these views, A/C Harold Godwin, a future Air Officer Commanding (AOC) of No.1 Air Division, wrote: "Hence our force would be dispersed in penny pockets, thereby losing its entity, lessening our control and reducing the magnitude of the RCAF effort in the eyes of the world."[14]

To get the Air Division operational, AFHQ created the RCAF Air Division (Europe) Planning Team in December 1951, under the leadership of wartime veteran and strategic planner G/C Keith Hodson. In January 1952, Hodson learned that SHAPE planned to assign the RCAF two wing locations in eastern France and two in southwestern Germany.[15] Ultimately, NATO gave the Air Division the airbases at Grostenquin and Marville, in France, and Zweibrücken and Baden-Soellingen, in West Germany. The next month, Hodson received more detailed briefings on Air Division operations

Sabres getting ready to depart Thule Air Force Base (Bluie West 1), Greenland, enroute to 1 Air Division squadrons in Europe.

and C2. While the Americans confirmed the need for air defence, the priority was to escort and protect the USAF's F-84 tactical nuclear fighter bombers. The commander of 4 ATAF, USAF Major General Dean Strother, assured Hodson that since the RCAF provided the bulk of air defence in Strother's command, he would delegate the Air Division's AOC considerable control of his wings. Hodson relayed this welcome news to AFHQ and also requested that Curtis assign RCAF officers to 4 ATAF's and AACFE's staffs to promote Canadian interests.[16] Curtis agreed. He approved the air power roles assigned to the Air Division, and he posted G/C Richard Cox to 4 ATAF.[17]

Most critical to Curtis was getting the Air Division's four bases established before the end of 1954. Alliance and national intelligence sources predicted that the Soviet economy would be able to support a prolonged war by this time.[18] The timely establishment of the Air Division was therefore an essential component of NATO's strategy to counter the Soviet's strategy as air power and American nuclear weapons were NATO's main hope in deterring and confronting the Soviet Union's

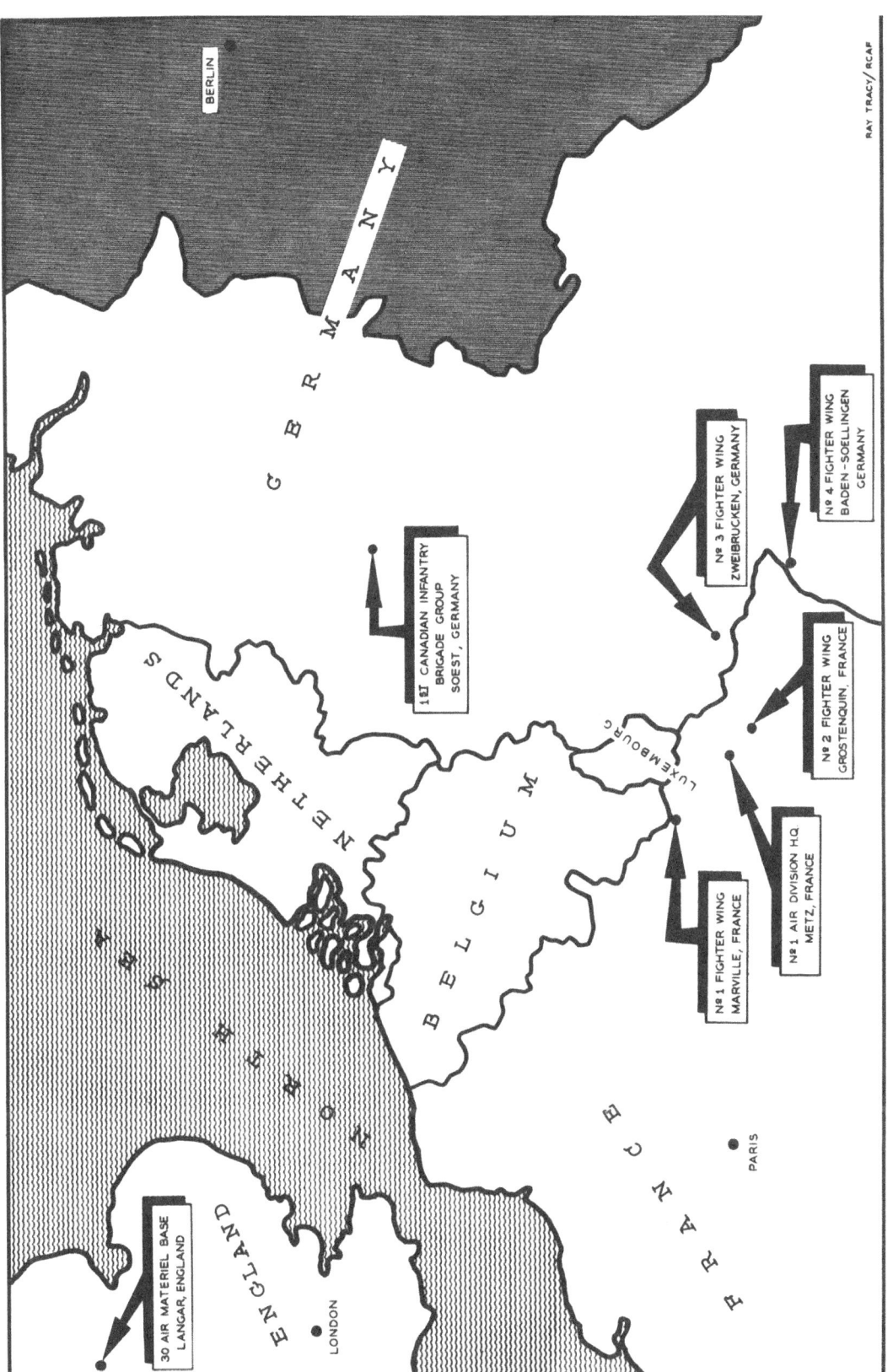

The map shows the four Fighter Wings stationed in France and Germany with their headquarters at Metz, France. All these bases were supplied by 40 Air Materiel Base in England. The First Canadian Infantry Brigade of the army is shown to the north in Germany.

numerically superior ground forces. Relying on superior air power, Alliance strategy had NATO forces meeting the enemy farther east in Germany rather than holding them at the Rhine, the latter situation placing the Air Division's four bases directly in the path of a Soviet thrust. Its 12 air defence squadrons were therefore crucial to defeating the enemy threat to 4 ATAF and NATO's Central Region.[19]

The RCAF completed the deployment of the Air Division according to NATO's desired timeline. On 1 October 1952, No.1 Air Division stood up in a ceremony in Paris. To protect RCAF institutional interests, Curtis selected A/V/M Hugh Campbell as the Air Division's first AOC. A future CAS, Campbell had worked for Curtis during the war, pushing for RCAF autonomy overseas. Important as well, Campbell's postwar, three-year tour in the US as chairman of the Canadian Joint Staff solidified RCAF-USAF cooperation.[20] Campbell's HQ was located at Mercy-Lès-Metz, near the great First World War battlefield at Verdun. On 11 October 1952, the AOC oversaw the official opening of No.2 (Fighter) Wing at Grostenquin, in Lorraine. No. 2 Wing became home to 416, 421, and 430 squadrons. On 7 April 1953, No. 3 (Fighter) Wing opened at Zweibrücken, Germany, with the arrival of 413, 427, and 434 squadrons. No.4 (Fighter) Wing officially opened at Baden-Soellingen, Germany, on 3 September 1953, with the arrival of 414, 422, and 444 squadrons. Finally, No.1 (Fighter) Wing departed North Luffenham in late 1954, but its three squadrons were temporarily dispersed at Zweibrücken and Baden-Soellingen until Marville, France, was cleared for operations in April 1955.[21]

The Early Years

The raison d'être of No. 1 Air Division was to protect and escort USAF F-84 fighter-bombers armed with tactical nuclear weapons. Therefore, the AOC's published roles for the Air Division, in descending priority, were escort of the 49th US Air Division (nuclear capable), air superiority, and offensive sweeps.[22] As confirmed by Air Division veterans, however, the emphasis at the wing and squadron levels was strictly on air defence. Even Lieutenant-General (retired) Chester Hull, the first wing commander of 3 (Fighter) Wing at Zweibrücken, was unfamiliar with the escort role of US strike aircraft.[23] As rationalized by an Air Staff officer at the time, "In every case the role is the same, that of destroying enemy fighters before they can attack the bombers."[24] Also, in a letter to G/C Hodson in February1952, A/M Curtis admitted that air defence was his Air Division's main role, but that he did not want to rule out performing other roles in the future.[25] The bottom line was that No.1 Air Division Sabre pilots trained to destroy enemy aircraft. While the genesis of the Air Division organization followed that of a wartime mobile tactical air force, the air

Scramble! Pilots from 414 Squadron, 4 (Fighter) Wing, Baden Soellingen, Germany, race to their aircraft during NATO Exercise Carte Blanche.

defence role was carried out from four static wings. Nevertheless, to increase survivability during war, each wing was assigned an alternate airfield. The Air Division was initially assigned four deployment airfields: Stuttgart in West Germany, Rocroi in France, and St. Hubert and Bertrix in Belgium.[26]

Initially flying the Canadair-manufactured Sabre 2, upgraded to the more capable Sabre 6 by 1956, Air Division Sabre pilots flew the best daytime air defence fighter in NATO at the time.[27] They engaged each other or flyers from other NATO air forces in dogfighting practice; however, the pilots also needed live-firing training. With limited airspace for military use over Western Europe, the Air Division conducted annual gunnery exercises at deployed bases. From 1954 to 1956, squadrons used a French air force base at Rabat, Morocco. After 1956 these squadrons used the more sophisticated gunnery range at Decimomannu, on the island of Sardinia.[28]

The air defence role required an integral warning and air traffic control function. Early on, this was provided by the French and the USAF. One Grostenquin

Aerial view of RCAF Station at Zweibrucken, Germany.

Sabre veteran, Roy "Mac" MacGregor, described his experience operating under French military radar: "Their control was perhaps a bit loose, but always enthusiastic and helpful, though differences in language didn't always help."[29] Thankfully for Air Division Sabre pilots, after 1 May 1955, they were directed by the RCAF's No. 61 Aircraft Control and Warning (AC&W) Squadron, equipped with the latest RAF-designed Type 80 radar.[30]

Another essential requirement for No. 1 Air Division was theatre-level logistics. As mentioned above, the RCAF insisted on maintaining national operational and administrative control over its forces in Europe.[31] To satisfy these ends, the RCAF established 30 Materiel Base, located at Langar in the UK. Langar hosted three RCAF units: 312 Supply Depot prepared shipments of aircraft, mobile equipment, and ground handling equipment; 314 Technical Support Unit looked after aircraft repair and overhaul contracts; 137 (Transport) Flight, equipped with five Bristol Freighters, and 12 C-47 Dakotas, gave the Air Division an integral air-transport capability. The flight moved freight and passengers between Langar and the four wings on the continent, as well between the wings and the gunnery ranges at Rabat and Decimomannu.[32]

With the introduction of Canadair CC-106 Yukon long-range passenger and transport aircraft in the fall of 1961, the RCAF established a direct supply and transportation link to Canadian-based national supply organizations. The 30 Air Materiel Base Langar was therefore closed and the number of Bristol and Dakota transport aircraft for intra-theatre airlift reduced. Beginning on 1 January 1962, 437 Squadron flew weekly missions between Trenton, Ontario, and No. 1 (Fighter) Wing at Marville. These included four freight flights that each carried 25,000 pounds and two passenger flights that each carried 120 individuals.[33]

Closely related to the improvement in air travel was the subject of the dependent families of the Air Division's military personnel. In April 1953, the Canadian government authorized dependents to accompany their military spouses to Europe. By 1956, married quarters were built at each wing, which pleased everyone. With this policy, military families enjoyed a higher quality of life than when living "on the economy" in civilian houses, and the military fixed a personnel problem. Military personnel accompanied by their dependents preferred a three-year posting. As such, the movement of dependents overseas eased manpower problems of the RCAF, since fewer members were required to provide a pool in Canada to furnish personnel for rotation.[34] In 1961, Defence Minister Douglas Harkness planned to repatriate all Air Division dependents and introduce a rotation concept for the Air Division's squadrons because of the need to cut defence costs. With the Yukon, the trip from Trenton to Marville took 12 hours instead of spending days crossing the Atlantic in a ship followed by a lengthy road trip to eastern France and Germany from the Channel. Since this air transport capability greatly reduced the cost of moving personnel to Europe, Harkness reversed course and did not to bring the dependents home.[35]

The Need for All-Weather Fighters

By late 1954, Soviet Tu-4 and IL-28 bombers, capable of operating at night and in poor weather, brought a new threat to NATO's nuclear forces. The Alliance desperately needed improved all-weather air defence in the Central Region,[36] Consequently, AAFCE requested that Canada replace four Sabre squadrons with the more sophisticated and all-weather capable Avro CF-100. The RCAF supported this plan, but only after the Canadian government and Alliance satisfied key operational and institutional demands. Most importantly, moving the four CF-100 squadrons to Europe could not come at the expense of the nine Canadian-based CF-100 air defence squadrons. Also, US Army General Alfred Gruenther, SACEUR, assured A/M Roy Slemon, who had replaced Curtis in 1953, that the

CF-100s would not be dispersed to units other than the Air Division. Gruenther also promised that the AOC, A/V/M Harold Godwin, would retain operational and administrative command over his RCAF units.[37] Between November 1956 and August 1957, each of the Air Division's bases saw one of its Sabre squadrons replaced by a CF-100 squadron from Canada. The Sabre squadrons all returned to the same RCAF station as their replacements and converted to CF-100s.[38] The Air Division henceforth protected 4 ATAF's tactical nuclear bombers around the clock and in poor weather.

The Changing Threat and a New Role

The CF-100s filled an operational void in NATO but changing Alliance air strategy put the future of air defence in doubt. In December 1955, the Cabinet agreed to NATO's increased reliance on tactical nuclear weapons in the interdiction and counter-air tasks.[39] By late 1957, NATO was emphasizing the use of strike and reconnaissance aircraft in coordination with the Alliance's missile capabilities. It was in the context of these changed roles for NATO's air forces that General Lauris Norstad, now SACEUR, pushed Canadian military authorities in 1957 for the Air Division to assume a strike role in addition to air defence.[40]

Slemon's successor, A/M Hugh Campbell, knew Norstad well, having just completed tours as No.1 Air Division's AOC, and SHAPE's Deputy Chief of Staff, Operations. While Campbell fully supported a strike role for the Air Division, he wanted the RCAF out of the European air defence role, which was increasingly being handled by each NATO member's own air forces. In December 1958, Campbell advised Gen Foulkes that this role should be undertaken by local European forces instead of the RCAF.[41] The institutional survival of the Air Division was also important to Campbell. In addition to satisfying changing NATO strategy, any contemplated air power role needed to assure the future of his beloved Air Division. Since the RCAF needed to replace its aging Sabres and CF-100s, Campbell's plan was to limit the replacement fighter to strike and reconnaissance (S/R). This strategy both satisfied changing Alliance air strategy and guaranteed a homogeneous, RCAF-led future Air Division. But this plan needed national support.

Fortunately for Campbell, in June 1958, the new Diefenbaker government announced it would continue the country's existing land and air commitments to NATO. This was no small commitment. Europe's postwar recovery was complete, while conversely, Canada was facing its first postwar recession and needed to cut defence expenditures.[42] A year later, General Norstad came to Ottawa to persuade the government to replace the Air Division's fighters with ones capable of

423 Squadron Canadair CF-100 Canuck at 2 (Fighter) Wing, Grostenquin, France. To augment the Air Division's all-weather capability, one Sabre squadron per wing was replaced by a CF-100 squadron in 1956.

performing the S/R role. SACEUR asked Diefenbaker not to increase Canada's land commitment at the expense of the Air Division.[43] On 2 July 1959, the Conservatives announced the procurement of 215 CF-104 Starfighters to replace the Air Division's Sabres. As requested by SACEUR, the CF-100s would continue to provide all-weather protection to NATO'S nuclear strike squadrons.

Campbell could not have been happier. With the strike role approved, and with the introduction of the CF-104, the national cohesion of the Air Division was extended. Better still, the government later agreed to relieve the Air Division of its air defence role in order to cut defence costs. On 1 June 1962, the government told NATO the four CF-100 Squadrons in No.1 Air Division and No.61 AC&W Sqn would be disbanded on 1 January 1963.[44] The 12 air defence squadrons were reduced to eight, albeit much more modern and lethal S/R organizations.

By the spring of 1963, the eight Starfighter squadrons were established in the Air Division: 439 and 441 Squadrons at Marville, 421 and 430 Squadrons at

The old and the new: An F-86 Sabre and CF-104 Starfighter in European skies.

Grostenquin, 427 and 434 Squadrons at Zweibrücken, and 422 and 444 Squadrons at Baden-Soellingen. Further, discussions were underway between A/V/M Larry Wray, the Air Division AOC, and 4 ATAF to ensure that the Canadian S/R squadrons could undertake their assigned roles by the expected operational date. Bases needed to increase security, including storage areas for the nuclear warheads. Pilots needed access to targeting data from 4 ATAF to create individual strike packages.[45] Unfortunately, there was one huge hiccup. The RCAF still did not have approval from Ottawa to use American-owned, tactical nuclear warheads on the Starfighters. Time was running out, and so was American and NATO patience.

To the frustration of the RCAF and NATO, the Diefenbaker government never did approve the use of nuclear weapons, even though that commitment was implicit in its approval of the strike role. Lester Pearson's Liberals defeated the Conservatives in the spring of 1963 in part because the incoming government promised to honour the country's commitment to arm its forces with American-supplied nuclear weapons.[46] To the relief of the RCAF, on 16 August 1963, the Liberal government signed the necessary US-Canadian agreement. But the contentious issue of nuclear weapons did not go away. Both Conservatives and Liberals were aware

Two 1 Air Division CF-104 Star Fighters.

that many Canadians did not support the idea of Canada being a nuclear-armed country. Nor were all Canadians comfortable with the corollary to this policy – closer dependence on the Americans.[47] More ominously for the RCAF, Pearson's commitment to nuclear weapons for the RCAF and Canadian Army was eclipsed by his subsequent goal to pursue a conventional role for the Canadian military.

As it was, the prime minister's plans for the Air Division proved consistent with extant NATO air doctrine. It incorporated the American strategy of "Flexible Response" that saw NATO less as a "trip wire," relying exclusively on nuclear weapons, and more as a holding force using conventional weapons.[48] As such, when 3 and 4 Wings passed the 4 ATAF tactical evaluations in June 1964, their squadrons were designated S/A – Strike/Attack. These squadrons met 4 ATAF's standard for both nuclear and conventional offensive roles. The two reconnaissance squadrons in 1 Wing, 439 and 441, passed their evaluation and were designated R/A – Recce/Attack. This achievement was remarkable given the RCAF's lack of postwar "recce" experience. Included in Central Region's 16 recce squadrons were 439 and 441

Squadrons. Competing against their fellow NATO recce squadrons in NATO's annual "Royal Flush" competitions, these two Air Division squadrons went from being dead last to winning each year between 1966–9.[49] Unfortunately for the RCAF, these tactical successes were overshadowed by institutional disappointment and uncertainty.

Within a year of achieving its coveted strike role in NATO, the RCAF learned that task would be of limited duration. In March 1964, Defence Minister Paul Hellyer confirmed that the Air Division's nuclear role would be terminated and replaced by conventional attack. Hellyer also announced that reduced defence funding precluded the purchase of attrition replacements for the Air Division's CF-104s.[50] Early maintenance and aircraft systems problems, as well as aircraft losses due to a worrisome accident rate, had quickly reduced the number of available aircraft. By the end of 1964, the RCAF had already lost 21 104s, with seven accidents resulting in the deaths of pilots.[51] Already angered that Hellyer was ending the Air Division's strike role, Canadian airmen went apoplectic with two further announcements from Hellyer. First, Canada would purchase the CF-5 Freedom Fighter to perform the conventional role. To CF-104 pilots the CF-5 was a "NATO joke" that would not have survived in the European theatre. For that reason, LGen (previously A/M) Fred Sharp, Vice Chief of the Defence Staff, rejected it as a replacement for the 104.[52] The CF-5 announcement was followed by the greatest bombshell of all: the RCAF's life as a separate service would end in 1968 as part of Hellyer's decision to integrate and unify the Canadian military. And there was more bad news. This time it came from France.

Unhappy with his country's participation in NATO, French President Charles de Gaulle made a series of demands on the Alliance, including national control over NATO nuclear weapons stored on French soil. This was unacceptable to NATO. Consequently, the Canadian government elected to move its two French-based Air Division wings as well as the HQ to West Germany. Grostenquin closed on 31 August 1964, and its two strike squadrons, 421 and 430, were "squeezed" into 4 and 3 Wings respectively. Marville's two reconnaissance squadrons, 439 and 441, and Air Division Headquarters moved to a newly allocated Canadian base in Lahr, West Germany, in April 1967. That same year, the AOC, A/V/M Reginald J. Lane, learned that the Air Division would be reduced to four S/A squadrons with the disbanding of 444 and 434 Squadrons. More reductions were to come.

In 1968, the new Liberal government led by Pierre Trudeau quickly delivered on its campaign promise to reduce Canada's NATO commitments. Canada's land force commitment was cut in half. No.1 Air Division was reduced to three squadrons, two strike and one reconnaissance. Operationally, Canada would be completely out of the nuclear role in Europe by 1972.[53] Trudeau had wanted to remove all Canadian forces from Europe, but he reconsidered when confronted with the resignations of his MND, Pierre Cadieux, and his external affairs minister, Mitchell Sharp, both veterans.[54] However, the chief of the defence staff, General Jean V. Allard, agreed with his prime minister. Allard believed Canada's continued presence in NATO's Central Region was only encouraged by the Europeans because it allowed the latter to minimize defence spending. Financial parsimony also underpinned the Europeans' preference for NATO's tactical nuclear forces. By comparison, building large, conventional forces was more expensive.[55] US Army General Lyman L. Lemnitzer, SACEUR, saw things differently than Allard. Lemnitzer pointed out that the Air Division's six S/A squadrons accounted for 33 per cent of 4 ATAF's total nuclear weapons delivery. This was a significant military contribution for a middle power, one that had raised Canada's profile at the North Atlantic Council level. In Lemnitzer's mind, withdrawing this RCAF capability would reduce Canada's political leverage in NATO.[56]

On 29 June 1970, No.1 Air Division was officially disbanded and renamed 1 Canadian Air Group. During the previous two years, the Air Division had closed 3 Wing, and Lahr ceased functioning as an operational fighter wing. What remained of an Air Division, once 12 squadrons strong with homes in four bases, had shrunk to three squadrons located at a single base. In 1972, 421 Squadron lost its strike role, and with its two sister reconnaissance squadrons, 439 and 441, converted to conventional attack operating out of Canada's only remaining European fighter base, Baden-Soellignen.

Conclusion

During its existence No.1 Air Division served both Canadian military and political ends. The latter proved overriding, as it should in a parliamentary democracy. On the other hand, the institutional aspirations of the postwar RCAF influenced how the Air Division was built, under what command it functioned, and what air power roles it fulfilled. But as shown, the realized designs of Canadian airmen were directly linked to the extent these were shared by their political masters.

If Canadian airmen relished the air defence role, flying the best daytime fighter at the time, and commanding their own national Air Division, these outcomes were equally satisfying to their political and alliance masters. Air power underpinned NATO's answer to a numerically superior Soviet military. The Air Division's Sabres, augmented by the all-weather and night capable CF-100s later on, were welcomed assets to SACEUR. Moreover, if NATO was happy, so were Canada's political leaders. The Air Division's success bought Canada international recognition.

With the election of John Diefenbaker's Conservatives, the RCAF's fortunes were less clear. At first, there was good news. The prime minister continued the country's alliance commitments, and he approved replacement fighters for the Air Division. Better yet, Diefenbaker approved the RCAF's coveted strike role, one that at once ensured continuation of a nationally cohesive Air Division and the RCAF's image as Canada's primary military service. Unfortunately for Canadian airmen, Diefenbaker never approved the American-owned nuclear warheads needed for the Air Division's strike role. If Canadian airmen saw the matter as simple military necessity, for Diefenbaker and his successor, Lester Pearson, it was no such thing. Many Canadians did not approve of nuclear weapons and the concomitant dependence on the Americans.

By signing the agreement to use American nuclear warheads, Pearson succeeded where Diefenbaker had failed. But the RCAF's positive reaction to this news was tempered by Pearson's subsequent direction that the Air Division was to move to a purely conventional role. The result was anger and embarrassment for the RCAF. Its coveted strike role lasted less than a decade. The RCAF's institutional powers waned in the face of increasing political oversight. The nadir came when Defence Minister Hellyer integrated and unified the military, ending the RCAF's stature as separate service. And just as Canadian airmen dealt with this blow to their beloved institution, Pierre Trudeau drove the last nail into the Air Division's coffin. The prime minister's force reductions led to the disbandment of No.1 Air Division, with the remaining squadrons in Baden-Soellingen limited to conventional attack.

While RCAF disappointment with its political masters was understandable, it was misguided. It was NATO, not Canadian policy, to wean the alliance off its exclusive dependence on tactical nuclear weapons in a confrontation with the Soviets. If replacing the S/R role with conventional attack satisfied successive Liberal governments, it was also consistent with an evolving NATO strategy. While the Alliance shared the RCAF's disappointment that Canada cut its forces in Europe, Canada's elected leaders, as opposed to the RCAF or NATO, decided national defence policy. It was also ironic that towards the end of the Air Division, its squadrons had become proficient in the conventional attack and recce roles. Their concerns for institutional independence aside, Canadian airmen could have done what they had avoided from the beginning – provide direct air support to the Canadian Army brigade.

In the end, unrealized RCAF institutional goals should not erase an impressive and important national contribution to the defence of NATO's Central Region for almost two decades. General Lemnitzer would have agreed with the Canadian political scientist, Joel Sokolsky, that the Air Division "symbolized Canada's commitment to NATO and the necessary minimum price for a seat at the [Alliance] table."[57]

NOTES

1 A/C H.B. Godwin, "Study of the Employment of RCAF Forces in Europe," March 10, 1951, RG 24, Vol. 6167, File 1, Library and Archives Canada (hereafter LAC).
2 Minutes of Cabinet Defence Committee (CDC) Meeting, October 12, 1950, RG 2, Series 18, Vol. 243 C-10-9, LAC.
3 Ambassador to Washington to SSEA, October 30, 1950, (telegram), DEA files, 50030-B-40, quoted in James Eayrs, *In Defence of Canada, Vol. IV: Growing Up Allied*, (Toronto: University of Toronto Press, 1980), 209.
4 CDC memo to General Charles Foulkes, Chairmen Chiefs of Staff Committee (COSC), February 19, 1951.
5 Minutes of Special Air Members Meeting with Sir John Slessor, Chief of Air Staff (CAS), RAF, held on October 11, 1950, File 73/1223, Raymont Papers, Vol. 1821, Directorate of History and Heritage (DHH).
6 Letter from A/M Curtis, CAS, to Air Member, Canadian Joint Staff, dated July 13, 1951, RG 24, Accession 1983-84/216, Box 3041, LAC.
7 Curtis, CAS, to Air Member, Canadian Joint Staff, dated July 13, 1951.
8 *The Times of London*, November 16, 1951, special correspondent at Stamford, Claxton Papers, RG 24, Vol. 110, LAC.
9 A/M Curtis reply to Gen Foulkes re: Air Division structure, dated April 9, 1951, RG 24, Vol. 6167, File 1, LAC.
10 Visit to SHAPE by A/V/M D.M. Smith, G/C C.A. Cook and G/C K.A. Hodson, May 1–12, 1951, RG 24, Vol. 6167, File 1, LAC.
11 Message from Maj Gen Smith to General Foulkes, dated September 14, 1951, File 73/1223, Raymont Papers, Series 9, Vol. 3233, DHH.
12 Address by A/C K. L. B. Hodson to the United Services Institute, London, Ontario, entitled "The RCAF Air Division in Europe," dated December 15, 1954, on file at Canadian Forces College (CFC) (Hodson) Library, Toronto, Ontario, 3–4.
13 Sean Maloney, *Learning to Love the Bomb: Canada's Nuclear Weapons during the Cold War* (Washington: Potomac Books, Inc., 2007), 20.
14 Study of the Employment of RCAF Forces in Europe, produced by A/C H.B. Godwin, D/AMAP/P, dated March 10, 1951, RG 24, Vol. 6167, File 1, LAC.
15 Letter from Hodson to CAS, dated January 28, 1952, RG 24, Vol. 6167, File 2, LAC.
16 Letter from Hodson to CAS, dated January 30, 1952, RG 24, Vol. 6167, File 2, LAC.
17 Letter from CAS to Hodson, dated February 10, 1952, RG 24, Vol. 6167, File 2, LAC.
18 Study of the Employment of RCAF Forces in Europe, produced by A/C H.B. Godwin, D/AMAP/P, dated March 10, 1951, RG 24, Vol. 6167, File 1, LAC.
19 Address by A/C K.L.B. Hodson to the United Services Institute …, dated December 15, 1954, on file at CFC (Hodson) Library, Toronto, Ontario.
20 Air Marshal Campbell, *Personnel Record*, LAC, Canada.
21 Message from Campbell to CAS, dated October 4, 1954, RG 24, Accession 1983–84/216, Box 3102, LAC.

22 Notes on discussion with LGen Norstad at SHAPE, October 26, 1954, File 73/1223, Raymont Papers, Box 132, DHH.
23 Interviews with Sabre veterans Roy "Mac" Macgregor, Leo Donovan, "Willy" Floyd, and Chester Hull, March and April 2004.
24 Staff paper written by Sqn Ldr Laubman, Director of Ops Research 3–5, dated March 5, 1954, RG 24, Series E-1-c, Accession 1983-84/049, Box 102, LAC.
25 Letter from Curtis to Hodson, dated February 19, 1952, RG 24, Vol. 6167, File 2, LAC.
26 Minutes of a Meeting of the Privy Council, dated March 18, 1958, File 73/1223, Raymont Papers, Series 9, Vol. 3233, DHH.
27 Laubman staff paper, dated March 5, 1954, RG 24 Series E-1-c Accession 1983-84/049 Box 102, LAC.
28 R.V. Dodds, "A Decade under NATO Flag," *The Roundel* 14, no.7 (September 1962): 13.
29 Interview with "Mac" MacGregor, Maxville, Ontario, April 26, 2004.
30 Minutes of the 200th Meeting of Air Members, Item 1086, held July 20, 1954, File 73/1223, Raymont Papers, Vol 1825, DHH.
31 Directorate of Public Relations, *Armed Forces News Release*, March 17, 1952, RG 24, Claxton Papers, Vol 110, LAC.
32 Internal Air Staff Memorandum, dated August 28, 1959, RG 24, File 096-56/1, Vol. 4, LAC.
33 Air Council Minutes, dated November 24, 1959, RG 24, File 096-100-56/1 Vol.10, LAC.
34 Minutes of the 93rd Meeting of the Cabinet Defence Committee: "Movement of Dependents Overseas," held on April 13, 1953, RG 2 Vol. 2749, LAC.
35 CAS letter to Douglas Harkness dated September 7, 1961, RG 24, File 096-100-56/1 Vol. 4, LAC.
36 Notes on Discussions with General Norstad at SHAPE, October 26, 1954, File 73/1223, Raymont Papers, Box 132, DHH.
37 SACEUR Message, SH 20911, dated June 6, 1955, File 73/1223, Raymont Papers, Vol. 132, DHH.
38 Air Staff meeting, dated April 1, 1955, RG 24, Vol. 6167, File 2, LAC.
39 Minutes of the 245th Meeting of Air Members, paragraph 1, held September 6, 1956, File 73/1223, Raymont Papers, Vol. 1826, DHH.
40 Chiefs of Staff Committee (CSC) memo for EA/CAS, "Air Division History," dated November 24, 1958, RG 24, File 096-100-56/1, Vol. 4, LAC.
41 Letter from Campbell to Foulkes, dated December 3, 1958, File 73/1223, Raymont Papers, Series 1, Box 363, DHH.
42 J.L. Granatstein, *Canada 1957–1967: The Years of Uncertainty and Innovation* (Toronto: McClelland & Stewart, 1986), 107.
43 Diefenbaker thanked SACEUR for convincing the CDC to place priority on the Air Division and to approve the Starfighter for the S/R role, 30 July1959, File 73/1223, Raymont Papers, Box 364, DHH.
44 Letter from CAS to all AOCs, dated August 13, 1962, RG 24, Accession 1983-84/049, Box 194, Vol. 12, LAC.
45 Detailed USAF operational instructions for "Nuclear Weapon Support of Canadian Nuclear Delivery Units Stationed in the Federal Republic of Germany", sent to A/V/M Bradshaw, AOC, No.1 Air Division, October 10, 1963, RG 24, G-13-10, Vol. 23319, LAC.
46 Granatstein, *Canada 1957–1967...*, 31–2.
47 Richard Preston, *Canada in World Affairs, 1959 to 1961,* (Toronto: Oxford University Press, 1965), 63–9.
48 Letter from George Drew, high commissioner for Canada in London, to Pearson dated October 8, 1963, DND, Hellyer Fonds, File entitled: "NATO 1963, Air Division in Europe – Equipment," MG 32, B-33, Vol. 74, LAC.

49 David Bashow, *Starfighter: A Loving Retrospective of the CF-104 Era in Canadian Fighter Aviation, 1961–1986*, (Stoney Creek: Fortress Publications, 1990), 52.
50 Douglas L. Bland, *Canada's National Defence, Volume I, Defence Policy*, (Kingston: Queen's School of Policy Studies, 1997), 58–60.
51 Memo written by G/C Smith, Director of Air Programmes, subject: "F-104 Deployment Update." dated November 29, 1963, RG 24, File 096-100-56/1 Vol. 4, LAC.
52 *CF-5: History of Events*, p. F-8, para 17(c), File 73/1223, Raymont Papers, Series V5, Vol. 2501, DHH.
53 J.L. Granatstein, *Who Killed the Canadian Military?* (Toronto: Harper Collins Publishers, 2004), 97.
54 J.L. Granatstein, *Canada's Army: Waging War and Keeping the Peace* (Toronto: University of Toronto Press, 2002), 361–3.
55 Unpublished paper written by Gen. J-V Allard: "Flexible Response and the Use of Nuclear Weapons in NATO, dated November 5, 1969, File 73/1223, Box 2528, DHH.
56 Maloney, *Learning to Love the Bomb…*, 330.
57 Joel Sokolsky, "A Seat at the Table: Canada and Its Alliances", in *Canada's Defence: Perspectives on Policy in the Twentieth Century*, eds B.D. Hunt and R.G. Haycock (Toronto: Copp Clark Pitman, LTD., 1993), 150.

CHAPTER THREE

THE RCAF, USAF, AND CONTINENTAL AIR DEFENCE, 1945–1957

RICHARD GOETTE

Introduction

The early Cold War period was uncharted waters for Canada-US continental defence collaboration. The two nations had come together to defend North America in 1940 because of wartime expediency. In September 1945, the Soviet threat remained distant – at least for the moment. Canadian and American planners had the luxury of time; nevertheless, there was a growing Soviet strategic bomber threat that required attentiveness to continental air defence needs. It grew to dominate the Canada-US continental defence relationship by the early 1950s.

Air force officers from both countries realized even in the first months of 1946 that the air defence challenge was a common one. The growing Soviet aerial threat required the RCAF and the USAF to work closely together to protect North America using a shared approach. Early cooperation between the RCAF and USAF's air defence systems was a positive development, but it was still insufficient. Proper protection of North America's populations and the USAF's Strategic Air Command (SAC) deterrent force necessitated, first, greater coordination, and then integration and centralization of bilateral air defences, which was achieved through the formation of the North American Air Defence Command (NORAD) in 1957. Simultaneously, Canada's air force professionals experienced a cultural paradigm shift from the RAF to the USAF as they worked closely with their American partners to gain a "seat at the console" for both planning and operations.[1]

General view of the Combat Operations Centre, Air Defence Command Headquarters.

Countering the Emerging Threat to North America

The development of a postwar Soviet aerial threat to North America provided the catalyst for Canada-US air defence cooperation. The USSR used American B-29 Superfortress bombers that had been forced to land in Soviet territory during the Second World War to reverse-engineer the aircraft. The resulting Tu-4 Bull was a virtual copy of the B-29 and was ready for service as a strategic bomber by the late 1940s. The Berlin Blockade, beginning in June 1948, brought the possibility of war – and a Soviet strike on North America – to the fore; and in August 1949, the threat became a nuclear one when the Soviets successfully tested an atomic bomb.[2] The USSR now had the capability to decisively attack North America via the northern approaches. How would Canada and the US respond?

Washington and Ottawa had formed the Canada-US Military Cooperation Committee (MCC) in 1946 to develop plans to counter the Soviet threat. The MCC consisted of Canadian and American service members plus one civilian representative from each of the Canadian Department of External Affairs and US State Department. Two of the RCAF members were A/V/M Wilfred Curtis and A/C C. R. "Larry" Dunlap.[3] Both would rise to the rank of air marshal and become the chief of the Air Staff. The future senior leadership of the RCAF thus had an intimate understanding of bilateral air defence planning in its infancy. Such awareness fostered the development of a close bond between Canadian and American aviators when it came to the requirement to integrate Canada-US continental air defences. A key MCC priority was to update the bilateral Canada-US Basic Security Plan (BSP). Defending against aerial attack was a vital consideration reflected in the BSP appendix entitled "Air Interceptor and Air Warning" (the AIAW plan).

Completed in December 1946, the AIAW plan had two distinct phases. Planners intended that Phase 1 actions, to be completed by 1950, would be adequate to counter both enemy bombers flying at subsonic speeds and short-ranged guided missiles armed with conventional explosives. It called for Canada and the US to construct an integrated early warning and ground control intercept system of radars and fighter-interceptor aircraft. Radar chains would be established throughout North America, including the coasts, northern regions, and near the continent's vital economic and population centres. It also called for an interceptor force of 975 American and 828 Canadian fighters. Planners expected the second phase, beginning in 1955, to respond to the more dangerous threat of large numbers of supersonic jet bombers and long-range guided missiles armed with atomic weapons. Air defences would move farther north with an early warning radar network in the Arctic augmented by increased interceptor aircraft and advanced surfaced-to-air missiles. Canadian and American command organizations would be responsible for the air defence of their own territory, and each headquarters would have liaison personnel from the other nation. The AIAW plan also called for the creation of a combined Canada-US Air Defence Command consisting of officers from both nations. It would be responsible for all Canadian and American air defence units deployed in North America with an American officer as its commander.[4]

The AIAW plan was ambitious, especially so soon after the Second World War when the Soviet threat was not fully apparent. Although both nations' chiefs of staff approved the AIAW plan in principle, they did little to implement it since it was only a planning document with no formal obligations for Canada or the US to act upon.[5] Even though the most grandiose aspects of the AIAW plan never came to fruition, it was remarkably predictive (albeit on a smaller scale) of the RCAF and USAF leaders' efforts to integrate North American air defences in the late 1950s. This work planted the seeds of North American air defence integration. In the late 1940s, the first step was to establish national air defence commands.

North American Mustang fighters belonging to 420 and 424 Auxiliary Fighter Squadrons. Along with the Vampire, these aircraft were committed to Canadian air defence in the early Cold War.

After the Second World War, the RCAF quickly demobilized and maintained only a minimal force with the Auxiliary (described in chapter 10) to provide protection against aerial attack. The RCAF Auxiliary had an authorized establishment of 4,500 with 15 squadrons located in large cities across the country. Most of its air personnel were fighter pilots from the Second World War, and the squadrons were equipped with P-51 Mustangs and later DH-100 Vampires (the first operational jet fighters in North America). Mobile radar units staffed by both Auxiliary and Regular Force personnel directed these aircraft in the interceptor role. However, these were rather rudimentary air defence measures.[6]

In response to the growing Cold War tensions of the late 1940s, the RCAF began to dedicate greater resources and attention to air defence. On 1 December 1948, it established No. 1 Air Defence Group (1 ADG) and charged it with protecting

United States Airforce B-36 of Strategic Air Command being escorted by a CF-100 Canuck.

the country from air attack. This included administration and control of both air defence operations (i.e., interceptors and the growing early warning network) and training. G/C W.R. MacBrien was 1 ADG's commander, and his first task was to prepare a comprehensive air defence plan for Canada.[7]

MacBrien presented his plan at the Air Members meeting on 27 January 1949. It came up against an alternative proposal developed by G/C E.H. Evans, the director of the RCAF Air Plans section. The plans represented different schools of thought regarding how to manage the RCAF's emerging air defence system. Evans's plan placed greater emphasis on point defence by recommending the stationing of RCAF fighter-interceptor bases closer to urban areas. However, the Air Members preferred MacBrien's plan because it was more consistent with the AIAW and its concept of air defence in depth.[8] MacBrien wanted bases located farther north. This would push the air battle away from North America's vital centres and allow

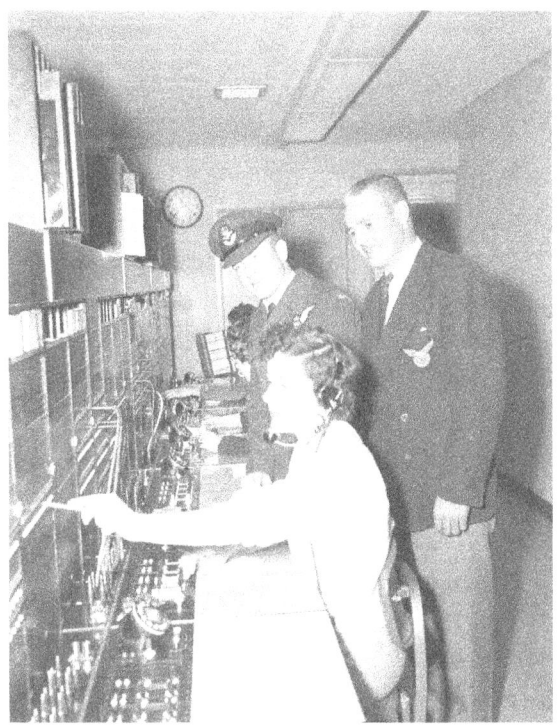

An often overlooked part of early Cold War Canadian air defence was the Ground Observer Corps, a primarily civilian organization that kept an eye skyward throughout the country. Here Miss Ann Davies, at the Northwest Telephone Company, can pass a flash message on an unidentified aircraft to the Corps Filter Centre in Vancouver in 15 seconds. Observing the process is L to R: Flying Officer J.R. Mungham of the Ground Observer Corps Headquarters in Vancouver, and Corps Regional Supervisor Lloyd Leishman.

interceptors to interdict enemy bombers quickly and effectively after detection by the continental radar network. The measures would also provide the USAF's Strategic Air Command (SAC) the warning time required to launch a nuclear counterstrike.[9] The importance of the RCAF air defence plan would soon become apparent.

The Soviet explosion of an atomic bomb in August 1949 and the outbreak of the Korean War in 1950 created an air defence crisis in North America that led to greater attention towards and funding for the RCAF's air defence mission. Canada centralized all of its air defences in June 1950 by placing the Canadian Army's Anti-Aircraft Command's units under the operational control of the 1 ADG commander and co-locating the Army air defence HQ with 1 ADG.[10] Additionally, the RCAF elevated 1 ADG to be the RCAF Air Defence Command

(ADC) in June 1951 and placed it under the command of A/V/M Dunlap, with MacBrien as his deputy.[11]

Headquartered in St. Hubert, Quebec, ADC benefitted greatly from the Canadian government's accelerated defence program. It grew steadily during the early 1950s; and by 1955, had reached its authorized strength of 19 fighter-interceptor squadrons (nine Regular Force and ten Auxiliary).[12] The Air Officer Commanding (AOC) ADC was responsible for Canada's air defence system, which included air defence planning and training, oversight of the radar network and control system (described below), and command of the Ground Observer Corps of civilian volunteers as well as RCAF fighter squadrons in Canada. Bilateral air defence exercises, a direct system of communications between St. Hubert and USAF Air Defense Command Headquarters in Colorado Springs, and daily briefings between the two air defence headquarters ensured greater RCAF-USAF cooperation than in earlier years. Additionally, ADC began sending liaison officers to Colorado Springs in 1951 to provide a more continental approach to air defence.[13] However, this was only the beginning of the growing institutional connection between the two air forces.

The RCAF's Cultural Integration with the USAF

Culture played an important role in the early Cold War RCAF-USAF air defence relationship. In addition to identifying themselves as military professionals, RCAF personnel also identified with service culture, in other words the customs and traditions, and in particular the institutional knowledge and skills associated with air power and air forces.[14] Professional military identity was also transnational. Joel Sokolsky has called this the "international fraternity of the uniform," which encompasses a "set of institutional and personal ties … [where] allegiance is to the common goal and the military means of implementing it."[15] RCAF personnel increasingly identified themselves with the USAF as part of the general cultural trend that moved away from British military traditions towards those of the US.

Many RCAF personnel found the USAF more welcoming than the RAF. Several RCAF officers had served in wartime British higher formations during the Second World War. Some remembered with distaste their subordinate position within the RAF commands, where they were shut out of senior leadership and staff positions.[16] For instance, during the mid-1950s there was talk of assigning the RCAF's No. 1 Air Division to the British sector in Europe. A/C Keith Hodson, who commanded a tactical fighter wing in Normandy and would become NORAD's first chief of operations, remarked that there was a Canadian "sentimental reluctance to joining the RAF to whom we surrendered our identity in the last war."[17] The USAF, by

Maintenance crew from 409 Squadron working on a CF-100 Canuck, RCAF Station Comox, BC.

contrast, was much more accepting of RCAF personnel. As Raymond Stouffer observes, because Canadian and American air force officers "came from similar social backgrounds," it "was less a cultural affront" for them to work together. Notably, the USAF treated their RCAF partners as peers instead of the "colonial" British attitude towards the Canadians during the war.[18]

In particular, the North American air defence mission was a culturally unifying force. The RCAF and the USAF ADCs saw air defence as a common continental problem. They agreed on the interrelated goals of defending people, cities, and industries from Soviet strategic bombers and of protecting the deterrent value of SAC as way to prevent the outbreak of a nuclear war.[19] Yet even with the RCAF's cultural shift towards the USAF, it was not at the expense of Canadian identity or Canada's unique national approach to military matters. Although RCAF air defence cooperation with the USAF was in direct support of (and therefore made an important contribution to) the overall American offensive strategic posture, the

RCAF's role in the continental air defence system was still doctrinally a defensive one that appealed to the Canadian public and politicians and served Canada's security interests.[20]

The RCAF was able to reinforce this support and raise the profile of its air defence mission via engagements with the public and important stakeholders. For instance, when speaking to the Trenton Chamber of Commerce A/C Clare Annis, the senior staff officer at ADC, likened the RCAF's contribution to continental air defence to a game of rugby to make it more understandable and justifiable to Canadian citizens.[21] There was an internal audience too and when speaking to the Canadian Army Staff College in 1955, Hodson outlined not only the value of air forces to armies for joint operations, but also how the destructive power of strategic bombers armed with nuclear weapons necessitated greater peacetime air defences to defend the continent's vital areas and protect the SAC deterrent.[22]

Canadian aviators were also not as engrossed by SAC nuclear bomber theory and doctrine as their USAF counterparts. Historian James Eayrs has credited the RCAF for its cautious approach of "capitalizing on (but not capitulating to) doctrines of air power sedulously propagated in the United States" and "reject[ing] the simplistic SAC approach to international problems."[23] J.I. Jackson, then a professor at the RCAF Staff College, echoes this sentiment, noting that the RCAF "avoid[ed] the USAF's excesses."[24] It was with these cultural factors in the background that the RCAF sought to integrate its air defence efforts with the USAF in the 1950s.

Steps towards Operational Integration

To ensure that both USAF and RCAF fighter-interceptors could effectively counter a Soviet bomber attack on North America, interception, engagement, and mutual reinforcement in each other's airspace would have to take place during a peacetime air defence emergency as well as during war. In 1951, both governments approved an agreement granting RCAF and USAF air defence commanders the authority to redeploy interceptors to either country in the event of war.[25] This arrangement allowed USAF interceptors to enter Canadian airspace and be redeployed to RCAF bases and vice versa if the progress of the air battle in a wartime emergency so dictated.[26] However, an agreement on cross-border interception and engagement proved to be more difficult.

Radar technology in the early 1950s necessitated collaboration between Canadian and American air defence forces because of the intricate cooperation required between interceptor pilots and air controllers on the ground. When ground radars picked up an intruding aircraft, interceptors scrambled, and the local Air Defence

Control Centre (ADCC) vectored them to the aircraft.[27] While simple in principle, the matter was made complex by the geographical location of certain elements of the Canadian and American air defence systems. ADCCs of one nation often had to vector interceptors from the other country in either country's airspace. This was especially true in the Prairies and Newfoundland, where the only nearby ADCCs were in the US, and the RCAF had no interceptor resources due to priorities elsewhere in Canada.[28] The prospect of the USAF vectoring American interceptors onto intruders in Canadian airspace also brought forth Canadian sovereignty concerns that needed to be addressed.

Completed in May 1951, the USAF was not satisfied with the initial agreement on cross-border intercepts and viewed it as only a temporary measure. Although it gave reciprocal permission to the USAF and the RCAF to cross each other's border and intercept unidentified aircraft, USAF interceptors had to wait until intruding aircraft entered American airspace before engaging them.[29] Negotiations for a new arrangement continued for several months, resulting in a compromise agreement in October 1953. USAF interceptors would have to adhere to RCAF Rules of Engagement (ROE) in Canadian airspace and vice versa; and the national air defence commander could delegate tactical control authority to order an engagement to an ADCC of the other country if there was no ADCC from that country nearby.[30] This agreement also complemented the mutual reinforcement provisions. However, the situation in Newfoundland, where American forces were located at bases gained from the British during the Second World War, required a separate arrangement.

In addition to being in the northeast approaches to North America, American bases in Newfoundland and Labrador also directly supported the US nuclear deterrent as a launching and refuelling point for SAC's bombers. Providing air defences for these bases was therefore a vital consideration for the Americans. The air defence mission in Canada's newest province (as of 1949) had to be a bilateral and collaborative one between the USAF and RCAF due to the unique status of the American bases and Canada's sovereignty concerns. When the Americans established a new command organization in Newfoundland in 1950, they negotiated an understanding with the Canadians that it would be called "*US* Northeast Command" to allay Canadian fears that the name "Northeast Command" might give the impression that the US was responsible for the defence of the entire northeastern part of the continent.[31] US Northeast Command (USNEC) stood up on 1 October 1950, at Fort Pepperrell, in St. John's, with USAF Major General Lyman T. Whitten as its commander-in-chief (CinC).[32]

In September 1952, the USAF began assigning fighter-interceptor squadrons to USNEC due to growing concerns that Soviet bombers might attack targets in

Two 421 Auxiliary Fighter Squadron Vampire aircraft airborne for a routine patrol.

Newfoundland and Labrador.[33] The RCAF did not have additional resources to defend its new province due to pressing concerns elsewhere in Canada as well as the requirement to provide fighters for the defence of Europe as part of Canada's commitment to the NATO (see chapter 2). Fearing that the air defence of Canadian territory in the Atlantic region would fall to the United States by default, Canada sought an RCAF contribution to USNEC to safeguard Canadian interests and sovereignty.[34] Initial ideas to have an RCAF officer serve as either USNEC's deputy commander (Canadian proposal) or as a senior staff officer (American proposal) proved unworkable.[35] The RCAF and USAF finally resolved the issue by viewing American air defence forces in Newfoundland as part of the overall system of continental air defence. In April 1953, the American Joint Chiefs of Staff (JCS) gave the AOC RCAF ADC operational control over USNEC's air defences, in peace or war, an arrangement that included American fighters adhering to RCAF ROEs.

However, there was a catch: the AOC was to designate a component commander to whom he would assign local operational control of USAF air defence forces in Newfoundland.[36] Since there were no RCAF ADC forces in Newfoundland, the only choice for a component commander was the USNEC commander. This arrangement resolved the air defence coordination issue in Newfoundland; however, for this and the other arrangements for mutual reinforcement and cross-border interception to function properly, the RCAF needed proper equipment and systems. The development of fighter-interceptor resources and the construction of a radar network was consequently an additional important feature of RCAF-USAF operational air defence integration.

The RCAF dedicated significant resources and attention to this integration with the Americans. In its early days, 1ADG equipped its squadrons initially with Vampires and then F-86 Sabres. In the early 1950s, the RCAF further contributed to North American air defence by designing and fielding the all-weather CF-100 Canuck interceptor and manufacturing American-designed F-86 Sabres by Canadair in Canada.[37] When the CF-100 became operational, ADC formed and deployed nine squadrons to defend vital areas throughout the country, with two Regular force squadrons each at Bagotville and St-Hubert, Quebec; North Bay and Uplands, Ontario; and one squadron at Comox, BC.[38]

The system to vector these interceptors towards intruding aircraft was another important operational feature of binational air defence cooperation. During the 1950s, Canada and the US built and operated a series of radar chains in Canada: the Pinetree Line, the Distant Early Warning (DEW) Line, and the Mid-Canada Line (MCL). The US and Canada agreed to construct the Pinetree Line in 1951 to protect North American industrial and population centres from the emerging Soviet atomic threat. By 1954, the two countries had built a total of 33 radar sites that were located close to the border, roughly along the 50° north latitude, to complement the USAF's Permanent radar system.[39] Canada financed 11 of the stations while the US funded the remainder. Although traditionally viewed as a radar network, Pinetree was "not solely a warning line but a command-and-control system for the identification and interception of unknown aircraft."[40] The USAF managed 17 of the American-built stations, while the rest were operated through a bilateral effort consisting of both USAF and RCAF personnel, including civilians. The Pinetree sites formed the Aircraft Control and Warning (AC&W) system that detected and plotted aircraft passing information to the regional ADCCs, and manually vectoring interceptors to the target.[41]

The Soviet Union's explosion of a thermonuclear bomb in 1953 (see below), caused great consternation in Canada and the US; it was recognized that the

The radar domes of RCAF Station Foymount, ON, on a typical northern Ontario winter day. A Pinetree Line radar site, Foymount was opened in 1952.

Pinetree system was insufficient to defend North America from the growing Soviet threat. The Canadian government agreed to expand its air defence relationship with the US, and this gave the RCAF an opportunity to make a larger contribution to North America's strategic defence. The resulting Mid-Canada and DEW Lines increased the ability to detect Soviet bombers in the Arctic approaches to North America.

Completed in 1957, the DEW Line was built north of the Arctic Circle in Alaska, Canada, and later Greenland, at approximately 70° north. It was an intricate system of radars spaced 80km apart, these supplemented at 160km intervals by auxiliary stations equipped with standard long-range radars.[42] The USAF funded the system and staffed it using civilian contract employees. These contractors were needed because of RCAF personnel shortages, but Canadian law applied to all Canadian stations, and Canada reserved the right to operate these stations as soon as the

An RCAF Sikorsky H-19 helicopter delivering supplies to the construction site for a Mid-Canada line radar installation.

RCAF had trained the necessary operators.[43] Meanwhile, Canada fully funded and built the MCL using Canadian technology and staffed it entirely with RCAF personnel. Finished in 1958 and located farther south, at approximately 55° north, it complemented the DEW Line. MCL radars tracked the intruding aircraft that had originally been detected by the DEW Line in the Arctic, thus providing RCAF and USAF fighters information on the direction of the target to aid vectoring and interception.[44]

Together, the MCL and DEW Line provided an effective "tripwire." Its purpose was threefold: provide warning to the civilian population and civil defence authorities to seek shelter or to begin evacuations; give interceptors the opportunity to destroy enemy bombers before they could strike North America's vital targets; and most importantly, protect the strategic deterrent by providing sufficient warning to SAC to launch a counter-attack.[45] The radar networks, the cross-border interception and mutual reinforcement protocols, and the Newfoundland arrangements all led to greater coordination of Canadian-American air defences. These adaptations respected the concept of air defence in depth, ensured that the air defence battle could be fought effectively regardless of the Canada-US border, and at the same time addressed sovereignty concerns. The next logical step in the RCAF-USAF air defence relationship was to achieve integration.

Integrating Canadian-American Air Defences: Establishing NORAD

The destructive power of Soviet thermonuclear bombs delivered by long-range jet bombers became the catalyst for the full integration of RCAF and USAF air defences. The coordination of two air defence systems, which had been the nucleus of continental air defence since the early 1950s, would no longer suffice against this new threat. In response, the Americans restructured their air defences by establishing the joint Continental Air Defense Command (CONAD) in September 1954, and in 1956 CONAD was given responsibility for all American air defence forces in North America. This included US bases in Newfoundland, and thus led to the closure of USNEC.[46] With US air defences integrated, the stage was set to make this a continental effort by bringing the RCAF into the fold.

In the spring of 1954, the commanders of USAF ADC and RCAF ADC established the Canada-US Air Defence Study Group (ADSG). Including staff from both air defence commands, ADSG explored the most effective way to protect North America from air attack.[47] The group concluded that the modern air defence battle required quick decision-making. This necessitated the creation of a combined Canada-US air defence command under one commander. This organization would be responsible to both governments and should be established in peacetime to be ready for an air defence emergency.[48] The CAS, A/M Roy Slemon, agreed.[49] However, the RCAF had to first overcome Canadian political sensitivities. Although cool to the idea of integrating Canadian and American air defences under one overall commander, Canadian government officials were not completely opposed to it. Military planners therefore needed to find the right arrangement that would safeguard Canadian sovereignty while simultaneously ensuring efficient continental air defence. The solution was to avoid using the term "command" and to instead use a concept known as "operational control."

In the summer of 1956, the Canadian Chiefs of Staff Committee (COSC) and the JCS agreed to form an ad hoc study group consisting of officers from the USAF, US Army, US Navy, RCAF, and Canadian Army. Its purpose was to study how to use operational control to facilitate integration of the two air defences.

Three CF-100 Canucks overflying the headquarters of Air Defence Command, RCAF Station St Hubert, QC.

The group's final report, in December 1956, recommended designating a single commander to exercise operational control over the air defences of both countries. CinC CONAD would become the new CinC Air Defence Canada-United States (CINCADCANUS). The new CinC would be responsible to COSC and the JCS, who would, in turn, be responsible to their respective political authorities. The report also proposed appointing an RCAF officer to be the Deputy CinC (DCinC). That officer would be in charge in the absence of the USAF CinC. An integrated headquarters would be established consisting of both Canadian and American personnel, making air defence a completely binational organization.[50] CINC ADCANUS would delegate operational control to subordinate component commanders of geographic areas, although these remained to be determined. Each service providing forces to the component commands would retain national command. This provision was particularly important for Canada, as RCAF ADC would be one of the proposed component commands. The AOC ADC would be responsible to CINC ADCANUS in Colorado Springs for operational control but would still be responsible to the CAS in Ottawa for operational command, thus maintaining national command of RCAF forces through the chain of command.[51] The emphasis was on the *authority* of the operational control of the CinC, not the establishment of a bilateral command organization, which was too politically sensitive.[52]

American approval of the proposal came in early 1957.[53] But while the COSC approved the plan in February, the Canadian government delayed its decision until after the federal election in June. This election resulted in a change in government, and approval fell to John Diefenbaker's new Progressive Conservative administration.[54] Diefenbaker approved the integration of the operational control of Canada-US air defences on 24 July.[55] On 1 August 1957, the minister of national defence and the US secretary of defense announced that they were "setting up a system of integrated operational control" of the nations' air defences under a new "integrated command" in Colorado Springs responsible to each nation's chiefs of staff.[56]

On 12 September 1957, the North American Air Defence Command officially stood up at Colorado Springs. The CinC CONAD, USAF General Earle Partridge, donned another "hat" as the new CinC NORAD with the authority to exercise operational control over Canadian and American air defence forces. A/M Slemon became DCinC NORAD and exercised operational control in Partridge's absence.[57] The name NORAD was the brainchild of General Partridge. "NORAD," he argued, "is punchy[,] forceful and conveys the idea with simplicity."[58] The JCS and CSC agreed. So too did the new Progressive Conservative government, which had minimal concerns with establishing a binational command organization.

Establishing NORAD's binational organizational structure proved an easy task. The new command was placed on top of the existing CONAD structure and RCAF ADC was simply plugged in as an additional component command. NORAD and CONAD still remained separate entities: a bilateral command with General Partridge wearing his CinC NORAD hat, exercising operational control over Canadian and American air defences for continental air defence; and a national JCS command with Partridge wearing his CinC CONAD hat exercising operational control over American air defences defending the US.[59] NORAD operated on an interim basis from its establishment in September 1957 until 12 May 1958, when Washington and Ottawa completed an official exchange of notes, known as the NORAD Agreement.[60]

From the beginning, General Partridge went out of his way to ensure Canada was an equal partner – an approach that ensured the binational features of NORAD that has lasted over six decades. As Slemon recalled, "although we were a little partner making a relatively small contribution to the operational capability of the joint effort, our views were considered in exactly the same light as our partners, the Americans."[61] In particular, Partridge took the Canadian DCinC position seriously. According to Slemon, shortly after NORAD's creation, Partridge told him "Roy, I'm supposed to be the Commander in Chief of NORAD and you're supposed to be the Deputy Commander in Chief. When I go out on a trip, inspecting units or go away to have a little fun, you have the responsibility and the authority," which also included access to America's tactical nuclear air defence weapons.[62] This clear understanding of the relationship between the CinC NORAD and his deputy, especially when the former was absent from headquarters, was essential for NORAD's success. When Partridge organized NORAD headquarters, he also ensured that Canadian officers had several of the most important positions. This included appointing A/V/M Hodson as NORAD's first Deputy Chief of Staff for Operations, a position Slemon considered "the guts of our joint effort."[63] A Canadian officer has subsequently always held this position at NORAD headquarters.

The practice of having appointments of importance in NORAD Headquarters allocated to Canadians continues today in Colorado Springs. It has given Canada what Joel Sokolsky has termed "a seat at the console," allowing Canadian officers to safeguard Canadian sovereignty while at the same time ensuring that Canada fulfils an important operational role in the defence of the continent.[64] This was important for Canadian personnel in NORAD during the Cold War, and it continues to be today.

Conclusion

NORAD's creation in 1957 was the culmination of over ten years' work by Canadian and American air force officers to first coordinate and then integrate and centralize RCAF and USAF air defences. These officers saw air defence as a common problem that required a common approach by Canadian and American air defence professionals working closely together to defend North America from the Soviet nuclear threat. NORAD embodied this realization.

The RCAF played a key role in realizing air defence integration under NORAD. That role included early national steps, such as the formation of 1ADG and its growth into ADC, as well as the building of RCAF air defence forces and systems. It also included key early connections with the USAF for air defence collaboration,

Two 440 Squadron CF-100 Canucks on patrol.

ranging from liaison officers in headquarters, cooperation in bilateral air defence exercises, and the vital role that RCAF personnel performed in the various bilateral committees and study groups to further coordinate continental air defence. The resulting RCAF cultural integration and partnership with the USAF has allowed Canadian and American personnel to work side by side to defend North America.

NOTES

1 Joel Sokolsky, "A Seat at the Table: Canada and Its Alliances," *Armed Forces and Society*, vol. 16, no. 1 (Fall 1999): 21–2.
2 Ann and John Tusa, *The Berlin Blockade* (Toronto: Hodder & Stoughton, 1988); Yefim Gordon and Vladimir Rigmant, *Tupolev Tu-4: Soviet Superfortress* (Hinkley, UK: Midland Publishing, 2002).
3 Col R.L. Raymont, *The Evolution of the Structure of The Department of National Defence 1945–1968, Report of the Task Force on Review of Unification of the Canadian Armed Forces* (November 30, 1979), Appendix A, "The Organization of Higher Control and Coordination in the formulation of Defence Policy, 1945–1964, 10, 27–28, File DHH 87/47.

4   AIAW Plan, December 9. 1946, DHH 112.3M2.009 (D106) Volume 1.
5   Minutes of the 400th Meeting of the COSC, September 4, 1947, COSC Minutes 1947, Raymont Collection, DHH 73/1223/1302.
6   Samuel Kostenuk and John Griffin, *RCAF Squadrons and Aircraft* (Toronto: A.M. Hakkert Ltd., 1977), 144; Mathias Joost, "The RCAF Auxiliary and the Air Defence of North America, 1948 to 1960," in *Proceedings*, 7th Annual Air Force Historical Conference: Canada in NORAD, Colorado Springs, Colorado, United States, June 4–8, 2001 (Winnipeg: Office of Air Force Heritage & History, 2001), 27.
7   DHH 74/649, F/O L.R.N. Ashley, "Air Defence of Canada" (1958), 66–9; RCAF ADC history "for background information purposes," entitled "Air Defence Command," n.d. [August 1953], LAC, RG 24, Acc. 1983-84/216, Box 3108, File HQS-895-100-69/14, Part 5.
8   Minutes of the 65 Meeting of Air Members, January 27, 1949, DHH 73/1223, Series 3, File 1820.
9   DHH 73/1501, *Nineteen Years of Air Defense*, NORAD Historical Reference Paper No. 11 (Colorado Springs: North American Air Defence Command, Ent Air Force Base, Colorado, 1965), 11–12; Andrew Richter, *Avoiding Armageddon: Canadian Military Strategy and Nuclear Weapons, 1950–63* (Vancouver: University of British Columbia Press, 2002), 41.
10 DHH 74/649, "Air Defence of Canada," 70; RCAF ADC history.
11 Joint Organization Order 14, May 23, 1951, LAC, RG 24, Acc. 1983-84/216, Box 3108, File HQS-895-100-69/14, Part 1.
12 Claxton Memorandum, "Acceleration of RCAF Programme," to Cabinet, July 19, 1950, LAC, MG 32, B5, Claxton Fonds, Volume 94, File Accelerated Defence Programme; Kostenuk and Griffin, *RCAF Squadrons and Aircraft*, 146, 208.
13 RCAF ADC history; Sean Maloney, *Learning to Love the Bomb: Canada's Nuclear Weapons during the Cold War* (Washington, DC: Potomac Books Inc., 2007), 100.
14 DND, *Duty with Honour: The Profession of Arms in Canada* (Kingston: Canadian Forces Leadership Institute, 2009), 17, 20–1, 55; Allan English, *Understanding Military Culture: A Canadian Perspective* (Montreal and Kingston: McGill-Queen's University Press, 2004), 89–97.
15 Joel J. Sokolsky, "Exporting the 'Gap': The American Influence," in *The Soldier and the State in the Post Cold War Era*, ed. by Albert Legault and Joel Sokolsky (Kingston: Queen's Quarterly Press, 2002), 213.
16 C.P. Stacey, *Arms, Men and Governments: The War Policies of Canada, 1939–1945* (Ottawa: Queen's Printer, 1970), 268.
17 K.L.B. Hodson, "The RCAF Air Division in Europe: Address to the United Services Institute, London, ON, December 15, 1954," Keith Hodson Memorial Library, Canadian Forces College (CFC).
18 Raymond Stouffer, *Swords, Clunks & Widowmakers: The Tumultuous Life of the RCAF's Original 1 Canadian Air Division* (Trenton: Canadian Forces Aerospace Warfare Centre, 2015), 166; C.P. Stacey, *A Date with History: Memoirs of a Canadian Historian* (Ottawa: Deneau Publishers, 1983), 258.
19 English, *Understanding Military Culture*, 95, 121; Richard Goette, "A Snapshot of Early Cold War RCAF Writing on Canadian Air Power and Doctrine," *RCAF Journal*, 1, 1 (Winter 2012): 53.
20 Goette, "Early Cold War RCAF Writing," 52–3; Richter, *Avoiding Armageddon*, 16–18, 42; Jockel, *No Boundaries Upstairs*, 7–8.
21 "The Role of the RCAF," (address, Trenton Chamber of Commerce, March 26, 1952) in *Air Power 1952: Three Speeches by Air Commodore Clare L. Annis*, CFC.
22 "The Role of Air Power" (address by Air Commodore K.L.B. Hodson to the Canadian Army Staff College, Kingston, April 18, 1955), CFC.
23 James Eayrs, *In Defence of Canada Volume III: Peacemaking and Deterrence* (Toronto: University of Toronto Press, 1972), 122.

24 J.I. Jackson to author, December 19, 2015.
25 PJBD Recommendation 51/6, November 12, 1951, DHH 79/35.
26 Claxton Memorandum, "Canada-United States Air Defence: Mutual Reinforcement," December 3, 1951, LAC, RG 2, Volume 2751; Secretary, US Section PJBD to Chairman, US Section PJBD, April 23, 1952, NARA, RG 333, PJBD, Entry 17-A, Box 4, File "Top Secret Correspondence, 1941–1956," Folder 23.
27 Jockel, *No Boundaries Upstairs*, 54; C.L. Grant, *The Development of Continental Air Defense to 1 September 1954*, USAF Historical Study No. 126 (Montgomery, Alabama: USAF Historical Division, Research Studies Institute, Air University [1954]), 54.
28 AMOT, to AMAP, May 14, 1951, LAC, RG 24, Volume 6172, File 15-73-3; Jockel, *No Boundaries Upstairs*, 50.
29 PJBD Recommendation 51/4, May 9, 1951, DHH 79/35.
30 PJBD Recommendation 53/1, October 1, 1953, DHH 79/35.
31 *Chronology of JCS Involvement in North American Air Defense 1946–1975* (Washington: Historical Division, Joint Secretariat, Joint Chiefs of Staff, March 20, 1976), 5–21; McNaughton to McKay, August 18, 1949, DHH 112.3M2.009 (D114); JCS Memorandum, "Establishment of the United States Northeast Command," December 2, 1949, Records of the JCS, Strategic Issues, Reel 9 (Section 2), Part 2, 1946–1953, copy at Massey Library (ML), Royal Military College of Canada (RMC).
32 USAF PJBD Member Progress Report, October 2, 1950, 59th Meeting of the PJBD October 2–5, 1950, DHH 82/196, File 8.
33 Lydus H. Buss, *U.S. Air Defense in the Northeast, 1940–1957*, CONAD Historical Reference Paper, No. 1 (Colorado Springs, CO: Directorate of Historical Information, Office of Information Services, Headquarters Air Defense Command, 1957), 16–17.
34 (Draft Plan) "Basic Provisions for Canada-US Collaboration on Defence in the Northeastern Areas of Canada," February 21, 1951, and Memorandum from Head, Defence Liaison (1) Division, April 17, 1951, *DCER*, Vol. 17, 1951, 1450–6.
35 JPC Report to the CSC, "Appointment of a Senior RCAF Officer to US North East Command," October 22, 1951, JPC Minutes to Meeting and Correspondence Volume 10, DHH 2002/17, Box 57, File 1; Memorandum by USAF COS for the JCS on Canadian Participation in the US Northeast Command, October 24, 1951, Records of the JCS, Strategic Issues, Reel 9 (Section 2), Part 2, 1946–1953, ML, RMC.
36 Memorandum from MND to CDC, January 8, 1953, *DCER*, Vol. 19, 1953, 1025–1026.
37 Randall Wakelam, *Cold War Fighters: Canadian Aircraft Procurement, 1945–54* (Vancouver: University of British Columbia Press, 2011).
38 NBC Group, *A History of the Air Defence of Canada 1948–1997* (Ottawa: Canadian Fighter Group, 1997), 9–10.
39 Gordon A. Wilson, *NORAD and the Soviet Nuclear Threat: Canada's Secret Electronic Air War* (Toronto: Dundurn, 2011), 100–3; NBC Group, *A History of the Air Defence of Canada*, 33–4.
40 Kostenuk and Griffin, *RCAF Squadrons and Aircraft*, 148n.
41 Wilson, *NORAD and the Soviet Nuclear Threat*, 100–3.
42 NBC Group, *A History of the Air Defence of Canada*, 39–40.
43 Wilson, *NORAD and the Soviet Nuclear Threat*, 106–7; Jockel, *No Boundaries Upstairs*, 83.
44 Wilson, *NORAD and the Soviet Nuclear Threat*, 108–9; Jockel, *No Boundaries Upstairs*, 84–5;
45 Andrew Burtch, *Give Me Shelter: The Failure of Canada's Cold War Civil Defence* (Vancouver: UBC Press, 2012), 86, 106; Wilson, *NORAD and the Soviet Nuclear Threat*, 106; NBC Group, *A History of the Air Defence of Canada*, 33–4.

46 *Chronology of JCS Involvement in North American Air Defense*, 52–70; DHH 73/1501, *Nineteen Years of Air Defense*, 37–46, 81.
47 DHH 73/1501, *Nineteen Years of Air Defense*, 47–8; Jockel, *Canada in NORAD*, 12.
48 AVM C.R. Dunlap, Chairman, Canadian Section MSG, to CSC Chairman, August 26, 1954, Raymont Collection, DHH 73/1223/89.
49 Extract from a Special CSC Meeting, April 6, 1955, Donaghy, ed., *DCER*, vol. 21, (1955): 709–12.
50 "Integration of Operational Control of the Continental Air Defenses of Canada and the United States in Peacetime," Ad Hoc MSG Committee Report, December 19, 1956, DHH 112.3M2 (D711).
51 Ibid.
52 Ibid.; Jockel, *No Boundaries Upstairs*, 102.
53 USAF COS Memorandum, "Integration of Operational Control of Canadian and Continental United States Air Defence Forces in Peacetime," to JCS, March 8, 1957, NARA, RG 218, JCS, Entry 943011, Box 8, File CCS 092 (9-10-45), Section 43.
54 604th and 605th Meetings of the CSC, February 1 and 15, 1957, DHH 2002/17, Box 87, File 2; Jockel, *No Boundaries Upstairs*, 104.
55 Pearkes note, "Discussed with P.M. and approved," 24 July 1957, on Index of documents relating to the integration of operational control of Canada-US continental air defence forces in peacetime, MND confirmation of PM approval on NORAD," DHH 73/1223/84.
56 Press Release by the Secretary of Defense of the United States and the Minister of National Defence of Canada, August 1, 1957, DHH 73/1223/84.
57 DHH 73/1501, *Nineteen Years of Air Defense*, 50.
58 CinC CONAD to CSC Chairman, August 13, 1957, DHH 73/1223/85.
59 JCS, Terms of Reference for CINCNORAD, January 8, 1958, NARA, RG 218, JCS, Entry 943011, Box 16, File CCS 092 (9-10-45), Section 47.
60 Text of Canadian Note, His Excellency N.A. Robertson, Canadian ambassador to the United States, to the Honourable John Foster Dulles, secretary of state of the United States, May 12, 1958, Canada Treaty Series 1958, copy in George Randolph Pearkes Papers, University of Victoria Archives, Accession 74-1, Box 26, File 26.3.
61 Slemon quoted in Kenneth Schaffel, *The Emerging Shield: The Air Force and the Evolution of Continental Air Defense, 1945–1960* (Washington, D.C.: Office of Air Force History, United States Air Force, 1991), 252.
62 DHH 79/128, Interview with Air Marshal Roy Slemon by W.A.B. Douglas and William McAndrew, October 20, 1978, 18.
63 Slemon quoted in Schaffel, *The Emerging Shield*, 252–3; "Organization for NORAD Headquarters," Appendix "A" to S964-104 (CAS), Campbell to Foulkes, March 8, 1958, DHH 73/1223/86.
64 Joel Sokolsky, "A Seat at the Table: Canada and Its Alliances," *Armed Forces and Society*, 16, 1 (Fall 1999): 21–2.

CHAPTER FOUR

NORAD PEAKS, 1957–1964

JOSEPH T. JOCKEL

In the seven years after NORAD's creation in 1957, Canada continued to be more tightly drawn into aerospace defence cooperation with the United States, above all for the further integration of the two countries' North American air defences.[1] As part of this evolution the RCAF acquired new American systems, including weapons. In 1958, the Diefenbaker government approved the Continental Air Defense Integration-North (CADIN) program, which provided for, first, adding additional radar sites to augment the Pinetree and Mid-Canada lines; second, controlling Canadian and US air defences with the Semi-Automatic Ground Environment (SAGE), which in turn led to redrawing functional air defence boundaries that diminished the importance of the international border; and third, equipping the RCAF with BOMARC surface-to air-missiles.

During this period, Canada also began to cooperate with the US in NORAD space surveillance, a mission the Command received from the US joint chiefs of staff (JCS) in 1960. The RCAF acquired a Baker-Nunn camera from the USAF in that same year, and installed the facility at RCAF Station Cold Lake, where it could directly contribute to NORAD's space surveillance efforts. This followed on the heels of the contributions to space tracking that a Canadian ADC radar laboratory at Prince Albert had already begun to make.

After the spectacular collapse of the Avro CF-105 Arrow interceptor program in 1959, the RCAF's ADC needed a replacement for the obsolescent CF-100s. The solution was to purchase 66 US-made F-101 Voodoo interceptors that were already in service with the USAF. The aircraft, new to Canada, were soon dubbed CF-101s and kept the name "Voodoo." This re-equipping was the result of the 1961

Two CF-101 Voodoo aircraft on patrol, Northern Quebec.

Triangular agreement between Washington and Ottawa. The shift to the Voodoo and the BOMARC surface-to-air missile, the latter having been envisaged some time before but never pursued, involved the use of nuclear warheads, but employing such weaponry in Canada and by Canadians was problematic. After much delay, Ottawa eventually agreed to give the Canadian-operated BOMARCs and CF-101s the ability to use US nuclear air defence weapons, which were then placed in Canada for that emergency purpose but stored under USAF control.

Upon coming to office in 1957, the Diefenbaker government firmly supported North American air defence cooperation with the US, swiftly agreeing to NORAD's creation and approving the CADIN integration package without difficulty the next year. It also approved the 1958 NORAD agreement that diplomats had negotiated. Washington had every reason to think that Ottawa's cooperative stance would continue. It did not. The first warning Washington received of this change was Ottawa's abrupt decision at the end of August 1959 to withhold Canadian participation in a

Armament technicians load a rocket pod on to a CF-100 Canuck air defence fighter.

long-planned NORAD air defence exercise called "Operation Skyhawk," which was to be held in October and would necessitate the grounding of all civil air traffic in North America for several hours.

The Diefenbaker government then dug in its heels with respect to giving the RCAF's BOMARCs and Voodoos, as well Canadian Army units in Europe, a nuclear capability. This in itself would have been enough to produce a row with the administration of President John F. Kennedy. Diefenbaker went much further during the Cuban Missile Crisis, though, refusing to allow RCAF forces in NORAD to be placed on alert for several days and to rhetorically support the Americans in their confrontation with the Soviets. A few months after the crisis, the Conservative minority government wound up in an extraordinarily rancorous public exchange with Washington over nuclear weapons. The Diefenbaker government subsequently fell apart, was defeated in the House of Commons, and lost the general election of 1963. The new Liberal government of Lester B. Pearson

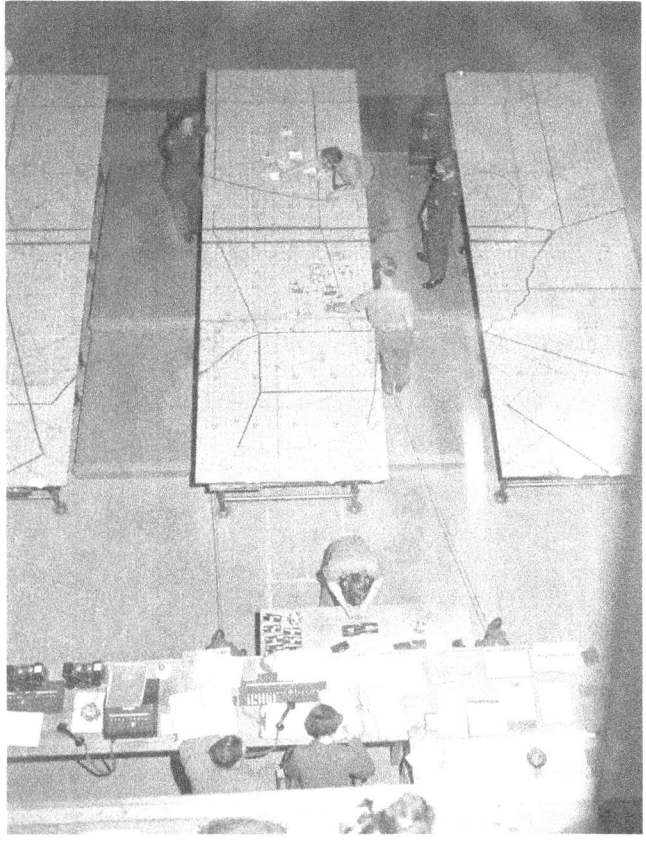
Bird's eye view of plotting tables at a radar warning site.

approved, albeit with reluctance, the nuclear capabilities for Canada's NORAD and NATO forces.

Just as political discord between Ottawa and Washington over North American aerospace defence peaked between 1957 and 1964, so did an unexpected divergence between the aerospace defence forces of the two countries. This working level variance was not a result of the Canada-US discord; there was no American decision not to trust or work with the Canadians. Nor was it a direct result of the lowering of East-West tensions that set in at almost exactly the same time. Never again did the Soviet Union challenge the US so audaciously and dangerously as it did during the Cuban Missile Crisis. The signing of the Nuclear Test Ban Treaty in 1964 marked the end of the coldest days of the Cold War. The conflict had peaked.

Rather, the decline in Canada-US aerospace defence cooperation was a result of the combined impact of technology and geography. The airplane, and in particular the intercontinental bomber, had made air defence, and Canada along with it, more important to the security of the United States in the late 1940s and the 1950s. Soviet long-range aviation could fly through Canada to strike at the United States, and presumably the cities of southern Canada, as well. That had led both countries to the deploy vast air defences, increasing cooperation between the air defenders (the RCAF and principally the USAF in the US), and eventually to NORAD. The intercontinental ballistic missile and, later, the submarine-launched ballistic missile made both air defence and Canada less important to the Americans. The Russians conducted their first test of an intercontinental ballistic missile ten days before NORAD stood up operations in September 1957. In 1964, the administration of President Lyndon B. Johnson decided to curb North American air defence, which would eventually shrink air defence capabilities vastly, in both the US and Canada. And it is worth mentioning in passing that to this day, Canadian northern territory and airspace, and the Canadian forces there, have never played a role in the detection or interception of ballistic missiles. It has made geographic sense for the US to place the most important missile early warning radars not in Canada, but in Alaska, Greenland, and the UK. A look at the globe shows why. By the end of the decade covered in this chapter, NORAD had peaked.

CADIN, SAGE, and the BOMARCs

Negotiations between the RCAF and USAF were underway between 1956 and 1958 over how to further improve Canadian air defences, and how to link them more tightly with US efforts even beyond simply creating a shared headquarters in Colorado Springs. The US National Security Council staff summarized the problem the two air forces had been addressing:

> The present air defence system in Canada does not provide sufficient radar coverage in depth for adequate protection of heavy industrial areas in Northeast Canada and the US and lack of radar coverage across the prairie Provinces [sic] leaves a large gap in the defence of the centre of the continent. We are therefore planning to integrate the Canadian and US air defence system by increasing Canadian radar coverage and adding BOMARC missiles to the Canadian system. This CADIN ... program is intended to increase defence in depth against attack from the North and to provide semi-automatic control of interceptor aircraft and BOMARC missiles.[2]

With the encouragement of the Diefenbaker government, a service-to service agreement was reached in 1958. It provided for three enhancements: improving the Pinetree radars (which were later renamed the CADIN/Pinetree Line) through the construction of new stations to fill the gap in Manitoba, Alberta, and Saskatchewan; giving extra warning and allowing US fighter interceptors based just to the south to move their operations into Canadian prairie skies; and by improving coverage in the Ottawa area.

Just as important, however, was the extension of SAGE into Canada. This was a computerized system that was highly advanced for its day and expensive. It was semi-automatic in that intricate plotting and telling functions were run electronically, while tactical decisions, such as which interceptor aircraft would fly where and which hostile aircraft the fighters would attack, were left in human hands. The first of the SAGE centres in the US became operational in 1958. The air defence radars in southern Canada were to be brought under SAGE control; however, Canada was prepared to fund just one SAGE centre on Canadian soil. That centre, which was eventually built at North Bay, would control the priority air defence operations in the populous eastern part of the country. With only one SAGE control centre in Canada, most Canadian airspace would have to be ground-controlled from air defence centres located in the US; operational control would be carried out by USAF officers with Canadian deputies, mirroring the situation at NORAD headquarters in Colorado Springs. The "Northern NORAD Region," controlled from the SAGE centre at North Bay appeared to be huge on official maps, because it included both eastern Canada and the north – where there were no ground control radars and so where fighter aircraft could not be deployed.

Canada's air defences had to this point been entirely based on the RCAF's fighter interceptors, without any surface-to-air missiles, but BOMARCs were also part of the package. The USAF's longer-range BOMARCs were one of three types of surface-to-air missiles that the US air defence intended to use against Soviet bombers; the other two were the US Army's shorter-range Nike-Hercules and Hawk missiles. In the west, the USAF was planning to deploy a line of BOMARC stations running just south of the 49th parallel. Deploying BOMARC missiles in central Ontario and Quebec made sense in order to continue to run the line straight eastward. George Pearkes, the first minister of national defence in the Diefenbaker government, encouraged this option because BOMARCs in Ontario and Quebec would provide additional protection for the Windsor-Quebec City axis and more coverage of the approaches to the US northeast. US air defence officials were, of course, also particularly interested in the latter, as a further strengthening of defence in depth. According to US plans, fighter interceptors "would strike first at incoming aircraft, then land on northern bases ... in order to clear the way for missiles. BOMARC, with its longer range, was expected to come into action first, then Nike-Hercules, with Hawk filling in as needed against low-flying aircraft."[3]

Technician in front of a Semi-Automatic Ground Environment (SAGE) computer system. The SAGE network would allow a single control station to monitor data from a number of different radar sites simultaneously.

Canadian Contributions to Military Space Surveillance; NORAD Receives the Mission

In the autumn of 1957, just as NORAD still was establishing itself (see chapter 3), the USAF installed its first Baker-Nunn optical satellite tracking camera at White Sands, New Mexico. This device was capable of outperforming radar in tracking satellites passing overhead in earth orbit. As a study written several years later by the Canadian Department of National Defence explained: "While the use of space vehicles in offensive systems did not appear likely in the near future, it was thought nonetheless that changing circumstances might make the employment of space vehicles in an offensive role more attractive in the more distant future."[4] One

Two BOMARC missiles in firing position in front of shelters, RCAF Station La Macaza, QC.

possibility was especially troubling for North American defence: the Soviets were researching a "fractional orbital bombardment" system that could deliver nuclear weapons to target from low earth orbit. Another concern was that NORAD, based solely on radar data, might mistake a satellite, especially one falling from earth orbit, for an incoming Soviet ballistic missile and give the alarm.

In June 1960, General Laurence Kuter, CINC NORAD, told the JCS that he strongly believed that they should give his command the task to operate a military space surveillance centre, which would, given NORAD's structure, make space surveillance a binational responsibility. As Kuter put it, "Our very survival may depend upon our ability to make vital decisions in a matter of minutes. To accomplish this, it is mandatory that all air and space be under continuing surveillance reporting to a single responsible commander who can correlate, evaluate and establish the credence of complementary sensors and intelligence information."[5]

A facility in Saskatchewan operated by the Defence Research Board, the Prince Albert Radar Laboratory (PARL), began a space tracking program in 1960 that focused on following the decaying orbit of Soviet satellites. PARL had been established in 1959 with the cooperation of the US military, which had furnished equipment, including a large parabolic antenna. The facility was opened with much ceremony by the local MP and most prominent citizen, Prime Minister John Diefenbaker. PARL was intended primarily to research the potentially negative impacts of the northern lights on the radar tracking of Soviet ballistic missiles attacking from over the pole. The facility was geographically well located for the task, and it could profit from researchers located at the University of Saskatchewan in nearby Saskatoon, whose studies centred on the northern lights.

Simultaneously and at NORAD's urging, the USAF turned over one surplus Baker-Nunn camera to the RCAF, which was installed and began operating at Cold Lake, Alberta. That same year, NORAD and its US sister command, the Continental Air Defense Command (CONAD), were given responsibility for operating the Space Detection and Tracking System (SPADATS) in their Colorado Springs, Colorado, headquarters. The system was stood up the next year with the participation of Canadian personnel. Among its many sources of data were the RCAF's Baker-Nunn camera at Cold Lake and PARL.

In 1963, a new CINC NORAD, General John Gerhart, asked the JCS and the Canadian COSC to amend his "terms of reference," (his instructions from the two chiefs of staff). He wanted to change the original 1958 version, which read "responsible for the air defence of the continental United States, Canada and Alaska" to read, "responsible for the aerospace defence" of those same regions. The formal names would stay the same: the "A" in "NORAD" and "CINC NORAD" would still stand for "Air." The Canadian chiefs endorsed the change. As A/C/M Frank Miller, the chairman of the Canadian chiefs, informed the Department of External Affairs, the change was intended to cover responsibilities CINC NORAD had already assumed for ballistic missile warning and the operation of SPADATS.[6] While the JCS pronounced themselves gratified by the decision of their Canadian counterparts, they dropped Gerhart's proposed change. To them, Gerhart seemed to be jumping the gun. No decision had been made in the US to actively "defend" against satellites or ballistic missiles, or for that matter, to entrust such defences to NORAD.

The problems of spelling out the command's responsibilities and of what to call NORAD would continue for decades. Not until 1981 was the "A" changed to "Aerospace." But the binational command, contrary to its own expectations, has never been given the responsibility to operate active defences against satellites or ballistic missiles. However, in 1959–1960 NORAD acquired the sensors and authority to undertake what would eclipse air defence and eventually become the command's most important mission: providing integrated warning and assessment of any attacks on the continent by airbreathing vehicles, ballistic missiles, and threats from space.

The Collapse of the Arrow Program and the "Triangular" Agreement

The story of the AV Roe CF-105 Arrow development program, which was intended to produce one of the world's most advanced fighter interceptors in Canada, has often been told, if only because it has become the subject of historical conspiracy theories. (A more detailed analysis follows in chapter 5 but short discussion is important here for context.) Building on its success with the development and production of the CF-100 interceptor, Avro Canada, and the RCAF along with it, were optimistic about its ability to produce the next generation of fighters. But the costs of production were high, and rose still higher, making the Arrow viable only if it could also be sold outside Canada. There was no sale in the US, though. This has led to one of the principal conspiracy theories, namely that the American were always out to get the Arrow. To be sure, the Americans were not inclined to purchase an expensive Canadian competitor. As one study put it: "Any realist would understand that the American government would be subject to strong pressure to put its taxpayers' money in American-made aircraft."[7] The British also lost their initial interest. Upon cancellation of the program the prototypes of the Arrow were destroyed, apparently on orders from Ottawa, which has also fuelled uncertainty.

John Diefenbaker tried to justify the cancellation. Announcing that the program was under review in September 1958 and, referring to the BOMARCs, he said:

> The government has concluded that missiles should be introduced into the Canadian air defence system and that the number of supersonic interceptor aircraft required for the RCAF air defence command will be substantially less than could have been foreseen a few years ago *if in fact such aircraft will be required at all* [emphasis added] in the 1960s in view of the rapid strides being made in missiles by both the USA and USSR.[8]

The prime minister's statement seemed to imply that the BOMARC, because it was a missile, offered some kind of response to the intercontinental ballistic missile. That was not so, of course; the BOMARC was a surface-to-air missile designed to destroy manned bombers. More serious was Diefenbaker's assertion that air defence fighter aircraft might not be needed at all within in the coming few years.

NORAD, Colorado Springs, October 1957. Seen left to right are: Air Marshal Roy Slemon, Deputy Commander of NORAD; General Nathan Twining, Chairman of the US Joint Chiefs of Staff; and General Earl C. Partridge, Commander in Chief of NORAD.

Neither the Canadian nor American air forces believed this. This was made publicly clear for Canadians in November 1958 when DCINC NORAD, Air Marshal Roy Slemon, with CINC NORAD, General Earl Partridge, standing next to him issued a public statement in Colorado Springs in reaction to the debate that had broken out in Canada. A manned interceptor, Slemon said, was an "unescapable requirement for as long as we can see."[9]

The case that the RCAF continued to make both publicly and privately for a manned interceptor still did not stop Diefenbaker from reiterating in his February 1959 announcement of the Arrow's cancellation that the advent of the ballistic missile had made the interceptor obsolete. As he put it, "the threat against which the CF-105 could be effective has not proved to be as serious as was forecast …. It is considered that the defence system of North America is adequate to meet this threat." Later in the debate, he argued that "There is no purpose manufacturing horse collars when horses no longer exist."[10]

John B. McLin, in his magisterial study, *Canada's Changing Defense Policy, 1957–1963: The Problems of a Middle Power of Alliance*, offered an explanation for the prime minister's obfuscations. McLin concluded that Diefenbaker could not bring himself to the "recognition, psychologically and politically difficult, that Canada could not no longer pay the price which advancing technology exacted to remain a producer of the more sophisticated military equipment. Unwilling to recognize the loss of power and prestige involved, the politically sensitive Diefenbaker obscured the issue."[11]

However, the RCAF still needed a new interceptor. In 1959, the USAF offered the Canadians 66 surplus F-101 Voodoos. Initially, the American proposal went nowhere in Ottawa. As Slemon explained to Partridge's successor, General Laurence Kuter:

> The reason is that it constitutes a major political headache, following as it does in the wake of cancellation by the government of the CF-105…. Procurement now of US interceptors of roughly the same performance as the 'Arrow' would place the Canadian government in an embarrassing spot, regardless of the nature or extent of any US-Canada cost-sharing arrangement.[12]

The embarrassment faded. More importantly, the Kennedy administration proposed in 1961 an attractive package to Ottawa with three elements. The RCAF would acquire the Voodoos. In return, Canada would not have to pay cash, but rather, take over sixteen stations of the Pinetree radar line that had been operated by the US. Canada also agreed to assume financial responsibility for some stations already being operated by the RCAF. Finally, aircraft manufacturer Canadiar gained a licence to build F-104 "Starfighter" aircraft in Canada and to provide them to NATO allies, with the US paying two-third of the cost and Canada the other third. Thus, "the Triangular" agreement solved the RCAF's interceptor problem, decreased the US military presence on Canadian soil (to the satisfaction of Canadians worried about sovereignty), and brought some welcome new business to the Canadian aircraft industry that had been so badly battered by the Arrow's cancellation.

Nuclear Air Defence Weapons in Canada, Part 1: Diefenbaker Stalls

To be most effective, the BOMARCs and the MB-1 "Genie" air-to-air rockets carried by the Voodoos required nuclear warheads. The story has often been told of Diefenbaker and the question of nuclear weapons for the Canadian military both

Accepting the first ex-USAF McDonnel F-101 Voodoo, 9 October 1961.

at home and in NATO Europe, and of the political fireworks he set off with his intransigence both in Ottawa and in Canada-US relations. At issue also were the arrangements for US interceptors based in Newfoundland to use nuclear weapons and, at one point, the nuclear arrangements for US interceptors, which could be temporarily deployed in Canada during a crisis.

In late 1958, the Eisenhower administration, with the president's approval, was prepared to turn the nuclear air defence warheads completely over to Canada. The text of the December 1958 decision directive of the US National Security Council observed that

> [O]ur North American continental defence relations with Canada were established outside of the NATO structure; and the peculiarities of geography, the defence structure we have established, the purely defence nature of the weapons under consideration, and the partnership of the United States and Canada in this defence undertaking,

provide a reasonable and logical basis for according Canada a favoured-nation status.[13]

This decision, in December 1958, coming soon after NORAD's creation the previous year, could be taken as the moment that continental defence relations peaked in Washington. Cooperating with Canada in NORAD would never again be seen in the American capital as quite so close and important.

The Eisenhower administration's idea of simply turning nuclear weapons over to Canada died quickly. As Diefenbaker told parliament in 1959, Canada did not want to own them. However, this did not mean that the RCAF still could not be quickly given access and authority to use them in the event of a real or imminently anticipated attack. But with no clear transfer of ownership from the US to Canada, negotiations between the two over the weapons would have to be conducted in the complicated legal, political, and military thicket of joint responsibility. Practical ways would have to be found to reconcile US legal custody and ownership of the warheads with Canadian sovereignty, as these issues would affect how the weapons would be stored in Canada, protected while in storage, released for potential use, and finally used. There was no reason, at first, for Washington to believe that they could not find an agreement amenable to both governments. As the prime minister's foreign policy advisor, Basil Robinson, later recalled in his memoir, the Diefenbaker government was consciously heading in the direction of acquiring nuclear weapons for its own forces, both in Europe and of allowing US forces stationed at or using bases in Canada to store nuclear weapons and equipment on them. The questions for discussion … in 1958 and 1959 had most to do with the how and the when rather than with the whether or the why.[14]

But then Diefenbaker began to stall in the negotiations and refused to budge from this position, (or non-position) as long as he managed to remain in power. Whatever doubts that the prime minister was acquiring about nuclear weapons were reinforced by the views of Howard Green, the new secretary of state for external affairs, who assumed the post in 1959. It has also frequently been argued that the bad personal relationship between Diefenbaker and Kennedy, who arrived in the White House in January 1961, also contributed to the prime minister's intransigence.

Yet, Green's influence and Diefenbaker's antipathy towards Kennedy cannot really suffice as explanations. A more likely interpretation is that Diefenbaker stalled and dodged because he came to fear that accepting nuclear weapons could endanger his chances at the ballot box. To be sure, he knew that most Canadians were initially in favour of such nuclearization. But the new and growing Canadian anti-nuclear movement might effectively mobilize opposition. Moreover, "the anti-nuclear movement was not Diefenbaker's only concern. He was plagued by fears

A CF-101 Voodoo on alert in the Quick Reaction Area hangar, RCAF Station Bagotville, QC.

that Liberal leader Lester Pearson would rally the anti-nuclear forces and take their support to victory in the next federal election."[15] He had good reason to do so. Pearson, who had held the external affairs portfolio from 1948 to the Liberal defeat in 1957, told the Commons in 1960 that his views on nuclear weapons in NATO had changed, and he was now opposed to equipping Canada's European forces with them. In January 1961, the Liberal Party convention adopted, in McLin's words "what was generally regarded as a resolution of general opposition to nuclear weapons for Canada," although it was hedged with qualifications.[16] The New Democratic Party also took a clear stance against the matter.

The Cuban Missile Crisis, Diefenbaker, and NORAD

While the government and official opposition continued to equivocate confusingly about equipping the Canadian military in Europe and at home with a nuclear capability, the world, and Canada along with it, was plunged into the Cuban Missile

Crisis in October 1962. The Soviets, recklessly seeking to undermine the credibility of the US extended nuclear deterrent, especially for the protection of Western Europe, secretly placed ballistic missiles in Cuba capable of delivering nuclear weapons swiftly to targets in the US. The Americans, caught by surprise, imposed what Kennedy called in an address to the nation on 22 October, a "strict quarantine" of ships carrying military equipment to the island. The possibility loomed of a direct clash between US and Soviet forces, which might escalate to nuclear war. The Soviets eventually flinched, agreeing to remove the missiles in Cuba, in return for the removal by the US of missiles in southern Europe.

Shortly before his address, Kennedy sent Livingston Merchant, a former ambassador to Canada, to Ottawa to brief Diefenbaker, along with the defence minister and the secretary of state for external affairs. While the prime minister received the special envoy politely, he was irritated. As Diefenbaker later described his own reaction, "We were not a satellite state at the beck and call of an imperial master."[17] Diefenbaker had had a reasonable expectation to be consulted by Washington and that expectation had not been met. In simply informing Ottawa of the steps it was on the verge of taking, the Kennedy administration had not honoured the pledges of consultation with Ottawa that the US government had made in the 1958 NORAD agreement, in a secret agreement reached that same year on protocols surrounding binational consultation, and in several other recent agreements for that matter. Nonetheless, as a study undertaken in the Privy Council Office immediately after the crisis concluded, "The NORAD Agreement does not seem to have worked properly during the crisis mainly because it was not designed for this sort of emergency when the US took the initiative after a period of secret planning…. In these circumstances proper consultation as required by the agreement is impossible."[18]

Diefenbaker infuriated the Kennedy administration with his refusal to publicly support the American position and stunned the US and Canadian military, as well as his own defence minister, Douglas Harkness, when he refused to allow the Canadian military, including RCAF elements under NORAD's operational control, to go on alert as the US was doing. CINC NORAD, General John Gerhart, thereupon scrupulously respected the bilateral procedures in place to protect Canadian sovereignty. On the evening of 22 October, he only put the American forces he had authority over on alert. He did so in his capacity as the commander-in-chief not of NORAD, but of CONAD.

Harkness, Pearkes's successor as minister of national defence, had expected Diefenbaker to approve a Canadian alert on the evening of 22 October. When approval did not come, he tried to force one at a cabinet meeting the next day, and still another one on 24 October. Backed by Green, Diefenbaker blocked the way.

Aerial view of the radar site at Hall Beach, NU, one of the Distant Early Waring (DEW) Line sites in the Canadian Arctic.

Harkness later recalled that at this second session, "I made a final effort with a rather angry outburst that we were failing in our responsibilities to the nation and *must* act, which produced an outburst from the prime minister to the effect that he would not be forced into any such action." Having had enough, Harkness simply authorized, on his own, the Canadian military to take such steps it could that moved it to a higher alert but not draw the attention of the public and prime minister, such as cancelling leaves. As he put it, "These measures accomplished the majority of the purposes of an alert – i.e., to get into a state of preparedness to meet an attack – but did not reassure the United States and our other allies, as an alert would have done, that we were prepared to fight."[19] However, later on October 24, Diefenbaker gave in, apparently being convinced that Canada's security was gravely endangered by preparations reportedly underway in the Soviet Union. While the formal proclamation of the Canadian alert was delayed for still another day, with Canadian permission now on hand, NORAD went on higher alert, two days after CONAD, and would remain on alert until the confrontation with the Soviet Union was over.

Nuclear Air Defence Weapons in Canada, Part 2: Nuclear Resolution

According to the Canadian historian John English, the Cuban missile crisis "stiffened Canadian spines, including some in Diefenbaker's [C]abinet" when it came to nuclearization of the Canadian military.[20] Almost as soon as the crisis was over, the Cabinet, pushed hard by Harkness, agreed to the reopening of negotiations with the US. A Cabinet committee soon concluded that an agreement should be reached with the US on nuclear air defence weapons and that Canada had committed itself to acquiring the weapons in Europe. Diefenbaker also came under pressure as a result of a surprising change of attitude by Pearson. It was not that the Liberal leader had changed his views on the strategic value of nuclear weapons in Canadian hands. Rather, he said, it was a matter of keeping promises. "As a Canadian I am ashamed if we accept commitments and then refuse to discharge them." The government, he went on, "should end at once its evasion of responsibility by discharging the commitments it has already accepted for Canada."[21]

Diefenbaker tried to get out from under the pressure with a speech on 25 January 1963, in the House of Commons that journalist Knowlton Nash later described as "a two-hour masterpiece of obfuscation filled with illusions, delusions and confusions."[22] As for air defence weapons for the RCAF in North America, he tried the same kind of argument he had used in 1959 to explain the cancellation of the Arrow: in negotiations just held in the Bahamas with the Americans, the British had agreed to replace their nuclear bombers with US-built Polaris submarine-launched ballistic missiles. This meant, Diefenbaker argued, that bombers were becoming obsolete; therefore, so was North American air defence.

The US government reacted to the prime minister's speech with an extraordinary press release, issued in both Washington and Ottawa, its text having been approved by the US ambassador in Canada, the secretary of state, and the president's national security advisor, McGeorge Bundy. It denied many of Diefenbaker's claims: "The agreements made at Nassau have been fully publicized. They raise no question of the appropriateness of nuclear weapons for Canadian forces in fulfilling their NATO or NORAD obligations." It also challenged Diefenbaker's good faith in the new negotiations over air defence weapons.[23]

On 4 February, Harkness resigned, taking two other ministers with him. The minority Conservative government, besieged and crumbling, was defeated the next day in a non-confidence motion in the House. McLin observed that "the ensuing election campaign was waged not so much on the specific defense issues as on the question of the Diefenbaker government's general incompetence to govern."[24]

In August 1963 the newly elected Pearson Liberal government reached an agreement with Washington on nuclear weapons for the Canadian forces in North America and Europe. Unless released for use, the nuclear weapons for the BOMARCs and the Genies would be in the legal custody of the US as well as in the physical custody of the US military at Canadian military bases. With Diefenbaker's defeat and the ensuing August agreement, contention between Washington and Ottawa over NORAD and air defence matters peaked and began to subside. While Canadians would, in the coming decades, argue among themselves over involvement in ballistic missile defence, and of course binational disputes still arose from time to time, never again would the two governments be so at odds over North American defence as they were in 1962–3. In other words, during the Diefenbaker years 1957–63, not only was NORAD created, but the politics of the NORAD relationship experienced historic peaks of both cooperation and discord.

The Thinning Out of North American Air Defence

In its 1964 Defence White Paper, the Pearson government sought to put a firm end to the notion, of which Diefenbaker had been so fond, that as the ballistic missile threat grew, Canada might very soon get entirely out of continental air defence. The White Paper stated that a "downtrend in continental defence forces seems likely, yet short of total disarmament one cannot foresee the day when Canada will not be directly involved in some form of air defence operations." But it added, "It seems probable however that, failing the wide-scale deployment of [missile defence] the proportion of Canada resources directed to air defence will gradually decline through the balance of the decade."[25] By the time the white paper appeared, the government had already made the decision to reduce the number of CF-101 squadrons to three, based at Comox, Bagotville, and Chatham, each with eighteen aircraft – a number that would drop over the coming few years. Four Pinetree radars were closed. And in 1965 Ottawa decided, over CINC NORAD's objections, to close the Mid-Canada Line.

At the end of 1964, US Secretary of Defense, Robert McNamara also addressed the issue of North American air defence. He wrote President Lydon B. Johnson that "At present, with no defence against ballistic missiles and only the beginning of a viable civil defence posture, our anti-bomber defence could operate on only a fraction of the damage inflicting forces in a Soviet attack." Such an attack, the secretary's analysts had calculated, would cost 90–120 million American lives. Deep cuts in air defence would increase that number "by perhaps 1 to 6 million persons; the Chief of Staff of the Army believes the difference would be less than 1.5 million

Aerial view of RCAF Station Moosonee, ON, a Pinetree Line radar site.

in the most plausible situations and I agree with his judgement." Therefore, McNamara concluded, "it no longer appears to be necessary or useful to retain our large interceptor force at its present size."[26] North American air defence had peaked. Diefenbaker had only exaggerated the anticipated speed and extent of its decline. NORAD was now well on its way to becoming a command whose most important task was not active defence, except for a vestigial air defence capability, but rather warning of and assessing an aerospace attack on the continent.

NOTES

1 This chapter draws substantially on Joseph T. Jockel, *Canada in NORAD, 1957–2007: A History*, Kingston: Queen's Centre for International Relations and the Queen's Defence Management Program, McGill-Queen's University Press, 2007.
2 Staff Notes, no. 443, October 22, 1958. Eisenhower Presidential Library, Ann Whitman papers.

3   Robert J. Watson, *History of the Office of the Secretary of Defense*, Vol IV, *Intro the Missile Age 1956–1960* (Washington: Historical Office of the Secretary of Defense, 1997), 423.
4   "Supporting Data for Memorandum to Defence Council on Space Detection and Tracking System," November 17, 1965, Raymont Fonds 219/110, DND Department of History and Heritage.
5   Message, CINCNORAD to JCS, cited in *NORAD and CONAD Historical Summary, Jan-Jun. 1960*. Copy in NORAD/USNORTHCOM History Office.
6   Miller, to N.A. Robertson, undersecretary of state for external affairs, August 9, 1963.Raymont Fonds 207/349 DND Department of History and Heritage.
7   Murray Peden, *Fall of an Arrow* (Toronto: Stoddard Publishing 1987), 6.
8   "Prime Minister Diefenbaker's Statement of September 23, 1958," annex II in John B. McLin, *Canada's Changing Defense Policy, 1957–1963: The Problems of a Middle Power in Alliance*. (Baltimore: The Johns Hopkins Press, 1967), 225–8.
9   "Prime Minister Diefenbaker's Statement of February 20, 1969," annex III in McLin, 229–34
10 Quoted in Peden, 148.
11 McLin, 84.
12 Slemon to CINC, "F-101Bs for the RCAF," January 23, 1960. Copy, Raymont Fonds 1/14, DND Directorate of History and Heritage.
13 "Canadian Access to Nuclear Weapons in Peacetime," Annex/Section E, to NSC 5822/1, "Certain Aspects of US Relations with Canada," December 30, 1958, *Foreign Relations of the United States, 1958–1960*, Vol VII, Part1 (USGPO, 1993): 740–74.
14 Basil Robinson, *Diefenbaker's World: A Populist in Foreign Affairs*, (Toronto: University of Toronto Press, 1989), 107.
15 Patricia I. McMahon, *Essence of Indecision: Diefenbaker's Nuclear Policy, 1957–1963*, (Montreal: McGill-Queen's University Press, 2009), 13.
16 McLin, 154.
17 John G. Diefenbaker, *One Canada: The Memoirs of the Right Honourable John G. Diefenbaker, Vol 3, The Tumultuous Years 1962–1967* (Toronto: Macmillan of Canada, 1977), 82.
18 From "D.B.D.," Privy Council Office, *Memorandum for Mr. Bryce: Lessons of the Cuban Crisis*, November 20, 1962, DND Directorate of History and Heritage, Raymont Fonds, 113/2503.
19 Harkness, "The Nuclear Arms Question and the Political Crisis Which Arose from It in January and February 1963, August 19–27, 1963." Library and Archives Canada, RG 32 B19, Harkness Papers, vol. 57, Jan–Feb 1963.
20 John English, *The Worldly Years: The Life of Lester Pearson* Vol II: *1949–1972*, (Toronto: Vintage Books, 1993), 248.
21 Quoted in English, 250.
22 Knowlton Nash, *Kennedy and Diefenbaker: Fear and Loathing Across the Undefended Border*, (Toronto: McClelland and Stewart, 1990), 235.
23 Quoted in McLin, 163.
24 McLin, 164.
25 Minister of National Defence, *White Paper on Defence*, 1964.
26 "McNamara to president, "Recommended FY 1966–1970 Programs for Strategic Offensive Forces, Continental Air and Missile Defense Forces, and Civil Defense" in the Johnson Library, National Security File, Agency File, Defense Budget – FY 1966, Box 16.

SECTION 2

INTRODUCTION

RANDALL WAKELAM

For the RCAF to make good on the obligations set out in NATO and NORAD agreements it would need both suitable aircraft as well as the people to operate them and the entire organization backing up those front-line efforts. If one thinks of a pilot, or a crew, in terms of a knight taking his charger into battle, an analogy springs to mind. That knight was not much to look at without a horse, without the equipment needed to keep himself and the horse healthy and protected, and without the training needed, both for himself and those providing the horse and equipment, so that he could do his job. In this section, then, we look personnel matters and at aircraft procurement.

This section begins with Russell Isinger's study of the Avro Arrow, which was and is arguably the most romanticized project in the RCAF's history. Isinger offers insights into many facets of the interplay between politicians, air force leaders, and industry, which are as relevant today as they were over half a century ago. For a nation that had virtually no design experience prior to 1945, the Arrow, and its forerunner, the CF-100 Canuck, were little short of amazing, but as Isinger shows, just being able to build an aircraft did not mean that it was a guaranteed military or economic success.

There were, however, many other aircraft that were designed and manufactured in Canada, and these are discussed in Sections One and Three of this volume. In Montreal, Canadair built aircraft, such as the F-86 and the F-104, under licence, adding Canadian improvements and selling many to allies in addition to supplying the RCAF. Canadair also skilfully Canadianized a number of American and British transport aircraft, both for the RCAF and for civilian operators. One of those transports, the Bristol Britannia, was used to design and manufacture the unique Canadair Yukon transport and the Argus long-range ASW aircraft, which set many records for range and endurance. In Toronto, De Havilland Canada excelled in designing and manufacturing short take-off and landing aircraft: the Beaver, Otter, and Caribou. But ironically while these aircraft were used extensively by allied air services, the RCAF purchased only handfuls of the latter two.

Buying necessary aircraft in necessary numbers and variants was central to a flying and fighting air arm, and yet those aircraft were stuck on the ground without the people to maintain and operate them and without the larger supporting system to sustain the flight lines. The chapters forming the balance of the section deal with what we might call people issues.

In the first of these, I examine the education both of young aspirants wanting to make the RCAF a career and of career officers as they undertook an expansive and intense year of intellectual activity at the RCAF Staff College. As you will see, the value of such education had been recognized in the interwar decades, but now the rapid expansion of the RCAF to meet the extraordinary challenges of the Cold War demanded a focus on creating the necessary intellectual competencies and broad range of knowledge that came with undergraduate degrees and with the honing of those qualities as officers moved into senior ranks.

Education was a necessary foundation for those destined to lead the RCAF, but these officers and others would need to be trained to sit astride their metal chargers. And it was not just the RCAF that needed to expand quickly. Rachel Heide looks at the vast experience that Canadians could offer to NATO nations during the buildup of the early 1950s, making the point that Canada had built a solid reputation and expertise during the preceding world wars. She traces the extensive diplomatic interactions between Canada and its allies and shows the details of the various flying courses that flyers from those nations and young Canadians had to pass through before joining their units.

Maintaining those training aircraft, and the fighters, transports and indeed all the various fleets that allowed the RCAF to do its job was the work of a vital technical organization and the thousands of technicians and technical officers who operated it. Terry Leversedge's chapter on maintenance organizations and maintainers of the RCAF, as well as concepts of supply, examines aspects of the air force often taken for granted. Indeed, we too often assume that the aircraft almost magically appear on the ramp ready for the crews, with all systems ready for flight, fuel tanks full, and weapons loaded.

The next chapter in this section examines another facet of the RCAF, one that until recently has received little attention – the Women's Division. Allan English's research looks at the work and contribution of the women who served the RCAF both in uniform and across the broader RCAF community. English explores these issues through another unique lens, the radar control system for NORAD and the parallel functions of the Air Division.

In the final chapter, Mathias Joost's examination of the Auxiliary Air Force is a study in the compromises involved in a part-time organization looking for a role and organizing the people and equipment to fulfill it. While RCAF HQ had many ideas, none of them bad or wrong, about what a part-time branch of the RCAF could do to underpin and, in some cases, take on front-line roles, the very part-time nature of the units and individuals meant that flying and maintaining increasingly complex aircraft and support equipment was a constant detractor from the utility of the units that made up "the Aux."

CHAPTER FIVE

HUBRIS: THE CF-105 AVRO ARROW PROGRAM AND THE END OF THE GOLDEN AGE OF THE ROYAL CANADIAN AIR FORCE

RUSSELL ISINGER AND DONALD C. STORY[1]

"For a force for which the sky was the environment, rather than the limit, nothing seemed impossible.... The cancellation of this project ... dealt to the prestige and morale of the Air Force a blow from which it never fully recovered. Pride led to *hubris*, *hubris* to the CF-105."[2] So assessed noted Canadian military historian James Eayrs when writing about the aircraft just a decade after the cancellation of the project. The Avro CF-105 Arrow was born into a dangerous atomic age.[3] The postwar ideological and military clash between the Western alliance and the Communist bloc spawned both an arms race and a game of brinksmanship where the Cold War could turn hot at any moment. The Soviet Union had broken the United States monopoly on the atomic bomb and had long-range bombers capable of raining radioactive destruction on targets in North America. Geography no longer provided protection from direct attack. As a result of the Korean War, the greatest peacetime military buildup in Canadian history was underway in the early 1950s, and as Liberal Prime Minister Louis St. Laurent's minister of national defence, Brooke Claxton, put it, "defence had become the single biggest industry in Canada."[4] But Canada was a strong and wealthy middle power whose economy was enjoying an unprecedented postwar boom, and it willingly took on the financial and other responsibilities entailed by the new national security requirements. As seen in the chapters of Section 1, political and military leaders, imbued with a sense of national pride arising from Canada's Second World War record, were solidly committed to collective defence, embodied in the North Atlantic Treaty Organization (NATO), as well as acting as a reliable ally of Canada's superpower neighbour, the US.

An overhead image of Arrow RL-201 during the official unveiling at the Avro Malton plant showing its futuristic lines.

In Canada, the control the military exercised over their political masters in establishing defence priorities was "a curious reversal of British and American experience between 1945 and 1958, in which military power had been steadily eroded by political authority ... the Canadian armed profession during roughly the same period exercised in terms of tasks, expertise, *and political influence a virtually unbridled control of foreign and defence policy.*"[5] The key elements of this integrated decision-making structure were the chiefs of staff committee (COSC, source of military and strategic advice), the Cabinet defence committee (CDC, ministers responsible for national security matters), and Cabinet itself.[6] The COSC comprised five members of equal rank: the chairman, the chiefs of the Air, Naval, and General Staffs, and the chairman of the Defence Research Board (DRB). The COSC chairman was the main contact point for the defence minister, but decisions were based on consensus; as a result, the COSC often presented a united front to government. Over the course of the Arrow program, Liberal and Conservative ministers tended to defer to the expert advice offered by the COSC. But within the COSC, it was the RCAF that was the most powerful of the services. Canada's defence agenda was dominated by the RCAF's operational, technological, strategic, and financial requirements as articulated by its chiefs of Air Staff during this period: Air Marshals Wilf Curtis, Roy Slemon, and Hugh Campbell. And at the top of the agenda was the Arrow.

With North America within striking distance of Soviet bombers, continental defence was the priority for the RCAF, which in turn drove aircraft procurement decisions. Canada had a well-developed aviation industry, but while companies like Canadair and De Havilland did well from boosts to defence spending in Canada and the US,[7] the chief beneficiaries of RCAF procurement were two privatized wartime Crown corporations, Avro Aircraft Limited and Orenda Engines Limited.[8] The first line of air defence for Canada throughout the 1950s was the CF-100 Canuck, a world-leading two-seat, twin-engine, all-weather, subsonic interceptor, designed and built by Avro and Orenda.[9] But production of the Canuck was barely underway in 1952 when the RCAF dispatched a team to evaluate allied supersonic interceptors capable of dealing with the anticipated enhanced performance and increased numbers of the next generation of Soviet bombers.

The team recommended that the Canuck's successor be another made-in-Canada interceptor as no suitable aircraft were in service or in the planning stages elsewhere. The recommendation was defensible, based as it was on the RCAF's stringent operational requirements: any interceptor had to carry a navigator/radar operator because the RCAF lacked a sophisticated ground control interception (GCI) capability, despite actions to build the air defence detection radars (described in earlier chapters). As well, the aircraft had to reach supersonic speeds rapidly to compensate for the short warning time provided by the Pinetree Line; and a second engine was needed as insurance against engine failure over Canada's north. Of key importance to the RCAF were the advanced technological specifications. The view at Avro was that the RCAF was "asking for the moon…. It was no small wonder that [the] team had failed to find any such aircraft on the drawing boards anywhere in the world."[10] But this was the so-called Golden Age of the RCAF: it was allotted nearly 50 per cent of the total defence budget and its personnel strength exceeded that of the army, reflecting the service's strategic importance; its NATO Air Division, deploying Canucks and Canadair-built and Orenda-engined CL-13 (F-86) Sabres, was arguably the best trained and equipped force in the world; its *esprit de corps* was high.[11] The RCAF would settle for nothing but the best.[12]

With the critically important support of the DRB, the RCAF convinced the COSC to proceed with the Arrow, and in December 1953, Cabinet awarded Avro a $27 million contract limited to the design of two prototype Arrows. The RCAF committed to purchase the Arrow's engines from the US or Britain and

CF-105 Arrow 201 is towed past an Avro CF-100 Canuck near the company plant.

its electronics system[13] and air-to-air missile armament from the US. It estimated around 500–600 Arrows would be needed to replace the Canuck in Canadian-based regular and auxiliary squadrons, with service entry by 1958–9. The COSC and Cabinet concurred that this number of aircraft justified setting up a development program and that it was achievable within forecast defence budgets.

The explosion of a Soviet hydrogen bomb and the growing alarm over a perceived "bomber gap" between East and the West led the RCAF to demand an expansion and acceleration of the Arrow program. In March 1955, Cabinet amended the Avro contract to $261 million for 40 development aircraft and engines. As the RCAF found the available engines for the aircraft wanting, a powerful engine under development at Orenda, the Iroquois, was selected. Cabinet also approved the RCAF's proposal to abandon the usual time-consuming process of hand-building prototype aircraft, testing them, and then setting up an assembly line. Instead, the RCAF and Avro would follow a new American procedure (called Cook-Craigie), whereby preliminary research validated the design, with all aircraft – prototype, pre-production, and production – then rolling off an already established assembly line. Both the RCAF and Avro tended to interpret Cabinet's approval of this procedure as tantamount to a commitment to produce the Arrow. But Cabinet was assured that any increases in up-front development costs would be offset by later savings in time and labour. In turn, Cabinet signalled to the RCAF that the project could be abandoned if deemed expedient or necessary.

The Arrow program was officially launched in June 1955. However, the Minister of Defence Production, C.D. Howe, did not inspire confidence when he stated, "I can now say that we have embarked on a program of development that frankly gives me the shudders."[14] Howe, who had been rattled by the cost of and teething problems with the Canuck, had actually opposed awarding Avro the follow-on contract, writing to Claxton in December 1952:

> I must say that I am frightened for the first time in my defence production experience … the design staff at Avro is far from competent to undertake work of this importance. Their designing record to date is very bad indeed, measured by any standard. If we must have further development work, let us contract it with a British firm which has the personnel, equipment, and experience that qualifies them to do work of this kind. Someone so equipped, can do the work for a fraction of the cost in making the attempt at A.V. Roe.[15]

But Claxton, more nationalistic and more supportive of securing domestic sources of supply, accepted the advice coming from the RCAF.[16]

Dissenting voices accompanied the Arrow's unveiling. Several retired army officers, led by Lieutenant-General Guy Simonds, former chief of the General Staff, took aim at the RCAF, proclaiming that missiles would soon render the Arrow obsolete, making it a billion-dollar boondoggle. This opinion mirrored a contemporary manned aircraft-versus-guided missile debate then raging – that in the coming era of "push-button" warfare, missiles would be more militarily effective and financially affordable.[17] In 1956, Simonds wrote scathingly that the "combined vested interests of the air force, the aircraft industry and defence research scientists, burning with zeal to participate in a project they could call their own … swept aside any opposition to this venture."[18]

The internal military consensus on the Arrow program also began to crack in 1955 as costs crept upward, a point driven home when Avro requested an extra $59 million to keep the project on schedule. In the aftermath of the Korean War, the St. Laurent government now demanded the military tighten its belt. The COSC, while continuing to support the RCAF's procurement goals, also began to question the

Avro Canada Plant, Malton, ON.

RCAF about the possibility of procuring an American interceptor instead of the Arrow. As the chairman, Army General Charles Foulkes later wrote:

> There would be definite budgetary advantage in purchasing a United States aircraft, since [they] would meet all development charges, take all the risks, and sell to Canada at a reduced price made possible by keeping their production line going a bit longer to satisfy Canadian needs. There was a distinct advantage of being able to assess the cost of Canada's air defence commitment instead of having every few months to face the harassment of the A.V. Roe Company for more and more development funds.[19]

The problem was that nobody in the military knew how many billions the Arrow program would likely cost, as the RCAF would not set up an overall project management office until 1957.

In December 1955, the CDC sought reassurance that the Arrow program was on the right track, so the COSC reappraised the project.[20] Their report led to a recommendation to press on, but proposed stretching the project out, a time-honoured military cost control method. Cabinet, eager for any savings, agreed, limiting funding to the first 11 prototypes, establishing a spending cap of $170 million for the next three years, slowing development until test flights proved the Arrow's airworthiness, and instituting a review process every six months. While supporting project continuation, Cabinet, however, also described the overall costs as "frightening."[21]

As Foulkes would later observe, the RCAF "clung tenaciously to their original concept of an interceptor which could navigate and control the firing of missiles without the need of a highly developed [GCI] environment."[22] In support of this goal, during 1956, the RCAF embraced the idea that proven (and cheaper) off-the-shelf equipment was not good enough. When the leading American defence contractor balked at meeting the electronics system requirements for the Arrow on the required timeline, the RCAF decided to fund the development of an unproven state-of-the-art system known as Astra. The RCAF also selected a complex US air-to-air missile, Sparrow II, as the preferred armament for the Arrow, only to have to take over its development when the missile was cancelled by the US Navy.[23] In both instances, the RCAF made the decision over Avro's opposition, the company presciently sensing that expanding the project beyond the original airframe would escalate costs. And while the RCAF was insisting on an "all-singing, all-dancing, gold-plated fighter,"[24] it also discovered that aircraft like the Canuck and Arrow were too technically complex for auxiliary squadrons to maintain and operate.[25] This had the effect of reducing the potential Arrow production run by more than half.

By February 1957, a nervous Cabinet, again acting on the advice of the RCAF and COSC, cut the number of prototypes from 11 to eight to further reduce costs. Squadron service was now not expected until 1961–2. The evidence suggests that by 1957, Cabinet and the military (the RCAF excepted) perceived the Arrow program to be in serious trouble because of its skyrocketing costs, and the St. Laurent government was contemplating the project's termination. For the Liberals, however, ending the RCAF's prestige project in 1957, an election year, was politically dangerous; any decision regarding cancellation would wait until after their expected election win. But in June 1957, to everyone's surprise, Canadians instead elected a Progressive Conservative government, and John Diefenbaker became prime minister.

The inexperienced Diefenbaker government's first encounter with the military was hardly encouraging.[26] The North American Air Defence (NORAD) agreement, negotiated but left unapproved by the St. Laurent government, established a US-Canada command to coordinate continental air defence. The RCAF, eager to further co-operation with the USAF, was pressing for final approval, so in July 1957 Foulkes brought it to the new minister of national defence, Major-General George Pearkes,[27] who took it straight to Diefenbaker, who signed it without

Air Marshal Hugh Campbell, Chief of the Air Staff, left, and George R. Pearkes, the Minister of National Defence in Diefenbaker's conservative government, decend from a CSR-110 Albatross amphibious aircraft after its inaugural flight. Pearkes was adamant that the cancellation of the Arrow program was the correct, albeit difficult, decision.

further consultation. The Opposition seized on the moment to criticize the casual manner of NORAD's approval, and the unwelcome political backlash deepened Diefenbaker's known mistrust of the senior ranks of the military. What NORAD did, as described in earlier chapters, was commit Canada to the integration of the RCAF and United States Air Force (USAF) air defence commands Beyond this functional integration there was an equally important political and financial advantage for both air arms. "Both the RCAF and the USAF were locked in struggles with their sister services for defence funds. [And] for the RCAF, the USAF was a source of funding for radar stations and a source of pressure on Ottawa to recognize the importance of air defence."[28] But the NORAD decision would have ramifications for the Arrow program, as partnering with the Americans drew the RCAF closer to USAF strategic doctrine and operational requirements.[29]

In October 1957, Cabinet dealt with the other thorny defence project inherited from the Liberals. On the advice of the RCAF and the COSC, it decided to continue the

Crowds mill about the new Canadian fighter after the official unveiling of Arrow RL-201.

Arrow development for another twelve months at a cost of an additional $173 million, whereupon Cabinet would review the project again. This was essentially a reprieve for the RCAF from further questions about costs. But the minority Conservative government was in a vulnerable political position, with the economy starting to go into decline, unemployment rising, and budgets under pressure. These circumstances led to this cautious decision to proceed, but all would have a bearing on the Arrow program.

The first Arrow rolled proudly out of its Avro hangar in October 1957, but on the same day the Soviet Union launched *Sputnik* into orbit, driving the Arrow story from the headlines and symbolically calling into question the interceptor as a leading-edge means of defence. *Sputnik* stunned the West: if the Soviets could launch a satellite, they could do the same with a nuclear warhead. Prior fears of a "bomber gap" were replaced with fears of a "missile gap," verified when secret American U-2 spy flights detected a Soviet shift of resources away from bombers towards missiles. With the menace of Soviet bomber attack appearing to recede, the US "New

Look" national security strategy placed an even greater emphasis on deterring attack – by ensuring the survival of the offensive retaliatory capability of the Strategic Air Command (SAC) largely through radar early warning, viewed by the US as Canada's most important contribution to continental defence.[30] The US, British, and other governments started to cancel or scale back redundant military aviation projects while their companies shifted into missiles or civil aviation.[31] The RCAF response was to stubbornly stay the course with the Arrow, while Avro, secure in its belief that it was "the industrial arm of the RCAF and servant of government,"[32] did not diversify.

By 1958, the combination of a diminishing threat and budgetary competition finally broke the military consensus on the Arrow. Interservice rivalry had intensified between the RCAF and the other two services as the latter increasingly came to realize their own procurement wish lists were at risk if the Arrow program went ahead. The army especially demanded that the RCAF explain how an advanced aircraft like the Arrow fit within the developing air defence concept for NORAD – something the RCAF struggled to do beyond claiming, as it always had, that the Canuck needed replacing and the Arrow represented the best contribution to continental defence. In another blow to the RCAF's ambitions, the DRB, which had been a driving force behind the project, announced in June 1958 that it would not support a full-scale deployment of the Arrow.[33] Complicating matters further for the RCAF, intraservice rivalry had arisen. In addition to insisting on a new NORAD interceptor, the RCAF also wanted to procure BOMARC-B[34] nuclear surface-to-air missiles from the US and reequip its NATO Canuck and Sabre squadrons, for which the Arrow was considered unsuitable.[35] The RCAF's impossible task was to reassure the army and navy that their budgets would not be cut if the Arrow program continued while also satisfying the rival equipment demands of its own officers – all within an evolving strategic situation.

As the end of Cabinet's extension approached, the COSC debated alternative air defence plans that would see the RCAF procure the Arrow in some quantity (37, 60, or 169 aircraft options were discussed, with or without Astra and Sparrow II). All such proposals came with exorbitant price tags for such small production runs, and the RCAF reluctantly admitted defeat. In August 1958, the COSC and Pearkes recommended to the CDC that the project be cancelled, the RCAF requesting instead approval for two BOMARC-B bases (plus their GCI environment and additional radars) and the procurement of approximately 100 comparable American-built interceptors for its NORAD squadrons.[36]

To the Conservatives, elected on the promise of decreased defence expenditures and lower taxes, the costs of the Arrow program were shocking, and they ordered the military to prepare another reappraisal report outlining all project decisions

An Arrow under construction, Avro Canada plant, Malton, ON.

made from 1952 until 1958 – essentially, they asked the military to prove matters were as bad as COSC claimed. The report was quickly prepared and confirmed that the greatest threat from the Soviet Union in the 1960s would not be from bombers but from intercontinental ballistic missiles (ICBMs), against which an interceptor like the Arrow could provide no defence. In this shifting strategic setting, it was questionable if the Arrow was worth the high cost of its production, which would entail an increase in the defence budget of $400 million a year for several years. The "figures," the report concluded, "speak for themselves."[37]

For the RCAF, the die was cast when the CAS agreed to the Arrow's cancellation – provided that a comparable US interceptor could be purchased instead. Cabinet had extensive discussions throughout August and September 1958, with Pearkes continuing to recommend that the Arrow program be cancelled. In September, Diefenbaker announced that, considering the expected reduction in the need for interceptors, it was inadvisable to put the Arrow into production; however, the government was deferring a final decision on the Arrow program for six months (though Astra and Sparrow II were cancelled, and establishing the BOMARC-B bases proceeded).[38] Troubled by an emerging crisis between Communist China and the US in the Formosa Strait – any escalation of which could drag in the Soviet Union and raise the possibility of an attack on North America – Diefenbaker believed it prudent to keep the Canadian defence industry operating in case of war. By the following spring, the government would also be better able to assess the evolving strategic situation and whether the Soviets were indeed pivoting into intercontinental missiles.[39]

After the announcement, Pearkes did make one last-ditch attempt to interest the US and Britain in the Arrow. As with previous attempts,[40] it failed, causing one writer to later quip: "had the Soviet Union itself come through with an offer, the Canadian government might have been tempted to accept."[41] A sizeable sale could have helped the Arrow program reach economies of scale, making production more economical, but when the St. Laurent and Diefenbaker governments attempted to sell the Arrow, they came up against the same logic that led Canada to build the Arrow in the first place: other countries had their own unique operational requirements to meet, and they had their own domestic manufacturers to support. Though US officials in particular were well informed about and expressed their admiration for the Arrow, and thought it would make a valuable contribution to continental defence (all taken by an ever-hopeful RCAF as evidence USAF would eventually buy it), they had also signalled as early as December 1955 that "it would be impossible for the US government to participate in developing the CF-105, or to commit themselves to buy it, because of the strong influence of the US aircraft industry…."[42] The Americans had their own priorities, including, as Canadian officials were told in January 1958, a proposed interceptor so leading edge that its cost made the Arrow "look like something which might be picked up in a department store."[43] On the other hand, US officials did make an offer to purchase and give to the RCAF a sufficient number of Arrow aircraft to equip several squadrons – bearing testimony to the often made false claim that the US was determined to undermine the Arrow program.[44]

By the end of 1958, the Arrow had undergone more flight tests and an Avro redesign had cut costs by accommodating an existing American electronics system and missile. However, few believed Avro's promise to deliver at a lower cost, or that there would be an end to their requests for more funding. In late February 1959, Cabinet met to confirm a decision that had essentially already been taken during the previous 60 days during a series of meetings where the ministers continued to agonize over the effects cancellation would have on the aircraft industry, the morale of the RCAF, the perception of Canada's commitment to its alliances, and Canada's sense of achievement and its sovereignty.[45] But the financial and strategic realities outlined by the COSC buried any of these considerations.

One of two specially modified Lancaster aircraft taking off from RCAF Station Cold Lake, AB, with two Ryan Aeronautical Firebee target drones under its wings. The drones were used to evaluate weapons systems for the Avro CF-100 Canuck and CF-105 Arrow.

On 20 February 1959, forever known to the Arrow faithful as "Black Friday," Diefenbaker announced the cancellation of the Arrow program; termination charges brought total expenditure to $470 million.[46] The RCAF's most-favoured companies had done little to prepare for the likelihood of cancellation, and they now suffered the consequences of gambling their future on a single defence order, with thousands of their technical personnel dispersing to other companies and agencies in Canada, the US, and Britain.[47] Despite the layoffs at Avro, Orenda, and other sub-contracting firms, and the expected flood of criticism from industry, unions, and the greater Toronto area municipalities, press reaction across Canada showed there were differing views: concerns about the increased integration of defence policy with the US; the loss of technical expertise; and an acknowledgment that the Arrow had been overtaken by the missile age and by the obvious advantages of pursuing shared defence production with the US.[48] As for the Opposition,

Prime Minister John Diefenbaker acknowledges the salute of an RCAF Honour Guard prior to his departure from RCAF Station Uplands, ON. Diefenbaker announced the cancellation of the Arrow project on 20 February 1959, a day that came to be known as "Black Friday."

while not disputing the problems with the Arrow program, it chose to focus its criticism on how the decision had been made. In private correspondence with the new Liberal Opposition leader, Lester Pearson, Howe (now out of office) wrote: "there is no doubt in my mind that the CF-105 should be terminated – costs are completely out of hand.... The proper line of attack should be directed to the Government's temporizing and fumbling with this decision."[49] The RCAF, for its part, remained wedded to the view that, while ICBMs would eclipse the Soviet bomber force in the coming decade, bombers were still a threat that needed to be met by deploying a combination of missiles like BOMARC-B, along with suitable advanced replacement interceptors for the Canuck (a request that Diefenbaker had noticeably left out his announcement). That such views were not grounded in financial or strategic realities were apparent when, in 1961, 66 surplus USAF McDonnell CF-101-B Voodoos arrived to more than satisfy the RCAF's NORAD requirements.

Canada's failed experiment with self-sufficiency in the production of modern weapons led to the realization that defence research and development in Canada was best served if it was integrated with the defence production resources of the US. As one contemporary American commentator admitted: "No one would ever deride the quality of Canadian research and weapons development, but the scale on which these programs must be conducted precludes most nations, including Canada, from participating meaningfully in the race."[50] With the cancellation of the Arrow, Canada abandoned the independent design of weapons systems, accepted the reality of procurement dependence on the US, and profited through guaranteed access to a larger and lucrative American market: "Canadian defense needs were satisfied with less costly American aircraft, and Canadian defence industrial needs were met by the conclusion of a defense production-sharing agreement with the United States [in 1959], and by the stipulation that weapons bought by Canada involve some manufacturing in Canada."[51]

But why did the experiment fail? Popular literature and culture have vilified Diefenbaker, holding him personally responsible for the Arrow's demise, ostensibly because of his lack of vision and his unconscionable acceptance of the dominance of the US in defence policy. But whatever form the mythic version of the Arrow's cancellation might take, the failure of the Arrow program can be attributed undeniably to the RCAF's fixation on the idea of flying the best interceptor in the world, an obsession based on visions of prestige and national pride that ignored the realities of a changing defence environment and the perils of insisting on incorporating the most sophisticated technology into the development of modern weapons.

The defence decision-making structure in Canada in the postwar years functioned so that defence procurement largely determined defence policy, rather than proceeding within a thoughtful defence strategy. But the RCAF, so expert at advancing its organizational interests within this structure, was considerably less adept at managing its homegrown weapons acquisition process. The crucial – and ultimately fatal – decisions regarding the project's acceleration and expansion from one to four state-of-the-art systems developed concurrently[52] – the Arrow airframe, the Iroquois engine, the Sparrow II missile, and the Astra electronics system – occurred on the St. Laurent government's watch, but at the RCAF's insistence. When the Arrow program arrived on the Diefenbaker government's desk, the damage was already done. Though the Diefenbaker government can be faulted for confusing the public with its muddled explanation of the consequences for the Arrow program of the arrival of the missile age, and for its part in exacerbating relations with Avro executives, in the end it made the right call – a decision that the RCAF and the COSC had already agreed was necessary.

Arrow RL-201 landing after a test flight. Note the drag chute deployed to slow the aircraft down.

Air-to-air image of Arrow RL-201 in flight.

A decisive contributing factor to the Arrow program's cancellation was harsh financial realities.[53] There was a lack of clarity, and considerable disagreement, about how costly the Arrow program would end up being throughout the procurement phases of conception, validation, development, production, and operation. It did not help that the RCAF was woefully deficient in estimating costs in the formative years of the Arrow program and only became concerned about its price when forced to by the other services. Nor that Avro and Orenda, with their "cost-plus" contract with the government, had little incentive to reign in costs. The Arrow was not substantively more expensive than comparable Western military aircraft, but the overarching truth, as one historian has put it, was that Canada learned the hard way that it "… simply could not afford to pay the costs involved in creating [such] a modern weapons system…. The only error in the government's decision was that it had not been made earlier."[54]

Such financial realities were made even harsher by the dramatic strategic shifts internationally, influenced by the rapid pace of development of modern weapons systems. The predicted growth in the strategic and tactical significance of the missile – superseding not only the bomber threat in the Soviet arsenal but the counter-threat posed by the interceptor – came at the expense of the Arrow, leading inexorably to a significantly reduced operational requirement for interceptors in 1959. The RCAF had poorly assessed the strategic horizon when it envisaged the Arrow, designed solely to meet a bomber attack, as the core of its air defences. In a nuclear conflict, protracted warfare would not take place; an interceptor would likely be used only once; and if even a few bombers or ICBMs got through, an unacceptable level of devastation would result. Strategic thinking therefore dictated that deterrence – achieved through the protection of the retaliatory capability of the USAF's SAC – was far more valuable than any defence that could be mounted. As a result, what the US wanted most from Canada was not so much an extensive and sophisticated RCAF air defence fleet as a robust system of early warning radars that ensured SAC bombers would have time to get off the ground. In such an air defence concept, the argument in favour of a trailblazing interceptor over a less advanced but still capable one – or a cheaper and efficient missile like BOMARC-B – was debatable. The RCAF's undoing was its insistence on the procurement of the world's best interceptor at an inopportune time of political, financial, and strategic uncertainty.

The poet Henry Wadsworth Longfellow once famously wrote: "I shot an arrow into the air, it fell to earth, I knew not where." The RCAF, filled with pride and confidence over its record, mission, and future, and blindly focused on its aircraft, in effect shot an Arrow into the air without knowing where it might fall. As it turned out, its hard landing signalled the end of the RCAF's pre-eminent role in the formulation and implementation of Canadian defence policy, and of its Golden Age.

NOTES

1 This chapter is based on Donald C. Story and Russell Isinger, "The Origins of the Cancellation of Canada's Avro CF-105 Arrow Fighter Program: A Failure of Strategy," *Journal of Strategic Studies* 30, no. 6 (December 2007): 1025–50; Russell Isinger, "The Avro Arrow," in *Canada: Confederation to Present*, CD-Rom textbook (Edmonton: Chinook Multimedia, Inc., 2001); Russell Isinger and Donald C. Story, "The Plane Truth: The Avro Canada CF-105 Arrow Program," in *The Diefenbaker Legacy. Canadian Politics, Law and Society since 1957*, ed. Donald C. Story and R. Bruce Shepard (Regina: Canadian Plains Research Centre, 1998), 43–55; and Russell Isinger, "The Avro Canada CF-105 Arrow Program: Decisions and Determinants," (MA thesis: University of Saskatchewan, 1997).
2 James Eayrs, *In Defence of Canada: Peacemaking and Deterrence* (Toronto: University of Toronto Press, 1972), 123.
3 The CF-105 designation was assigned only in 1957, but the aircraft will be referred to as the Arrow here.
4 Canada, House of Commons, *Debates*, 27 November 27, 1952, 136–7.
5 Adrian Preston, "The Profession of Arms in Postwar Canada, 1945–1970. Political Authority as a Military Problem," *World Politics. A Quarterly Journal of International Relations* 23, no. 2 (January 1971): 201.
6 This chapter draws extensively upon the minutes and supporting documents of COSC, CDC, and Cabinet meetings. On the defence decision-making structure of this period, see Douglas Bland, *The Administration of Defence Policy in Canada 1947 to 1985* (Kingston: Ronald P. Frye & Company, 1987), 151–2, and Lawrence R. Aronsen, "Canada's Postwar Re-armament: Another Look at American Theories of the Military-Industrial Complex," *Historical Papers* (1981): 175–96.
7 See Lawrence R. Aronsen, "'A Leading Arsenal of Democracy:' American Rearmament and the Continental Integration of the Canadian Aircraft Industry, 1948–1953," *The International History Review* 13, no.3 (August 1991): 481–501.
8 Divisions of A.V. Roe Canada Limited, they were based in Malton, Ontario. For pre-Arrow RCAF aircraft procurement, see Randall Wakelam, *Cold War Fighters. Canadian Aircraft Procurement, 1945–54* (Vancouver, University of British Columbia Press, 2011).
9 Though not without its problems, the Canuck program was a success, and Avro built 692 examples. See Wakelam.
10 Greig Stewart, *Shutting Down the National Dream: A.V. Roe and the Tragedy of the Avro Arrow*, 2d. ed. (Toronto: McGraw-Hill Ryerson Limited,1997), 180, quoting Jim Floyd, Avro's vice-president of engineering.
11 See Jeff Rankin-Lowe, "A Decade of Air Power. Royal Canadian Air Force 1950–1959: Part I and Part II" *Wings of Fame. The Journal of Classic Combat Aircraft*, 2 and 3 (1996): 142–57.
12 The team's report led to a 1952 operational requirement designated OR 1/1-63 "Supersonic All-Weather Interceptor Aircraft," and a 1953 design study designated AIR 7-3 "Design Studies of a Prototype Supersonic All-Weather Aircraft."
13 The electronics system encompassed a radar fire control, navigation, communications, and flight control system.
14 Canada, House of Commons, *Debates*, June 28, 1955, 5380.
15 C.D. Howe to Brooke Claxton, December 19, 1952, Clarence Decatur Howe Papers, MG 27, III, B20 (hereafter Howe Papers), vol. 48, file 4, A.V. Roe Canada Limited, 1952, LAC.
16 For Claxton's influence on defence policy, see David Jay Bercuson, *True Patriot. The Life of Brooke Claxton 1898–1960* (Toronto: University of Toronto Press, 1993).

17 For the missile vs. aircraft debate, see Lewis Betts, *Duncan Sandys and British Nuclear Policy-Making* (London: Palgrave Macmillan, 2016).
18 Lieutenant-General Guy Simonds, "Where We've Gone Wrong on Defence," *Maclean's*, June 23, 1956, 66. See also Lieutenant-General Guy Simonds, "We're Wasting Millions on an Obsolete Air Force," *Maclean's*, August 4, 1956, 39.
19 General Charles A. Foulkes, "The Story of the CF-105 Avro 'Arrow,' 1952–1962," 8–9. Foulkes Papers (hereafter Foulkes Papers), file 14-2 Arrow DHH,
20 A valuable report, its appendices contain individual reports from the Plans Analysis and Requirements Group, Comparison Group (Fighters), Comparison Group (Missiles), Cost Analysis Group, on US and British aircraft design and development programs, and on the phasing in of weapons in air defence system with relation to the enemy threat. LAC, DND, 83-84/226, vol. 20886, file COSC 10:9, pt. 4, Canada, Manufacture of Aircraft, 1948–1964, (Top Secret) 1948–1955, "Report by the Working Group to the Ad Hoc Departmental Committee for the Reappraisal of the CF105 Development Programme," n.d.
21 LAC, RG2, Records of the Privy Council Office, Cabinet Conclusions (hereafter CC), 11–15, December 7, 1955.
22 Foulkes Papers, 13.
23 Foulkes Papers, 7, 11–13.
24 Danford W. Middlemiss, "A Pattern of Cooperation: The Case of the Canadian-American Defence Production and Development Sharing Agreements, 1958–1963" (PhD Dissertation, University of Toronto, 1975), 188.
25 For more on the auxiliary squadrons, see Sandy Babcock, "Whithered on the Vine: The Postwar RCAF Auxiliary," in *Canadian Military History since the 17th Century*, Proceedings of the Canadian Military History Conference, Ottawa, May 5–9, 2000 (Ottawa: DHH/DND, 2001): 395–404.
26 For an overview of the Diefenbaker government's defence challenges, see Isabel Campbell, "The Defence Dilemma, 1957–1963. Reconsidering the Strategic, Technological, and Operational Contexts," in *Reassessing the Rogue Tory: Canadian Foreign Relations in the Diefenbaker Era*, ed. Janice Cavell and Ryan M. Touhey (Vancouver: University of British Columbia Press, 2018), 123–42.
27 For Pearkes's time as defence minister, see Reginald Roy, *For Most Conspicuous Bravery: A Biography of Major General George R. Pearkes, V.C., Through Two World Wars* (Vancouver: University of British Columbia Press, 1977).
28 Joseph T. Jockel, *No Boundaries Upstairs: Canada, the United States, and the Origins of North American Air Defense, 1945–1958* (Vancouver: University of British Columbia Press, 1987), 56.
29 For the US perspective on continental defence, see Kenneth Schaffel, *The Emerging Shield. The Air Force and the Evolution of Continental Air Defence, 1945–60* (Washington, DC: Office of Air Force History, United States Air Force, 1991), and for the Canadian view, see Richard Goette, *Sovereignty and Command in US-Canada Continental Defence, 1940–1957* (Vancouver: UBC Press, 2018).
30 For more on the air defence debate, see Andrew Richter, *Avoiding Armageddon: Canadian Military Strategy and Nuclear Weapons, 1950–1963* (Vancouver, University of British Columbia Press, 2002), and Patrick I. McMahon, *Essence of Indecision: Diefenbaker's Nuclear Policy, 1957–1963* (Montreal and Kingston: McGill-Queen's University Press, 2009).
31 See Robert Jackson, *Cold War Combat Prototypes* (Ramsbury: The Crowood Press Ltd., 2005); Erik Simonsen, *Project Terminated: Famous Military Aircraft Cancellations of the Cold War and What Might Have Been* (Manchester: Crécy Publishing Limited, 2013); and Derek Wood,

Project Cancelled: The Disaster of Britain's Abandoned Aircraft Projects, rev. ed. (London: Jane's Publishing Company Limited, 1986).

32 Fred Smye (former vice president and general manager of Avro), *Canadian Aviation and the Avro Arrow* (Oakville: Randy Smye, 1989), 83.

33 DHH/DND, the Raymont Collection, Chairman, Chiefs of Staff Committee, series 1, 73/1223, file 10, Air Defence Requirements, Defence against the Manned Bomber: Appreciation by DRB, July 1958.

34 See Sean Maloney, "Secrets of the Bomarc: Re-examining Canada's Misunderstood Missile, pts. 1 and 2, *Royal Canadian Air Force Journal*, vols. 3 and 4 (2014): 33–45, 65–78, and Christopher J. Bright, *Continental Defense in the Eisenhower Era. Nuclear Antiaircraft Arms and the Cold War* (New York: Palgrave Macmillan, 2010).

35 The Lockheed CF-104G Starfighter would be chosen for the NATO nuclear strike-reconnaissance role, built under licence by Canadair and Orenda.

36 A critical meeting, see LAC, Records of the Privy Council Office, RG2, Cabinet Defence Committee Conclusions, August 15, 1958, with reference to Minister's Memorandum, August 8, 1958, D9-58.

37 Another valuable report, its appendices contain letters, memoranda, and extracts from Hansard as well as summaries of expenditures, key decisions of the COSC, the CDC, and Cabinet, and of discussions with the US and Britain. DHH/DND, the Raymont Collection, Chairman, Chiefs of Staff Committee, series 1, 73/1223, file 632, CF-105 Aircraft 01/30/58-08/19/58, "Report on the Development of the CF105 Aircraft and Associated Weapon System 1952–1958," August 19, 1958 (hereafter COSC Report).

38 Diefenbaker's statement is reproduced in Jon B. McLin, *Canada's Changing Defence Policy, 1957–1963: The Problems of a Middle Power in Alliance* (Baltimore: The Johns Hopkins Press, 1967), 225–8.

39 LAC, CC, September 21, 1958, 2–3. On the crisis over the islands of Quemoy and Matsu, see the memoranda sent to Diefenbaker in *Documents on Canadian External Relations*, ed. Michael D. Stevenson, vol. 25, 1957–1958, part II (Ottawa: Foreign Affairs and International Trade, 2004), 212–13 and 852–7.

40 DHH/DND, COSC Report, Appendix G, contains a summary of sales efforts in the US and Britain.

41 James Eayrs, "Canadian Defence Polices Since 1867," in Canada, *House of Commons Special Studies Prepared for the Special Committee of the House of Commons on Matters Relating o Defence, Supplement 1964–1965*, 20.

42 LAC, CC, December 7, 1955, 12.

43 DHH/DND, COSC Report, Appendix G, Annex I, 1.

44 This offer was rejected as being politically unacceptable as Canada did not accept military aid, but it also would not have produced the economies of scale needed to make production viable. For a discussion of US and British interest in the Arrow program, see Brad W. Gladman and Peter M. Archambault, "Advancing the Canada-US Alliance: The Use of History in Decision Support," *Journal of Military and Strategic Studies*, 14, no. 3 and 4 (2012): 18–24.

45 The meetings were LAC, CC, January 13, 1959, 8–9; January 28, 1959, 6; February 3, 1959, 4–5; February 4, 1959, 3–4; 10 February 1959, 2–3; 14 February 1959, 3–5; 17 February 1959, 4–5; 19 February 1959, 2; and February 23, 1959, 2–4.

46 Diefenbaker's statement is reproduced in McLin, 229–39.

47 The Arrows were subsequently scrapped according to standard bureaucratic operating procedure. DHH/DND, file 79/333, NDHQ, DHIST, March 13, 1959–January 11, 1980, Eyes

Only – Director, DHIST, re. responsibility for scrapping Arrow prototypes, Air Marshal Hugh Campbell, Chief of the Air Staff, "Memorandum. The Minister (Through the Deputy Minister). Arrow Cancellation – Disposal of Material," March 26, 1959.

48 "Press Views on the Arrow and Defence," *Globe and Mail*, February 25, 1959.
49 LAC, Howe Papers, vol. 149, file 75–7 Political – General, C.D Howe to Mike Pearson, January 22, 1959.
50 Melvin Conant, "Canada and Continental Defense: An American View," *International Journal* XV, no. 3 (Summer 1960): 226.
51 Robert Bothwell, "Defense and Industry in Canada, 1935–1970," in *War, Business, And World Military-Industrial Complexes*, ed. Benjamin Franklin Cooling (Port Washington: Kennikat Press Corp, 1981), 117–18. See also Middlemiss.
52 For an evaluation of concurrency, see Michael E. Brown, *Flying Blind. The Politics of the U.S. Strategic Bomber Program* (Ithaca: Cornell University Press, 1992), 21.
53 Isinger, "The Avro Canada CF-105 Arrow Program: Decisions and Determinants," and Bryn Rees, "Neo-Classical Realism and the Avro CF-105 Arrow" (MA Thesis: University of Saskatchewan, 2016), argued that, while the external strategic realities of the missile age dictated the likelihood of the Arrow's cancellation, they were not determinative until reinforced by affordability.
54 J.L. Granatstein, *Canada. 1957–1967: The Years of Uncertainty and Innovation*. The Canadian Centenary Series, ed. Ramsey Cook, vol. 19 (Toronto: McClelland and Stewart Limited, 1986), 109.

CHAPTER SIX

EDUCATING AIR POWER PRACTITIONERS

RANDALL WAKELAM

During the interwar years, with no real threats to national security and obliged to operate on a shoestring budget, the air force found itself having to prove its utility to a civilian population in peacetime. At the same time, the RCAF was limited to a small personnel establishment with little need for a steady intake of new officers or staff-trained officers.[1] In these circumstances professional education was of lesser importance than many other pressing matters, but this was to change dramatically at the end of the Second World War as the threat to national security placed a focus squarely on the ability of the RCAF to manage organizations of growing size and complexity. Providing leaders for this new RCAF required education and training both for young men starting their service and for mid-career officers moving into demanding leadership and staff appointments. This chapter will examine how the RCAF responded to these needs with an examination of the programs offered by the Canadian Services Colleges and of the policies and curricula of the schools of the RCAF College. The story begins with a brief look at education programs prior to 1945.

Interwar and Wartime Education

By the middle of the 1920s, absorbed by the Department of National Defence, the RCAF, like the militia and the Royal Canadian Navy, drew its career officers largely from the graduates of the Royal Military College at Kingston, where a university-like, army-focused program had been the norm since the college's opening in 1876. While the curriculum did not lead to a degree, the four-year program did

Founded in 1876, the Royal Military College (RMC) of Canada is located in Kingston, ON. Although a handful of graduates entered the RCAF in the 1920s and 1930s, it was after the Second World War when RMC re-opened as a Canadian Services College (CSC) that substantial numbers of air force cadets attended this educational institution. There were two other CSCs: HMCS Royal Roads, Victoria, BC, and Le Collège militaire royal de Saint-Jean, QC.

provide a useful blend of engineering, military training, and liberal arts courses. Those few destined for the RCAF undertook air force training during summer training periods.[2]

Not until 1931 did the RCAF place an officer on the RMC staff. The first was Squadron Leader C.M. McEwen, an ace in the Royal Flying Corps during the First World War and an interwar graduate of the RAF Staff College, who would go on to command No. 6 Group (RCAF) during the Second World War. When McEwen left RMC, he was replaced by Squadron Leader George Wait, who also had combat flying experience as well as a year at the RAF College.[3] Wait would become the first commandant of the RCAF war staff course described later in this chapter. McEwen, and later Wait, gave all RCAF cadets lectures on air force history and air tactics, and they were also able to instruct air force officers taking the RAF Staff College preparatory course.[4]

Throughout the interwar years graduates joining the RCAF made up no more than 20 per cent of their classes.[5] That statistic changed in 1938 when 12 RCAF commissions were offered to the 40 young men seeking a permanent appointment.[6] Interest in the RCAF, no doubt the result of expansion plans,[7] contributed to a rethinking of the RMC curriculum in 1937 which, had it been implemented would have seen a range of air force-oriented courses introduced in the Fourth Year curriculum.[8] The commandant's report of that year noted: "In view of the fact that more graduates of the College are taking commissions in the RCAF than in any other branch of the services, it is thought that the time has come when we must consider whether we are doing everything we should in the way of preparing potential Air Force candidates."[9]

In terms of mid-career education, the RCAF had no capacity for operating a staff college in the interwar period, but it did send one or two officers to the RAF Staff College each year. Group Captain J.S. Scott, appointed the RCAF's first full-time director in 1925, had been the first Canadian to attend that program.[10] These graduates enabled the RCAF, in the words of the official history, to maintain "a measure of military identity."[11] But this exposure did little to foster the creation of Canadian airpower concepts or instil a service culture, as the RCAF official history points out:

> Very few had ever worked on air staffs at all. They have been combat flyers and now they were "bush pilots in uniform," their minds focused on the practical, technical, and administrative problems which beset them on every side. There was no RCAF Staff College to stimulate their thinking on strategy and doctrine, and when merit and good fortune took one or two a year to the RAF Staff College in England, it must have been an exhilarating experience.[12]

By 1939, twenty-two RCAF officers had passed through the RAF Staff College and another five had attended the Imperial Defence College, which focused on strategic issues.[13] This latter education, while a good broadening experience for those working at the strategic level, would be less useful for officers charged with the practical administration surrounding the wartime expansion of the RCAF.

Indeed, once the war began, the RCAF grew rapidly in both numbers and responsibilities, all of which demanded officers with advanced professional education. As in the United Kingdom and Australia, by the middle of the war, the need for staff-trained officers was acute. In November 1942, the minister of national

Visit by RCAF Staff College staff and students to the Avro Canada plant to view the assembly line for CF-105 Avro Arrow interceptors.

defence for air, C.G. "Chubby" Power, directed the Air Council to develop a war staff course for the RCAF. Like the RAF and RAAF war staff courses, the Canadian version was short – just ten weeks of curriculum – and used experienced officers to instruct students on the problems of administering a modern air force.[14]

The first Canadian air war staff course commenced in October 1943 and was watched closely by now Air Commodore Wait and his staff to ensure that they had it right, in terms of both quality and compatibility. Some weeks later, Wait had an opportunity to offer his thoughts on the content and conduct of the program, as well as the professional development philosophy that combined training and education: "The backbone of the course consists of a series of lectures on staff duties given by the Directing Staff, which leads students through service writing, precis writing, appreciations and orders and instructions. The students then put their knowledge to work by doing a series of practical problems on the employment of air power."[15]

Aerial view of the Strathrobyn estate, Armour Heights, north Toronto, taken from an aircraft belonging to Bishop-Barker Aeroplanes Limited in 1920. The estate would be acquired by the Department of National Defence in 1943 to house the RCAF Staff College.

To give this routine staff training some added richness, however, the program of studies also included lectures given by well-qualified visiting speakers, both officers and civilian officials, on a variety of topics, including other services, allied and enemy forces, strategic direction of the war, and war production. Similar enrichment could be achieved by exposing RCAF officers to members of Canada's other services and to allied aviators. Some initial success was achieved by including an army officer as a member of the directing staff and by taking students to the army war staff course in Kingston to participate in a joint exercise. "Only by such a means," Wait emphasized in his correspondence with Ottawa, "can the students be given the broader and more authoritative outlook that they will require in staff positions."[16] Wait's overall philosophy was clear: staff officers, although expected to produce standardized staff solutions, needed a breadth of knowledge in order to develop those products.

In the period between 1919 and 1945, the RCAF had had supporting roles and financial constraints during the peace, and had not been able to create an independent junior officer educational program. Nor had it been seen as necessary or feasible to establish a domestic staff college during the interwar years, with reliance on the RAF for roughly a score of staff-educated officers who could provide some degree of air power thinking for the respective air forces. Things were to change with the peace of 1945 and the coming of the Cold War. Even in the closing months of the war RCAF leaders recognized that they would need a better educated junior officer population and, having seen the benefits of a domestic staff college, a senior officer curriculum that offered both staff skills training and broad education for high level decision making.

Educating the New Entrant: Postwar Education Policies and Programs

Both the Royal Canadian Navy (RCN) and the RCAF had recognized that not having their own cadet colleges in the interwar period had left them with insufficient junior officer cadres in 1939, when rapid expansion was needed. To redress this problem during the war, the RCN had opened a college on the west coast, HMCS *Royal Roads*, and so with the future of the Royal Military College in Kingston still uncertain in 1946, the navy and air force decided to send cadets to the *Royal Roads* instead.[17] But the command and control of the two-service college and the details of the cadets' education led to discord. Differences between the RCAF and the RCN over admissions, terms of service, and pay were stumbling blocks, and a joint meeting of the Air Council and the Naval Board was convened on 23 May 1946, with Minister of National Defence Brooke Claxton presiding. All but one of the issues were quickly worked out and, intriguingly, the notion of a common cadet uniform, to avoid creating a social divide, was adopted. The one issue on which consensus could not be achieved concerned admissions standards. The RCN planned to continue accepting cadets who passed a "qualifying examination on a Senior Matriculation level," while the RCAF wanted only candidates who actually had a senior matriculation.[18] In this, the air force was placing emphasis on having cadets enter military college with a solid educational foundation.

Soon after, Claxton called on the three services to adopt a philosophy of joint education so that officers would, by the time they reached executive positions, have served with colleagues from the other services. He also wanted officers to have sufficient postsecondary and professional education to deal with complex and ambiguous problems that they would encounter during their careers.[19] To define a common educational philosophy, Claxton appointed recently retired Air Vice-Marshal Ernest Stedman, formerly the RCAF's head of research and development, to lead a tri-service committee on cadet education. Stedman reported that the army sought a full undergraduate degree, the RCAF wanted something close to a baccalaureate degree, and the navy was content with less. An observer might have concluded that the RCAF was shortchanging its institutional need for officers with sufficient education to become senior leaders twenty years after graduation.[20]

At this point, the task of developing an implementation plan for cadet education was given to Air Vice-Marshal Wilf Curtis, then the air member for Air Staff and soon to be CAS. Curtis proposed a blend of existing concepts such that RCAF officers, like their peers in the other Canadian services, would complete a four-year program at RMC Kingston. While not leading to a degree, the syllabus had the content and rigour of undergraduate degrees in the province of Ontario, where the RMC was located. Four summers of training would be sufficient for air force officer cadets destined for flying jobs to graduate with their wings.[21] Between the agreement with the navy at *Royal Roads* and the subsequent tri-service philosophy and concept, both developed by senior RCAF officers, one gets the clear sense that the Canadian air arm was content with, or at least accepted, an integrated approach to entry-level officer education.

Some sense of the general modalities of Curtis's common educational program can be seen in a multiyear (1948–53) commandant's report from RMC Kingston.[22] The college had adopted a four-year program, which was conducted at the university level and which gave cadets a liberal education with sufficient math and sciences to be effective in the highly technical worlds of the services. For those actually going into the technical fields, an engineering program enabled them to gain an engineering degree by attending a civilian university for an additional year. Cadets spent their summers with the service that they would join after graduation. For the RCAF, that meant summers of flying training for aircrew leading up to the awarding of their wings (pilots) the fall after graduation, navigators (initially called "observers") in the summer prior to their last academic year[23]; for non-flying air force officers, it meant a similar period in technical schools or working in their fields in the air force.

While RMC would not reopen until 1948, *Royal Roads* was fully operational. A variety of *Roads*' commandant's reports through the late 1940s provide some comments on cross-college activities but not on focused unique professional development for air force cadets. For example, the May 1948 report says that air force cadets spent the day on a submarine while their naval counterparts were flown to

Comox on Vancouver Island. Both groups apparently enjoyed the experiences, but perhaps soon-to-be air force officers might have gained more by experiencing the flying operations. That same month naval cadets were given a one-day series of lectures on a range of historical and contemporary air force topics by RCAF staff at the college. The report of September 1949 states that the student body consists of 62 navy, 45 army, and 33 air force cadets and signalled the shift to a tri-service institution.[24]

A third Canadian Services, College le Collège Militaire Royal (CMR) de St-Jean, opened in 1952 with an objective, among other purposes, to attract young Francophone Canadians in greater number. The CMR yearbook noted the amazing task of creating the third cadet college in the span of a summer. The program was drawn up along academic lines but, as significantly, this was truly a tri-service institution. The commandant was an army officer, his deputy was from the RCAF, and the director of studies was a naval officer. Similarly, the three squadrons of cadets had commanders representing the three services. Of the student body, approximately 40 per cent was RCAF, reflecting the rapid expansion of that service in the first years of the Cold War.[25] As important as the bilingual nature of CMR was its preparatory year, which accommodated students from the Quebec secondary education system, young men from across Canada with only a junior matriculation, and non-commissioned Airmen seeking advancement to officer status.[26]

Opening opportunities for Francophones did not mean that the RCAF was becoming a bilingual service. During the Second World War, with the RCAF integrated with British personnel both in Europe and even in the British Commonwealth Air Training Plan (BCATP), working in French had been considered a difficulty and even an operational risk given the difficulty of understanding British pronunciation. Rather than employ French Canadians in their first language, English language instruction was set up. Nevertheless, one French-speaking (i.e., French Canadian) squadron had been formed, 425 Squadron within Bomber Command. Despite good intentions, even 18 months after the squadron's activation only half the personnel were Francophone.[27]

During the 1950s RCAF leadership continued to see the service as an English-speaking institution where Francophones would be expected, after language training, to work in English. Despite the opening of CMR for the purpose of attracting French Canadians a Defence Research Board study in 1956 noted that if the RCAF did not reconsider its recruiting policies generally "it would continue to attract few French speaking career volunteers which might have unfortunate consequences in the event of mobilization."[28] A further study concluded that Francophones scored lower during courses because they were forced to learn and be assessed in their

Two officer cadets attending the Royal Military College (RMC), Kingston, ON, hard at work in an engineering workshop. Throughout the 1950s and 60s, many RCAF personnel attended RMC as part of the Regular Officer Training Plan pursuing degrees in science and engineering.

second language.[29] Perhaps the results of these studies drew attention to the fact that young Francophones entering CMR could only complete the first two years of their university program in English. This led the MND, Douglas Harkness, to announce in 1960 that a study would be conducted to look at the feasibility of introducing a full four-year degree program at CMR.[30] It would be almost a decade later, in 1969, that this proposal was made good. And it was only after the adoption of the bilingualism and biculturalism policy across the forces that French-language flying and support units would be mandated in the early 1970s.

Returning to entry level officer education in 1952, the three colleges were not the only entry path for would-be officers. The same year that CMR opened, the Services introduced the Regular Officer Training Plan (ROTP), which allowed those selected to undertake either a four year program at one of the colleges; mirroring it were the University Reserve Training Plan, which allowed students to attend a civilian university with all costs covered by the Crown and the Subsidization of Serving Airmen

Plan.³¹ By 1960 there were some 1,500 cadets within the program: 780 at the three colleges, 600 in 17 university "squadrons," and finally 60 airmen students.³²

RCAF-bound cadets did not see much RCAF-oriented training except in the summers and the training regime varied over time. At one point all aircrew training to wings standard (the earning of flying qualifications) was completed before graduation but this practice changed in 1960, at which time all officers experienced the full range of air force officer employment fields so that, once commissioned, they would have a better sense of how their work fit into the larger air force.

Staff Education for the Cold War

While entry-level education operated in a tri-service system, the staff college was destined to maintain its air force focus. In early 1945, with the end of hostilities on the horizon, the Air Council decided that it would be appropriate to look at options for extending the war staff course to a more comprehensive six-month program of studies. Air Commodore Wait responded that this would be an ambitious but worthwhile undertaking. He did not feel that the overall thrust of the curriculum needed to be changed, but that additions should be made to the air power concepts and air force organizations phases of the course. His staff provided detail: if Canada was to educate its air force leaders, the curriculum needed to include the doctrine of air power as well as the roles, structures, and functions that would enable the RCAF to live up to it. Such changes, they stated, would produce well-polished senior officers who would "be able effectively and efficiently to perform staff duties at the level of [their] rank or one rank higher."³³ Wait added his personal thoughts to the staff's commentary, emphasizing a graduate's ability to deal with complexity:

> The course is designed to make an officer think straight and to get his thoughts down clearly on paper. The amount and depth of his thinking will depend entirely upon himself. There will be little use for anyone to come on the Course expecting to do only the bare minimum of work and to get by. The candidate must want to make the Service a career; want to take the Course; have a high level of ability to learn; and have a reasonable education (minimum Senior Matriculation). Given student officers of this calibre, the 6 months Course should be of great value to the R.C.A.F.³⁴

Expanding to a 10-month curriculum, the college continued throughout the 1950s to focus on the theme of professional development as a sort of multiplier in which competent graduates would not just increase their own professional competence but would then use these new skills and knowledge to help ensure the effectiveness of the RCAF. The program of study included active learning activities, all

Air Commodore Keith Hodson (left) Commandant, RCAF Staff College, with the Chief of the Air Staff, Air Marshal C.R. Slemon.

pitched at a graduate level and involving many inter-service learning events with the Canadian Army Staff College in Kingston.[35] The commandant's foreword to the 1958–9 calendar stated: "You are being given the opportunity to learn more about the Services and their relationships to each other, and as well to read, write, speak and think in such a manner as to improve your professional competence and hence your usefulness to the Air Force."[36] The curriculum continued to reinforce the themes of effective thinking and communications; general knowledge of the air force and of world affairs; an understanding of personnel matters and of leadership; and a firm grasp of those issues involved in generating, sustaining, and employing air forces in both multi-service and international scenarios.[37] The concluding entry in the calendar reminded students of the philosophy of the College, one which continued to emphasize Wait's initial acceptance of education as an equal and increasingly senior partner to staff training.

Students and staffs "hosted" guest speakers at the RCAF Staff College providing an opportunity for one-on-one conversation. The guest at this table is John Holmes, who served as Assistant Under-Secretary of State for External Affairs (1953–1960) and then as President Canadian Institute of International Affairs (1960–1973).

The RCAF Staff College makes no attempt to graduate experts in a particular field, nor does it expound any easy universally applicable doctrines. Rather by providing its graduates with an *education of the broadest scope* and by *developing habits of clear thinking*, it attempts to provide them with the breadth of interest, *openness of mind, reasoning ability, and a broad view of their Service and profession*, which will enable them to *master the specific tasks of any appointment and to make sound decisions in any situation*.[38]

There was substance behind the philosophy. One of the most tangible indicators was the *RCAF Staff College Journal* (later renamed the *Air Force College Journal*), which appeared annually between 1956 and 1964. Describing the complex world of the Cold War and the still difficult task of optimizing air power, the first editorial called on officers to examine general and specific problems of the use of air forces as well as the technical aspects of air power from as many perspectives as possible. The Staff College was one forum for competing arguments and the journal was seen as another.

R.C.A.F. STAFF COLLEGE JOURNAL

1959

CONTENTS

	PAGE
NATIONAL STRATEGY AND THE ARMED SERVICES — *Air Vice-Marshal E. J. Kingston-McCloughry, C.B., C.B.E., D.S.O., D.F.C., R.A.F. (Retired)*	9
SURPRISE AND BLITZKRIEG IN SOVIET EYES — *Dr. Raymond L. Garthoff*	16
LIMITED WAR STRATEGY IN THE NUCLEAR ERA — *Aquila*	25
LOGISTICS IN THE MISSILE AGE — *Maj. Gen. F. S. Besson, Jr.*	37
UNITED NATIONS ARMED FORCE "THE GREAT ILLUSION" — *Mr. Peter Stursberg*	44
NATIONAL POLICIES AND ARMED FORCE — *W/C John Gellner, D.F.C., C.D. (Retired)*	53
CIVIL DEFENCE ROUNDUP — *Maj. Gen. M. H. S. Penhale, C.B.E., C.D. (Retired)*	59
HUMAN NATURE AND WAR — *Dr. Marcus Long*	68
THE DISCUSSION AND FORMULATION OF NATIONAL SECURITY POLICY — *Prof. Richard A. Preston*	74
A CONCEPT FOR CANADA'S MILITARY ORGANIZATION — *Prize Winning Essay — F/L J. R. Rundle*	85
THE EFFECT OF ENVIRONMENTAL CONDITIONS IN SPACE ON MATERIALS FOR SPACE TRAVEL — *H. P. Tardif*	91
IS ALLOUT NUCLEAR WAR FEASIBLE? — *CDR B. C. Thillaye*	96
PERSPECTIVE ON WAR — *Capt. R. H. Murphy*	101
A COMPARISON OF NINETEENTH AND TWENTIETH CENTURY BALANCE OF POWER — *LCDR J. W. B. Buckingham*	106
BOOK REVIEWS	116

PRICE ONE DOLLAR

A yearly RCAF Staff College *Journal* was published containing not only material about the academic year, students, and staff, but also featuring articles on various political, military, and scientific topics.

The curriculum at the RCAF Staff College included presentations by distinguished speakers such as Field Marshal B.L. Montgomery shown here in 1953 with College Commandant Air Commodore J.L. Hurley.

…the [*Journal*'s] aim is to encourage professional writing on military matters, particularly those of an air nature, and in so doing to generate ideas and to allow these ideas to be assessed through the medium of objective discussion. In this manner a useful contribution can be made towards an understanding of the complex and dangerous forces which threaten national security and of the defence measures best calculated to support the attainment of an honourable, prosperous and secure existence.[39]

Contributors included members of the college, both staff and students, personnel from the RCAF and other Canadian military Services, and civilian defence commentators. The value and stature of the journal were enhanced by a number of internationally respected thinkers, and the list of contributors included such notables as Bernard Brodie, S.L.A. Marshall, Basil Liddell Hart, Melvin Conant, and James Eayrs.

As well as inviting debate and discourse, the college benefited from a number of well-qualified aviators who also knew how to think and to educate. From 1956 to 1958, Wing Commander John Gellner was a key player among the directing staff. A Czech lawyer before the war, in 1939 Gellner had fled to Canada and joined the RCAF; eventually becoming a pilot, he won two Distinguished Flying Crosses during combat operations. When the first edition of the journal was published, in 1956, it was Gellner whose article on leadership in modern war appeared immediately after the editorial. He would go on to publish material on a range of topics including air power and deterrence, officership, national security policies, and the armed forces and NATO, providing articles well after his retirement in 1958.[40] Gellner went on to write for a range of magazines, including *Canadian Aviation, Canadian Commentator, Maclean's Magazine* and *Saturday Night*. In the latter he was a regular contributor throughout the 1960s. In 1967, for example, he wrote on such diverse topics as Eastern Europe, Gaullism, lunar exploration, and Vietnam.[41] In 1971 he became the first editor of the resurrected *Canadian Defence Quarterly*, which had ceased publication during the war, and remained at the controls for 16 years. His intent, spelled out in editorials during the first year, was to recreate the "standard of excellence" established by the original *Quarterly* in the inter-war decades.[42] By the end of that first year he was able to praise the submissions from serving officers, but reminded readers that "there is much fresh ground to be broken in areas which do not swarm with academic theoreticians, those of tactics, organization, weaponry, logistics, or military leadership and training. This is particularly true in Canada, where so many aspects of national defence have never yet been expertly addressed."[43] Gellner's message repeated what the air force had been trying to do all along – engage officers in probing their profession; make them think and then articulate their thoughts for the betterment of the profession and the institution.

The RCAF College: An Expanded Education Envelope

Despite the quality of the education being offered at the Staff College, the effectiveness and efficiency of the professional development continuum within the air force was not as well honed. Various courses, run by various agencies across the air force, seemed to be operating with overlapping, or worse, underlapping curricula. In June 1958, the RCAF Staff College board of governors had recommended the establishment of an ad-hoc committee "to review professional education in the RCAF."[44] Mandated by the vice chief of the Air Staff (VCAS) on 29 September of that year, the committee set about to examine "the implications of coordinating the existing agencies of professional education in the RCAF." The committee's finding on "control" was that a "professional education process can be composed of a number of

Students at the RCAF Staff College had access to a well-stocked library and were encouraged to broaden their knowledge across a range of subjects.

courses, examinations, and other instructional agencies. But as all contribute to a single aim and exist to fulfil this aim, the coordination between all agencies is essential. The best coordination would be provided by having all agencies of education controlled by a commander with that responsibility alone."

Expressing this notion more forcefully in their conclusion they said: "The process of educating is [being] … done piecemeal and cannot be anything but inefficient, uneconomical, and inadequate." The recommended solution for this situation was the creation of an RCAF Air University that would ensure "unified control and continuous coordination" and hence the "most suitable and efficient means of RCAF professional education today and in the future."[45]

In June of the next year another senior-level conference was convened in Toronto to review, among other matters, the process of creating the Air Force College, which had meanwhile been approved by the Air Council.[46] The record of the Air Council decision reflected that while giving its blessing for the college, the Council had "not been definite" on command-and-control arrangements. There were two options for how things should run: the college could report directly to Air Force HQ; or it could become a subordinate component of Training Command. Minutes of the Toronto meeting suggest that the level of discussion degenerated from the difficult overarching question to a more mundane debate, with speakers worrying that young officers attending courses might find Toronto too distracting and that the cost of living was high for permanent staff. The VCAS closed the discussion saying that it had not been intended to come to any firm decision, but merely to explore the matter.[47] Clearly, however, there had been a desire to find a means of grouping professional education under one organization, thus improving effectiveness and efficiency. The fact that senior commanders and staff could not find an agreed approach was indicative of the complexity and uniqueness of the question.

By 1961, the Air Force College had been activated, and personnel were busy trying to define the optimum internal structure to provide a Staff College for mid-career professional development, a Staff School for junior officer professional development, planning and research activities and, eventually, an extension program – formally known as the Graduate Assistance Program or GAP (described below). A comprehensive internal study (cited and described in the next section) focused on planning and coordination issues, and the report reflected the nature of the challenge.

Syllabus Planning, Coordination, and Education Planning

> The activities of defining the basic professional syllabus, of developing study requirements for individual courses, and for planning changes to the education system are all intimately related to research and study of the professional field of knowledge. Yet these activities are all coordinating activities in the sense that they determine the relationship of one course to another within the education system, and that they show a need for change or the establishment of new courses. Thus it seems unwise to separate coordination or education system planning as distinct administrative functions which can be performed by administrative methods divorced from a knowledge of the syllabus and a close familiarity with the instructional methods available.[48]

In terms of who would do what, the study's authors proposed that the syllabus planning function be folded into the instructional organizations, making course development and delivery the task of the Staff College and Staff School. At the same time the Air Force College headquarters would be responsible for a variety of tasks including "developing RCAF educational concepts, policies, plans and programs; developing Air Force College operating policies; helping develop, and approving,

Tours were a large part of the RCAF Staff College curriculum. Here RCAF students are shown the intricacies of the NORAD underground complex at RCAF Station North Bay, ON.

program outlines; and carrying out advanced syllabus and doctrine research."[49] In short, the task of the teaching units was to execute the courses by building and delivering effective curricula. The headquarters, staffed by officers well versed in these content and delivery issues, would establish broad learning outcomes as well as the policies and processes needed for effective curriculum delivery. If it worked, the system would ensure that students got the right curriculum at the right time taught by the right people and in the right way. It was to be a coherent education continuum designed to meet the needs of air force professionals and the RCAF.[50] By 1962, AVM H.M. Carcallen, the commander of RCAF Training Command, could confidently report that the Air Force College was indeed running effectively, and by then perhaps that was actually the case.[51]

Two years earlier, the confusion over the nature of the extension program was indicative of the sorts of problems that the Air Force College had been established to correct. From the outset it was not clear to those working within the college just what the course was to include or for whom it was intended. The college's director of plans and requirements prepared a report at the end of 1960 that talked about a "staff school correspondence course," the aim of which was to "prepare junior officers during their first tour of duty for higher appointment. The syllabus is to be designed to help junior officers to think logically and to express themselves clearly, to know RCAF organization, administrative procedures and management practices, and to understand the Service's basic operational doctrine."[52] It was understood by the staff that this course had initially been seen as a distributed version of the actual staff school program, but that the requirement was now "reduced."[53] Reduced perhaps, but from what or to what were not defined. Strangely, considering that each course was intended to complement the others in the continuum, the director of plans and requirements seemed to be intent on creating nothing more than a distance version of the Staff School program.[54]

A more logical extension concept appeared in late May 1962 when the Air-Officer-Commanding Training Command issued a directive creating a Graduate Assistance Program (GAP) intended to provide a "professional education link" between staff school and staff college curricula. According to the directive, the aims of the program were to contribute to life-long learning and to the effectiveness of the officer corps and the air force. Specific aims were "to direct private study in subjects that contribute to professional development; to make officers' private study as productive as possible; to promote the habit of private study of professional literature; [and] to provide an additional measurement of achievement as an aid to selection for career progression."[55]

Initially voluntary, until a multi-year phase-in was completed, GAP was to comprise four courses, two common and two of four electives. The common courses would fall under the rubric of "military studies" including "military theory; writing, logic, and problem solving; the effects of science and technology on military forces; and world conflict and strategies." The electives would be chosen from "the Individual in Society" – a psychology and sociology primer; "Modern Political Systems" – political philosophies and their associated forms of government; "Canada" – Canadian history and national resources; and "Management – the principles relevant to marshalling resources for the accomplishment of a task."[56] These electives were to be developed by the University of Toronto but be administered by the Air Force College. Despite the source of these courses and the fees charged by the university, no credit was offered or apparently sought.[57]

Amazingly, the staff at the Air Force College were able to react to the Training Command directive almost literally overnight, if one is to believe the 1 June 1962 date on the cover of the first GAP handbook. More reasonably, the directive was likely promulgated as a finishing touch to a program that had been in development for several months, possibly in lieu of attempts by the director of plans and requirements. The handbook's foreword indicated the newness of the program which was to be administered by the Air Force College's Extension School. The message conveyed the same education philosophy seen many times before: "The program's subject matter is *designed not for rote memorization but to stimulate and enlighten*, and thus *provide each officer with new insights and understanding to improve his immediate performance and prepare him for the future*."[58] The handbook also succinctly laid out the philosophy, curriculum themes, and component courses of the revised air force professional development scheme. Any officer reading through its dozen pages could not fail to grasp the RCAF's educational concept – liberal education, scientia, remained at the core of the learning philosophy.

The End of Single Service Education

In 1963, however, initiatives like the GAP were somewhat moot and certainly of minor importance in relation to a more general turmoil in defence policy. The clouds of integration and eventual unification of the three services were contributing to widespread confusion. For instance, there were three unique and not easily integrated philosophies of officer development. In 1965, a working group delegated to develop a program for "Integrated Staff Training" concluded that "All in all, it is apparent that the professional education of the three services, taken in aggregate, shows no discernible similarities…. It is apparent that … a great distance must be travelled before a fully integrated program can be achieved."[59]

For the RCN, the "training" of naval officers dealt uniquely with junior officer training. An article, written by the Staff Officer Training Publications from the Directorate of Naval Training, concentrated on the complexities of life at sea for a new member of the naval service and described how one became, through a multi-year process, a competent junior naval officer, progressing from general sea-going abilities to specific advanced duties such as navigation or anti-submarine warfare.[60] What the article did not say was that the navy still did not have its own staff college and continued to send students to the Royal Naval College at Greenwich.

The army conducted its own year-long program for officers approaching the mid-career point at Canadian Army Staff College. The curriculum focused on field operations. Students graduated with a "thorough understanding of the principles and techniques" of land operations, including "specialized staff skills, a knowledge of military management, and the functions of the staff." The latter included an introduction to logical and critical thinking as well as communications skills. Graduates would also be given an exposure to issues impacting on military operations – national security studies in their broadest sense. At the heart of the course, however, was the opportunity for the practice of staff skills in the solving of "typical command and staff problems encountered in war and situations short of war throughout the world, with emphasis on the divisional level and below."[61] While the Army course was seen as the peer to the RCAF Staff College, it was the latter which would be deemed the better model for a post-Unification vehicle for mid-career education. While on the face of it this could be considered a good outcome for the future of air force professional education, one commentator sees it otherwise. "In retrospect, the conversion of the RCAF Staff College to a tri-service institution marked the demise of Air Force professional military education until the twenty-first century. Air Force education became a victim of its own success."[62]

It was not until 1967 that the senior leaders of the now integrated Canadian Forces were able to turn to the question of a common officer development and education system. In that year an Officer Development Board was established under Major General Roger Rowley.[63] Rowley's team used the next 18 months first to develop a definition of "an officer" and then to plot out the professional development and education requirements for the officer corps. From these requirements a suite of harmonized courses for officers, from captain to general, was defined, with some of the courses largely unchanged from those offered by the Air Force College. Moreover the whole notion of one central organization, a Canadian Defence Education Centre, charged with the policy, plans, and operations of officer development was a pivotal element of the board's proposal. The Centre, with its undergraduate and professional colleges, was not established; however, many of the board's recommendations have seen at least partial implementation over the past 30 years. In this way the shadow of the Air Force College has in some way been perpetuated.

NOTES

1 See W.A.B. Douglas, *The Creation of a National Air Force* (Toronto: University of Toronto Press, 1986), 48–59. By comparison, the Army has a permanent establishment of approximately 3,500 and the RCN just over 400, enough to operate two destroyers.
2 Richard Preston, *Canada's RMC: A History of the Royal Military College* (Toronto: University of Toronto Press, 1970), 251–3.
3 "RCAF SC Service Experiences Report S/L C.M. McEwen, RCAF, Andover, September 1930," UK National Archives (hereafter TNA), Air 1 2391-228-11-151. "Service Experiences Report S/L G.L. Wait, RCAF, Andover, March 1931, TNA, Air 1 2392-228-11-175."

4   "Report of the Commandant," Royal Military College of Canada, 1931–1932," n.d., file 171.013 (D4), "RMC Commandants reports 1917/47," Directorate of History and Heritage, National Defence Headquarters, Ottawa (DHH).
5   Preston, *Canada's RMC,* 281–2.
6   See Douglas, *The Creation of a National Air Force,* 48–59.
7   Untitled memorandum, Senior Air Officer to MND, September 6, 1936, file DHH 76/32, "Royal Canadian Air Force Three Year Expansion Plan." The memo indicates a 120 per cent increase in officer positions and the need to strip non-operational billets to contribute to the expansion.
8   "The Organization and Syllabus of Military Instruction at the Royal Military College," April 1937, file DHH 113.1009 (D5), "Recommendations Regarding the Re-introduction of Special and Optional Courses in the Final Year at the Royal Military College," DHH.
9   "The Organization and Syllabus of Military Instruction at the Royal Military College," April 1937,10.
10   Douglas, *A National Air Force,* 63.
11   Douglas, *A National Air Force,* 36. The term "military" may seem curious when the topic is air power, but the RCAF of the period was largely a paramilitary service and thus a program like that at Andover offered, broadly speaking, exposure to a military way of thinking and operating.
12   Douglas, *A National Air Force,* 120.
13   Douglas, *A National Air Force,* 145.
14   William Shields and Dace Sefers, *Canadian Forces Command and Staff College: A History 1797–1946* (Toronto: Canadian Forces College, 1987), 4-2-4-3.
15   Shields and Sefers, *Canadian Forces Command and Staff College,* 4–15.
16   Shields and Sefers, *Canadian Forces Command and Staff College,* 4–16.
17   Preston, *Canada's RMC,* 322–4.
18   "Minutes of Air Council," May 23, 1946, "Minutes of Air Council 1946," file 180.009 (D62), DHH.
19   Preston, *Canada's RMC,* 320.
20   Preston, *Canada's RMC,* 325–6.
21   Preston, *Canada's RMC,* 328–9.
22   "Royal Military College of Canada Canadian Services Colleges Annual Report of the Commandant Consolidated for the Years 1948–1953." Copy held at Massey Library, RMC Kingston.
23   "Education for Responsibility," *The Roundel,* (May 1958): 9.
24   LAC RG 24 17756 "Progress Reports, Canadian Services College Royal Roads."
25   DHH 171.009 (D196) "La Revue du Collège Militaire Royal de Saint-Jean, 1952–53."
26   D.E. Hamilton, "The Canadian Services Colleges, Part One: College [sic] Militaire Royal de Saint-Jean," *The Roundel,* (April 1955), 33–6.
27   Jean Pariseau and Serge Bernier, *French Canadians and Bilingualism in the Canadian Armed Forces Volume 1* (Ottawa: Directorate of History, Department of National Defence, 1988) 133–6.
28   Jean Pariseau and Serge Bernier, *French Canadians and Bilingualism in the Canadian Armed Forces,* 164.
29   Jean Pariseau and Serge Bernier, *French Canadians and Bilingualism in the Canadian Armed Forces,* 165.
30   Jean Pariseau and Serge Bernier, *French Canadians and Bilingualism in the Canadian Armed Forces,* 170.
31   "Education for Responsibility," *The Roundel,* (May 1958): 6–9. See also A/V/M H.M. Carcallen, "The Evolution and Current Status of Training Command," *The Roundel,* July–August 1962, 9–10.

32 "Working Their Way Through College," *The Roundel*, (June 1960): 9.
33 Shields and Sefers, *Canadian Forces Command and Staff College*, 4–16.
34 Shields and Sefers, *Canadian Forces Command and Staff College*, 4–28. Emphasis added.
35 For more detail see Howard Coombs, "Interests Aligned but Not Integrated: The Royal Canadian Air Force Staff College and Inter-Service Staff Education After the Second World War," in *Educating Air Forces*, Randall Wakelam et al., (Lexington Ky: University Press of Kentucky, 2020).
36 Canada, Department of National Defence. *R.C.A.F. Staff College Calendar Course 23: 1958–59*, "Introduction."
37 *R.C.A.F. Staff College Calendar Course 23*, "Staff Training Studies."
38 *R.C.A.F. Staff College Calendar Course 23*, "Conclusion." Emphasis added.
39 Air Commodore K.L. Hodson, "Editorial," *RCAF Staff College Journal No 1*, (RCAF Staff College: Toronto, 1956), 8.
40 "Contents," *Air Force College Journal – 1964* (Air Force College: Toronto, 1964) 100–1.
41 M.A. Wodehouse and M.C. Wilson, eds., *Canadian Periodical Index, Authors and Subjects 1967, Volume 20* (Ottawa: National Library of Canada, 1968), 203.
42 John Gellner, "Editorial" *Canadian Defence Quarterly*, 1, 1 (Summer 1971): 5.
43 John Gellner, "Editorial" *Canadian Defence Quarterly*, 1, 4 (Spring 1972): 4.
44 Canada, Department of National Defence, Various working papers of the Officer Development Board (ODB Papers). "C470-1 (CTrain), A Report on RCAF Professional Education prepared for the Vice-Chief of the Air Staff by an Ad Hoc Committee November 1958," 1. These papers were donated to DHH by LCol (retd) Laurence Motiuk who was a member of the ODB. Directorate of History and Heritage (DHH).
45 "C470-1 (CTrain), A Report on RCAF Professional Education prepared for the Vice-Chief of the Air Staff by an Ad Hoc Committee November 1958," 1,6,11, 15. DHH, ODB Papers.
46 "C9-03 (RTH) Minutes of a Conference held at RCAF Staff College at 0900 hours 12 Jun 59 to Review the Function of the Staff College," 3. DHH, ODB Papers.
47 "C9-03 (RTH) Minutes of a Conference held at RCAF Staff College at 0900 hours 12 Jun 59 to Review the Function of the Staff College," 3–4. DHH, ODB Papers.
48 "2-01(RJG) A Report on Air Force College Organization Prepared for the Commandant by a Working Group," March 20, 1961, 4. DHH, ODB Papers.
49 "2-01(RJG) A Report on Air Force College Organization Prepared for the Commandant by a Working Group," March 20, 1961, 12. DHH, ODB Papers.
50 Wing Commander G.K. Murray, "Professional Education in the RCAF," *The Roundel*, (April 1963): 8–12.
51 A/V/M H.M. Carcallen, "The Evolution and Current Status of Training Command," *The Roundel*, (July–August 1962): 10–11.
52 From the personal papers of Dr. Stephen Harris. Currently the senior historian at the DHH, Dr. Harris was a member of the Extension staff in Toronto in the early 1970s. The document in question is a memo from the Director of the Plans and Requirements to the Acting Commandant, "9-02-02 (Dir P&R) Air Force College – Correspondence Course," December 9, 1960, 1.
53 Harris Papers. "9-02-02 (Dir P&R) Air Force College – Correspondence Course," December 9, 1960.
54 Harris Papers. "9-02-02 (Dir P&R) Air Force College – Correspondence Course," December 9, 1960, 3–5.
55 Harris Papers, "TCHQ 470-14 (SGTSO) Professional Education – Officers Graduate Assistance Program," A.-O.-C. Training Command to Commandant Air Force College, May 29, 1962, 1.

56 Harris Papers, "TCHQ 470-14 (SGTSO) Professional Education – Officers Graduate Assistance Program," A.-O.-C. Training Command to Commandant Air Force College, May 29, 1962, 3.
57 Harris Papers, Chief of the Air Staff to University of Toronto Department of Extension, file number illegible, no subject, April 12, 1962.
58 RCAF Extension School, *Graduate Assistance Program* (Toronto: Air Force College, June 1, 1962), Foreword. Emphasis added.
59 Canada, Department of National Defence, *A Program for Professional Military Education for the Canadian Defence Force, A Report by the Working Group* (Ottawa, March 19, 1965), 8–9.
60 Lt H.R. Percy, "Training the Navy's Officers," *Canadian Army Journal* 17/3 (1963), 57–69.
61 Brigadier General W.A. Milroy, DSO, CD, "The Course," *Snowy Owl*, 4/2 1967–8, 2–3. *Snowy Owl* was the journal of the Canadian Army Staff College.
62 Coombs, "Interests Aligned but Not Integrated," 144.
63 Canada, Department of National Defence, *Report of the Officer Development Board* (Ottawa: DND, 1969). The Report was issued in three volumes, which looked in depth at the full gamut of the military profession and the requirements for officer education across all ranks.

CHAPTER SEVEN

TRAINING THE FLYERS: THE LEGACY OF CANADA'S INTERNATIONAL AIR TRAINING SCHEMES AND THE NATO AIR TRAINING PLAN

RACHEL LEA HEIDE

Introduction

Generations of Canadian children have grown up with their gaze fixed on the sky, watching as aircraft flew overhead with passengers learning to be military aircrew. These trainees were not only young Canadian men learning to defy gravity; thousands of recruits came from Allied and Commonwealth nations to participate in the air training programs Canada has hosted during the international crises of the first half of the twentieth century. Most widely known is the training program of the Second World War: the British Commonwealth Air Training Plan (BCATP). Nonetheless, this was not the first – nor the last – international training scheme run on Canadian soil. The precursor to the BCATP was the RFC Canada air training program, where flying schools built in Canada trained airmen for the Royal Flying Corps (RFC) and the Royal Air Force (RAF) during the First World War. Even less commonly known is Canada's Cold War air training activity: the North Atlantic Treaty Organization (NATO) Air Training Plan, which taught aircrew from ten other nations in the 1950s.

Although fundamental characteristics about each training plan were decidedly different – the numbers of aircrew trained, the technology used, the length of courses, and the nationality of foreign students – a common thread ran through the three training plans spanning four decades. Canada's military stepped up in the time of need, participated in these internationally attended flying training plans, and created a positive reputation for the nation among her allies.

Student pilots bearing flags from their respective NATO countries before an advanced jet training course, RCAF Station Portage la Prairie, 19 August 1960.

First World War Training: Royal Flying Corps and Royal Air Force Canada

Until mid-1916, the Canadian government saw no need for a significant Canadian aerial contribution to Imperial flying services in the First World War. Early in the war, Canadians interested in joining the Royal Flying Corps (RFC) or the Royal Naval Air Service (RNAS) had to fund their own training at one of a small number of private flying schools in Canada or the United States. When the Curtiss school in Toronto could not continue to train over the winter of 1915, Sam Hughes, the minister of militia, offered no support or encouragement to the 100 RFC and 150 RNAS candidates waiting to commence training. Instead of financing the recruits' passage overseas to train in England, Hughes suggested that the men "forget all about this aeroplane business and join the army." Being more sympathetic, the British War Office and Admiralty arranged for all these candidates to come to Britain.[1]

The British government, from the beginning of the war, tried to secure the Canadian government's cooperation in running an air training program, but Canada's government officials were not immediately willing to take on the responsibility of providing training for the nascent aeroplane technology and its usage in war. The first proposal for a training wing in Canada (made up of 6 officers, 150 non-commissioned officers, and 15 aircraft, costing £50,000) came from a Lieutenant-Colonel C.J. Burke while he was in Canada recruiting for the RFC in November 1915. When Sir George Perley, the Canadian high commissioner in London, informed his own government in May 1916 that Britain "would welcome a Canadian government flying school," Loring Christie, legal advisor for the department of external affairs, concluded that "the needs of the war are not such as to demand the immediate organization of a distinct Canadian flying service." Later in 1916, the British government's subsequent proposals for flying training schools on Canadian soil continued to hold little appeal to Canadian politicians when the British government offered only to cover a per capita grant of £250 per graduate, while the Canadian government would become responsible for both the $500,000 training plan establishment costs and annual operational costs of $500,000. Canadian officials wanted the financing burden to be Great Britain's responsibility.[2]

As casualties among flyers were extremely high in 1916, the British government found it necessary to authorize an expansion of the RFC in order to meet frontline needs. This meant that more pilots had to be trained, but there was no room for new training sites in Great Britain. Canada seemed the best alternative. It was relatively close to Great Britain (compared to the other parts of the Empire); North American production could supply the materials needed to build and run the schools; and more manpower was available in Canada than in Great Britain to get the schools underway. Furthermore, British officials believed that there was "a large reservoir of pilot material in Canada."[3]

Under pressure from the British Air Board and Canadian aviation enthusiasts, Hughes finally relented in September 1916, advising the British that a Canadian air training plan could be worked out. Imperial authorities would oversee the schools because Canada lacked experience in running a project of this type and magnitude, while on a repayment basis, the Canadian government would supply food, clothing, gasoline, oil, and medical services. Canada would also provide $1 million for an aircraft plant to fill British orders. Although managed by Britain's Imperial Munitions Board[4] during the war, the factory would belong to Canada. After months of resistance, on 21 December 1916, the Canadian government finally agreed to train thousands of men for the air war.[5]

The next challenge was turning a paper agreement into an actual air training program and building a home for the 20 training squadrons to be stationed in Canada. With Toronto chosen as RFC Canada's headquarters, the stations were selected in the general vicinity: Camp Borden, Deseronto (with its two airfields being Rathburn and Mohawk), and North Toronto (with fields at Leaside and Armour Heights). The first cadets arrived at Camp Borden on 19 March 1917, of whom 18 graduated three months later. A restructuring took place over the summer with the stations taking on wing status, each wing providing both elementary and advanced training.[6]

The trainer used by RFC Canada was the Curtiss JN4 Canuck, a two-seater biplane. The 2,100-pound (950 kg) aircraft had a maximum speed of 75 mph (120 kph), and an American-built Curtiss OX-5 90 horsepower engine. In winter, because the maximum depth of snow that the JN4's undercarriage could handle in training was six inches, a toboggan-like ski was used in place of the wheels. During the cold winter months, the gasoline, oil, and water had to be drained each night. In the morning, mechanics would heat the oil and water before returning the fluids to the aeroplane.[7]

Despite this protocol to keep the aircraft engines from freezing in the winter, the harsh Canadian elements led RFC Canada officials to arrange to continue most of the 1917–18 winter training in the warmer climate afforded by Fort Worth, Texas. In return for the use of American facilities, RFC Canada would train American airmen. The Canadian training school in Texas was named Camp Taliaferro, and it was comprised of three airfields, providing homes for the Borden and Deseronto Wings. The North Toronto Wing, the Cadet Wing, and the School of Aeronautics remained in Canada throughout the winter. Upon RFC Canada's return to Ontario in April 1918, 67,000 flying hours had been flown in Texas, 1,960 pilots had been trained, and 69 ground officers and 4,150 others received training in ground trades and skills.[8]

In April 1918 the RFC and RNAS had amalgamated and formed the Royal Air Force (RAF). Consequently, the name RFC Canada changed to RAF Canada. The curriculum responsibilities of schools also changed numerous times (table 7.1 lists the RAF Canada schools' responsibilities as of November 1918). The final training pattern for recruits in 1918 began with new trainees spending two weeks at the Recruits' Depot, where they received lectures on hygiene, discipline, and the air force. They also received their first lessons on wireless equipment and infantry training. Subsequently, the trainees completed eight weeks of training at the Cadet Wing, where they studied signalling, navigation, and map reading. More ground training was provided at the School of Military Aeronautics, where lessons focused on artillery cooperation, bombing, and photography. Trainees then spent four to

Table 7.1. RAF Canada schools (November 1918)

Headquarters: Toronto
Aeroplane Repair Park
Engine Repair Park
Mechanical Transport Section
Stores Depot
Recruits' Depot: Toronto
Cadet Wing: Long Branch
#4 School of Military Aeronautics: Toronto
Armament School: Hamilton
#42 Wing: Deseronto (Rathburn & Mohawk)
#43 Wing: North Toronto (Leaside & Armour Heights)
#44 Wing: Camp Borden
School of Aerial Fighting: Beamsville
School of Special Flying: Armour Heights

Sources: S.F. Wise, "The Official History of the Royal Canadian Air Force," vol. 1, 29–33; R.V. Dodds, "Canada's First Air Training Plan," *The Roundel* (four parts spanning November 1962 to March 1963).

five weeks at the Armament School learning about the Vickers and Lewis machine guns, as well as bomb loading, aiming, and release.[9]

Finally, recruits arrived at the Borden or Deseronto Wing to commence flying training. Elementary flying was taught by a Lower Training Squadron, where students were given two to three hours of dual instruction before soloing, five to six hours solo time, and 30 to 40 practice landings. After this, the trainee would move onto a Higher Training Squadron to learn about photography, air-to-ground signalling, cross-country flying, and formation flying. At Leaside's School of Artillery Cooperation, students used large maps with light bulbs to practice locating shell bursts. Trainees were also taken on flying exercises where shell bursts (actually smoke puffs) had to be located and communicated to ground receiving stations. Students completed their training at the School of Aerial Fighting, located at Beamsville, near Lake Ontario; here, students trained with moving targets: drogues towed by aircraft and silhouettes floating on the lake. Observers underwent similar training, except they did not receive flying instruction.[10]

By the end of the First World War, RFC Canada had 11,928 trainees and staff on strength (993 officers, 6,158 NCOs, 4,333 cadet pilots, 444 cadet observers). While consistent breakdown numbers are hard to come by, it has been estimated that Canada's training program produced approximately 10,500 graduates, which included pilots, mechanics, and aircraftmen; thousands more were still in training when the war ended. Fortunately, the training plan, which cost $40,000,000, suffered only 130 training fatalities. Ultimately, Canadians and the RFC-RAF Canada program made a significant contribution to the air war. A quarter of RAF officers serving at the end of the war were identified as Canadians. Over the course of the Great War, more than 22,000 Canadians served with the RNAS, RFC, and RAF in air and ground trades; at least two-thirds of those had joined through the Canadian air training plan.[11] Undertaking this international training scheme not only provided Canada with air training experience and facilities, but it also gave Canada a reputation (and experience) for training allies that would not be forgotten with the coming of the Second World War.

Second World War Training: The British Commonwealth Air Training Plan

When the winds of war began to blow with serious strength in the mid-1930s, Great Britain knew it needed to commence building its air power strength. But there was simply not enough land and air space to build the required number of training and operational aerodromes necessary for protecting the nation from a German attack. In an effort to avoid congestion, protect recruits from enemy attack, and create a psychological weapon against the Germans – meaning an air power source that could not be easily attacked because of the distances involved – the British government looked to its dominions for help.[12] Because Canada had hosted an air training scheme during the First World War, and because the Canadian government and the RCAF had agreed to a 1935 proposal to train 15 Canadians annually for service with the RAF,[13] the British government hoped that Canada would be willing to expand these precedents.

Prime Minister King was reluctant to accept the British Air Ministry's training plan proposals during peacetime for three key reasons: asserting Canadian autonomy from British imperialism, avoiding automatic commitments to future wars, and dividing French-English Canada over conscription fears. Hence, he did not accept British proposals in 1936,[14] 1937,[15] or 1938.[16] While refusing to fund British training schools on Canadian soil, and despite resisting pressure to provide Canadian recruits for the RAF, King's government did invite British pilots to attend Canadian air training schools, which were both owned and operated by the RCAF. This offer was meant to forestall any British plan to train only Canadians for RAF expansion.[17] King's intransigence shaped the agreement that was ultimately reached in April 1939: for a trial period of three years, Canadian schools would provide intermediate and advanced training to 126 pilots annually. Fifty of these pilots would be Britons, their costs being fully covered by the British government; the remaining seventy-six recruits would be Canadians' training for the RCAF. The first seventeen British pilots of the new accord were scheduled to arrive in the last week of September 1939.[18]

The outbreak of war at the beginning of that month removed King's reservations and also resulted in the British government's wanting an even larger air training commitment than what was then in effect. Following the suggestion on 16 September by Vincent Massey, high commissioner of Canada in London, and Stanley Bruce, high commissioner of Australia in London, that the dominions could "make a decisive contribution to the common war effort by training Commonwealth [Canadian, Australian, New Zealand] airmen" in Canada,[19] British Prime Minister Neville Chamberlain officially requested that Canada annually provide intermediate and advanced training for 20,000 pilots and 30,000 other aircrew. Because Britain could provide less than half of these numbers, most of the pilots would come from the Dominions.[20]

Although the British government planned to set up part of the training infrastructure in Great Britain, planners anticipated needing a training organization that was more than double the UK's capacity. Establishing training schools in the various Dominions meant they were beyond the reach of enemy interference, but Canada provided special advantages: proximity to the United Kingdom, capacity to manufacture aircraft, and access to aircraft parts available on American markets. Chamberlain hoped "the knowledge that a vast air potential was being built up in the Dominions where no German air activity could interfere with expansion might well have a psychological effect on the Germans equal to that produced by the intervention of the United States in the last war with its vast resources."[21]

With the world at war, King no longer portrayed Commonwealth air training as dangerous to Canadian independence. Instead, he embraced the proposal as a means of limiting and controlling Canada's war involvement. When the Emergency Council of Cabinet met on 27 September 1939, it came to a consensus that the training plan's importance would diminish the need to send large numbers of ground forces overseas. King consequently accepted the plan in principle on 28 September 1939.[22] Once the details were finally worked out, representatives of Great Britain, Canada, Australia, and New Zealand signed the BCATP Agreement on 17 December 1939. The plan established the percentage of trainees each country would send, the percentage of the cost each would share, the training schedule, and the aerodrome opening schedule, among other details.[23] King's tenacious negotiations resulted in an air training plan that embodied Canada's initial military position: willingness to provide manpower contributions, but not at the expense of national sovereignty or national unity.

After an intense winter of surveying sites, drawing up plans, and constructing aerodromes (see table 7.2),[24] the BCATP started training the first recruits in the spring of 1940. At Initial Training Schools (ITS), recruits were introduced to the

Table 7.2. BCATP schools under RCAF control, 1940-1945

7 Initial Training Schools (ITS)
30 Elementary Flying Training Schools (EFTS)
29 Service Flying Training Schools (SFTS)
3 Flying Instructors Schools (FIS)
10 Air Observer Schools (AOS)
11 Bombing and Gunnery Schools (BGS)
5 Wireless Training Schools (WTS)
4 Air Navigation Schools (ANS)
1 Naval Air Gunner School (NAGS)
2 General Reconnaissance Schools (GRS)
1 Instrument Flying School (IFS)
1 Flight Engineers School (FES)
7 Operational Training Units (OTU)

Source: W.A.B. Douglas, *The Official History of the Royal Canadian Air Force*, Vol 2, maps in between pages 236–7.

theory of flight, navigation, armaments, meteorology, and aircraft recognition. Other introductions included the Link Trainer – a flight simulator – and physical training. Recruits selected for pilot training would then attend an Elementary Flying Training School (EFTS) for eight weeks. Here, half days were spent on ground school where students encountered aircraft engines, morse code, and more practice on the Link trainer. The other half of students' days was taken up with flying instruction. A student had to solo before he reached 12 hours of dual instruction; otherwise, he would be "ceased training." A total of 50–60 hours of flying time was logged at the EFTS where pilots, early in the plan, were taught on DeHavilland Tiger Moths and Fleet Finches; later, the Fairchild Cornell became the standard EFTS trainer.[25]

Successful trainees then progressed to a Service Flying Training School (SFTS) for advanced instruction. Ground school taught such subjects as navigation, aircraft engines, and fuel systems. The type of aircraft that a pilot trainee flew depended on whether he was at a single-engine or twin-engine SFTS. Potential fighter pilots were trained on the single-engine North American Harvard. Pilots selected for bomber, coastal, or transport operations learned on twin-engine Avro Ansons, and later Cessna Cranes. Because syllabus revisions were made throughout the war, the course lengths varied from 10 to 16 weeks, and flying time from 75 to 100 hours.[26]

Other aircrew trainees attended Bombing and Gunnery Schools (BGS) where instruction covered bombing, navigation, wireless telegraphy, and gunnery. Aircraft used included the Fairey Battle, Avro Anson, Bristol Bolingbroke (a Canadian-built version of the Bristol Blenheim), and the Westland Lysander.[27]

The Air Observer was one type of recruit who attended BGSs. Observers first received five weeks of theoretical training at an ITS before attending a 12-week course at an Air Observer School (AOS). Instruction here included aerial photography, reconnaissance, and air navigation, as well as 60–70 hours of practical experience in the air (often in Anson aircraft). Observers would then spend ten weeks at a BGS, and an additional four weeks at an Air Navigation School (ANS) where the recruit learned dead-reckoning, astro-navigation, and flight plan preparation. After October 1942, the Observer category ceased to exist, the duties having been divided between Navigators and Air Bombers (also known as Bomb Aimers).[28]

Students selected for bombing employment needed to spend eight weeks at a BGS and 12 weeks at an AOS before qualifying as Navigators or Bomb Aimers. Navigators specializing as wireless operators received 28 weeks' training at a Wireless Training School (WTS), where subjects covered included radio transmitting and morse code. This was followed by a 22-week course at an AOS, thus qualifying these men in the dual role of Navigator and Wireless Operator. Bomb Aimers required five weeks' ITS, eight to 12 weeks' BGS, and six weeks' AOS training. Meanwhile, those selected for Wireless Operator-Air Gunner employment attended 28 weeks of WTS to become proficient in radio work and wireless communications before undergoing six weeks of gunnery training at a BGS. Straight Air Gunners spent 12 weeks at a BGS: six weeks in ground school and six weeks performing air exercises. Later in the war, a flight engineer was added to the crews of heavy bombers. In addition to being an aero-engine technician, he was also trained to replace the pilot at the controls if need be.[29]

The successful set up and operation of the BCATP was a feat in itself. In less than six years, 131,553 airmen from 11 different countries were trained, from Canada, Great Britain, Australia, New Zealand, the United States, Poland, Norway, Belgium, Holland, Czechoslovakia, and France (see table 7.3). Integral to the implementation of this international air training scheme was the modification of existing airfields and the construction of over 100 new aerodromes and emergency landing fields. When the BCATP came to an end on 31 March 1945, $2,331,129,039.06 had been spent, $1.6 billion of which was Canada's responsibility.[30] Prime Minister King had been loath to contribute money to Britain's defence when the British government first proposed an air training scheme in the 1930s, but the advent of war brought a reversal to the government policy. Not only did the BCATP become an attractive and effective means of contributing to the air war, but it also helped create an international reputation for the RCAF, a reputation that would soon be remembered as Cold War tensions escalated.

Table 7.3. Nationality of BCATP graduates, 1940–1945

Royal Canadian Air Force (RCAF):	72,835	
Royal Australian Air Force (RAAF):	9,606	
Royal New Zealand Air Force (RNZAF):	7,002	
Royal Air Force (RAF): included	42,110	448 Poles 677 Norwegians 800 Belgian/Dutch 900 Czechs 2,600 Free French
Royal Navy Fleet Air Arm also trained at BCATP schools:		5,296

Categories of 131,553 Air Crew Graduates
(October 1940–March 1945)

	Pilot	Nav B	Nav W	Nav	AB	WO/AG	AG	Naval AG	FE
RCAF	25,747	5,154	421	7,280	6,659	12,744	12,917	0	1,913
RAF	17,796	3,113	3,847	6,922	7,581	755	1,392	704	0
RAAF	4,045	699	0	944	799	2,875	244	0	0
RNZAF	2,220	829	30	724	634	2,122	443	0	0
Total	49,808	9,795	4,298	15,870	15,673	18,496	14,996	704	1,913

Legend:
Nav B: Navigator Bomber   WO/AG: Wireless Operator/Air Gunner
Nav W: Navigator Wireless   AG: Air Gunner
Nav: Navigator   Naval AG: Naval Air Gunner
AB: Air Bomber   FE: Flight Engineer

Source: F.J. Hatch, *Aerodrome of Democracy*, p. 206.

Cold War Training: NATO Air Training Plan

Just as the BCATP had grown out of the RFC Canada venture, so too was the NATO Air Training Plan a natural extension of the wartime air training plan since much of the instructing experience, teaching pedagogy, aircraft, and infrastructure were transferable. Little has been published on the NATO plan, but this Cold War air training scheme was equally as important as the previous two: it contributed to international defence needs, demonstrated Canada's desire to make a meaningful contribution on the international stage, and highlighted to Canada's allies the RCAF's expertise in air training.

The desire of NATO signatories to establish aircrew training in Canada – far away from the expected battlefront – existed even before the Soviet Union exploded its first atomic bomb on 22 September 1949. While the CAS, A/M W.A. Curtis, visited France, Sweden, Norway, and the United Kingdom in April and May

Lineup of Canadair T-33 Silver Star jet trainers at No. 3 Advanced Flying School, RCAF Station Gimli, MB.

of 1949, he was approached about training British aircrew in Canadian schools: "The Air Ministry is most anxious for assurance from us that some arrangement can be made for training RAF aircrew in Canada."[31] Understanding how it would be impossible to carry out aircrew training in the United Kingdom in the event of hostilities, Canadian military officials took the RAF's request under serious consideration. As early as June 1949, the CoSC identified the most likely region in which to set up air training schools: the prairie sections of Canada, away from operational zones such as the Atlantic and Pacific coasts and central Ontario.[32]

In addition to responding favourably to the CAS's training proposal, the government's Cabinet Defence Committee agreed that providing aircrew training for NATO signatories could be a practical and affordable means of helping Western Europe and NATO defences. Indeed, because the value to NATO would be greater than the actual cost to Canadians, in November 1949, the committee authorized the minister of defence, Brooke Claxton, to informally explore the issue at the upcoming North Atlantic Defence Committee meeting scheduled for December 1949. Upon his return, Claxton reported enthusiastically that France, Belgium, the Netherlands, and the United Kingdom were interested in the proposal: "Everything I heard and saw pointed to this being an important provision which we could make without great expense and without additional commitment."[33]

On 17 March 1950, the minister announced to the House of Commons that he had officially offered to train 100 aircrew (50 pilots and 50 navigators) from NATO nations. The country of origin would be responsible for the trainees' pay, allowances, clothing, and transportation to Canada. The Canadian government would provide training tuition, food, accommodation, transportation in Canada, and medical services. This offer was extended to the United Kingdom, France, Belgium, Norway, Luxembourg, Denmark, Portugal, Italy, and the Netherlands.[34] While Luxembourg, Denmark, and Portugal declined for this first year, the six other nations eagerly submitted their requests. In fact, even before specifying its desired number of vacancies, the United Kingdom intimated that it would want even more spots than had been made available.[35] The first trainees arrived in July 1950, and the first graduation ceremony to include NATO airmen occurred on 4 May 1951 at the Air Navigation School in Summerside, Prince Edward Island. The first NATO pilots graduated two weeks later.[36]

These NATO flyers were graduating from a "pipeline" that in the five years since the end of the war had been operating quietly, but now expanded quickly. Peacetime RCAF aircrew selection and flying training had at first been limited to three locations in southern Ontario – London, Centralia, and Clinton – as well as Summerside, PEI, but the influx of NATO trainees and the RCAF's own buildup required the reactivation of a number of stations across the West. Selection and ground training activities and some flying remained in Centralia, with the bulk basic pilot training moving to Moose Jaw and Penhold, Alberta. Advanced training on T-33 jets took place at Portage La Prairie, Manitoba, and multiengine flying was conducted at Saskatoon. Observer training, a trade replacing both Navigator and Radio Operator, was now centralized at Winnipeg where after a common introduction advanced courses were conducted: Observer (Navigator), Observer (Air Interceptor) and Observer (Radio).[37]

Before a Canadian ever reached a flying school he needed first to meet the basic recruiting standards administered by 22 recruiting stations located throughout the

Three Harvards from the Central Flying School in formation.

country where he encountered the first of many tests and evaluations that formed a rigorous recruiting process, which consisted of three phases: selection, classification, and assignment. "Selection" testing, which started at the recruiting office and continued at No. 2 Personnel Selection Unit (Officers) at RCAF London, confirmed that the individual had the potential both for successful aircrew employment and for service as a commissioned officer. "Classification" assessment determined which flying trade the candidate was best suited for. And finally, "assignment" paired a selected candidate with the expected employment needs of the RCAF awaiting him at the end of the training pipeline.[38]

Maintaining flying standards, thus ensuring that all graduates had identical skills and competency in the air, was the task of the Central Flying School and the associated Flying Instructor Schools, as well as the Central Navigation School. These agencies developed training syllabi and conducted "standards" tests, both on

The three aircraft that many of the NATO pilot candidates would have trained on. From bottom to top: de Havilland Chipmunk, North American Harvard, and the Canadair T-33 Silver Star.

the ground and in the air, of the actual instructors who in turn taught the flying candidates. Quite appropriately, the motto of the CFS was: "We teach today that they may teach tomorrow."[39]

All of these schools were part of Training Command, headquartered in Trenton, which was also responsible for non-commissioned technical trades training as well as the training of all other support trades. Most of this training took place at RCAF Station Borden, the former home of RFC Canada operations, but there were schools in Centralia and Clinton as well as St-Jean Quebec. Even as the 1950s drew to a close there were some 4,000 technical students in training annually. Training Command was also responsible for the service training of officer cadets attending the three Services Colleges and those young men attending civilian universities. By the end of the 1950s the command was coordinating the

Operations Room at RCAF Station Centralia, ON, one of the NATO training sites.

training of 1,500 young men each summer: 350 ROTP in aircrew training, 600 cadets in various technical and non-technical courses, and another 500 undertaking on job training.[40]

RCAF requirements were not uppermost in the minds of British; indeed, the RAF was serious in 1950 about securing more aircrew vacancies for itself. By August, the RAF had arranged for 200 aircrew (150 pilots and 50 navigators) to attend Canadian schools in 1951; starting 15 January 1951, 25 trainees would arrive in Canada every six weeks.[41] Even this was not enough. In December 1950, the RAF indicated that it wanted to expand the number of pilots and navigators trained in Canada on an annual basis (table 7.4). Because the initial cost of this expansion would be $68 million, the recurring annual cost $43 million, and 2,826 additional uniformed personnel would be required to support all aspects of the increased

Table 7.4. RAF plan for expanded annual NATO training in Canada (December 1950)

Flying Training School	Intake 520
	Output 350
Air Navigation School	Intake 900
	Output 768
Personnel Requirements	Officers 921
	Airmen 1,905
	Civilians 695
Aircraft Requirements	Basic Trainers 178
	Advanced Trainers 79
	Navigation Trainers 88
Initial Cost	$68 million
Recurring Cost	$43 million

Source: Extract from Minutes of Meeting of Panel on Economic Aspects of Defence Questions, Document 567 in *DCER XVI*, December 15, 1950, pages 997–9.

throughput, Cabinet decided that Canada could not assume such responsibility without any financial assistance from the beneficiaries.[42]

The British high commissioner approached Brooke Claxton in February 1951, again raising the issue of additional RAF trainees. This time, the RAF proposed that the 1,100 NATO vacancies in the new Flying Training School, Advanced Flying School, and Air Navigation School, soon to be opened, should all be allocated to RAF trainees. Canadian authorities hesitated to make such a decision, for vacancies were being allocated to various countries by NATO's Standing Group, not by Canada's Defence Department. Much to Great Britain's relief, the Standing Group recommended that all available training positions be given to the RAF until the end of 1951.[43]

As early as June 1951, the NATO nations realized and acknowledged that achieving the 1954 Medium Term Plan requirements would not be possible unless training was accelerated. This plan, approved in October 1950, had called for 9,212 front-line aircraft in Europe by December 1954. Consequently, Canada was asked by its NATO allies to open more schools and provide more vacancies. In April 1952, Claxton announced to the House of Commons that the RCAF was prepared to train 1,400 aircrew annually for NATO. December 1952 found the chiefs of staff considering training proposals for the period beyond 1954 because "the North Atlantic Treaty nations will not achieve their goals by 1954, and it may be 1955 or 1956 before the original goals ... are reached." In 1954, Canada agreed to a three-year commitment to train 1,200 NATO airmen a year. The annual cost was estimated at $55 million.[44]

NATO pilots undergoing flight training, RCAF Station Centralia, ON. From left to right: Steiner Wang of Norway, Andre Maes of Belgium, Norman Ronaasen of Canada, Manlio Quarantelli of Italy, and Frank Van Der Vlught of the Netherlands.

The NATO Air Training Plan came to the forefront of the government's attention in 1956 when it was time to decide what should happen once the agreement expired in 1957. Two motivating factors fuelled the Canadian government's desire to not renew the plan. First, front-line goals would be met by the end of 1957, and most of the participating countries had achieved acceptable aircrew levels. The Supreme Allied Commander of Europe (SACEUR) advised that most NATO nations could now replace their own aircrew attrition in training facilities on their own soil. The second motivation to not extend the air training plan was the manpower savings of 495 officers, 1,870 airmen, and 580 civilians; additionally, $31 million dollars annually would be free for reallocation towards operational commitments.[45] Indeed, SACEUR had advised that the resources Canada had put into the air training plan were needed in defence of North America against nuclear attack. Discussions and

A formation of de Havilland Chipmunk basic training aircraft.

decisions to end the NATO Training Plan occurred even before the Soviet Union launched its first satellite in October 1957, thus ushering in the ballistic missile age and a shift, if temporary, away from piloted interceptors.

While considering the formal termination of NATO aircrew training, Canadian officials recognized that not all the nations could meet their aircrew needs on their own. Because Denmark and Norway did not have any training facilities (the weather was too adverse, and numbers were too small to allow a school to be economically feasible), and because Dutch training facilities were not large enough for the number of graduates desired, Canada signed bilateral agreements with the three nations in order to accommodate their needs. For a token payment of $5,000 per pilot and $2,000 per navigator trainee, Canada committed to train aircrew for three years, the offer being renewable for four-year periods.[46]

Turkey also secured an agreement to have five officers annually receive advanced flying training. Additionally, West Germany arranged to have 360 pilots, at a total

Three members of the Turkish Air Force, Lieutenants Ferit Yeselguldem, Omer Yavuz, and Umit Atak, after having completed a training flight, RCAF Station, Gimli, Manitoba.

cost of $12 million, trained by the RCAF. Canada had been reluctant in years previous to accept German recruits for fear of possible clashes with Canadians if German airmen happened to meet relatives of prisoners shot by General Kurt Meyer. The Department of External Affairs had toyed with the possibility of reaching "some secret understanding with the Standing Group that German aircrew should be trained elsewhere than in Canada;" the US, for instance, had more people of German extraction than Canada. This course of action – the secret agreement – was not pursued, for it would be discriminatory towards a fellow NATO signatory, and justifying it would be difficult if the secret arrangement were ever leaked. Instead, for as long as possible, "appropriate but tactful steps [would] be taken to avoid vacancies in the aircrew training program being allotted to students from ... the Federal German Republic's NATO forces." In 1956, Ottawa apparently ran out of tactful excuses to put off accepting German recruits and allowed them to begin training.[47]

Table 7.5. Pre-flight orientation course at RCAF Station London (as of June 1954)

Subjects of Instruction	Films Utilized in the Course
3 hours Canadian History	NFB Film *River of Canada*
5 hours Canadian Geography	NFB Film *Newfoundland: Sentinel of Canada*
9 hours Introduction to the Canadian Way of Life	NFB Film *Prince Edward Island*
21 hours Introduction to the RCAF	Encyclopaedia Britannica Film *Industrial Provinces*
8 hours Drill and Sports	Encyclopaedia Britannica Film *Prairie Provinces*
3 hours Miscellaneous Subjects	NFB Film *Peace River*
12 hours Visits to Industrial and Cultural Centres	NFB Film *People of Canada*
10 hours Educational Films	NFB Film *Banff School of Fine Arts*
19 hours Language Training and Testing	NFB Film *Skiing in the Valley of the Saints (Sports)*
120 hours total	*Scenic Highway*
	NFB Film *Ottawa on the River*
	NFB Film *Jasper National Park*
	NFB Film *Song of the Mountains*
	Ontario Hydro Electric Power Film *Niagara the Powerful*
	Ontario Hydro Electric Power Film *Romance of a River*
	CPR Film *Across Canada*
	CPR Film *Snow-Time Holiday*
	CPR Film *High Powder*

Source: Letter from Squadron Leader E.R. McEwen, June 23, 1954, RG 25 Vol. 6556 File 10548-AT-40.

The actual training regime and schools used changed over time as the NATO Air Training Plan expanded throughout the 1950s. Upon arrival in Canada, NATO recruits would spend approximately five weeks at the RCAF Station in London, Ontario for a Pre-Flight Orientation course where they were introduced to the history, culture, and manners of Canada and the RCAF. As English was not the first language of many of these airmen, much time was spent learning terminology relating to flight, navigation, meteorology, and aircraft controls and parts. Students also worked on speech technique, so they could be understood when communicating over the radio during flight. In addition to these language lessons, the recruits participated in sporting events, went on local tours, and watched many films so as to familiarize themselves with the host country (see table 7.5 for sample film titles).[48]

Pilot trainees would then attend a Flying Training School for 30 weeks where they were taught to fly on Harvards. Ground training included flight instruments, meteorology, and Link Trainer practice. Like his RCAF colleague, once a pilot was ready to move to an Advanced Flying School, he would be selected for either single-engine jet training on T-33 or multi-engine training on Beechcraft Expeditors or North American Mitchells; tutelage spanned approximately four to five months.[49]

Navigators' training followed the Canadian curriculum and could take up to nine months; the first 20 weeks were spent on a basic course, and then the students

A Canadair T-33 advanced jet trainer in flight.

would specialize in radios, air interception, or navigation. Here, while studying dead-reckoning, radar, celestial navigation, and morse code, students' exercises were flown in Expeditors or Douglas Dakotas.[50]

The most substantial change to the training regime of the NATO Air Training Plan came with the introduction of the de Havilland Chipmunk aircraft. In 1952, a debate arose between proponents of teaching students entirely on Harvards and those wanting to introduce trainees to the Chipmunk before giving instruction on the Harvard. Those favouring using Harvards all the way through primary and basic training believed this saved time and money since no conversion training had to be provided. Believers in providing primary training argued that the Chipmunk would build confidence, identify washouts earlier, and save expenses since the Harvard would be flown for fewer hours. When the issue came to an impasse, a trial was initiated. Half of the trial class learned on Harvards from the beginning of their training; the other half of the class received 25 to 30 hours on Chipmunks before progressing to Harvards. Due to the success of those receiving

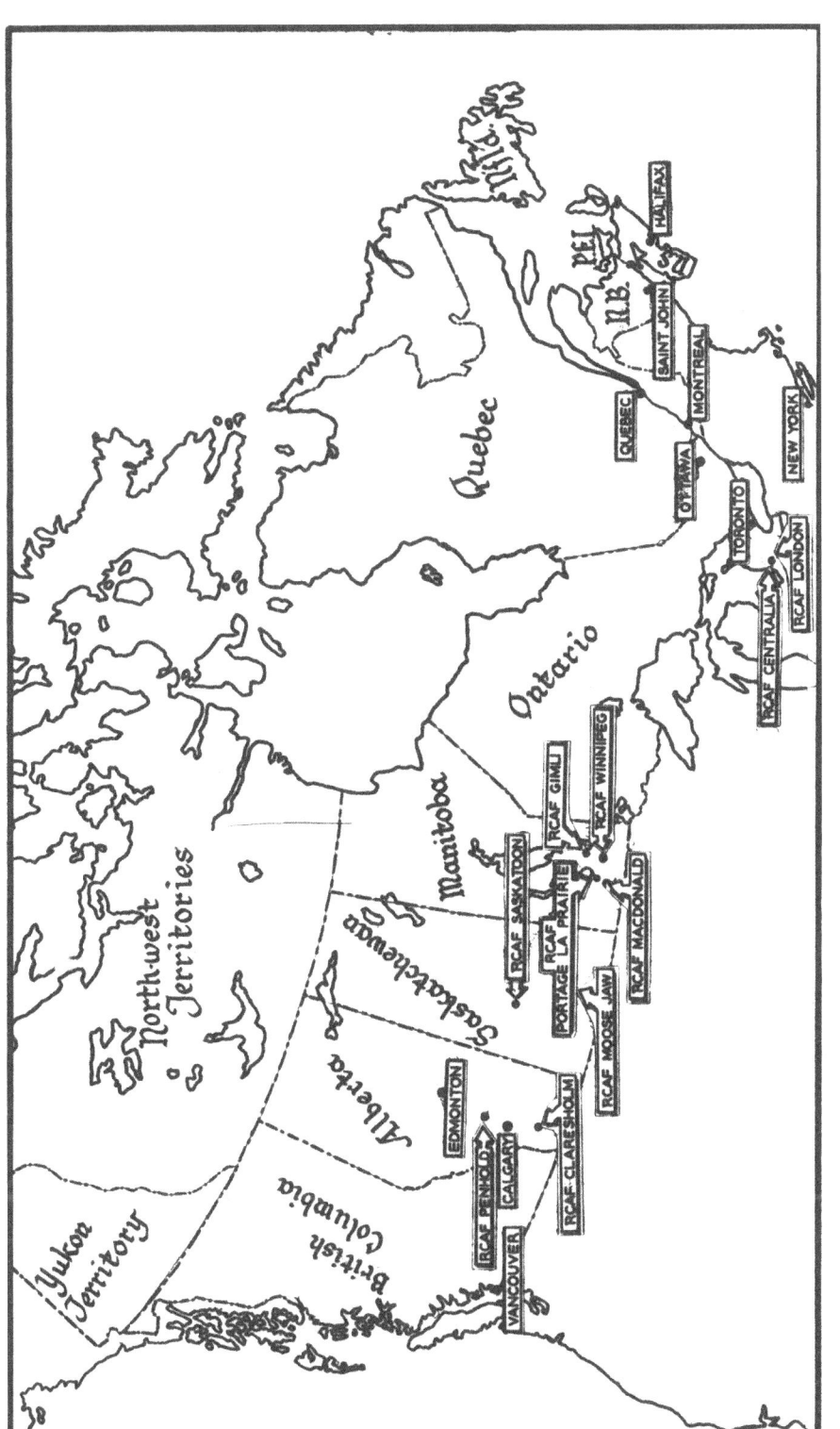

A contemporary map showing the major NATO training facilities: RCAF Stations Penhold and Claresholm, AB; Saskatoon and Moose Jaw, SK; Portage La Prairie, Gimli, Winnipeg and MacDonald, MB; and Centralia and London, ON.

Table 7.6. NATO air training plan schools

#1 Flying Training School Centralia, Ontario
(later became Preliminary Flying Training School)
#2 Flying Training School Gimli, Manitoba
(later moved to Penhold, Alberta)
#3 Flying Training School Claresholm, Alberta
#4 Flying Training School Calgary, Alberta
(later moved to Moose Jaw)
#1 Advanced Flying School Saskatoon, Saskatchewan
#2 Advanced Flying School MacDonald, Manitoba
(later moved to Portage La Prairie, Manitoba)
#3 Advanced Flying School Gimli, Manitoba
#1 Air Gunnery School MacDonald, Manitoba
#1 Air Navigation School Summerside, PEI
#2 Air Navigation School Winnipeg, Manitoba

Source: "Aircrew for NATO: SHAPE to Honour Canada's Effort at Winnipeg Wings Parade July 19" in *The Roundel* 10.5 (June–July 1958): 2–6.

primary training first, the Chipmunk was permanently adopted, thus removing 18 hours of Harvard instruction. Beginning in 1956, trainees would begin flying at the Preliminary Flying Training School in Centralia, where they received 25 hours on the Chipmunk, learning how to take-off, fly, and land safely. Students then received 155 hours on Harvards at one of the three Flying Training Schools. Pilots selected for multi-engine training went on to the Advanced Flying School in Saskatoon. Those trained on jets would fly 125 hours on T-33 Silver Stars at one of the other two Advanced Flying Schools (see table 7.6 for a list of all NATO Training Plan schools established in Canada). After 75 weeks and 305 flying hours, RCAF students, who followed the identical training regime, would then attend an RCAF Operational Training Unit prior to posting to their first squadron; NATO recruits returned home.[51]

A total of 11 NATO nations (including Canada) had students in the NATO Air Training Plan between 1950 and 1958. The first NATO trainees arrived in July 1950 and graduated in May 1951. The last class began its training in July 1957 and graduated the following summer. In addition to training over 3,200 airmen for Canada, the RCAF trained 5,575 pilots and navigators from NATO nations at a total cost of over $402 million (table 7.7).

Post-training plan bilateral agreements saw Malaysian, Jamaican, Tanzanian, Turkish, Danish Norwegian, and Dutch airmen attend RCAF schools throughout the 1960s. In fact, the bilateral agreements between Canada and the Netherlands did not come to an end until 1983.[52]

Table 7.7. NATO air training plan totals (1 May 1951–31 March 1958)

# Trained by Country of Origin	
Canada	3,218
United Kingdom	3,042
Belgium	170
France	1,096
Denmark	307
Greece	12
Holland	205
Italy	101
Norway	259
Portugal	21
Turkey	86

# Trained for RCAF by Fiscal Year		# Trained by Year for 10 NATO Nations	
1951–2	260	1951	184
1952–3	622	1952	1,076
1953–4	536	1953	1,253
1954–5	476	1954	719
1955–6	395	1955	631
1956–7	426	1956	620
1957–8	503	1957	692
Total:	3,218	1958	124
		Total	5,299

Canadian Mutual Aid Expenditures on the NATO Air Training Plan	
1951–2	$ 42,552,000
1952–3	$ 104,628,000
1953–4	$ 71,340,000
1954–5	$ 52,890,000
1955–6	$ 51,056,000
1956–7	$ 47,753,000
1957–8	$ 26,418,000
Total	$ 402,637,000

Sources: "Aircrew for NATO: SHAPE to Honour Canada's Effort at Winnipeg Wings Parade July 19" in *The Roundel*, vol. 10, no. 5 (June–July 1958): 6; "End of NATO Training" in *The Roundel*, vol. 10, no. 7 (September 1958): 2.

Conclusion

In all three air training programs,[53] Canada made a global name for itself and demonstrated that its allies were not mistaken or misguided in asking Canadians to take on the task of providing pilot and aircrew training during three crises. In all three instances, it was recognized that Canada had suitable geography: vast spaces far away from theatres of war. British politicians trying to convince Canada to undertake the BCATP often made mention of Canada's air training experience during the First World War. The RFC Canada venture did not really prepare the RCAF for the BCATP: too much time had elapsed, technology had radically changed, new aerodromes had to be built, and new instructors had to be trained. On the other hand, BCATP experience was easily transferable to the NATO Air Training Plan. Some old technology was still useful; Second World War training aerodromes were easily updated; BCATP courses provided example lesson plans; and demobilized BCATP graduates existed as a ready pool of instructors.

On three occasions, the United Kingdom approached Canada concerning flying training; Canadian politicians were initially reluctant to accept the First and Second World War commitments, and government officials were consistently working to keep expenditures to a minimum during the NATO Air Training Plan. Nonetheless, despite hesitancies, Canada successfully carried out its commitments in an exemplary fashion, building not only three training plans, but also an international reputation, not forgotten by NATO allies. The legacy of these training plans paved the way of the current day NATO Flying Training in Canada (NFTC) program.[54] Although the acquisition of next generation fighters among NATO allies and partners will necessitate a revision of pilot training courses and contracts with industry, the precedent of carrying out military flying training in Canada for international students was established even before the birth of the RCAF, repeated in follow-on times of international conflict and unrest, and is still ongoing in the twenty-first century. Little did those who proposed the RFC Canada training scheme imagine that over 100 years later, Canada's air force would still be proudly providing flying training to its allies – what an amazing long-term strategic outcome that grew from the initial Great War vision.

NOTES

1 S.F. Wise, *The Official History of the Royal Canadian Air Force*. Vol. 1: *Canadian Airmen and the First World War* (Toronto: University of Toronto Press, 1980), 29–33; R.V. Dodds, "Canada's First Air Training Plan: Part I," *The Roundel* 14, no. 9 (Nov. 1962): 9.
2 Wise, 44–5, 60–1 (quote), 62–4; Dodds (1), 10.
3 Wise, 74; Dodds (1), 8, 10.
4 The Imperial Munitions Board was established in Canada by the British Ministry of Munitions to secure war material contracts in Canada on behalf of the British Government. The IMB was led by Toronto businessman J.V. Flavelle. See D.J. Bercuson, "Imperial Munitions Board," *The Canadian Encyclopedia*, March 4, 2015. https://www.thecanadianencyclopedia.ca/en/article/imperial-munitions-board [accessed 6 Sept. 2021].
5 Wise, 70, 75; Dodds (1), 10.
6 Wise, 77–8, 80; R.V. Dodds, "Canada's First Air Training Plan: Part II," *The Roundel* vol. 14, no. 10 (Dec. 1962): 17–21.
7 Wise, 83; Dodds (2), 16; R.V. Dodds, "Canada's First Air Training Plan: Part III," *The Roundel* vol. 15, no, 1 (Jan./Feb. 1963): 20.
8 Wise, 93–4; Dodds (2), 20–1; Dodds (3), 18–19.
9 Dodds, "Canada's First Air Training Plan: Part IV," *The Roundel* 15, no. 2 (Mar. 1963): 20–1.

10 Wise, 98, 102–3; Dodds (4), 20–1.
11 Wise, 114–7, 120; Dodds (1), 7; Glenn B. Foulds and Jonathan Scotland, "Royal Flying Corps," *The Canadian Encyclopedia*, Feb. 7, 2006. https://www.thecanadianencyclopedia.ca/en/article/royal-flying-corps [accessed 26 Oct. 2021]; "Air Training in Canada," The Canadian War Museum, https://www.warmuseum.ca/firstworldwar/history/battles-and-fighting/air-war/ [accessed 26 Oct. 2021].
12 British Air Ministry, *The Second World War 1939–1945: Flying Training – Policy and Planning* (London: Air Ministry Air Historical Board, 1952) 74, 76, 87; Ted Barris, *Behind the Glory* (Toronto: Macmillan Canada, 1992), 13.
13 April 22, 1937, Telegram from Dominions Secretary, May 6, 1937, Memo from Joint Staff Committee, Doc. #143-144 in *Documents on Canadian External Relations [DCER]* Vol. VI (Ottawa: Dept of External Affairs, 1972), 192–5; W.A.B. Douglas, *The Official History of the Royal Canadian Air Force*, Vol. 2: *The Creation of a National Air Force* (Toronto: University of Toronto Press), 194, 196.
14 Sept. 4, 1936, Letter from Ian Mackenzie (Minister of National Defence), King Papers MG 26 J1 Reel 3690 Vol. 220, 189790-1; J.L. Granatstein, *Canada's War: The Politics of the Mackenzie King Government 1939–1945* (Toronto: Oxford University Press, 1975), 43; Sept. 11, 1939, Memo by E.A. Pickering (Dept of External Affairs), Doc. #136 in *DCER VI*, 175–6.
15 James Eayrs, *In Defence of Canada*, Vol. 2: *Appeasement and Rearmament* (Toronto: University of Toronto Press, 1965), 92; 23 Feb. 1939, *Dominion of Canada Official Report of Debates of House of Commons* (HoC Debates) (Ottawa: J.O. Patenaude, Printer to the King's Most Excellent Majesty, 1939), 2049–50; May 6, 1937, Memo by Joint Staff Committee, Doc. #144 in *DCER VI*, 193–5.
16 July 1, 1938, *HoC Debates*, 4523–4; 13 [sic 16] May 1938 Memo from W.L.M. King (Prime Minister), July 2, 1938, Memo from O.D. Skelton (Undersecretary of State for External Affairs), June 19, 1938, Memo by L.C Christie (Dept of External Affairs), Doc. #152, 153, 159 in *DCER VI*, 206–10, 217–18.
17 July 1, 1938, *HoC Debates*, 4527–9; July 1, 1938, King Diary, LAC, MG 26 J13 Microfiche T123 509; Dec. 9, 1938, Letter from Gerald Campbell (British High Commissioner), Doc. #168 in *DCER VI*, 227–8; Dec. 9, 1938, Memo from British Government, RG 25 Vol. 1858 File 72-T-38C; Dec. 21, 1938, King Diary LAC MG 26 J13 Microfiche T129 p. 1031; Dec. 31, 1938 Letter from W.L.M. King, Doc. #169 in *DCER VI*, 230–2.
18 Eayrs, 103; C.P. Stacey, *Arms, Men, and Government: The War Policies of Canada 1939–1945* (Toronto: University of Toronto Press, 1965), 89; Douglas, 203; May 1, 1939 Letter from Gerald Campbell, RG 25 Vol. 1858 File 72-T-38C.
19 Vincent Massey, *What's Past is Prologue: The Memoirs of the Right Honourable Vincent Massey* (Toronto: The Macmillan Company of Canada Limited, 1963), 303–4l; Douglas, 207.
20 Sept. 26, 1939 Telegram from Dominions Secretary, LAC RG 25 Vol. 1858 File 72-T-38C; Brereton Greenhous, *The Official History of the Royal Canadian Air Force*, Vol. 3: *The Crucible of War* (Toronto: University of Toronto Press, 1994), 20.
21 Ibid.
22 Sept. 26, 1939 Telegram from Dominions Secretary, LAC, RG 25 Vol. 1858 File 72-T-38C; Sept. 28, 1939 Minutes of Emergency Council of Cabinet, Sept. 28, 1939 Telegram from Secretary of State for External Affairs, Doc. #689-690 in *DCER VII* (1974), 552–7.
23 Dec.17, 1939 BCATP Agreement, LAC, RG 25 Vol. 1858A File 72-T-38.
24 Rachel Lea Heide, "Technocracy at Work: Why Political Lobbying Failed," in *The Politics of British Commonwealth Air Training Plan Base Selection in Western Canada* (Ottawa: Carleton University MA Thesis, 2000), 93–140.

25 F.J. Hatch, *Aerodrome of Democracy: Canada and the British Commonwealth Air Training Plan 1939–1945* (Ottawa: Cdn Govt Publishing Centre, 1983), 14; Heide correspondence with Charles Birch, Roy Brown, Allen Burgham, Borden Fawcett, William Fuller, Peter James, Richard Jones, Ross Lennox, Jack Rathburn.

26 Ibid.

27 Rachel Lea Heide, "Fallen Planes – The Cause of Training Accidents at #5 Bombing and Gunnery School, Dafoe, Saskatchewan" (Ottawa: Carleton University BA Honours Research Paper, 1998), 31–6; Heide correspondence with Greville Fox, Ignatius Green, Richard Jones, John Pite.

28 Hatch, 165–8; Norman I, Smith, *The British Commonwealth Air Training Plan* (Toronto: The Macmillan Company of Canada Limited, 1941), 6; Heide correspondence with Colin Smith, Ignatius Green, John Griesbach, Harold Smoker.

29 Hatch, 169–70, 173–6; Heide correspondence with Malcolm Holliday, Elmer Kerr, Gene Steeves, Gord Wallace.

30 Hatch, 199.

31 Report to Cabinet Defence Committee on Visit of A/M W.A. Curtis to France, Sweden, Norway, and the United Kingdom April–May 1949, LAC, RG 24 Vol. 5185 File 15-9-58 Part 2.

32 June 21, 1949 Memo from A/V/M C.R. Slemon (Air Member of Organization and Training), July 8, 1949 Memo from Secretary of Chiefs of Staff Committee, July 21, 1949 Extract of Minutes of 450th Meeting of Chiefs of Staff Committee, LAC, RG 24 Vol. 5185 File 15-9-58 Part 2; June 23, 1949 Memo from Captain C.N. Lentaigne (Royal Navy Assistant Chief of Naval Staff Air), July 8, 1949 Memo from RCAF CAS, LAC, RG 24 Vol. 8097 File 1280-14 Part 1.

33 Nov. 23, 1949, Extract from Minutes of Cabinet Defence Committee Meeting, Nov 29, 1949 Memo from Under-Secretary of State for External, Dec. 1949 Extract from Report of Minister of National Defence, Dec. 21–2, 1949 Extract from Cabinet Conclusions, Doc.#404, 407, 418, 419 in *DCER XV* (1994), 698, 701, 725–34.

34 Mar. 17, 1950 *HoC Debates*, 852–3; Jan. 5, 1950 Memo from Military Secretary Cabinet Defence Committee, Jan. 18, 1950 Memo from Defence Liaison Division, Doc. #500-501 in *DCER XVI* (1995), 876–81; Mar. 17, 1950, Letter from Brooke Claxton (Minister of National Defence), Mar. 17, 1950, Message from Secretary of State of External Affairs, June 24, 1950, RCAF Administrative Instructions Re: Aircrew Training Personnel of Member Nations of NATO, Claxton Papers MG 32 B6 Vol. 113 File 2.

35 June 13, 1950, Memo from A/ M W.A. Curtis, June 15, 1950, Letter from Brig. J.D.B. Smith (Secretary), June 21 Cypher from High Commissioner for Canada in London, Claxton Papers LAC, MG 32 B6 Vol. 113 File 2.

36 David Fletcher and Doug MacPhail, *Harvard! The North American Trainers in Canada* (Dundas: DCR Flying Books, 1990), 126–7; Mar. 8, 1955, RCAF Press Release from R.V. Dodds (Director of Public Relations RCAF), LAC, RG 25 Vol. 6556 File 10548-AT-40.

37 "The R.C.A.F. Today," *The Roundel*, 11 no. 1 (Jan–Feb 1959): 26.

38 S/L E.P. Sloan, "The Party Line: Aircrew Selection in the R.C.A.F.," *The Roundel*, 6, no. 11 (December 1954): 4–7.

39 F/L J.A. Emery, "Between the Lines: A Resume of Flying Instructor Training in the R.C.A.F.," *The Roundel*, 6, no. 6 (June 1954): 11–12.

40 A/V/M H.M. Carscallen, AOC Training Command, "The Evolution and Current Status of Training Command," *The Roundel*, 14, no. 6 (July–August 1962): 7–10.

41 Aug. 22, 1950, Signal from RCAF CAS, Aug. 28, 1950, Memo from A/VM A.I. James (Acting CAS), Claxton Papers LAC MG 32 B6 Vol. 113 File 1; July 27, 1950 Letter from High Commissioner in United Kingdom, Doc. #533 in *DCER XVI*, 945.

42 Dec. 13, 1950, Minutes of 477th Meeting of Chiefs of Staff Committee, LAC, RG 24 Vol. 21814 Part 12; Dec. 15, 1950, Extract from Minutes of Meeting of Panel on Economic Aspects of Defence Questions, Doc. #567 in *DCER XVI*, 997–9; Feb. 13, 1951, Letter from Deputy Minister of National Defence, Claxton Papers LAC, MG 32 B6 Vol. 113 File 1.

43 Jan. 15, 1951, Minutes of Cabinet Defence Committee Meeting, Doc. #636 in *DCER XVI*, 1162–71; Jan. 25, 1951, Letter from Cdre H.S. Rayner (Royal Canadian Navy Secretary), Feb. 6, 1951, Letter from Arthur Henderson (British High Commissioner), Claxton Papers LAC, MG 32 B6 Vol. 113 File 1; Feb. 15, 1951, Extract from Cabinet Conclusions, Feb. 20, 1951, Extract from Minutes of Cabinet Defence Committee Meeting, Doc. #362, 364 in *DCER XVII* (1996), 635–6, 641–3; Mar. 21, 1951, *HoC Debates*, 1485–6.

44 June 26, 1951, Memo from Minister of National Defence, Doc. #384 in *DCER XVII*, pp. 695–8; April 3, 1952, *HoC Debates*, 1085; Dec. 30, 1952, Letter from Lt-Gen. Charles Foulkes (Chairman Chiefs of Staff Committee), Claxton Papers MG 32 B6 Vol. 113 File 1; May 13, 1954, Letter from Defence Liaison Benjamin Rogers, LAC, RG 25 Vol. 6556 File 10548-AT-40; Nov. 8, 1954, Memo from Minister of National Defence, Doc. #260 in *DCER XX* (1997), 490–6.

45 April 16, 1956, Memo from Minister of National Defence, April 18, 1956, Memo from Under-Secretary of State for External Affairs, April 19, 1956, Extract from Minutes of Meeting of Cabinet Defence Committee, Letter from High Commissioner in United Kindgom, May 8, 1956, Letter from Under-Secretary of State for External Affairs, May 9, 1956, Letter from Chairman of Chiefs of Staff Committee, 14 May 1956 Extract from Minutes of Meeting of Panel on Economic Aspects of Defence Questions, June 14, 1956, Letter from Secretary of State for External Affairs, June 14, 1956, Letter from Secretary of State for External Affairs, Doc. #443-450 in *DCER XXII* (2001), 831–45.

46 Mar. 28, 1960, Memo from Canadian Ambassador in Denmark, Mar. 25, 1960, Note from Jens Otto Krag (Minister for Foreign Affairs, Denmark), Mar. 25, 1960, Note from Jens Otto Krag, Jan. 21, 1960, Note by the Canadian Ambassador in Norway, May 26, 1960, Memo from W/C S.S. Farrell, LAC, RG 24 1983-84/216 Vol. 2820 File 871-9.00.22 File 2.

47 Nov. 9, 1954, Memo from Under-Secretary of State for External Affairs, Nov. 10, 1954, Memo from Under-Secretary of State for External Affairs, Doc. #261-262 in *DCER XX*, 494–501; Sept. 14, 1956, Note from Dept of External Affairs in Ottawa, Undated Memo from A/M Hugh Campbell (RAF), July 7, 1958, Letter from Minister of National Defence, May 26, 1960, Memo from W/C S.S. Farrell, LAC, RG 24 Accession 1983-84/216 Vol. 2820 File 871-9.00.22 File 2.

48 L.P. Valiquet, "RCAF Station Cosmopolis: NATO Training at London," in *The Roundel* 2 no. 12 (Nov. 1950): 9–13; "Aircrew for NATO: SHAPE to Honour Canada's Effort at Winnipeg Wings Parade July 19," *The Roundel* 10, no. 5 (June–July 1958): 4; June 23, 1954, Letter from S/L E.R. McEwen, LAC, RG 25 Vol. 6556 File 10548-AT-40.

49 Heide Correspondence with Eric Beeby, Ken Castle, Russell Manson, Roger Turner.

50 "Aircrew for NATO," 5; Heide correspondence with Grant Baker, Ken Castle, Jack Rathburn, Ross Truemner, Greg Vincent, Don Wilson.

51 Fletcher, 131–2; S/L E.P. Sloan, "RCAF Experience with the Training of NATP Aircrew," in *Defence Psychology* (London: Pergamon Press, 1961), p. 114; "Aircrew Training for NATO," *The Roundel* 4, no. 6 (June 1952): 19; Heide correspondence with Grant Baker, Ken Castle, Ross Truemner, Greg Vincent.

52 Larry Milberry, *Sixty Years: The RCAF and CF Air Command 1924–1984* (Toronto: Canav Books, 1984), 346, 471; "Aircrew for NATO," 6; "End of NATO Training," *The Roundel* 10, no. 7 (Sept. 1958): 2; NATO Flying Training in Canada, April 3, 2002, http://www.nftc.com/Concept/History.html [accessed 2002]; Heide correspondence with Ken Castle, Bert Clark, Russell Manson, Stuart Poulin.

53 A very special thanks to the following RCAF veterans for their correspondence answering questions posted by the author: Grant Baker (NATO), Eric Beeby (NATO), Charles Birch (BCATP), Roy Brown (BCATP), Allen Burgham (BCATP), Ken Castle (NATO), H.F. Clark (BCATP and NATO) Borden Fawcett (BCATP), Greville Fox (BCATP), William Fuller (BCATP), Ernie Glozier (BCATP), Ignatius Green (BCATP), John Griesbach (BCATP), Malcolm Holliday (BCATP), Peter James (BCATP), Richard Jones (BCATP), Elmer Kerr (BCATP), Ross Lennox (BCATP), Hector MacGregor (BCATP), Russell Manson (BCATP and NATO), John McCullough (BCATP), Tom Murphy (BCATP), John Pite (BCATP), William Pearson (BCATP), Archie Pennie (BCATP), William Peppler (BCATP), Stuart Poulin (NATO), Jack Rathburn (BCATP and NATO), Colin Smith (BCATP), Harold Smoker (BCATP), Gene Steeves (BCATP), Robert Tait (BCATP), Ross Truemner (BCATP and NATO), Roger Turner (NATO), Greg Vincent (NATO), Dennis Wagner (BCATP and NATO), Gord Wallace (BCATP), Fred Willing (BCATP), Don Wilson (NATO).

54 "NATO Flying Training in Canada (NFTC) Now Operational." Canadian Department of National Defence (Cdn DND) Press Release, July 6, 2000. http://www.defense-aerospace.com/article-view/release/2584/canada-opens-nato-pilot-training-center-(july-7).html [accessed July 3, 2021]; "NATO Flying Training In Canada Now Operational At Moose Jaw." Cdn DND Press Release, July 6, 2000. http://www.defense-aerospace.com/article-view/release/2584/canada-opens-nato-pilot-training-center-(july-7).html [accessed July 3, 2021]; "NATO Flying Training in Canada: An Innovative Solution for NATO Flying Training Requirements." Cdn DND Press Release, July 6, 2000. http://www.defense-aerospace.com/article-view/release/2584/canada-opens-nato-pilot-training-center-(july-7).html [accessed July 3, 2021]; "Italy Signs on to NATO Flying Training in Canada." Cdn DND Press Release, July 6, 2000. http://www.defense-aerospace.com/article-view/release/2584/canada-opens-nato-pilot-training-center-(july-7).html [accessed July 3, 2021]; Major Petra Smith. "NATO Flying Training in Canada Program Makes History." *Skies Magazine*, April 20, 2018. https://skiesmag.com/news/nato-flying-training-canada-program-makes-history/ [accessed July 3, 2021]; "NATO Flying Training in Canada (NFTC) Program Contract Modification." Canadian Armed Forces Press Release, January 25, 2017. https://www.canada.ca/en/department-national-defence/news/2017/01/nato-flying-training-canada-nftc-program-contract-modification.html [accessed July 3, 2021]; "NATO Flying Training in Canada (NFTC)." CAE, 2021. https://www.cae.com/defence-security/what-we-do/training-centres/nato-flying-training-in-canada-nftc/ [accessed July 3, 2021].

CHAPTER EIGHT

RCAF AIR MAINTENANCE

TERRY LEVERSEDGE

Introduction

While the context, approach, and technologies involved in aircraft maintenance and engineering have changed drastically over the decades, the fundamental requirements and underlying characteristics have remained relatively constant. Airworthiness, engineering, and technical competence in support of air operations rely directly on the personnel cadre of the day. The organizational structures, engineering and technical trades, technologies, and reliance on civilian industry have all constantly evolved, in most cases, in a cyclical pattern of expansion and contraction due either to budget restrictions or operational necessity.[1]

The RCAF maintenance community emerged from the Second World War with conflicting priorities and mixed experiences. Before 1939, the RCAF had focused almost exclusively on aircraft and equipment designed in the United Kingdom.[2] Procurement options available to the federal government involved a hard compromise: either buy in the United States and risk an embargo in the event of participation in a European war, once American neutrality legislation came into effect; purchase in the UK and wait until after deliveries to the Royal Air Force (RAF) were completed; or purchase in Canada and wait for many months until the existing and limited industrial base could begin to produce aircraft of foreign design. According to the CAS, Air Commodore G.M. Croil, there was only one solution to the problem, and that was the production of equipment destined for the RCAF, albeit of British design, in Canada.[3] By awarding these contracts, the Department

Aero engine technicians in a trade advancement class.

of National Defence hoped that Canadian aviation companies would gain experience in the large-scale production of modern combat aircraft. This decision also cemented that the RCAF's third- and fourth-line[4] support would be from Canadian industry.

The RCAF consequently aligned itself with the RAF in terms of equipment selection but also in organizational structure and maintenance support approaches. However, with the rapid progress of technology, and as the UK struggled to survive during the first two years of the Second World War, both the RAF and RCAF needed additional support. As the war unfolded, the RCAF at home had no choice but to look south of the border and to re-equip using American-designed aircraft in both the combat and training roles. Overseas, the RCAF still relied primarily on British designs to equip its deployed combat squadrons, most of which were supplied from UK stocks. The standards, specifications, and maintenance approach to these British and American designs were, however, in most cases quite different.

Non-commissioned Officers, Trades, and Technical Officers

The evolution of the RCAF's maintenance non-commissioned officer NCO trade structure was driven by technology. Originally, RCAF trade structures simply mirrored those of the Royal Flying Corps (RFC) / RAF with riggers, fitters,[5] carpenters, blacksmiths, and stores persons. An armament trade was then developed to look after weapons, such as machine guns, bombs, and torpedoes. Additional specialists were also needed to service evolving technology, such as aviation instruments, cameras, and wireless transmitters. These trades remained largely unchanged during the interwar decades.

The RCAF's only technical training school was a small establishment at RCAF Station Camp Borden, Ontario, which had been formed in the early 1920s.[6] Happily, as part of the pre-war expansion in the late 1930s, No. 1 Technical Training School (1 TTS) had been created at RCAF Station Trenton, Ontario, while the school at Borden was retained for specialist training and became No. 2 Technical Training School (2 TTS). These two small facilities could now train the riggers, fitters, and other technical specialists (armament, instrument repair, wireless technicians, welders, etc.) required by the RCAF for its modest operations up to September 1939, but the need was almost immediately to grow.

Throughout the 1930s, the RCAF had fewer than 1,500 fully trained tradesmen, but with the outbreak of the Second World War the RCAF was faced with training huge numbers of personnel. The war also brought further complexities as additional technical specialists were needed for newly developed avionics and installations such as radar, electronic warfare countermeasures, identification friend or foe (IFF) systems, autopilot, and bombing systems. The British Commonwealth Air Training Plan (BCATP) scheme further added to the enormous nature of the task. Not only did the aircrew have to be trained but the requisite support staff required to facilitate these operations had to be recruited, trained, and distributed to both operational and training units. The solution for the RCAF was to create a massive technical training facility suited to the task. Both existing schools were closed, and a new No. 1 TTS was opened on the campus of a former hospital in St. Thomas, Ontario, as the year came to a close.[7]

The former St. Thomas Psychiatric Hospital had opened its doors for the first time on 1 April 1939, and soon was at its capacity with over 2,400 patients. Built at a cost of more than $7 million, the hospital, with its elaborate limestone buildings, was known as a first-class institution. The site also included 460 acres (186 hectares) of additional land for the facility's produce needs. But shortly after Canada's declaration of war, in September 1939, the province quickly agreed to lease the entire complex to the RCAF in support of the war effort.[8]

Leading Aircraftsman J.R. Kennedy checks a torpedo for leaks in the seals between the different components.

Most of the hospital buildings were re-purposed. Hangars were rapidly constructed, equipped, and staffed for the instruction of a series of practical courses in aircraft maintenance and repair, which typically lasted from 18 to 26 weeks. Graduating students were not intended to be technical experts, but rather qualified basic aviation mechanics who had been competently trained in the various basic aspects of engine and airframe servicing, maintenance, and repair.

The task of creating a modern technical training establishment from scratch in a new location was not without significant challenges. No. 1 TTS was initially designed to take a complement of 2,500 military students, but the buildings used for barracks could accommodate as many as 3,500 students. Of the planned cadre of 2,500 students, approximately 1,100 were to be trained as engine mechanics, 1,100 as airframe mechanics, and the remainder as electrical and instrument workers, fabric workers, parachute packers, and metal workers. Initially, there were shortages of virtually everything needed: experienced personnel, instructors, and even uniforms.[9]

Wartime graduating class from 1 Technical Training School, RCAF Station St. Thomas, ON, 30 October 1942. These personnel supported the British Commonwealth Air Training Plan and RCAF operations at home and abroad.

A critical problem for the school from the outset, however, was the acquisition of suitable training aids for the courses. The obsolete wood and fabric biplanes that made up a large portion of the RCAF's peacetime inventory were not representative of the modern aircraft the tradesmen would be working on. The initial courses had to make do with rudimentary training aids or poor specimens of actual aircraft. Gradually, more representative state-of-the-art airframes and engines were made available for training.

As the expansion of the RCAF accelerated, A/V/M Ernest W. Stedman, a First World War aviator and the service's senior engineering officer during the interwar period, recognized that the RCAF needed more aeronautical engineers to fill positions at the BCATP schools and HWE stations as well as all the various aircraft repair depots and technical detachments. Unfortunately, there were very few qualified aeronautical engineers in Canada, and the only university that provided training was the School of Applied Science at the University of Toronto. Its production up to 1939 had been very small. The RCAF, at Stedman's prompting, consequently established a School of Aeronautical Engineering (AE) in Montreal where it could train graduate engineers from any discipline in the aeronautical sciences. The syllabus for the course was similar to the RAF's wartime engineering "E" course, with heavy doses of lectures but also with a large amount of practical aircraft work and laboratories.[10]

On Stedman's suggestion, the RCAF also recruited T.R. Louden, the professor in charge of Toronto University's aeronautical school, as a direct-entry[11] squadron leader, and he became the first commanding officer of the AE School. Louden's appointment was significant as it indicated Stedman's desire to have properly trained, qualified engineers in the supervisory positions at all levels – from stations through to AFHQ. There was, however, another school of thought, one supported by the CAS, A/M Robert Leckie, that believed scientific principles and engineering had a place, but that the primary need was for "practically experienced" officers who could manage the technical affairs of a flying station. The argument continued in one form or another through the war years and resurrected itself many times during the postwar years.[12] This same debate was closely connected to much later arguments associated with the commissioning of technicians from the ranks (CFR) within the engineering branch.

The first AE School was small, with staff of just seven officers, 29 airmen and 13 civilians. Initially, the total student population consisted of 48 officers, grouped in classes of roughly 15. The first class started on 1 April 1940, and graduated in September. While it was a small school, it was busy, and by the time it disbanded in July 1944 it had trained over 1,000 officers.[13] Besides training engineering officers, the school also provided some specialist airmen training. The original concept of accepting only graduate engineers did not last because the supply was quickly exhausted. Consequently, early on, the RCAF agreed to the idea of taking talented personnel from any academic background and also to accepting above-average airmen. The school also adjusted the syllabus of the course to provide more emphasis on engineering theory for these pools of candidates.[14]

Practical workshops covered all aspects from basic fitting and metalworking through airframe rigging and engine running. The aspiring engineering officers got their hands dirty at almost every shop job or flight-line task that their mechanics would do at a station. As their instructors were NCOs, students also came to understand something of the character of the people they would work with. The 40 hours of lectures on administration provided insight into the organization of the air force, salvage procedures, the supply organization, publications, responsibilities and duties of an engineering officer, engineering administration, and regulations for workshops including safety. With this knowledge, personnel who completed the course could then carry out the duties of a junior engineering officer.

Postwar RCAF Technical Training Schools

By early 1944, the Allies knew they would win the war. As the BCATP and HWE activities scaled back, the RCAF did not need additional ground crew or engineers, and it drastically cut back production from all technical training schools. Some, like the Officers' AE School, were completely disbanded, and No. 1 TTS St. Thomas was turned back over the province to again become a mental health hospital. For the remainder of the war, and during the early postwar period as the RCAF downsized, the air force had ample aeronautical engineering personnel to meet requirements.

However, the RCAF could not ignore training for long. It enrolled its first post-war recruits to fill vacancies in various ground trades starting in February 1946, with technical training for both officers and NCMs re-established at RCAF Station Aylmer, Ontario. Also, as of 1947, the RCAF started summer employment schemes for reserve officers who were studying in technical programs at Canadian universities. Many of these were veterans would later re-join the regular RCAF on completion of their university training.

RCAF Station Aylmer officially became the home of the RCAF Technical and Engineering School on 1 April 1945. As the name implied, all technical training was originally intended to take place at this school and, for a short time, AFHQ used the title of "RCAF Technical College." The planners believed that half of the postwar RCAF strength would be ground tradesmen and anticipated that the school would train 300 students per year. The original plan was that tradesmen would undergo a two-year apprentice program. The first year would consist of common training and the second of trade specific training, with radio tradesmen taking their second year at the RCAF Radio School at RCAF Station Clinton. Besides the apprentice training, the RCAF Technical College planned to conduct advanced NCO courses and aircraft engineering officer training as well as flight engineer and several miscellaneous specialist courses. The staff, under a wing commander, consisted of 51 personnel with the lowest rank being flight sergeant. Most of the instructors were technical officers and senior NCOs; however, two education branch officers looked after academic subjects such as shop mathematics, science, physics, and administration. As the technical complexity of aircraft grew with the introduction of jets by the end of the 1940s, so too did the number of RCAF aviation technical trades, which increased to over 11 separate trades with further specialties.[15]

Ground training. Equipped with "hangar queens," the massive hangars at Camp Borden give 2 Technical Training School students a chance to put textbook theories to work under actual conditions encountered in Air Force maintenance sections across the nation and overseas.

Because of budgetary constraints, however, the proposed apprentice training scheme for tradesmen did not materialize. While Aylmer remained as the technical training school, new recruits instead received the previous wartime trade courses rather than going through the planned apprentice program. Shortly after its formation, the RCAF designated the Aylmer School as No. 1 TTS and, in 1946, No. 2 TTS re-opened at RCAF Station Camp Borden. As well, the Radar and Communication School at RCAF Station Clinton provided telecommunications and electronics training. The long-term plan developed by Central Air Command involved No. 2 TTS Camp Borden becoming the school for aircraft trades, while No. 1 TTS would concentrate on non-aircraft trades. In a round of further consolidations, both for budget and administrative efficiency reasons, by 1958, all NCO aircraft technical trades training (except for refinisher, safety equipment, and technical officer aircraft engineering training) had left Aylmer, and Camp Borden became the main school for aircraft technical trades training.[16]

Officer training did not start immediately after the war, and many wartime veterans entered the technical branch without any engineering training. The Technical Aeronautical Engineering (Tech AE) School initially followed the previous pattern of the wartime training. It occupied its own hangar at Aylmer, and most of the course (with generally 30 officers per course) was practical work supervised by NCOs on instructional aircraft. The Supply Officers School was in the same hangar, and both syllabi involved cross training – the Tech AE officers getting an exposure to supply practice and accounting, and the supply officers to aircraft engineering. In 1960, Training Command Headquarters (TCHQ) transferred all technical officer training to RCAF Station Centralia, Ontario.[17]

Squadron versus Centralized Maintenance

The debate surrounding the merits of centralized aircraft maintenance, where all the technical work on the station was done by a centralized organization, versus squadron maintenance, with each squadron having its own technical personnel, began during the Second World. Before 1939, the RCAF relied almost exclusively on squadron-level maintenance for aircraft first- and second-line aircraft maintenance, which handled day to day servicing and relatively straight forward repair work. Squadrons were backed by a small number of centralized in-house third-line units, such as repair depots that conducted major periodic overhauls and complex repairs. These depots were further aided by civilian companies that were contracted to complete still more complicated repairs or overhauls.

The merits of a squadron-level maintenance cadre, such as unit cohesiveness, esprit-de-corps, and unit mobility, were well understood and appreciated by most. But wartime demands had also revealed some of its weaknesses. The lack of highly skilled or experienced tradesmen and engineering officers compounded by limited resources, such as facilities, tool kits, and spare parts, initially meant that some units suffered more than others. Furthermore, the remoteness, or isolation, of bases and stations was another major influencing factor.[18]

During the war, as the pressure to increase the scope and pace of operations in both the HWE and Overseas War Establishment grew dramatically, so did the need to increase the efficiency and productivity of aircraft maintenance activities. This pressure was particularly noticeable in the RCAF's No. 6 Bomber Group based in the UK. The need to turn around large numbers of bombers for daily or nightly sorties resulted in the squadrons adopting a centralized approach to maintenance

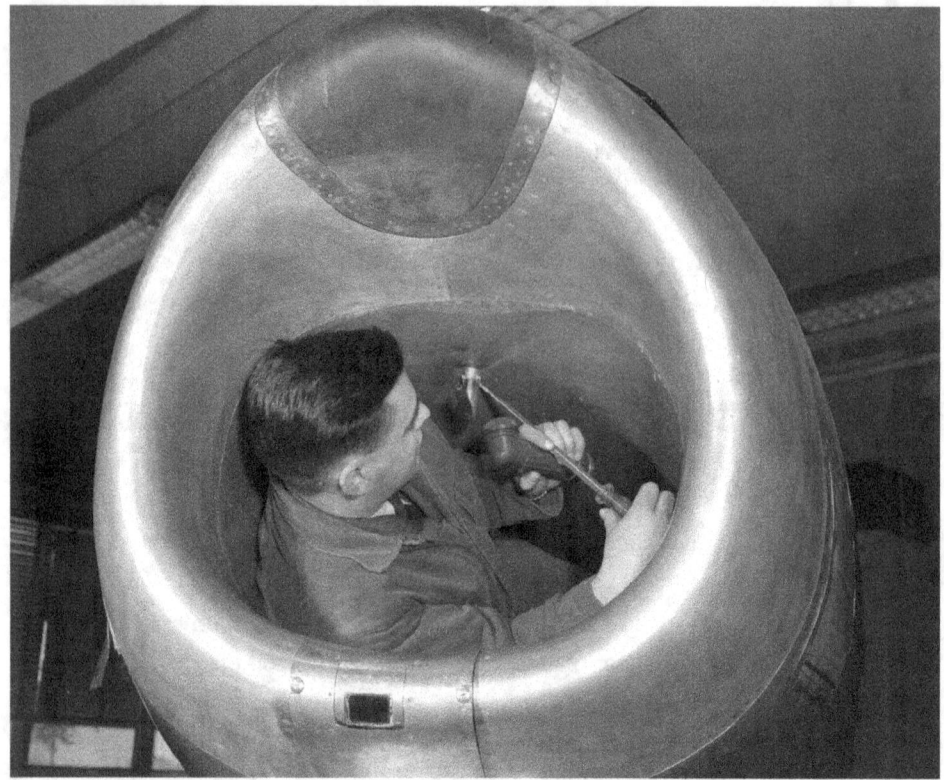

Aircraftsman Second Class James R. MacKenzie, a student at the Technical Training School, RCAF Station Camp Borden, installing a pitot head in the air scoop of an F-86 Sabre.

as was practiced by the RAF. The squadrons retained a small number of personnel to perform first-line servicing including pre- and post-flight checks, "starts and parks," refuelling, and rearming. Meanwhile all second-line functions, including material repairs, overhauls, and specialized support shops, were conducted by a centralized organization commanded by an engineering officer. Third-line and fourth-line activities, depot-level repair, and overhauls relied almost exclusively on civilian industry.[19]

Within the HWE, the exact same pressures existed, particularly within the units supporting the massive BCATP structure. The pressure to increase efficiencies and generate greater numbers of sorties eventually resulted in the adoption of a centralized maintenance approach for all BCATP stations. There was initially considerable grumbling by squadron commanding officers as maintenance personnel and resources were pulled away from their units, but the ensuing rise in maintenance output and sortie generation capability generally put any further objections to rest.[20]

Aerial view of 2 Technical Training School at Camp Borden.

In the postwar decades, a pattern of retaining a mix of squadron-level maintenance organizations for smaller stations, while forming centralized maintenance organizations on larger stations, became the norm within the RCAF.

RCAF Logistics and Maintenance Organizational Structures

From 1923 to 1936, No. 1 (Aircraft) Depot was the RCAF's sole permanent supply and repair depot. By 1936, the first separate supply depot, No. 2 (Equipment) Depot, was formed at Winnipeg. Then in 1937, the first separate repair depot, No. 3 (Repair) Depot, came into being at Vancouver. The number of these units continued to expand through the Second World War with repair and equipment depots spread across Canada.[21]

By 1938, the volume of production and repair in support of the RCAF had grown so much that it was decided to set up air force units in the areas where contractors were most concentrated so that technically experienced service personnel could optimize a number of activities. Principally, these officers and NCOs would assist the contractors in interpreting specifications, report technical progress back to AFHQ, inspect the quality of work as it progressed, and safeguard the Crown in RCAF materiel being supplied to the contractor. The first such unit, No. 11 Technical Detachment (TD), was formed in Montreal in 1938 and, shortly thereafter, No. 12 TD was formed in Toronto. During the war, these types of units were subsumed into various Aeronautical Inspection Districts (AID).

Between 1945 and 1965 the AID organizational structure and nomenclature disappeared but the RCAF retained Technical Service Detachments (TSDs) and Technical Service Units (TSUs) across the country and in the US. These were staffed by a combination of military and civil servant technical personnel whose offices were located at major aircraft manufacturer's plants doing contract work for the RCAF. At the same time the third-line repair and overhaul work done within the RCAF migrated to these civilian firms, and all the military-manned repair depots disappeared except for one. The RCAF was now supported by a singular third-line unit, known initially as No. 6 Repair Depot at RCAF Station Trenton.[22]

RCAF Maintenance Command

Although RCAF technical organizations had been expanded during the war, by 1944 separate aircraft engineering, supply, and construction engineering divisions were merged to become sub-divisions under the Air Member for Support and Organization (AMSO) controlled by an A/V/M. At the same time, the pressures to form a dedicated Maintenance Command Headquarters (MCHQ) became intense. Although forming this new headquarters would reduce the number of personnel at AFHQ, the primary reason behind setting up the new command was to remove from AFHQ the responsibility for the materiel management plan for scaling back the huge inventories of wartime materiel back to a peacetime level with just 14,000 personnel and eight operational squadrons.[23]

The physical management of the vast stocks of materiel, which had been accumulated over five years, had now become a major problem. Accordingly, Reserve Equipment Maintenance Units (REMUs), Reserve Equipment Holding Units (REHUs) for storing aircraft and vehicles, and Surplus Equipment Holding Units for other materiel were established on many of the now defunct flying stations from which aircrew training had been withdrawn. There was a peak of 23 such units in 1945/46. The REMUs later simply became known as "Storage Sites" while the REHUs and SEHUs disappeared entirely.[24]

As AFHQ wanted to devote as much of its energies as possible to policies, planning, and procurement for the postwar period, Maintenance Command (MC) was tasked with the provisioning and supplying of technical instructions, spares, and other direct and indirect support materiel to the other commands in order to enable them to do their own first- and second-line maintenance. It was also tasked with carrying out or managing a range of other functions: third-line maintenance; inspection and acceptance of all contract materiel coming into the RCAF's inventory; and operation of the RCAF third-line (i.e., wholesale level) supply system. A Research & Development (R&D) Division was first created at AFHQ in May 1945 from the AE elements in the AMSO Division. Given its responsibilities, MC Headquarters (MCHQ) was to be staffed by extracting and transferring the majority of the remaining technical elements from AMSO. Therefore, when MCHQ was established, its principal functional staffs were maintenance engineering, construction engineering, and supply.[25]

Maintenance Command was officially established on 6 August 1945, and commenced operations two months later. It had required the intervening weeks to rehabilitate wartime buildings at Uplands, to make and implement detailed organization establishment and procedural decisions, and to segregate and shift the appropriate elements of the various AFHQ staffs and voluminous records from their previous AFHQ offices. Maintenance Command HQ subsequently moved close to AFHQ, relocating to No. 8 Temporary Building, on Dow's Lake in central Ottawa on 1 April 1947.

RCAF Air Material Command

In 1949, Maintenance Command was renamed Air Materiel Command (AMC) and, by 1 September 1954, AMC had relocated to Building 155, a brand new, purpose-built building located at RCAF Station Rockcliffe. The planned role of AMC was to provide materiel logistic support for the RCAF's operational and training commands and the stations and other units which these commands comprised. The purpose of the command, commonly understood, was to ensure "the right thing in the right place at the right time – with utmost economy." The broader function of AMC was to carry out the logistical policies and plans for AFHQ and to provide logistics support for all RCAF activities and organizations.[26]

Although a separate command, AMC ensured that its activities were closely integrated with the Air Member for Technical Services (AMTS) at AFHQ. An intimate relationship was necessary between these two organizations as AMTS staff dealt with logistics and engineering plans and policies. as well as overseeing the purse strings associated with the procurement and construction-engineering budgets. AMC also established and maintained a firm relationship with the Department of Defence Production. This was a necessary interface as Defence Production was the conduit for the procurement of materiel from civilian industry and AMC had a limited, but essential role in representing the RCAF in that conduit.[27]

Factors such as complexity, cost, personnel, and location were key considerations in RCAF logistics and engineering functional support. Operational commands, such as Air Defence, Maritime, and Tactical, were organized and staffed to provide first-line support within squadrons, with second-line support undertaken by their respective stations. Third-line support, however, was the responsibility of AMC depots and units. Much like the policy in previous eras, fourth-line support was arranged by AMC through contracts with domestic or, if required, international commercial aviation firms.[28]

The original plan for AMC's operational structure was to establish two large Air Material Bases (AMB) in Canada, with a third in Europe to serve 1 Air Division. The bases' purpose would be "to combine, at one location, the functions performed by a supply depot, repair depot, construction engineering unit, explosives depot and technical services unit." The RCAF's wartime No. 1 Supply Depot at Downsview, Ontario, would become the AMB, serving eastern Canada, while No. 7 Supply Depot at Namao, Alberta, was designated as the western base. The third AMB, No. 30 AMB at Langar in Nottinghamshire, England, was activated in September 1952. The AMB's in Canada were, however, never were fully set up as a result of budget constraints that began that same year. Consequently, miscellaneous AMC units remained scattered across the country.[29]

Naval Air Service Aircraft Engineering and Maintenance[30]

Prior to integration, the Royal Canadian Navy's (RCN) postwar aviation training and career patterns were largely patterned after that of the Royal Navy's (RN) Fleet Air Arm (FAA). In 1945, when the Air Branch was formed at RCN Air Station (RCNAS) *Dartmouth*,[31] there were only a few technicians with any background in naval aviation, and most were either transfers from the RCAF or on loan from the RN. This meant training a large number of new recruits as air mechanics. After some initial training in metal work at HMCS *Stadacona*, these recruits were sent to the United Kingdom in 1946 for training as air mechanics or riggers. Depending on their actual trade, the sailors remained in the UK for approximately nine months, after which they returned to HMCS *Shearwater* for on-type experience. In 1947-8, another group was sent to Scotland to train as "air artificers," with further training

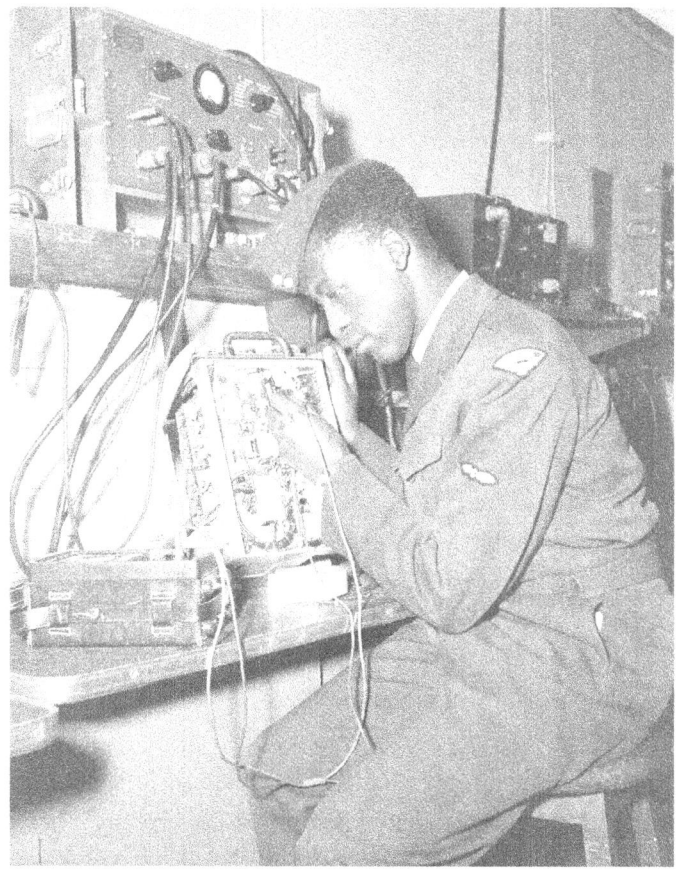

Leading Aircraftsman Whitfield Grant, Communication Technician (Air), stationed at RCAF Station Rockcliffe, checks the VHF Transceiver of the Beechcraft.

for a select number who were to become electricians. These personnel became the nucleus of the RCN's Air Branch technicians who went on to train those that followed as the branch expanded. The establishment of Naval Aircraft Maintenance School (NAMS) enabled the RCN to train its own thereafter, although electrical and radio technicians received most of their training in HMC Electrical School at *Stadacona*.[32]

The officer's air engineering branch was an integral part of the regular RCN career structure, and as such an individual first received training in a number of pure naval fields before deciding on becoming an air engineering officer. As well as an Air Engineering Officer (AEO) branch there was an Air Electrical Engineering

(ALO) branch, and each squadron would have both an AEO and an ALO. There were also a smaller number of officers in the Air Armament and Safety Systems Branches who worked for base support and not directly for any squadron; these two branches were not considered separate engineering fields. After completing his training, an air engineer would be sent to a naval air base at either HMCS *Shearwater, Patricia Bay*, or possibly a reserve unit, and would be attached to a flying squadron at which squadron=level maintenance took place.

A typical base organization consisted of one air engineer commanding officer position, three or four lieutenant commanders, who would be in charge of major repairs and overhaul, and an AEO and ALO Lieutenant (Navy) for each squadron. On each base, there were three types of naval squadrons: training, utility, and operational. An air engineering officer would start his career with either a training or utility squadron and would not serve with an operational land-based or carrier squadron until he had at least two years' experience.

The squadron air engineering officer was expected to be the expert on all the aircraft in his squadron. With no centralized maintenance, the AEO was in charge of both servicing and maintenance. In addition to these roles, each of the AEOs took turns acting as duty engineering officer in the tower. This meant that they were the first line of expertise when a pilot had an in-flight emergency and, therefore, they had to be knowledgeable on all types of aircraft on the base. The air engineer was also typically among the first on the scene for any accident investigation or salvage.

The squadrons themselves were not assigned to any one location but would rotate between base and carrier operations. When the squadron was deployed to a carrier all the squadron personnel, including the engineers, would go with it. A carrier would, in addition, have one AEO and one ALO attached to it, in charge of workshops and support facilities.

There does not appear to have been any formal continuous coordination or co-operation between the RCN air service and the RCAF. At times, however, the RCAF would loan aircraft to the RCN and, under such circumstances, the RCN would have to follow RCAF engineering orders and tie into the RCAF logistics system. Ordinarily, however, because of the aircraft types employed, the air support requirements of RCN would be met by direct logistic pipelines to the Royal Navy or the US Navy.

Army Aviation Maintenance

In the immediate postwar period, because there was no full-time group of aviators within the Canadian Army, aviation had a different status than it did in the RCN

During NATO Exercise Carte Blanche, a 4 (Fighter) Wing maintenance crew remove the tail section of a Sabre to locate a problem with the engine.

and RCAF. The Canadian Army trained people as professionals within their corps or regiment first and then trained some to be flyers as a specialist function. Within this system, it was convenient to rely upon the RCAF for maintenance services.

The air force, thus, accepted the responsibility for army aircraft repair and maintenance including spares provisions, preparation of maintenance schedules, modifications, overhaul, maintenance, and servicing. While this approach was essentially a continuation of the scheme developed for the Air Observation Post (AOP) squadrons during the Second World War, it did not include a dedicated cadre of maintainers. Rather than provide flight line, or squadron maintenance organizations for army aircraft, the RCAF took the alternative approach of assigning maintenance tasks to its already existing air force maintenance organizations. There does not appear to have been any vigorous action on the part of the army to repatriate aviation maintenance so long as the equipment involved was a handful of wartime Auster aircraft used in the immediate postwar period.[33]

One of the first RCAF C-130B Hercules undergoing routine maintenance at RCAF Station Namao, AB.

During the 1950s, however, the Canadian Army decided they needed both more and better aviation support. The 1957 DND budget included an army-funded project to buy both transport and light observation helicopters, as discussed elsewhere in this volume. The increase in number and complexity of army aircraft led directly to the need for an organic army maintenance capability. To meet the army's needs the RCAF technical wing at the Canadian Joint Air Training Centre, RCAF Station Rivers, Manitoba, was given the task of training army personnel in all aircraft trades. And thus, during the autumn of 1961, 52 Royal Canadian Electrical Mechanical Engineers (RCEME) craftsmen and two officers were trained on aircraft maintenance. Highly qualified RCEME vehicle technicians were selected for conversion training, including some who had entered the army through the apprentice training program. The practice of training its aviation maintenance officers as pilots to carry out test flying was also adopted by the RCEME Corps.[34]

In early 1963, the Army created a new unit at Rivers known as the Army Aircraft Maintenance Unit (AAMU). It was to function both as a basic-skills training unit for army aviation tradesmen and as a logistics support unit for all army aircraft at Rivers. In addition, it provided assistance and detailed advice to the army quartermaster general organization in Ottawa on a wide variety of issues including spares scaling. The initial establishment was 168 people, however, by 1964 that number had grown to 210. The army did not skimp on training for its mechanics, and the bulk of the aviation craftsmen could count upon numerous specialist courses with the US Army, principally at Fort Rucker, Alabama.[35]

The maintenance concept followed a traditional RCEME light forward aid detachment (LAD) and backup workshop approach to providing aircraft maintenance. Several aircraft field maintenance squadrons were established as support units that would deploy as and when required. The squadron organizations would provide a first-level servicing and limited repair (typically called "snag" recovery) capability. The field maintenance squadrons also included a number of specialized and special-purpose vehicles in order to provide mobile maintenance facilities.

Impact of Unification[36]

On 1 February 1968, the separate military services were unified into the Canadian Armed Forces with six functional commands: Mobile Command, Maritime Command, Air Defence Command, Air Transport Command, Material Command, and Training Command.[37] All aviation assets were amalgamated within a newly established "Air Element" and, with respect to air maintenance, this created a hybrid of the RCAF, RCN, and Canadian Army approaches, as well as NCM and officer technical trades.

Greater numbers of helicopters were purchased and delivered throughout the early integration years and personnel familiar with helicopter maintenance were as a result initially in short supply for the increased demand. The RCN had the bulk of practiced helicopter maintainers and, therefore, contributed a great deal to the early success of the early Mobile Command helicopter operations. To meet service needs, the former naval helicopter maintenance personnel shifted between the various land-based squadrons, the naval support activities at the newly christened Canadian Forces Base (CFB) Shearwater, or deployment with ships at sea.

The elaborate split in responsibilities for the large postwar RCAF technical trade structure, with 11 separate trades, did not adapt well to smaller and more nimble rotary-wing operations. Consequently, relying on pre-integration army and navy air maintenance approaches, there was a tendency to cross-train technicians to accomplish multiple tasks as opposed the more specialist air force approach. Cross-training also became common on less sophisticated fleets such as Chipmunk and Tutor training aircraft.

The Aerospace Engineer Classification[38]

Pre-integration RCAF engineering officers were either held engineering degress upon entry into the classification or were commissioned from the ranks. With integration, there came a new requirement to create an engineering cadre that drew upon the expertise provided by all three services. As part of the new Air Operations Branch an Aerospace Engineering (AERE) classification was initially formed, retaining the old RCAF sub-specialty classifications of Technical Aeronautical Engineer (Tech AE), Technical Telecommunications (Tech Tel), Technical Armament (Tech Arm) and Technical Photography (Tech Photo). These previous classifications did not, however, restrict the employment of any officer in the new classification.

With integration, RCNAS Air Engineer (similar to Tech AE) and Electrical Air Engineer (corresponding roughly to roles performed by Tech Tel, Tech Arm and Tech Photo) officers were also selected for the AERE classification. Similarly, officers with the Royal Canadian Electrical and Mechanical Engineers (RCEME) having light aircraft and helicopter experience, were offered an option to become AERE officers.

The basic criterion for AERE selection was an involvement, or background, in aircraft maintenance. However, some of the previously mentioned categories were given the option of being assigned to other occupational classifications. For example, Tech Tel officers had the option of becoming AERE or Communication and Electronics Engineer (CELE) officers. Overall, the result of unification was that those classifications previously employed in air maintenance support roles such as electrical, photo and armament officers now could find themselves playing a more direct role in general aircraft maintenance activities.

Training in the four RCAF engineering disciplines, Tech AE, Tech Tel, Tech Photo, and Tech Arm had been carried out at Clinton since 1967 after moving there from RCAF Station Centralia. In June 1969, the Aerospace Engineering Officer Training Company (AOTC) moved to CFB Borden from the Radar and Communications School (R&CS) at Clinton, to become part of the Canadian Forces Aircraft Trades School (CFATS). The decision to relocate to Borden was driven by the desire to amalgamate all air trades training for both officers and NCMs at one location for efficiency and administrative support purposes.

Seen working on an Orenda jet engine from a Sabre jet fighter is Corporal Tom Blyth, an aero engine technician.

Canadian Forces Material Command

By the early 1960s, the RCAF logistics system was the most advanced among the three services and became the model for the Canadian Forces during integration and unification. AMC was disbanded as an RCAF Command on 1 August 1965, on the formation of the new integrated Canadian Forces Materiel Command Headquarters at Rockcliffe. The new organization amalgamated elements of the former RCN and Canadian Army logistics organizations within the RCAF's AMC. The command was charged with providing necessary supply and maintenance support to the other operational commands. Thus, Materiel Command was presented with one of the most formidable tasks of the integration period involving moulding the three dissimilar service systems into a single automated CF supply system. Unlike AMC, the new command had no operational air element units assigned to it.[39]

Aircraft maintenance within Material Command was represented by the Directorate of Aircraft Engineering (DAE) in Building 155 in Rockcliffe; its functions reflected those of previous wartime counterparts, included both aeronautical engineering as well as supply and logistics components. The directorate's responsibilities later expanded to include both air and ground-based communications and radar systems for the "Air Element." After the formation of Air Command in 1975, a corresponding operations-focused maintenance staff was created under the auspices of the deputy chief of staff (maintenance) or DCOS Maint at Air Command HQ in Winnipeg.

Conclusion

While the organizational structure for military aircraft maintenance expanded and contracted during postwar decades, the basic composition, responsibilities, and scope for the staffs involved remained relatively constant. Despite plans for improvements and expanded mandates, the same held true for the ancillary support structures and organizations that followed past philosophy and practice. Operationally, a mix of centralized and squadron-level maintenance organizations were retained. To keep up with the increasing sophistication of technology, however, the number of officer and NCO occupations increased dramatically with up to four different RCAF technical officer sub-categories and more than 11 NCO trades and specialties. The RCN and Canadian Army each developed their own unique approach to maintenance and personnel training. The effect of unification, however, was to simply hybridize the existing aircraft maintenance approaches and practices between the services with increased cross-training of the NCO trades and the creation of a unified AERE officer classification. Regardless of the upheaval brought on by unification, air maintenance personnel, and indeed the entire aerospace organization, adapted to ensure that a high degree of efficiency and professionalism was maintained. No pun intended.

NOTES

1 Information drawn from Fortier, Rénald, *And Look After Our Coasts – The Royal Canadian Air Force and the Production of Coastal Defence Aircraft in Canada, 1936–1939* (Ottawa: Canada Aviation & Space Museum, 2007).

2 W.A.B. Douglas, *The Official History of the Royal Canadian Air Force, Volume II, The Creation of a National Air Force* (Toronto: University of Toronto Press, 1986), 141. It had been the unofficial policy in all branches of the military that their combat equipment should be identical to that used by the British forces.

3   Ibid., 140.
4   Levels of support are defined as follows: first-line support as maintenance capabilities that are organic to a unit or a squadron; second-line support capabilities that are organic to a wing / main operating base; Third-line support capabilities include major repairs or refurbishment by military organic to the service or by civilian technical personal; and fourth-line support capabilities are provided by national-level resources, such as national depots, contractors, and industry.
5   In the earliest days of aircraft maintenance, riggers dealt with the riggings of airframes, ensuring that the wings, fuselage, and other control surfaces were properly joined by rigging wires, etc. Fitters were responsible for the fitting of the engines as well as the fittings between various other parts of the power train.
6   Camp Borden was officially opened on 11 July 1916 as a militia training area, while the associated RFC (Canada) airfield was stood up in February 1917. The RCAF subsequently took over the airfield in the earliest days of this service.
7   T.F.J. Leversedge, "The Forgotten Legacy – 1 TTS," *Airforce Magazine*, 39, no. 1 (June 2015): 34–7.
8   Author's collection, Herbert Sutherland, "Saturday's Children – The Story of People Who Look After Airplanes: A Recollected History of Canadian Military Aviation Maintenance," unpublished manuscript, 188–94.
9   Ibid.
10 Directorate of History and Heritage (DHH), File 74/21, "Airmen's Technical Training, 1920–1944."
11 Direct entry officers were recruited for their existing qualifications. Apart from orientation to the military, these officers required no additional technical or skills training.
12 DHH, File 74-21, "The School of Aeronautical Engineering, Officers, Senior N.C.O.'s and W.O.'s, 1940–1944," 1–3. Leckie, a highly decorated flying-boat pilot in the First World War, remained with the RAF after the Great War, and returned to Canada early in 1940 where he served as Air Member for Training, 1940–4 and oversaw the BCATP. He transferred to the RCAF in 1942 and was appointed CAS, 1944–7.
13 Ibid., 11.
14 "Saturday's Children…," 196–8.
15 Ibid., 198–201. The RCAF trades at this time consisted of Airframe, Aero-Engine, Integral Systems, Communications & Radar, Avionics, Instrumental Electrical, Safety Systems, Armament, Metals, Machinist and Refinishing technicians along with further specialties in Photo, Explosive Ordnance Disposal and eventually Non-Destructive Testing.
16 Ibid.
17 Ibid.
18 G/C J.A. Verner, "Maintenance of Technical Equipment in the R.C.A.F.," *The Roundel* 4, no. 1 (April 1952).
19 Author's Collection, Canada, Department of National Defence, "AERE History Brief," 4640-2574-83 (AERE), Borden, ON, Canada, 1980.
20 Ibid.
21 For additional detail for this section see A/V/M C.L. Annis, "The Evolution of Air Material Command," *The Roundel* 14, no. 4 (May 1962): 4–10.
22 Later known as the Aerospace Maintenance & Development Unit (AMDU).
23 Annis, 10.
24 Ibid., 8.
25 Ibid., 9–10.

26 Ibid., 4.
27 Bertram C. Frandsen, "The Rise and Fall of Canada's Cold War Air Force, 1948–1968" (PhD Diss., Wilfrid Laurier University, 2015), 201.
28 Ibid.
29 Ibid., 202.
30 Unless otherwise noted, material in this section is taken from Author's Collection, Canada, Department of National Defence, "AERE History Brief" 4640-2574-83 (AERE), Borden, ON, Canada, 1980.
31 The RCN followed RN naming traditions; therefore, shore establishments, such as *Dartmouth*, *Stadacona*, etc., are referred to as "ships," hence the names are italicized. The RCN Air Stations were also known as HMCS "*name.*"
32 Eric Edgar, "A Story of the Technicians of the Canadian Naval Air Branch," *Warrior*, (Spring, 2010): 35.
33 Sutherland, 230.
34 Ibid., 230–1.
35 Ibid., 231.
36 Unless otherwise noted, material in this section is drawn from Sutherland, *Saturday's Children*.
37 Allan English and John Westrop, *Canadian Air Force Leadership and Command: The Human Dimension of Expeditionary Air Operations* (Trenton, Ontario: CF Aerospace Warfare Centre, 2007), 47.
38 Unless otherwise noted, material in this section is taken from Author's Collection, Canada, Department of National Defence, "AERE History Brief," 4640-2574-83 (AERE), Borden, ON, Canada, 1980.
39 Paul Hellyer, "Address on the Canadian Forces Reorganization Act, December 7, 1966, quote in Douglas L. Bland, editor, *Canada's National Defence*, Volume 2, *Defence Organization* (Kingston, Ontario: Queen's University School of Policy Studies, 1998), 126–7.

CHAPTER NINE

THE FORGOTTEN DECADE: WOMEN AND THE RCAF, 1952–1962

ALLAN ENGLISH

During the 1950s and early 1960s thousands of young Canadian women served in the Royal Canadian Air Force. The over 17,000 women who served in the RCAF Women's Division (WD) in the Second World War blazed a trail for them, but those who served in the early days of the Cold War carved out their own paths. In so doing, they helped to transform the RCAF from a tiny pre-1939 group of "bush pilots in uniform" into a large, modern force that assumed responsibility for the welfare of thousands of families whose well-being was critical to the morale of its skilled personnel and was an important factor in reducing attrition.[1] However, the story of these women has been largely forgotten as there is no comprehensive history of the RCAF during the Cold War, as other chapters in this volume and other works on the RCAF during the Cold War make little mention of airwomen and only minor references to families.[2] Looking at the RCAF through a different lens, this chapter, therefore, provides a preliminary examination of some of their experiences in the hope that it will encourage others to tell their story in more detail.

Women's wartime service in the WDs was always understood to be for the duration of the war only; therefore, after the war, with the government planning to reduce the military to pre-war levels, the last WD was discharged from the RCAF in December 1946. A small number of women did remain, serving in the RCAF medical branch as nurses.[3] As seen in Section 1, however, with the increasing tensions of the Cold War, the government decided to allocate a considerable portion of its defence resources to the air force, especially in the roles of protecting North America from Soviet nuclear-armed bomber attack and defending Western Europe, through NATO, from Warsaw Pact attacks. Consequently, the RCAF

Leading Airwoman Mary Honeyman, an aircraft refinisher at 104 Composite Flight, St Hubert, QC, putting the finishing touches to the maple lead insignia on a Dakota.

expanded rapidly, increasing fourfold in size in seven years, becoming Canada's largest fighting service by 1955, and remaining so until unification in 1969, reaching a Cold War peak of 53,119 in 1962.[4] Due to manpower shortages and their impressive service during the war, the RCAF decided that bringing women into the air force was essential to its successful expansion, thus up to 10 per cent or about 5,000 of the RCAF's strength, was authorized to be women.[5] Despite this goal, the service was hard pressed to maintain its airwomen strength at 60 per cent of that number. Nonetheless, this was significantly more than the small number of women in the other two services (90 in the army in 1954 and 400 in the navy in 1955).[6] Despite early successes in employing women, by 1966 there were fewer than 600 still serving in the air force.[7]

Many questions remain to be answered about the RCAF's employment of women in the 1950s and early 1960s. For example, why did it not recruit women up to the authorized strength in the 1950s, and why did it decide to stop recruiting women in 1962? And, why, despite opening most trades to women, did it stop employing women in roles where in wartime and in the 1950s they had already proved themselves capable? This chapter will offer answers to some of these questions; however, it is only a first step towards understanding the part women played in the RCAF at the beginning of the Cold War. This chapter, as reflected in its title, is about women *and* the RCAF because it examines the contributions of not only those women who served in uniform, but also some of the contributions the wives of airmen made to the RCAF. A significant number of these wives were airwomen who met their future spouses while serving and, once married, remained part of the air force community. They often raised their children in air force married quarters, sent them to air force administered schools, especially overseas and on semi-remote stations in Canada, and maintained social contacts through mess events and recreation and sports activities held in the station facilities where they lived. The story of Leading Airwoman (LAW) May Beaverstock (née LaPierre) is an example of an airwoman's experience at the time. She was in the first draft of women sent to RCAF Station Grostenquin, France, where she worked as a Telecom Performance Checker (Ground) in 1953. She recounted later that "I worked in the Telecommunication area and my main responsibility was installation and repair of the phones on the station. So mostly I was climbing to tops of hangars, poles, etc…" Eight months after arriving at Grostenquin she married an airman she met there and then left the RCAF. She had her first child in the station hospital in September 1954, 10 months after her marriage. Beaverstock left Grostenquin in November 1955 with her husband and child when he was posted back to Canada, "…in a much different way than when I arrived as a single serviceperson. I was now married with one son and another on the way."[8]

The RCAF and the Employment of Women

Policies regulating the participation of women in Canada's armed forces have evolved over time in response to changes in Canadian society and the need for human resources. For example, in the First World War, unlike Britain where, between 1918 and 1920, 32,000 served in the Women's Royal Air Force, other than nurses, no women served in the Canadian military.[9] However, while Canadian women did serve in auxiliary roles such as volunteer nurses' aides, ambulance drivers, and clerical staff, a remarkable story is found in their participation in the Royal Flying Corps/Royal Air Force Canada (RFC/RAF Canada) flying training scheme, the predecessor of the British Commonwealth Air Training Plan of the Second World

Airwoman Elizabeth Boyko, an air control operator with 418 Squadron, works the tower at RCAF Station Rivers, Manitoba.

War. Due to a shortage of men, almost 2,000 women were employed in a civilian capacity by RFC/RAF Canada; some were clerks and drivers, but the majority were employed in the "technical trades" with almost 600 classed as "mechanics."[10] The acceptance of women in these roles was in stark contrast to the prevailing Canadian attitude that women should remain in the domestic sphere and not work outside the home, especially in jobs usually reserved for men like aircraft mechanics. This is an early example where the demand for workers transcended the prevailing social mores, which was demonstrated in the Second World War when airwomen were eligible to work in 69 of 102 RCAF trades, including traditionally male-dominated occupations such as aircraft maintenance and air traffic control. Nevertheless, they were initially paid only two-thirds of what men received in the same occupation, until, at the urging of RCAF senior officers, in July 1943 their pay was raised to 80 per cent of an airman's wage. While they were banned from combat and from flying in general, some WDs, such as photographers, did perform flying duties wearing "one-piece coveralls, armed with a camera and a heavy parachute on her back that hung down to her knees."[11]

During the war, many Canadian parents feared that a woman's reputation would suffer if she joined the military and was unsupervised by her family. These views led to whisper campaigns accusing women in the service of leading immoral lives. Therefore, the commander of the RCAF (WD), Wing Officer Willa Walker, crisscrossed the country speaking to groups and organizations in an effort to change the public perception of women in uniform. One of her most persuasive arguments to get parents to let their daughters join the RCAF was that "Life in the air force is a wonderful background for marriage …A marriage is going to mean so much more, because of the experience the man and woman have shared together in uniform. A girl who has been in the service will be able to understand her husband better – because she'll know what he's been through." In a testament to Walker's success in raising and training this rapidly expanding organization, the head of the British Women's Auxiliary Air Force, after which the RCAF WD was modelled, on an inspection visit to Canada called the WDs' performance "absolutely first-class. The thing that has impressed me is their enthusiasm…their cheerful, keen attitude to do the job they are doing. People still don't realize just how colossal it is."[12]

Canada's postwar economic boom led to high employment and prosperity. After the war women working outside the home were more accepted by society, and, while women's participation in the Canadian workforce declined by 9 per cent from 1945–7, the increasing demand for workers meant that women quickly re-entered the workforce, including married women whose participation more than doubled from less than 4 per cent in 1941 to 11 per cent in 1951and doubled again to 22 per cent by 1961.[13]

This time of full employment made the RCAF's enormous Cold War expansion difficult. The air force had reached its postwar nadir of 12,017 in 1948 and in 1951 it was authorized to increase its strength to 50,000. One strategy to achieve its expansion goals was the enrol women to comprise up to 10 per cent of this number.[14] Unlike the Second World War, women were no longer enrolled in a separate division of the air force but joined the regular RCAF with the same rates of pay as men. At first 28 trades were open to them, but by 1958, 63 trades were open to

RCAF Nursing Sister E.R. Kelly at the station hospital, Trenton, Ontario.

women.[15] During the 1950s and early 1960s, most airwomen worked at semi-isolated Canadian radar sites and in Europe, as Fighter Control Operators (FCOps) or "Fighter Cops." This was considered to be a "prestigious" job as it required passing a demanding 20-week course followed by numerous other courses to update skills as technology changed.[16] FCOps were a key part of a largely manual air defence command and control system (described elsewhere in this volume), similar to that used in the Battle of Britain, that tracked aircraft in areas of radar coverage, identified those that might be hostile, and then dispatched and directed fighters to intercept "hostiles." With the introduction of the computer assisted Semi-Automatic Ground Environment (SAGE) air defence system starting in the late 1950s, the FCOp trade was phased out.[17] However, the RCAF continued to recruit and train female FCOps until 1 January 1963, when it stopped recruiting women entirely, and by 1966 there were only 530 women still serving.[18] The closing of the FCOp trade provides one explanation for the reduced employment opportunities for women, but why, despite opening most trades to women, did the RCAF stop employing women in jobs where they had already proven themselves capable? One answer is the high attrition rate among airwomen in the 1950s.

Why Women Joined the Air Force

Some may wonder why women joined the RCAF given the military discipline and, by today's standards, lack of freedom. Looking back from the early twentieth century, the glass of RCAF service for women may look half empty, but for those who were attracted to the air force, the glass looked half full. Many of the women who joined the RCAF in these years were born between 1933 and 1944 and grew up during both the Depression and the Second World War. Life was not always easy for them as many families faced employment challenges, shortages of food and clothing, and rationing during the war. Living conditions could be primitive by today's standards, with crowded accommodation, limited entertainment opportunities, and often insufficient medical and dental care.[19] During this era, young women had few opportunities for travel, and it was not unusual for them to live in communities where their behaviour was under constant scrutiny by their parents, relatives, and neighbours. Interactions with men were closely controlled, and women often had a limited choice of potential partners, usually men from their local area.[20] Rita Jordan provides an example of this life as she lived in several communities in Alberta before she joined the RCAF. She tells us that if she wanted to spend any time with a young man, she had to ask her parents' permission. She considered joining the air force to get away from the constraints of life in a small community, and her parents were not happy when, on turning 18, Rita announced that she had decided to join the air force. But join she did and went to St-Jean, Quebec for her basic training in January 1952. After training as a FCOp she served at a semi-isolated radar site, RCAF Station Lac St. Denis, Quebec, 60 miles north of Montreal. Rita left the air force in 1954, after two years of service, to marry her civilian boyfriend back in Medicine Hat, Alberta.[21]

According to research done by the RCAF in the mid 1950s, some young women, like Rita, were looking to get away from home, to travel, to meet new people and to do meaningful work. The air force offered these opportunities plus pay and amenities that might seem appealing to women living at home with little disposable income.[22] They saw air force life as a chance to meet, work, and socialize with young people their own age from all over Canada, a new experience for most. Also, their basic needs were taken care of by the air force – three meals a day, free medical and dental care (in Canada's pre-Medicare days this was unusual), employment

Four styles of Airwomen's uniforms displayed during a fashion show at Rockcliffe. Left to right: summer dress uniform, summer cotton working dress, slacks and shirts for special trades, blue dress uniform.

in challenging jobs, and a good salary.[23] Outside of duty hours, the RCAF exercised very little control over women's social lives. There was some supervision when participating in activities on station like sports (including organized station teams) dances, section parties, movies at the station cinema, and watching TV in the messes and quarters, but even given this supervision these sorts of amenities were simply unavailable to many Canadian women living at home at the time.[24] Service life, despite these sorts of drawbacks, was seen by many women who joined the RCAF as better than the life they would have at home. In addition, when not on duty or on leave, women were free to go off station in civilian clothes and many had access to cars, enabling them to socialize away from any direct supervision. Trips to the beach or travel to cities in Canada and Europe in "civvies" meant that they were anonymous and free to do many things they could not do at home, including

RCAF Fighter Control Operators in action, January 1956.

drinking, smoking, and engaging in intimate relationships if they wished. On base, the "wet canteen" (for junior ranks), where there was little enforcement of provincial drinking age limits, served beer and wine and was the site of many informal parties where frequently lots of alcohol was consumed.[25] Intimate partners were easy to meet and access to contraceptives, through the station clinic or hospital, was relatively easy compared to civilian society, as contraception was technically illegal in Canada until 1969.[26]

Another indication of airwomen's independence and resistance to social control was very low church attendance by single service members. During the Second World War, attendance at church was often compulsory, enforced by weekly "church parades," the intent being to demonstrate to the public that servicewomen were respectable, moral young ladies, like their female counterparts in civilian life.[27] After the war such parades were rare, and one station Commanding Officer said that without families church services would be "very sparsely attended" as "the younger element" displayed "a certain apathy" towards attending "religious services."[28] Despite this newfound freedom, women in the RCAF were generally portrayed very favourably in the media, with stories in two of Canada's largest circulation weekend magazines declaring that an airwoman's life included "Good pay and lots of fun" and "They find good companionship while working and playing together."[29] The RCAF reinforced this impression by co-operating with filmmakers. In one instance, the 1955 documentary-style film *Radar Station*, airwomen are portrayed as vital members of the air defence team protecting North America from the Soviet bomber threat.[30] The 1957 film *Airwomen* made in a promotional style, begins with an attractive airwoman being driven to a radar station by a handsome young man in a sports car. It then shows her working as a FCOp there, participating in social events like dances, and ends with her posting to Germany where she visits some tourist attractions with another airwoman and meets her brother and his fighter pilot squadron mates who are also stationed there.[31] As depicted in *Airwomen*, many of those serving in the RCAF found that their independence from their families gave them the ability to choose a spouse from a much wider pool than would be available at home.

Marriage: Finding a Spouse or a "Short-Cut to Release"?

Many young people at this time aspired to have some time in their late teens and early 20s to experience life on their own followed by marriage, settling down, and raising a family. In the 1950s, the average age of marriage for women in Canada was 23 and remained so "well into the 1970s."[32] In 1957, there were 325 airwomen (average age 23) and 500 fighter pilots (average age 23) on the strength of the RCAF Air Division in Europe.[33] Contemporary sources, including RCAF surveys of airwomen, stated that most women did not want to make the air force a career but were keen to be independent and meet others their age outside of their existing social circle, and perhaps a spouse, because, for this generation, "marriage, for both men and women, signified maturity, responsibility, and an end to the dependency of childhood."[34] As we have seen, the RCAF provided an environment where they could meet these aspirations.

Airwomen frequently married airmen they met while in the service, and then settled down to raise a family. Marrying an airman came with many advantages: for example, a partner who shared the same interests and military experience, financial security, good accommodation, access to medical care, recreation facilities for families, and children's educational needs provided by the RCAF in many places. Another advantage was continued access to a mess-based social life with many

A class of Fighter Control Operators are seen plotting during a practical operations class.

friends who also lived in military accommodation. At the time, there was also a reasonable chance of a posting to Europe and the chance to sample living and travelling abroad. Not all was rosy, however, as frequent postings and the absence of a spouse on courses or detachments could be a hardship. But with moves paid for by the service and many amenities provided by the air force on stations, life as a service spouse could be a very attractive option compared to Civvy street.[35]

Following policies first introduced during the war, in most cases women had to leave the service after they married, and this led to very high attrition rates among airwomen. Air force regulations were changed in December 1953, allowing a trade-qualified married airwoman to remain in the service as long as her marriage would not "interfere with her usefulness to the service."[36] However, she had to leave the air force if she became pregnant, and the continuing high attrition rate among airwomen was a serious personnel resource problem for the RCAF in the 1950s and early 1960s.[37] Much more research needs to be done in this area, but fragmentary data shows that between March 1951, when Cabinet officially approved the recruitment of women into the RCAF, and February 1954, of the 1,713 airwomen who were released from the RCAF, 1,351 or 80 per cent were "released as unsuitable for reasons other than misconduct, inefficiency or medical unfitness," a category that until October 1952 included release for marriage. Thereafter, between 1952 and 1954, 307 women were released for marriage and "the release of airwomen peaked with 1,137 releases between January 1953 and February 1954."[38]

We can also get clues to the reasons for this attrition from the records of No. 31 Aircraft Control and Warning (AC&W) Squadron at RCAF Station Edgar, located 20 km northeast of Barrie, Ontario. The records show that the air force initially embraced with enthusiasm the employment of women. For example, on 31 May 1954, just as the station was becoming operational, the squadron reported its "operational strength" as 158 personnel.[39] Of the 129 below the rank of corporal almost 80 per cent (102 airwomen and 27 airmen) were female, most of them FCOps.[40] As late as 1961, women still comprised a large majority of the "operational strength" of some radar sites; for example RCAF Station St. Sylvestre, Quebec, reported that almost 70 per cent of its "operations crew" below the rank of corporal was female.[41] This is a situation unique in Canadian military history, where a large majority of personnel on an operational unit was women. Yet, one year after Edgar reported an "operational strength" that was 80 per cent women, that dropped to 40 per cent and fluctuated between about 20 per cent and 40 per cent thereafter, until the station closed in 1964.[42] Why this precipitous drop? Part of the answer can be found in some of the official reports from Edgar, which illustrate conditions at many new semi-isolated stations. They tell us that in the first year or so of its existence, the conditions at Edgar, like many others radar stations being built at the time, were "intolerable."[43] Delays in construction and poor planning led to overcrowded accommodation, high sick rates, poor food, misemployment of junior ranks (i.e., doing menial tasks instead of the technical duties for which they had been trained), and a general lack of amenities. This situation must have been a great disappointment to new members of the air force, and it resulted in poor morale and discipline at Edgar. While airmen had no choice but to serve out their engagements, airwomen had a way out of these conditions – announcing that they were getting married. The precipitous drop in the number of airwomen on the squadron is explained in a November 1953 official report that showed that 50 per cent of No. 31 AC&W Squadron's airwoman strength had applied for release since the unit had been activated 20 months previously, most giving intended marriage as a reason. Subsequent investigations by the station found that many of these women did not marry but used it as a "short-cut to

Airwomen in training practice their drill. Female recruits made up a substantial portion of new inductees into the RCAF during the 1950s.

release."[44] The policy of not allowing married women to serve appears to have caused, at least in this case, an untenable personnel situation for the station, leading to fewer airwomen and more airmen being posted into the unit subsequently. If other units' experiences reflect the situation at Edgar, and some official reports suggest that they did (for example in 1953 the attrition of airwomen at RCAF Station Whitehorse was 40 per cent)[45] it would provide one reason why the RCAF decided not to recruit women to their authorized strength and to stop recruiting them once there were enough men available to fill its ranks.

The high attrition rate caused by airwomen requesting release for marriage was compounded by their terms of service. They were engaged for 36 months, but it took between 18 and 22 months to fully train them for many trades, including FCOps. In the late 1950s the RCAF found that women served on average for 30 to

36 months; therefore, women were only being gainfully employed in their chosen trade for between 8 to 18 months. Men in the same occupations, because of their five-year engagement contract, were generally employed for at least 36 months. The RCAF examined the possibility of longer contracts for women but no action was taken.[46] Nonetheless, the RCAF often found creative ways to keep married airwomen on strength. For example, LAW Dorine Roberts (née Weagle) was an accounts clerk at RCAF Station Grostenquin. She arrived with the first draft of airwomen in March 1953 and married an airman she met there in February 1955, but to keep her working in her job until her replacement arrived, she recounts that "with some possible collusion between the Senior Accounts Officer and the Senior Medical Officer, it seems that my records were misplaced so that I remained in the RCAF" until November 1955 at which point she was seven months pregnant.[47]

More research needs to be done on this topic, but what we do know from the limited information on the attrition of airwomen in the 1950s and early 1960s is that a significant proportion of the female strength of the RCAF was leaving every year. Attrition peaked at 35 per cent in 1953, and the attrition rate for airwomen was four to five times higher than for airmen. This problem could not be resolved by the air force and was a key reason for the decision to stop recruiting women in 1962.[48] But for many airwomen, marriage did not end their connection with the RCAF. They continued to be part of a large air force community of families that produced a transformation in the air force unparalleled in its history.

Families

For most of its history, Canada's small peacetime armed forces had treated family welfare as an afterthought, at best. That changed after the Second World War with the creation of large standing armed forces that included significant numbers of married servicemen with families. In 1953, in response to the Soviet and Warsaw Pact threat, Canada began to increase its military strength significantly to over 100,000 and maintained this strength for the next 15 years, reaching its peak of 126,474 in 1962.[49] These larger forces required many new bases both in Canada and overseas.

The unprecedented peacetime expansion of Canada's armed forces presented particular problems for the RCAF as it depended on a stable, highly skilled workforce to operate and maintain its aircraft, radars, and other technical systems. It recognized that to limit attrition in a workforce whose members moved to new bases every few years, it had to invest in making the service an attractive career for married servicemen. One way of doing this was to provide accommodation and amenities

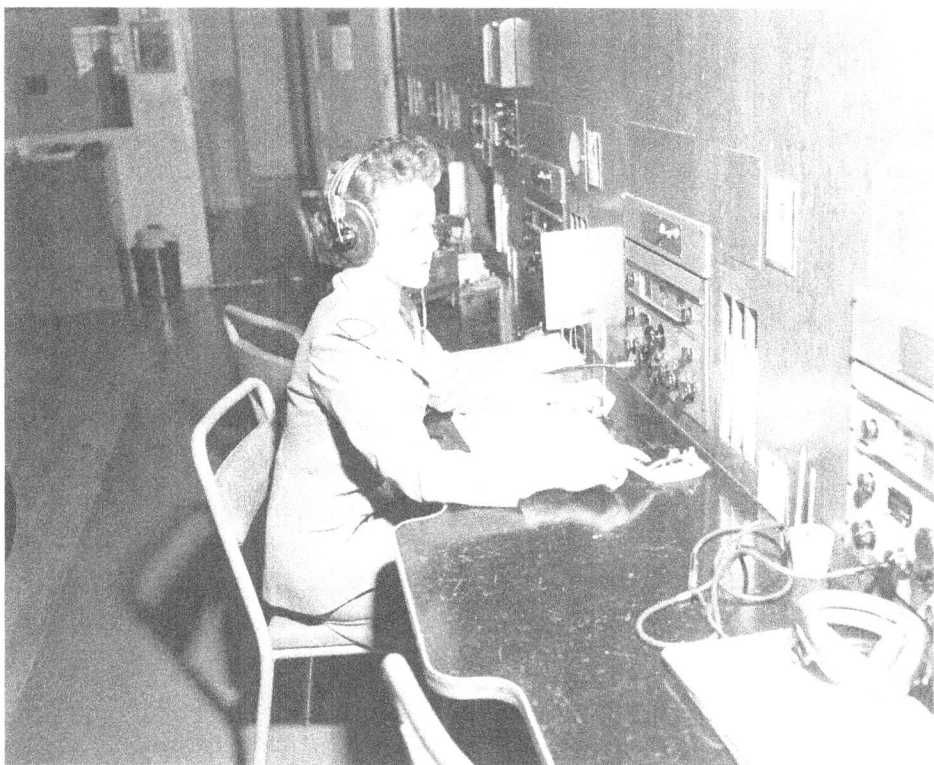

Leading Airwoman D. Crouset at the Morse-code key in the operations room, RCAF Station Greenwood, NS.

for families at all bases and schools for dependent children, where there were no local public schools.[50] One of the RCAF's Cold War challenges was staffing some 44 semi-isolated radar stations across Canada. These stations comprised small communities of up to 600 people, with about 150 to 200 servicemen and servicewomen, and about 85 civilian employees, plus families.[51] Due to their remote locations, they were "self-contained" towns with RCAF standard pattern "military housing and barracks, a school, a recreation centre with a bowling alley and swimming pool, an infirmary, a chapel, a firehall, a water treatment and distribution facility, a central heating plant, auto repair shops, cafeteria facilities and sports fields."[52]

In addition to the new bases in Canada, in the early 1950s the Air Division, described in chapter 2 of this collection, began to arrive in Europe, based at first temporarily in the United Kingdom and then permanently on the continent. At full strength in 1957, the RCAF's No. 1 Air Division was a very large organization consisting of four wings of 12 squadrons located at four main bases, two in France and two in Germany. Throughout most of its existence from 1952–67 it had an authorized strength of about 6,000 personnel of which approximately 5 per cent (over 300) were servicewomen. In addition, there were about 1,600 civilian employees and 5,300 families (2,200 wives and 3,100 children).[53] Initially the air force hoped to avoid the cost and effort of dealing with families in Europe by posting servicemen there for short, unaccompanied tours of duty. Despite this policy, "many wives with children followed their husbands to France and Germany at their own expense, calculating that six months" to one year "in Europe was likely to be more stimulating and educational then waiting with the kids on a base somewhere in Canada."[54] However, in the 1950s, France and Germany were still recovering from the devastation of the Second World War, and life was not easy for families arriving in Europe on their own as rationing was still in effect for some "luxury" items, such as coffee, tea, nylons, cigarettes, and liquor. Therefore, while rationed items could be purchased duty free, amounts were limited to prevent black market re-selling; for example, cigarette purchases were limited to 200 per week, alcohol to two bottles of liquor per week, coffee to one pound per adult per month, and nylons to two pairs monthly to women over 18 years of age. Despite these hardships, there were perks. Automobiles could be purchased tax free, either in Canada and shipped overseas or in Europe, and in Europe gasoline could be purchased on Canadian or American bases at one half the rate on the "open market."[55]

Housing was in short supply because government-provided accommodation such as married quarters did not exist. Therefore, the first families to arrive had to take what they could find, either apartments rented "on the local economy" or in temporary accommodation at trailer parks near the bases.[56] Four months after the RCAF station at Grostenquin opened, "there were 53 children of school age living in a big trailer camp next to the Base with no education facilities available to them and the nearest French town with schools was 10 miles away."[57] To meet the need for schooling the children "temporary ad hoc schools [were] started with mothers with teaching experience as volunteer teachers."[58]

At first, the service was not concerned with this state of affairs because, officially, there were no Canadian families overseas; however, RCAF station commanders reported that the lack of facilities for families was causing morale and welfare problems that were affecting the performance of airmen at work, and therefore the effectiveness of the Air Division. The RCAF at this point realized that it had to deal with this problem, and in August 1953 it changed its posting policy to four years for those married servicemen accompanied by dependents. The policy did not apply to airwomen as they had to remain single or, if later married to an airman at the same station,

Aircraftsman G.D. Flanna is shown how to check a CF-100 Canuck fighter electrical system by Leading Airwoman J. Wennick.

to remain in the air force. This policy change had an immediate effect on those already in Europe as "many officers and airmen indicated their desire to extend their tour …."[59] With the rapid influx of families, the building of married quarters and schools was then "given a high priority," with "unused barrack blocks" being converted into schools while new ones were being built. Thereafter, the Canadian military dependents' school system in Europe continued to grow, reaching its peak in the academic year 1968–69 with 8,676 students enrolled in 22 Canadian schools, staffed by 530 teachers who were hired on contract from provincial school boards to teach curricula equivalent to those taught in Canada.[60] An illustration of how this new posting policy affected the RCAF's responsibility for families overseas is that in 1959, seven years after the first group of RCAF personnel arrived, the Air Division reported that there were 4,699 families with 8,652 children housed in 2,015 newly constructed married quarters. Typical amenities for families to be found at an RCAF station in

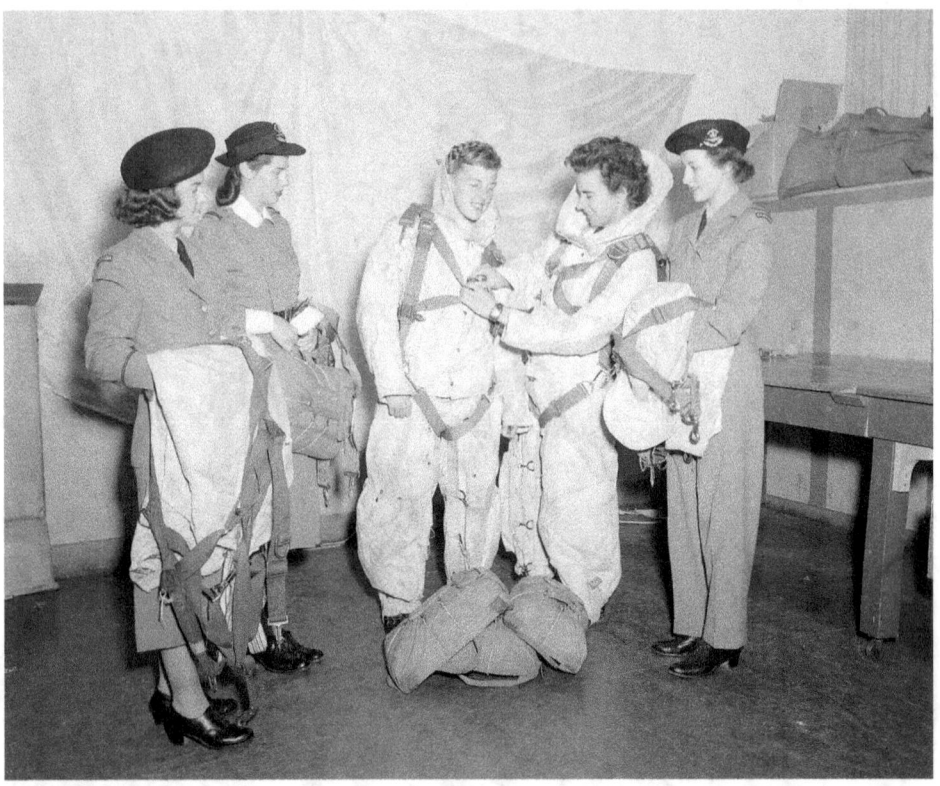

RCAF Nursing Sisters being fitted for para-rescue clothing in preparation for undertaking the para-rescue course. Qualified Nursing Sisters were expected to jump into crash sites to treat casualties as part of RCAF search and rescue operations.

Europe were "Station Store (PX), Grocery and butcher store, Snack Bar, Airmen's Canteen, Corporals Club, Theatre, Auto Club, Dental Clinic, Bowling alleys, Barber and Beauty Parlour, Hobby Shop."[61] By 1963, there were as many as 31 different amenities available for families at most RCAF stations.[62] As the families arrived in number, a major challenge for the RCAF was the provision of medical and dental care for them as local health care, with different professional practice customs and standards given in a foreign language, was deemed unsuitable for Canadian dependents. Consequently, the RCAF established an extensive medical and dental care system at all wings that included out-patient clinics with "pre- and post-natal baby care," station hospitals with "full obstetric and nursery facilities," a free school health service, and a dental clinic. In addition, the station hospital at 3 (F) Wing, Zweibrücken, Germany, had a "surgical-obstetrical specialist team that will take care of cases beyond the capabilities of other wings." Furthermore, cases beyond the capability of RCAF specialists could be referred to large US military hospitals in the area. The cost of all care was subsidized by the government and generally dependents were charged two-thirds of the Department of Veterans Affairs rates. Many of these costs could be covered by private medical insurance, which was compulsory for all dependents proceeding overseas.[63] The RCAF also provided trained social workers, many of them in uniform, to assist families where needed.[64]

Former airwomen were a significant, but as yet untold, part of this story of the Cold War transformation of the RCAF from an organization that paid little attention to families to one that provided a substantial range of amenities, both in Canada and overseas, for them. This newfound concern for family welfare was born of the necessity of maintaining the morale and efficiency of service personnel and of retaining them in the air force, something that was key to the RCAF's Cold War successes.

Conclusion

Between 1952 and 1962 as many as 10,000, or perhaps more, women served in the RCAF.[65] The experiences of these airwomen, and former airwomen who remained in the air force community after marrying and leaving the service, might not be described as halcyon, but they were unique in the annals of Canadian military history. For some writers today, the RCAF in the 1950s was a glass-half-empty situation for airwomen because not all occupations were open to them, and it was difficult for them to make the RCAF a career. However, for some young women at the time it was a glass-half-full situation because they had more work opportunities than in civilian life, were paid well, had all their basic needs provided by the air force, and had the chance to enjoy freedoms they could not in their home communities. Many only wanted to serve in the air force for a short period of time before marrying and raising a family, with matrimony seen by both men and women at the time as a rite of passage to adulthood and independence. Despite the short time most airwomen served, they made a vital contribution to the RCAF during its rapid Cold War expansion.

Furthermore, many airwomen married airmen they met when posted to semi-isolated stations or to Europe. When married, these women, for the most part, did not return to their, or their husbands', hometown but joined the RCAF community of families moving from station to station every two to four years. Despite the moves, they enjoyed a measure of stability in their lives as almost all RCAF stations provided for most of their family's needs. The 1950s marked a new era for the RCAF when, for the first time, it found it necessary to invest substantial resources to provide for the welfare of the families of its servicemen. It is somewhat ironic that the Canadian Armed Forces today is beginning to emphasize the importance of supporting families to ensure the well being of servicemembers[66] – a lesson the RCAF learned almost 70 years ago.

NOTES

1 W.A.B. Douglas, *The Official History of the Royal Canadian Air Force. Vol. 2: The Creation of a National Air Force* (Toronto: University of Toronto Press, 1986), 91–118.
2 Raymond Stouffer, *Swords, Clunks and Widowmakers: The Tumultuous Life of the RCAF's Original 1 Canadian Air Division* (Trenton, ON: Canadian Forces Aerospace Warfare Centre, 2015); Bertram Frandsen, "The Rise and Fall of Canada's Cold War Air Force, 1948–1968" (unpublished PhD thesis, Wilfrid Laurier University, 2015).
3 "RCAF Women's Division," *The Canadian Encyclopedia* at https://www.thecanadianencyclopedia.ca/en/article/rcaf-womens-division; Sarah Hogenbirk, "Women inside the Canadian Military, 1938–1966" (unpublished PhD thesis, Carleton University 2017), 251.
4 René Morin, *DND Dependants' Schools, 1921–1983* (Ottawa: Directorate of History, National Defence Headquarters, 1986), 174.
5 Patricia A. Power, "'With Their Feet on the Ground': Women's Lives and Work in the Royal Canadian Air Force, 1951–1966" (unpublished MA thesis, University of Ottawa, 1998), 27.
6 Hogenbirk, "Women inside the Canadian Military, 1938–1966," 279.
7 Power, "'With Their Feet on the Ground,'" 81.
8 May LaPierre, "Historical Information, Grostenquin, France, 1953 – Airwomen Arrive at Grostenquin – May LaPierre (now Beaverstock)," personal account at http://www.c-and-e-museum.org/grostenquin/other/airwomen-5.html.
9 "Women's Royal Air Force (WRAF) 1918–1920," RAF Museum at https://www.rafmuseum.org.uk/research/online-exhibitions/women-of-the-air-force/womens-royal-air-force-wraf-1918-1920/.
10 Alan Sullivan, *Aviation in Canada 1917–18* (Toronto: Rous & Mann, 1919), 144–5.
11 "RCAF Women's Division," *The Canadian Encyclopedia*; Elinor Florence, "Lou Marr: farm girl turned RCAF photographer," *East Kootenay News Online Weekly*, November 5, 2017, at https://www.e-know.ca/regions/east-kootenay/lou-marr-farm-girl-turned-rcaf-photographer/.
12 Elinor Florence, "Willa Walker blazed the trail for RCAF airwomen," *RCAF News and Publications*, March 7, 2019, at http://www.rcaf-arc.forces.gc.ca/en/article-template-standard.page?doc=willa-walker-blazed-the-trail-for-rcaf-airwomen/jskwdczn.
13 Power, "'With Their Feet on the Ground,'" 20–1.
14 Morin, *DND Dependants' Schools, 1921–1983*, 174; Power, "'With Their Feet on the Ground,'" 27
15 Hogenbirk, "Women inside the Canadian Military, 1938–1966," 279; "A Brief History," RCAF Airwomen at https://www.rcafairwomen.ca/About_Us.php#:~:text=In%201958%20there%20were%2063,and%20Air%20Force%20were%20unified.&text=The%20reunions%20were%20originally%20held,in%20contact%20over%20the%20years.
16 Power, "'With Their Feet on the Ground,'" 31, 33, 43.
17 An excellent description and history of FCOps' work is in "50 Years RCAF Airwomen 1951–2001," (n.d.), 21–34, copy at http://www.c-and-e-museum.org/Pinetreeline/misc/misc14.html.

18 "50 Years RCAF Airwomen 1951–2001," 29; Power, "'With Their Feet on the Ground,'" 81.
19 Lara Campbell, *Respectable Citizens: Gender, Family, and Unemployment in Ontario's Great Depression* (Toronto: University of Toronto Press, 2009).
20 Power, "'With Their Feet on the Ground,'" 17.
21 Susan Weisenburger, "Fighter Control Operator with Rita Jordan," *Parkland Community Compass*, July 24, 2018, at https://parklandcc.ca/stories-from-seniors/fighter-control-operator-with-rita-jordan/.
22 Hogenbirk, "Women inside the Canadian Military, 1938–1966," 75, 291; Power, "'With Their Feet on the Ground,'" 41. The *Star Weekly* had an extensive article on FCOps that showed their life "at work and at play," emphasizing the many positive aspects of life in the RCAF. "Fighter Control Operator," *Star Weekly*, February 28, 1959, at http://www.c-and-e-museum.org/Pinetreeline/misc/misc14.html.
23 Hogenbirk, "Women inside the Canadian Military, 1938–1966," 79.
24 "Fighter Control Operator," *Star Weekly*; Robert McKeown and Louis Jacques, "These Girls Make Fighters Scramble," *Weekend Picture Magazine* 13, no. 4 (1954) at http://www.c-and-e-museum.org/Pinetreeline/misc/misc14.html; "50 Years RCAF Airwomen 1951–2001," 28.
25 Hogenbirk, "Women inside the Canadian Military, 1938–1966," 153, 164; Power, "'With Their Feet on the Ground,'" 64. Numerous photos on the Communications and Electronics Museum, Pinetree Line website illustrate their social lives; for example, "Airwomen from [RCAF Station] Edgar enjoying a day at the beach – July 1954," at http://www.c-and-e-museum.org/Pinetreeline/photos/edgar/edgar276.jpg; "RCAF personnel snuggling at Christmas – December 1957," at http://www.c-and-e-museum.org/Pinetreeline/photos/montap/monta505.jpg.
26 "History of Family Planning in Canada," Canadian Public Health Association (n.d.) at https://www.cpha.ca/history-family-planning-canada; Hogenbirk, "Women inside the Canadian Military, 1938–1966," 180, 398–9; Ruth Roach Pierson, *They're Still Women After All* (Toronto, McClelland and Stewart, 1986), 200.
27 Rosamond Greer, *The Girls of the King's Navy* (Victoria, BC: Sono Nis Press, 1983), 89; "Proudly She Marches," The National Film Board (1943) at http://www.nfb.ca/film/proudly_she_marches/.
28 Historical Record, 31 Aircraft Control & Warning Squadron, Edgar, Ontario, Period Dec. 1, '54, to May 31, '55, Inclusive, LAC, copy at http://www.c-and-e-museum.org/Pinetreeline/other/other14/other14h.html.
29 "Fighter Control Operator," *Star Weekly*. "Good pay and lots of fun" at http://www.c-and-e-museum.org/Pinetreeline/misc/other/misc14i.jpg; McKeown and Jacques, "These Girls Make Fighters Scramble." "They find good companionship …" at http://www.c-and-e-museum.org/Pinetreeline/misc/other/misc14x.jpg.
30 "Radar Station," National Film Board (1953) at https://www.nfb.ca/film/radar_station/.
31 "Airwomen," National Film Board (1957) at https://www.nfb.ca/film/frontiers-to-guard/.
32 Hogenbirk, "Women inside the Canadian Military, 1938–1966," 285–6, 294, 300, 364.
33 Metz, France, 1957 – 1 Air Division Statistics, LAC, copy at http://www.c-and-e-museum.org/Pinetreeline/metz/otherm1/otherm1-15.html.
34 Campbell, *Respectable Citizens*, 101.
35 Al Gay, "Metz, France1956 – Memories of Metz" personal account at http://www.c-and-e-museum.org/Pinetreeline/metz/other/otherm75.html.
36 Karen D. Davis, "Organizational Environment and Turnover: Understanding Women's Exit from the Canadian Forces" (unpublished MA thesis, McGill University, 1994), 14–15.
37 Hogenbirk, "Women inside the Canadian Military, 1938–1966," 293, 336, 713.
38 Davis, "Organizational Environment and Turnover," 15.

39 "Operational strength" refers to those personnel on strength with No. 31 AC&W Squadron working directly in the aircraft warning and control mission. It does not include station technical or support personnel.

40 Historical Record, 31 Aircraft Control & Warning Squadron, Edgar, Ontario, Period Dec 1, '53 to May 31, '54, 16, LAC, Reel 12184 from Royal Canadian Air Force operations record books at https://heritage.canadiana.ca/view/oocihm.lac_mikan_135766.

41 Operations Crew Listing, St. Sylvestre, Quebec, September 1, 1961 at http://www.c-and-e-museum.org/Pinetreeline/other/other40/other40ai.html.

42 Historical Records at Edgar, ON, Pinetree Line Locations, Edgar ON, Additional Information at http://www.c-and-e-museum.org/Pinetreeline/other/other14.html.

43 Power, "'With Their Feet on the Ground,'" 60–1.

44 Historical Record, 31 Aircraft Control & Warning Squadron, Edgar, Ontario, Period Jun 1, '53 to Nov 30, '53, Incl., LAC, copy at http://www.c-and-e-museum.org/Pinetreeline/other/other14/other14g.html; Historical Record, 31 Aircraft Control & Warning Squadron, Edgar, Ontario, Period 1 Dec 54 to 31 May 55, Inclusive; Power, "'With Their Feet on the Ground,'" 72.

45 Power, "'With Their Feet on the Ground,'" 72.

46 Hogenbirk, "Women inside the Canadian Military, 1938–1966," 319; Power, "'With Their Feet on the Ground,'" 81–2.

47 Dorine Weagle, "Grostenquin, France, Historical Information, Grostenquin, France 1953 – Airwomen Arrive at Grostenquin – Dorine Weagle (now Roberts)," personal account at http://www.c-and-e-museum.org/grostenquin/other/airwomen-1.html.

48 Hogenbirk, "Women inside the Canadian Military, 1938–1966," 350; Power, "'With Their Feet on the Ground,'" 80, 88.

49 Morin, *DND Dependants' Schools, 1921–1983*, 173–4.

50 Morin, *DND Dependants' Schools, 1921–1983*, 13, 20, 25.

51 A Programme for Two Heavy Radars and Six Gap Filler Radars, S955-110, Ottawa, Ont. Oct 14, '58, LAC, copy at http://www.c-and-e-museum.org/Pinetreeline/gap/gap17.html.

52 "Edgar station has storied history," *Barrie Advance* (December 15, 2006) at https://www.simcoe.com/community-story/1990981-edgar-station-has-storied-history/.

53 Metz, France, 1957 – 1 Air Division Statistics http://www.c-and-e-museum.org/Pinetreeline/metz/otherm1/otherm1-15.html. For more statistics see the division's historical reports at Metz, France 1 Air Division Headquarters at http://www.c-and-e-museum.org/Pinetreeline/metz/otherm1.html.

54 Gordon MacKinnon, "General Navereau Schools at Metz, 1955–1967," personal account at http://www.navereau.org/about/history-of-the-schools/.

55 RCAF, "1 Air Division Information Pamphlet" (1955), 9, 11-12 at http://www.c-and-e-museum.org/marville/articles/rcaf1/rcaf1.html.

56 MacKinnon, "General Navereau Schools at Metz, 1955–1967"; Metz anniversary booklet (1977), "Family Life with the RCAF in France," 40–4 at http://www.c-and-e-museum.org/Pinetreeline/metz/otherm1/otherm1-6.html.

57 Morin, *DND Dependants' Schools*, 35–6.

58 MacKinnon, "General Navereau Schools at Metz, 1955–1967."

59 1 Air Division HQ Historical Record, December 1, 1953, to May 31, 1954, LAC, copy at http://www.c-and-e-museum.org/Pinetreeline/metz/otherm1/otherm1-8.html.

60 Morin, *DND Dependants' Schools*, 37–8, 40–1.

61 Historical Record, 1 Air Division HQ for the Period June 1, 1957, to November 30, 1957, Personnel, LAC, copy at http://www.c-and-e-museum.org/Pinetreeline/metz/otherm1/otherm1-13.html.
62 "Welcome to 1 Air Division Europe" (1963), 14–15 at http://www.c-and-e-museum.org/marville/articles/welcome.html.
63 "Welcome to 1 Air Division Europe" (1963), 35 at http://www.c-and-e-museum.org/marville/articles/welcome.html.
64 RCAF, "1 Air Division Information Pamphlet" (1955), 12–13.
65 A rough calculation based on an annual intake of about 1,000 women per year to build up to a steady state of around 3,000 and then a continued intake of about 1,000 per year to replace attrition. See, for example, Power, "'With Their Feet on the Ground,'" 81; Davis, "Organizational Environment and Turnover," 15.
66 DND, *Strong, Secure, Engaged: Canada's Defence Policy* (Ottawa: Queen's Printer, 1917), chapter 1 at https://www.canada.ca/en/department-national-defence/corporate/reports-publications/canada-defence-policy.html.

CHAPTER TEN

THE AIR RESERVES: A FUNCTIONAL SECOND LINE OF DEFENCE?

MATHIAS JOOST

As the RCAF began its postwar planning, a part-time force was included and was considered for a prominent role, similar to the functions assigned to the pre-war Auxiliary Active Air Force. The first squadrons of the RCAF Auxiliary, as the new organization was called, were authorized on 15 April 1946. From these beginnings the organization would rise to a strength of 5,774 personnel at the end of 1955. The Auxiliary was in fact almost its own mini-air force, with intelligence and medical units, radar units, and training units for its personnel, all in addition to its operational flying squadrons.[1] From 1948 to 1955, the Auxiliary fighter squadrons were the front-line of defence for Canada while the non-flying units provided needed personnel to augment the Regular Force or to support the flying squadrons' and radar units' activities. By 1967 the Auxiliary was down to less than 800 personnel: only six flying squadrons remained and these in a transport and emergency operations role in support of the Army.

The RCAF Auxiliary played an important but hereto unrecognized role in the air defence of Canada in the early 1950s as a second line of defence. But it had its problems, not the least of which was that it became operationally irrelevant. The question thus arises as to whether the RCAF Auxiliary was an effective second line of defence. This chapter examines the roles of the Auxiliary, how its squadrons and units operated, and how effective they were. To assess this second line of defence, the emphasis will be on the units that directly contributed to the air defence of Canada and North America. Examining the shortfalls and benefits as assessed by the RCAF leadership will allow an understanding of the decisions taken with respect to the Auxiliary. It will become apparent that many factors were in play, including manning and changes in technology that in turn affected readiness, training and operations, and budgets.

Pilot Officer J.G. McLaws and a contingent of 403 Auxiliary Squadron Mustangs at Rockcliffe, Ontario, for their two-week summer training period, July 1953.

A First Auxiliary Role: Tactical Support to the Army, but Some Air Defence

When the government approved Plan B for the RCAF in 1946 the Auxiliary's "function" was "to provide a first-line reserve of fully organized, manned and equipped squadrons which can be mobilized on short notice into a tactical air component." The Auxiliary, equipped with Second World War aircraft, would provide the front-line air defence for Canada as well as army support.[2] This organizational and operational structure did not envision an enemy who might fly over the Arctic Ocean and attack North America. At best, it was considered that the Soviets might try to establish a base on the continent from which to attack the United States.[3] The tactical air nature of the Auxiliary suggested a force capable of fighting much as the RCAF had done in supporting army operations in Europe in 1944–5.

To meet this mandate 11 Auxiliary fighter, fighter-bomber, and light bomber squadrons were formed between April 1946 and 1948, with one additional fighter

B-25 Mitchel Bomber, 406 Auxiliary Squadron.

squadron added in September 1951.⁴ To support these flying squadrons with a detection capability the RCAF formed No. 1 Radar and Communications Unit (RCU) in 1947 and 2401 Radar Squadron (Auxiliary) in December 1948, both in Montreal. The RCU trained Auxiliary personnel in maintaining and operating communications and radar equipment while the Radar Squadron maintained and operated a British Air Ministry Experimental Station mobile radar system to conduct ground-controlled interception training with the fighter squadrons.

It is important to understand that during these years the Auxiliary was the only organization capable of providing air defence for Canada, no Regular Force fighter squadrons having been formed yet. Auxiliary aircrew trained to the same standards as their Regular Force counterparts; they attended Regular Force pilot training and specialist courses. As for the airmen who conducted maintenance, they too were expected to have the same standards as the Regular Force and initially attended Regular Force trades courses.

Once activated, each squadron generally spent its first year getting organized, recruiting, and training for flying. In its second year a squadron would participate in exercises, normally against other Auxiliary squadrons. Some outstanding rivalries were soon developed, such as between 401 and 438 Squadrons in Montreal and 400 and 411 in Toronto, or 402 in Winnipeg and 403 in Calgary. There were, however, problems in bringing many of the squadrons up to strength both for the officers and the skilled technical trades.

Plan G: Growth and Re-equipment

Manpower was an issue from the start. While the Auxiliary was able to enlist sufficient personnel in the non-skilled trades, it was observed that "it was practically impossible to get men for the skilled technical trades." A recruiting campaign was therefore recommended,[5] but it resulted in limited success. In June 1949, the lack of groundcrew and their poor attendance at training sessions were two issues contributing to a low standard of Auxiliary effectiveness; another was the poor utilization of aircraft. While there was no shortage of former wartime pilots, the groundcrew problem was serious enough that it was seen as a potentially significant negative impact on the Auxiliary's role in the event of an emergency. To address this situation various measures were recommended and implemented, including better pay and some pay incentives, as well as a revised trade structure. All measures were intended to increase the attendance and technical qualifications of the aircraft maintainers. The period also saw the commissioning of the first of many studies to examine the Auxiliary, including at this time the possibility of "reroling" some squadrons from air defence to transport.[6]

Squadrons had been initially equipped with North American Harvard training aircraft, but in March 1948 the de Havilland Vampire began to enter Auxiliary service in five fighter squadrons, with the other units receiving the North American P-51 Mustang. The two light bomber squadrons, 406 and 418, received the North American B-25 Mitchell in June 1948 and January 1947 respectively. Future plans called for all Auxiliary squadrons, including the light-bomber ones, to receive the Avro CF-100 Canuck once these new Canadian fighters had equipped the Regular Force Squadrons.[7] The Auxiliary was thus ultimately intended to be an organization on par with the Regular Force, except for its part-time nature.

There were to be 19 squadrons defending Canada, nine Regular Force and ten Auxiliary. The Auxiliary's role was two-fold: to provide trained personnel to bring the RCAF up to war establishment strength on mobilization and to supply trained personnel to augment training and logistics activities.[8] The RCAF's intentions were clear: Auxiliary flying squadrons that could be ready at a moment's notice, and personnel from Auxiliary headquarters and ground units that could augment the Regular Force in the non-flying operations.

A de Havilland Vampire jet fighter. This type of aircraft equipped many of the auxiliary fighter squadrons during the early Cold War.

Plan G envisioned an Auxiliary of 10,800 personnel supported by a cadre of 1,300 Regular Force personnel and civilians. The augmentation role of the Auxiliary was readily apparent in the RCAF's commitment to new Auxiliary units such as the Medical and Wing Headquarters units, which were intended to support the Regular Force. Seen in raw numbers, the Auxiliary was to be broken down as follows:

Flying squadrons	3,500
Radar and communications units	5,100
Technical training units	1,600
Medical units	300
Wing headquarters	300[9]

The Aircraft Control and Warning (AC&W) squadrons, which began to form in October 1950, would provide radar services, especially fighter control and

Class Instructor Flying Officer John L. Den Ouden supervises radar plotting exercise during practical exercise at 2405 AC&W Auxiliary Squadron.

interception, to the Auxiliary fighter squadrons. This interception function involved manually guiding fighters towards incoming bombers or hostile aircraft, much has had been done a decade earlier during the Battle of Britain. Meanwhile, technical training units (TTU) were created to train tradesmen, and later tradeswomen, to the Group 1 level, which was the basic level of trades skill. One TTU was collocated with each flying squadron. Medical units were established to support and supplement the RCAF medical branch, providing a nucleus of medical personnel for the RCAF on mobilization. During peacetime these units and their clinicians were to provide medical services to the Auxiliary, such as recruit and aircrew medicals, and X-ray and pharmacy services. Some medical units participated at Auxiliary summer camps or assisted air cadet summer programs. From an operational perspective, air evacuation teams at some medical units assisted in medical mercy flights conducted by both Regular and Auxiliary flying units.

The Auxiliary also needed a means to retain senior RCAF officers and non-commissioned officers. The wing headquarters, and later the technical trade unit headquarters would allow senior personnel to advance beyond what squadrons and units could provide. These headquarters would be the training grounds for staff-qualified officers in the event of an emergency.

Not part of Plan G, but created to augment the Regular Force, were four Auxiliary Intelligence Units formed on 1 September 1951. Their role was to support Auxiliary units during peacetime and to augment the Regular Force on mobilization. The units, in particular No. 5000 IU in Toronto, also provided intelligence products to the Directorate of Air Intelligence at RCAF Headquarters. In the case of No. 5001 IU in Montreal, it had extra personnel so it could provide technical intelligence to Air Defence Command on such topics as armaments, aircraft engineering, and communications.[10]

The basis for any effective force is training, and from the very start the flying squadrons conducted tactical exercises involving air interceptions and ground attacks. Some of the training exercises were large-scale activities that involved Regular squadrons as well as the Canadian Army and even the United States Air Force (USAF). For example, in October 1949 the air defence system was tested during Operation Metropolis, a joint USAF/RCAF exercise. The exercise was small in scale, involving only 401 and 438 Squadrons and the radar from No. 1 Radar and Communications Unit plus a few USAF National Guard squadrons, but it did test the interoperability of the two services and laid the groundwork for future cooperation. This was also the first test of the Vampire in RCAF service, which served as part of the defending force alongside USAF F-47 Thunderbolts protecting New York City from attacking USAF bombers.[11]

The Auxiliary fighter-bomber and light bomber squadrons supporting the Tactical Air Group were also active in a major exercise – Exercise EAGLE – held in Northern British Columbia and Yukon in August 1949. The exercise was also a test of the Army's Mobile Striking Force concept, which also involved the RCAF's support of the Army. The 402 and 442 Squadrons participated with their Harvards and 406 and 418 with their Mitchells; 402 Squadron's radar section provided radar coverage. The fighters were employed in air defence of their respective airfields while the bombers provided ground attack in support of the Army.

By the end of 1949 the RCAF Auxiliary had assumed the roles of air defence against enemy bombers and support of the Army in dislodging any enemy bases that might be created in Canada. These roles fit the threat assessments of the time. Importantly, as there was only one Regular Force fighter squadron in operation, the Auxiliary was the RCAF component responsible for air defence and, in fact, the first and only line of defence.

Mark V Sabre flown by 411 Auxiliary Fighter Squadron.

The 1950s: More Capable, but Still Part-Time

With the start of a new decade, the RCAF Auxiliary began to hit its stride. Additional units were activated, and the AC&W units and fighter squadrons began to have a real impact on operational capability. The first new units were the AC&W squadrons, which were formed in August 1950 and started aircraft control exercises the following summer. By July 1952, four AC&W units in eastern Canada, augmented by personnel from five other AC&W units across Canada, were able to participate in a major air defence exercise, Exercise SIGNPOST.[12] This was the RCAF's first major postwar air defence exercise and included USAF aircraft and headquarters. By 1954, the AC&W squadrons were cooperating regularly with their USAF counterparts.[13]

The AC&W units also had an additional warning role as they were equipped with the British Air Ministry Experimental Set Mk II (AMES II), a mobile radar system transported on specially modified trucks. AMES II could be deployed to fill gaps in the Pinetree radar warning line or around major cities.[14] While AMES II had range and altitude limitations, the mobile sets did provide a valuable training capability.

The flying squadrons normally operated every second weekend and conducted a variety of necessary training: armament weekends at an approved range, high- and low-level navigation, radio compass let-downs, formation flying, flying in clouds, and air-to-air gunnery (using cine cameras). For new pilots the purpose of the flying was to qualify on the squadron aircraft after completion of basic pilot training with the Regular Force. More experienced pilots participated in operationally focused exercises like those mentioned above, these often held with nearby USAF squadrons. The exercises could be quite large, such as Operation PHOENIX held in November 1951, which involved 401, 411, 416, 420, 424 and 438 Squadrons along with USAF squadrons and 418 Squadron providing Mitchells as part of the attacking force.[15] All of these exercises led up to the summer camps, at which the AC&W squadrons operated with the flying squadrons while staff from Auxiliary headquarters, intelligence, and medical personnel deployed in varying numbers in support.

Squadrons designated to support Army operations, wholly or in part, participated in exercises with the Canadian Army or conducted training on bombing ranges. One of the first major joint exercises was Operation ARCHITECT, which took place near Edmonton in May 1951, with 402, 403, 406 and 418 Squadrons participating in support of 5 Brigade. Such training continued into 1953, after which all the Auxiliary fighter-bomber squadrons were converted to the air defence role.[16] The two light bomber squadrons, 406 and 418, continued to support army exercises, which even took on an international flavour with Operation Lockstep, held across the Prairies in May 1954, involving western units in Canada and some from the United States.[17]

The formation of NATO in 1949 and subsequently the RCAF Air Division in Europe had a significant effect upon the Auxiliary. Initial plans had called for nine Regular Force fighter squadrons to be the first line of defence for Canada, but they were now committed to the Air Division. Thus, the Auxiliary, which was to have been the second line of defence, now became the first, and it was crucial that it prepare for this commitment.

Starting in 1952, the Auxiliary fighter squadrons participated in three major joint exercises involving the RCAF and the USAF – Exercise SIGNPOST (July 1952), Exercise TAILWIND (July 1953), and Exercise CHECKPOINT (July 1954) – designed to test the air defence system of eastern North America. These exercises constituted the summer camps for the Auxiliary flying squadrons but had a more important role – they helped iron out problems in aircraft control, interception,

Exercise SIGNPOST. Loading 20mm ammo into a 411 County of York Auxiliary Squadron Vampire. Maintenance and armament for most auxiliary squadrons was carried out by reserve personnel supported by a small cadre of regular air force maintainers.

and communications that would later facilitate the establishment of the formal North American air defence system. Unlike Exercise METROPOLIS in 1949, these exercises involved the majority of the Auxiliary fighter and AC&W squadrons, with wing headquarters providing personnel and intelligence units providing support at the station and squadron level. In all of these national / bi-lateral exercises, the Auxiliary units attempted to intercept USAF bombers acting as the enemy force with the AC&W squadrons using their AMES II radar units to locate the enemy force and then vectoring the Auxiliary fighters for an attack.

Some observations on the Auxiliary can be made from the after-exercise reports on Exercise CHECKPOINT. Wing Commander R.W. McNair, sector commander of No. 1 Air Defence Control Centre, noted that the AC&W personnel performed very well in deploying to radar stations and directing interceptions of the "enemy"

Air-to-air view of a 102 Composite Flight North American Mustang. This aircraft would be a mainstay of the RCAF auxiliary fighter squadrons during the early Cold War.

aircraft, but also that the lack of sufficient trained personnel among the Auxiliary and Regular flying squadrons hindered their capabilities. Group Captain Miller, commanding officer of RCAF Station St-Hubert, thought that despite the exercise being a "no warning" one, which handicapped the Auxiliary, he and other commanders believed the Auxiliary made a great contribution to the effectiveness of Air Defence Command.[18]

W/C McNair's remarks about the flying squadrons were a reminder of the issue of manning of groundcrew technical positions. This was still a problem despite the fact that there was sufficient technical training capacity, with Auxiliary tradesmen being offered space on Regular Force courses, as well as at the Auxiliary TTUs, but often individuals were not able to take the courses because of their civilian work commitments.[19] Additionally, despite recruiting efforts and training opportunities, there were still not enough personnel, especially in the higher trade groups. Typically, new groundcrew would remain with the Auxiliary for only a year or two before taking their release, resulting in insufficient Auxiliary personnel to man all the advanced qualification trade levels. This typically resulted in senior Regular technicians being attached to the Auxiliary to fill supervisory functions.

There was another issue that W/C McNair's remarks highlighted. Besides honing squadron skills, the exercises also highlighted areas where additional training or changes were required. One observation that came out of the exercises as early as 1952 pointed to the effectiveness of the Auxiliary fighter squadrons. As the first line of air defence, anything that affected the efficacy of the Auxiliary fighter squadrons affected the efficacy of the air defence of Canada.

These early exercises did suggest one thing to RCAF Headquarters – that in the event of emergency the state of training of the Auxiliary would not allow them to be ready for mobilization. An insufficient number of Auxiliary pilots were trained to full operational capability, while there were not enough trained maintainers at the higher trade levels. Operationally ready pilots and sufficient trained maintenance personnel would be a definite requirement if the Auxiliary were to receive the CF-100, as was the eventual goal. For the moment this meant that that the number of Regular pilots assigned to Auxiliary squadrons had to be increased and significantly, so too the number of Regular groundcrew; only with these Regular augmentees could the Auxiliary have the expertise to meet their operational commitments.

The Mid-1950s: Revised Roles for Better Effectiveness

Starting in May 1952, the Air Council directed the first of a series of studies to improve the operational effectiveness of the Auxiliary flying squadrons. Various proposals were put forward, all of which were rejected as being too intensive (read expensive) in terms of Regular Force augmentation and in one case would lead to a loss of Auxiliary identity. By January 1954, the Air Council recognized that they were expecting too much from the flying Auxiliary.[20] But there seemed no way around augmenting the Auxiliary with more Regular Force air and groundcrew if the Auxiliary was going to operate the CF-100. While there was still some time to make changes, given delays in CF 100 production, there was some urgency as the Auxiliary fighter squadrons were slated to receive the Canuck as of June 1955.[21] In October 1954 most Auxiliary flying squadrons began to receive the Canadair-built Lockheed T-33 jet trainer in preparation for conversion to the CF-100.[22]

By mid-1955 the Air Council came to accept that air defence was no longer a viable role for the 10 Auxiliary fighter squadrons. In September 1955 the RCAF presented to the COSC a proposal that some squadrons should be converted to the air transport role while others would provide jet flying instructors to be used at RCAF Regular Force flying training schools. Alternately, all flying operations could be taken away from the Auxiliary. Regardless, it was recognized that by removing these squadrons from air defence duties Regular Force squadrons would need to be created to replace them. The COSC agreed.[23] The minister of national defence, Ralph Campney, was not, however, so enthusiastic about the proposal or about creating new Regular Force squadrons.

At the same time, the minister suggested keeping a limited number of Auxiliary fighter squadrons. Based on Campney's thinking, the CAS, Air Marshal C.R. Slemon, ordered the development of another proposal for the Auxiliary flying squadrons, in which some squadrons would be equipped with the F-86 and T-33 so that they could then augment the Regular Force. The remaining fighter squadrons would be re-roled as "disaster and rescue" squadrons in support of civil authorities in the event of national disaster and search and rescue operations on a more regular basis. The four fighter squadrons to be converted were to receive four helicopters and four light transport aircraft each. At the same time, the two tactical bomber squadrons were to retain their role. However, the CAS's proposal to create the four light transport squadrons was rejected at the next chiefs of staff meeting.[24] With no decision being taken, the role of the Auxiliary fighter squadrons remained in limbo as there was no viable alternative to allow a cost effective and meaningful role. The plan therefore remained to provide six squadrons with the Sabre (these being older models being replaced in Europe) in the air defence role and to convert four others to light transport.

The AC&W squadrons would also undergo a change. With the construction of the Mid-Canada and Pinetree radar lines, the Auxiliary personnel would be tasked to augment the Regular Force units serving on those lines, as these were only sufficiently manned for eight hours of operation per day in times of emergency. With the change in role the Auxiliary AC&W squadrons began to provide individual or small group augmentation to these units. Eventually there were cases where Auxiliary crews were able to take over operations completely for a weekend at a time.[25]

It would not be until the end of 1956 that the new roles came into effect, and then it was the CAS's proposal from the fall of the previous year that partially won out. Three squadrons, 402, 403, and 424, became light transport units with the role of training a reserve of aircrew for the Auxiliary and Regular Force. For this they received the twin-engine Beech Expeditor, of which the RCAF had ample numbers, hence there was no cost for the change of equipment. In addition, 402 Squadron was given the specific task of training navigators. Meanwhile, 420 Squadron was disbanded.[26] Organizationally, the squadrons were transferred to Transport

Sabres from 1 Air Division transported to Canada on the Royal Canadian Navy carrier, HMCS *Magnificent*. Replaced by newer models, these Sabres are destined for RCAF auxiliary squadrons.

Command. The six Vampire squadrons, which had retained an air defence role, began to receive Sabre Mk Vs repatriated from the Air Division between August and November 1956. These six transitioned to the training role in February 1957, qualifying air and groundcrew for T-33s and F-86s.[27] While the three initial squadrons became part of Training Command in January and September 1957, 400 and 411 transferred to Air Transport Command (ATC) in October 1958, while 401, 438, 442 and 443 Squadrons remained under Air Defence Command until April 1961.

The light transport squadrons spent their first year in the new role primarily in converting to the Expeditor, with the pilots learning to function as a crew and

University Reserve Training Plan (URTP) officer candidates at RCAF Station Centralia, ON, 8 July 1959. They are spending their summers training for possible Air Force careers. Left to right are Flight Cadets Sandra Blaine, Dianne Walker, Margaret Hitchins, and Jane Stobbe.

learning the flying standards required by ATC compared to those of Air Defence Command. There was also a return to the units' previous support of the Canadian Army, a role that they had given up only three years earlier. Meanwhile the six jet-flying squadrons began to learn to operate their Sabres; however, further changes were in store for them.[28]

In early 1957, the chiefs of staff accepted a proposal to employ the transport squadrons in the national survival role. Here, in the event of a nuclear war, the Auxiliary would be used to help the Army in supporting those civil authorities mandated with providing aid, rescue services, and policing to areas hit by nuclear weapons.[29] At the same time as this new role was proposed it was decided that equipping Auxiliary squadrons with Sabres was impractical and not cost effective, and so these units would also would be re-rolled as transport squadrons. Search and Rescue and short-haul transport for the RCAF and Canadian Army continued to be included in the Auxiliary's mandate, as was transport of other reserves and the Air Cadets.[30] The change in government in June 1957 and the economics of the new government lent credence to this decision.

Other changes were also on the table. In June 1957, the COSC saw no further reason why 406 and 418 Squadrons should continue to be equipped with the Mitchell as the Service heads perceived the risk of enemy lodgements as being very limited.[31] This change in thinking reflected the assessment that nuclear war was more likely than a Soviet effort to attack North America through the creation of a base on the continent. It was decided that these two squadrons would join the other Auxiliary squadrons in the National Survival, search and rescue, and transport roles.[32]

As the end of the decade approached, the Auxiliary remained relatively unchanged in its composition and work. The flying squadrons had gone through a role change with some being re-equipped and one squadron being disbanded. The AC&W squadrons, intelligence, medical and technical training units, and the various Auxiliary headquarters all continued to function as they had since the early 1950s. There were local exercises, summer camps, support of the Regular Force and augmentation of the Regular Force by the AC&W squadrons. Despite change to flying roles on the whole, the Auxiliary looked and operated much as it had, but other major changes were in store.

A National Survival Role for the '60s

In 1958 the RCAF had its first budget reduction of the 1950s. Among the first casualties were the Auxiliary Intelligence units. Despite the fact that Auxiliary intelligence personnel had augmented both the Regular Force in Canada and at the Air Division and had provided valuable intelligence products to the Directorate of Air Intelligence, the units themselves did not directly support operations and were therefore deemed expendable.[33]

In contrast, the Auxiliary's national survival role was firmly set, and in June of the same year consideration was given to making best use of the organization. This included replacement aircraft, with consideration given to de Havilland Otter, and the resurrection of a proposal made in February 1956 for the acquisition of helicopters.[34] The use of helicopters was further confirmed in March 1959 when A/V/M D.M. Smith, the vice chief of the Air Staff, advised the Air Officers' Conference that this would be the case. The only question was one of which helicopter would be chosen – the Bell 47 or the Vertol 107. The first was a small bubble helicopter, while the Vertol was a much larger and robust twin engine aircraft. A decision had been delayed so that standardization with the Army and Navy could be achieved over the Bell 47. Smith also noted that "This will provide not only training but also a heavy-lift capability to the Auxiliary squadrons in their role of emergency rescue."[35] The Otters were approved and began to arrive at the squadrons in October 1960.

While the COSC approved the purchase of the helicopters in May 1959, fiscal restraint put a hold on this purchase for Auxiliary units even though helicopters were considered essential to the Auxiliary's role in survival operations.[36] When the Auxiliary's helicopter requirement was again examined in May 1961, questions arose surrounding the organization's ability to maintain and operate the Vertols, which were fairly complicated pieces of equipment.[37] This concern appears not to have raised much question, as the Air Council approved the purchase of 15 Hiller 12E (these being equivalent to the Bell aircraft and having been selected by the Army for its reconnaissance flights) and 16 Vertol 107 helicopters for use by the Auxiliary just a few months later, in September 1961. The associated operating concept was accepted as long as there would be no additional need for Regular Force personnel at the Auxiliary squadrons.[38] Whether an Auxiliary-only helicopter capability might have worked was not tested as there simply was not sufficient money in the DND budget for these aircraft when there were higher priorities for the Regular Force.

Money was not the only problem. As early as March 1960 the Air Council had accepted that the Auxiliary was of limited use in the event of mobilization and that its main role was to maintain a community presence. And having a presence in Canadian society was important to the RCAF leadership, not just for recruiting but also to maintain an air-minded public. Disbanding the Auxiliary was not an option as it would allow the Army a monopoly on Canadians' perceptions of the armed services.[39]

While the RCAF was forced to find a role and equipment for the Auxiliary flying squadrons to keep them flying, other events necessitated the disbanding of other units. As early as 1955 the RCAF was aware that automation would eventually reduce the manpower requirement at radar stations.[40] The Semi-Automated Ground Environment (SAGE) system, under development in the US, would allow automated tracking and interception of hostile aircraft and would be ready for use by the end of the decade. This new system would replace manual tracking and thus have a significant negative impact on the Auxiliary AC&W squadrons.[41] In 1960 the first AC&W units were disbanded, followed by the remainder in 1961, as SAGE came into use at RCAF radar sites.

This left only the flying squadrons, the headquarters, the technical training, and medical units on the Auxiliary's establishment. With an Auxiliary that was now not contributing to air defence but rather supporting Army operations and national survival, RCAF leaders began to ask whether the air force should maintain an organization that was not contributing to operational capabilities and mission. In March 1960, the Air Council and AOCs examined this question. Discussion ranged from disbanding the entire Auxiliary, to reorganizing it to provide a community presence. The solution was ... another study.[42] As with past studies, no action was taken after the study was completed.

By 1963 the RCAF had seen more than six years of declining budgets even as new roles and equipment were being added. Twice that year and again in 1964, the RCAF comptroller suggested disbanding the Auxiliary as a way to make ends meet.[43] Yet, there were positive aspects to the organization. In 1963 at its annual briefing to the Air Council, ATC noted the Auxiliary had flown 100 per cent of its allocated hours in 1962 and that officer establishments were full. ATC had developed training plans for the Auxiliary's role in national survival operations in support of the Army and received permission to purchase cameras for this role. The Otter, of which there were only two in each squadron, was considered a good aircraft in the National Survival role. By comparison the Expeditor was inadequate and the de Havilland Caribou was suggested as a replacement aircraft.

While the squadrons were thus performing well, the long-time shortage of technicians continued. Both manning and trade qualification status were below required levels, with only 54 per cent of the airmen positions filled at flying squadrons. In fact, for ATC, the status of the Auxiliary airmen trades was fourth on its list of critical factors in the Command. ATC was, however, pleased with the Auxiliary: "[t]he Auxiliary Squadrons are now making a significant contribution to the RCAF despite the limitations of their equipment, and there is ample room for further exploitation of their capability, particularly if they are re-equipped with Caribou aircraft."[44]

The suggestion of purchasing the Caribou was a new one. The Otter was already in service, while the Hillers were now being used for training of the Regular Force and the Vertols had been left to the Army. Despite previous recommendations to disband the Auxiliary, the RCAF clearly believed it was still useful.

Another major study of the role of Auxiliary was undertaken in early 1964 at the request of the new Liberal minister of national defence, Paul Hellyer. Group Captain J.W.P. Draper led the ministerial committee that in the end recommended that the Auxiliary be equipped to provide greater support to the Army in the areas of mobility and tactical and logistical support and should, as a result, receive new aircraft. The Air Council saw it differently and indicated that the Auxiliary would maintain six flying squadrons in four locations, co-located with Regular Force RCAF stations, that its national survival, transport, and search and rescue

418 City of Edmonton Auxiliary Squadron Expeditor aircraft over its namesake city. By the early 1960s the auxiliary squadrons had been re-purposed from fighter operations to flying light transport aircraft.

roles remain the same, and that it would continue with its current aircraft. The Air Council believed that the Auxiliary was providing good value for the $3 million being spent on it annually and saw no reason to expand its roles or provide new equipment. As for the medical and technical training units, it was agreed that there was no reason, or funding, to retain them.[45]

Despite the views of the Air Council, Air Commodore R.J. Lane, Air Officer Commanding ATC, saw potential in the Auxiliary as a solution to the RCAF's shortage of medium transport capability. The Auxiliary had, he observed, the ability but not the capability, and would require replacing the Expeditors with four Dakotas or Caribous at each squadron.[46] Lane suggested that new aircraft would "provide an urgently needed manifestation of a firm policy on the future of the Auxiliaries, which is now lacking, and would give the Auxiliary a real sense of purpose as an integral and essential component of the Air Transport System." But with no spare Dakotas and the Caribous at a premium, this suggestion was not viable.

Integration and Unification: An End to the Auxiliary Air Force

With integration of the three Canadian services looming, there was yet another study of the Auxiliary. In January 1967 the RCAF Auxiliary Consulting Group completed its report, recommending a role of "close logistic and utility air support" for Mobile Command. Lieutenant-General W. Anderson, Commander, Mobile Command, as the Army was now called, agreed with this role for the Auxiliary, while ATC indicated they had no further requirement for the Air Reserve, as it had been renamed on 17 October 1967.[47] Thus, the RCAF Auxiliary, now the Air Reserve, became part of Mobile Command on 1 February 1968.

Looking back over the two decades of the Auxiliary Air Force, we can conclude that the Auxiliary squadrons were never really the second line of defence that had been envisaged. In the early 1950s they were, for a short time, in fact a first line of defence, albeit with a number of deficiencies, not the least of which was that the RCAF leadership was expecting too much of them. The Auxiliary of those years suffered a chronic insufficiency of technicians and a lack of proper equipment for the fighter role. Thus, as a first line of defence, the organization was not properly organized or equipped. And when the Regular Force began to take on the air defence function, the deficiencies in the Auxiliary fighter squadrons were such that the decision was made not to provide the front-line aircraft they needed to be effective. The result was that by 1956 their role was changed to provision of augmentee aircrew for the Regular Air Force. In this sense they were not even a second line of defence and would not provide any first- or second-line air defence thereafter. Considerations to rectify the Auxiliary issues ran into the problem of cost – finding means to attract and hold on to part-time personnel seemed problematic, and adding Regular Force manpower to bring auxiliary units up to operational strength was simply too expensive.

There was a bright spot for the Auxiliary in the 1950s. The Auxiliary Aircraft and Control Warning squadrons offered key support in the opening and operation of the radar lines, and their contribution proved to be a boon to both their status and that of the Auxiliary. This was where the Auxiliary provided an effective second line of defence. But it was not a lasting contribution.

NOTES

1 Starting in 1950 and continuing through to 1956, 69 units were formed: 12 flying squadrons, 14 Aircraft Control and Warning Units, 18 Medical Units, eight Technical Training Units, four Intelligence Units and two Radar and Communications squadrons. Overseeing the operations of local Auxiliary units were nine Wing Headquarters (Auxiliary) and two Technical Training Wing Headquarters (Auxiliary).

2 "Plan B," *Post-War Plan for the Royal Canadian Air Force*, April 1946, chapter III, Para 28.01 and 28.02 and chapter 1, Para 2.01 and 4.02, DHH 181.004 (D44). These aircraft were Vampire, Mosquito, and Mitchell.

3 This lodgement possibility was a concern for Canadian military planners and led to the Mobile Striking Force concept. Dislodging such an enemy was one of the elements of the RCAF's Exercise Eagle conducted in northern British Columbia and Yukon in 1949.

4 Fighter squadrons formed in 1946 were 400, 401, 402, 424, 438 and 442, plus 418 as the light-bomber. The 406 squadron was the lone one formed in 1948, while 403, 411, and 420 were formed in 1948.

5 Minutes of the Meeting of Defence Council held in Room 2200 "A" Building, Department of National Defence, at 1000 hours, Thursday, 12th June 1947, Item 3, DHH, 73/1223. File 1373.

6 Minutes of the Meeting of the Air Officers Commanding Conference, June 27–9, 1949, Item 3, DHH, 73/1223, File 2000.

7 Minutes of the 115th Meeting of Air Members held at 1430 Hours, Friday, September 8, 1950, Item 877 DHH, 73/1223, File 1821; and Minutes of the 121st Meeting of Air Members Held at 1430 Hours Wednesday, Jan 10, '51, Item 705 DHH 73/1223, File 1822. The 406 and 418 squadrons were to receive machine gun-equipped versions of the Canuck to replace their Mitchells.

8 "Plan "G" for the Royal Canadian Air Force" September 1, 1950, revision, Section A, Green Tab 1, para 7, Section C, Pink Tab 1, para 3 and Section C, Pink Tab 2, paras 13 and 21.

9 "Plan "G" for the Royal Canadian Air Force" 1 September 1950 revision, Section C, Pink Tab 2, para 10.

10 Based on author's research to be published as part of a history of the RCAF Intelligence service.

11 "Raiders 'Shot Down' in Operation Metropolis," *Ottawa Citizen*, October 24, 1949, 14; "U.S. – Canada Cooperate in Air Maneuvers," *Sarasota Herald Tribune*, October 12, 1946, 6; "Montreal R.C.A.F. Reserve Units To Take Part in 'Raid' on N.Y.," *Montreal Gazette*, October 12, 1949, 3; Local Flier Heads Manoeuvre Force," *Montreal Gazette*, October 18, 1949, 3; "Mock New York Attack Brings Heavy Air Loss," *Calgary Herald*, October 24, 1949, 9.

12 "Final Report on Exercise Signpost," 2–3, DHH, 181.009 (D319).

13 See for example 2424 AC&W Squadron, Daily Diary, 24 Feb 24, and May 17, 1954, LAC, Microfilm C12403.

14 LAC, RG 24, Volume 5258, TS 19-80-7 (DOE), 20 Nov 50, paras 2–4.

15 Historical Report of 401 "F" Squadron Auxiliary, 4 (Period Jun 1, '51 to Nov 30, '51), and Appendix reports, LAC Microfilm Reel C12266.

16 Dr. Leo Pettipas, "402 Squadron, 1946–1968," *402 "City of Winnipeg" Squadron History*, Pat McNorgan, editor (Winnipeg, MB: The 402 Squadron Association, 2007) 118.

17 406 Squadron, "Semi-Annual Historical Returns Dec 53 to May 54 Inclusive," 2, LAC Microfilm Roll C12273.

18 Air Defence Command Operation Order 11/54, "Exercise Check Point,"111600Z Jun 54, para 3 (b), 34, 42, 46 and 52; and S4-4-42, Jul 30, '54, Minutes of a Meeting to Discuss Exercise Check

Point Held at the Theatre at RCAF Stn St. Hubert, on Thurs. Jul 15, '54, para 34, 36.and 42, DHH, 181.002 (D343).
19 Government of Canada, *The Canada Year Book 1954* (Ottawa: Edmond Cloutier, King's Printer and Controller of Stationery, 1954) 1195.
20 "Decisions and Subjects Requiring action raised at the AOsC and Air Members Conference, Jan 13 and 14. '54, Item 1, DHH, 73/1223, File 2000.
21 Minutes of the 190th Meeting of the Air Members held in CAS' Office, 1000 Hours, Dec 14, '53 and continued at 1430 Hours Dec 15, '53, Item 1037, para 5, DHH, 73/1223, File 1824.
22 These squadrons were, all but 442 and 443 Squadrons, based in Vancouver.
23 Memorandum for the COSC: Role of the RCAF Auxiliary Flying Squadrons, Sep 21, '55, DHH, 2002/17, Box 90, File 13; COSC, Minutes of a Special Meeting held on Friday, September 23, 1955, in the office of the Chairman, Chiefs of Staff, National Defence Headquarters, DHH 73/1223. File 1308; and Records of the 584th COSC meeting, Nov 1, '55, DHH 73/1223, File 1308.
24 COSC, Minutes of the 586th Meeting held on Tuesday, February 21, 1956, in the Office of the Chairman, Chiefs of Staff, National Defence Headquarters, Item VIII and Minutes of the 590th Meeting held on Monday, March 5, 1956, in the Office of the Chairman, Chiefs of Staff, National Defence Headquarters DHH, 2002/17 Box 71, File 3; and Memorandum to Cabinet Defence Committee: New Roles for the RCAF Auxiliary (draft), DHH 2002/17 Box 90, File 13.
25 For examples of the latter, see 2420 AC&W Squadron, Historical Record, Jun 1, '57–Nov 30, '57, June 30, and July 1, 1957, and 2405 AC&W Squadron, Historical Narrative, Jun 1 '57–Nov 30, '57, LAC, Microfilm C12403.
26 895-64/402 (DOE) Dec 21, '56, Organization Order R5.0.17.1, 402 City of Winnipeg Transport Squadron (Auxiliary), RCAF, Winnipeg, Manitoba and 895-64/403 (DOE) Dec 21, '56, Organization Order R6.0.30.1, 403 Transport Squadron (Auxiliary), RCAF, Calgary, Alta.
27 895-64/438 (DOE), Feb 19, '57, Organization Order R2.0.11.2, 438 City of Montreal Fighter Squadron (Auxiliary) RCAF, St-Hubert, PQ and 895-64/442 (DOE) Jul 9, '56, Amendment List 2 to Organization Order R3.0.19.1, 442 City of Vancouver Fighter Squadron (Auxiliary), RCAF, Vancouver, BC. (400, 411 and 443 Org orders not found.)
28 These were the 400, 401, 411, 438, 442, and 443 squadrons. However, it should be noted that no Sabres were on the strength of 442 Squadron, which had to use those of 443 Squadron.
29 For information on the national survival role see Major-General A.E. Wrinch, "The Role of the Army in National Survival," *Canadian Medical Association Journal*, vol. 87 (December 1962): 1146–53, and J. Mackay Hitsman, *Report No. 96, Historical Section Army Headquarters, The Canadian Army's Role in Survival Operations*. The Auxiliary's role would be to provide transport, provide assessments of damage, monitor radiation levels and fallout areas.
30 COSC, Minutes of the 604th Meeting held at 0930, Friday, February 1, 1957, in the office of the chairman, chiefs of staff, National Defence Headquarters, Item V, DHH, 2002/17, Box 71, File 4.
31 COSC, Minutes of a Special Meeting held at 0930 on Wednesday, June 26, 1957, in the office of the chairman, chiefs of staff, National Defence Headquarters, paras 47 and 49 (c), DHH, 2002/17. Box 71, File 4.
32 895-64/418 (DOE), Feb 19, '58, Organization Order R10.0.18.1, 418 Squadron (Auxiliary) RCAF, Namao, Alberta; 895-64/424 (DOE), Jun 1, '58, Organization Order R3.19.1, 424 Squadron (Auxiliary) RCAF, Vancouver, BC; 443 also Jun 1, '58; 895-64/438 (DOE), Jun 16, '58, Organization Order R2.11.2, 438 Squadron (Auxiliary) RCAF, Montreal, PQ.
33 Based on author's research for forthcoming book on the RCAF Intelligence service.
34 COSC, Minutes of a SPECIAL Meeting Held on June 25, 26 and 27, 1958, in the office of the chairman, chiefs of staff, National Defence Headquarters, paras 9 (a)(iii)(G) and 9 (a)(iii)(L) DHH, 73/1223, File 1313.

35 "Briefing by AVM DM Smith, CBE, CD, Vice Chief of the Air Staff to the Air Officers Conference, March 17, 1959, para 42 and S000-109-59(A/CAS) Summary of Major RCAF Programs, March 18, 1959, para 4, DHH, 73/1223, File 2005.
36 Two Bells and two Vertols were to be on the strength of six Auxiliary squadrons. COSC, Minutes of the 63lst Meeting Held at 0930 hours on May 14, 1959, in the office of the chairman, chiefs of staff, National Defence Headquarters, Para 27 (c) and (e). DHH, 73/1223, File 1310; and COSC, Minutes of the 648th Meeting held at 0930 hours on November 5, 1959, in the office of the chairman, chiefs of staff, National Defence Headquarters, para 7, and para 9 (a) and (c), DHH, 73/1223, File 1310A.
37 Minutes of the Air Council Meeting 18/61 held in the Air Council Room, at 0900 Hrs, May 3, 1961, and continued at 0900, May 4, 1961, Item 77, DHH, 73/1223, File 1837.
38 "Minutes of the Air Council Meeting 35/61 Held in the Air Council Room at 0900 Hrs, Sep 6, 1961, Item 159, DHH, 73/1223, File 1837-2. In 1959, the three services signed an agreement on joint helicopter requirements. The procurement of the Hiller 12E had been ongoing since early 1959 with the Army and RCAF to receive this aircraft.
39 RCAF Auxiliary Brief for the AOsC Conference to be held March 15–17, 1960, 1, DHH, 73/1223, File 2007.
40 Records of the 584th COSC meeting, Nov 1, '55, DHH, 73/1223, File 2500.
41 895-91/97 (DOE) Oct 3, '60, Organization Order R2.0.6, Disbandment of 2400 Aircraft Control and Warning Squadron LAC, Microfilm 12403. Other Auxiliary AC&W disbandment orders state the same thing.
42 Minutes of the 1960 Conference of Air Officers Commanding and Air Officers held in the Air Council Room at Air Force Headquarters, Ottawa, Mar 15–17, 1960, Item 7, DHH, 73/1223, File 2000.
43 S895-100-125, Compt, Feb 15, '63, Supporting Data for Air Council: RCAF Military Manpower Requirements FY 63/64 to FY 67/68, Appendix B, Item 7, DHH, 73/1223, File 1874; S895-100-125, Compt, 16 May 16, '63, Supporting Data for Air Council: RCAF Military Manpower Requirements Status Report on Reduction Programme, Appendix, Item 7 DHH 73/1223, File 1887; Minutes of the Special Air Council Meeting held in the Air Council Room at 1100 hrs, Jul 29, 1963 and File 1835, Summary Record of Decisions of Special Air Council Meeting held in the Air Council Room at 1400 hrs, Jan 9, 1964, para 6, DHH 73/1223, File 1834.
44 "ATC Effectiveness Evaluation Briefing, Air Council, 15 May 15, 1963, 8, 10, 14 and 15–16, DHH, 73/1223, File 1886.
45 A/V/CAS "Supporting Data for Air Council: RCAF Auxiliary – Impending Meeting with Auxiliary Squadron Representatives," paras 1, 2, 3, 5 and 6, DHH, 73/1223, File 1942; and S895-100-91, March 23, 1964, "Minutes of the Air Council Meeting 7/64 held in the Air Council Room at 1145 hrs, Feb 19, 1964 and continued at 1600 hrs, Feb 19, '64, Item 30, DHH 73/1223, File 1947.
46 ATC Stewardship Briefing to Air Council, Jun 24, '64, paras 59 and 60, DHH 73/1223, File 1957.
47 Memorandum to Defence Council from Chief of Defence Staff: Air Reserve Study, paras 3–5, June 5, 1968, DHH, 73/1223, File 2125; and Minutes of the Chief of Defence Staff – Staff Meeting 22/67 held in the CDS Conference Room at 0900 hours on October 18, 1967. Para 21 (c) The designation Royal Canadian Air Force Auxiliary be replaced by "Air Reserve Squadrons," V1901-3091/00 (DLANDR), DHH, 73/1223, File 1617.

SECTION 3

INTRODUCTION

WILLIAM MARCH

At first glance it might be difficult to identify a unifying theme for the six chapters contained in this section, as they run the gamut from reaching for the stars to plumbing the depths of the world's oceans. However, the material provided allows the reader to appreciate the breadth of activities undertaken by the RCAF in the period between the end of the Second World War and its dissolution in 1967. It does so by studiously ignoring the primary focus of Canada's air force during its "golden age" – fighters. There is no doubt that the provision of fighters for North American air defence and European security drove the evolution of the RCAF during the first two decades of the Cold War, but it is equally true that the ancillary, or secondary, tasks undertaken during this period were extremely important to the nation. In the post-unification era, in areas such as search and rescue (SAR), transport, or support to peacekeeping, air force organizations and their aviators undertaking these tasks have arguably eclipsed the pre-eminence within the Canadian consciousness once enjoyed by fighter units and personnel. Yet, the bulk of RCAF historical writing deals briefly, if it addresses them at all, with the subjects covered in the following chapters.

There are exceptions to this mild condemnation. Andrew Godefroy's *Defence & Discovery: Canada's Military Space Program, 1945–1974* and James Perotti's *Becoming a No-Fail Mission: The Origins of Search and Rescue in Canada* are two studies that shed light on aspects of the RCAF that, while perhaps well known, such as SAR, have never been examined with academic rigour. In their respective chapters, both these scholars make excellent use of their in-depth knowledge and delve into the how space and SAR became an integral part of RCAF institutional growth.

Studies of Canada's involvement with peacekeeping have become something of a cottage industry. Although many of the papers and books on this subject deal with this endeavour from a political perspective, most military-oriented treatments examine peacekeeping from the angle of Canadian land forces. This latter viewpoint is not surprising as the RCAF major contribution, airlift, was seen as routine task for the air force's air transport squadrons. Routine could also be used to describe the RCAF's numerous humanitarian flights undertaken prior to unification. And yet, as described below, these unplanned missions were an important part of Canada's foreign policy and diplomatic efforts in the 1950s and 1960s.

The chapter on maritime aviation examines a so-called second-tier community within the RCAF. Although the bulk of RCAF North American-based resources may have flowed to air defence organizations, the need to provide a land-based maritime air capability to safeguard the shipping lanes that had proved so vital in the Second World War was never in doubt. During the Cold War, Canadian maritime aviation became a key element in defending Canada and its allies against Soviet nuclear and conventional submarines. The postwar reconstitution, growth, employment, and impact on the RCAF's inter-service relations is a complex subject as reflected by Ernest Cable's comprehensive examination.

Dean Black's look at Canadian army aviation adds another important element to RCAF historiography – how the services interacted with respect to the broader notion of military aviation. The retention of an aviation element after the Second World War, employment in Korea, and introduction of a rotary-wing capability by the Canadian Army resulted in both cooperation and conflict with the RCAF. The areas of friction, whose underlying cause was a basic desire to control direct aviation support to land forces, has not gone away, and a comprehensive understanding of how both the debate and the capability waxed and waned during the early years of the Cold War can only enhance our understanding.

And what of Canadian naval aviation? The trials and tribulations of the Royal Canadian Naval Aviation Branch and its often-tumultuous relationship with the RCAF have been dealt with in numerous studies, such as J.D.F. Kealy and E.C. Russell's *A History of Canadian Naval Aviation 1918–1962* and Shawn Cafferky's excellent *Uncharted Waters: A History of the Canadian Helicopter Carrying Destroyer*. The story with respect to army aviation in Canada has yet to be told in any detail.

The same lack of historical attention afflicts the evolution of RCAF air transport. Air Transport Command's responsibilities were truly global in nature while underpinning virtually all the RCAF's Cold War commitments. And while often categorized as routine, its activities and contributions to the Canadians and the nation writ large were, and are, extremely important. Bert Frandsen's examination of the RCAF air transport provides an intriguing glimpse into how this capability grew from humble wartime beginnings to become a key ingredient in Canadian domestic, international, and defence policy.

The six chapters of this section will fill in some of the historiographical blanks that exist within the history of the RCAF and Canadian military aviation, but there is still much work to be done. The authors and editors collectively hope that the information provided will elicit a broader understanding of the RCAF's contributions as an element of national power, and will also stimulate curiosity, debate, and a desire for further research and analysis. The chapters contained herein are but the start of a much larger story. Enjoy the read.

CHAPTER ELEVEN

THE RCAF AT THE DAWN OF THE SPACE AGE, 1958–1965

ANDREW GODEFROY

At the height of the Cold War, the central role of the RCAF in Canada's early forays into the militarization and weaponization of outer space was something of a natural evolution. Already closely linked to emerging US programs, thanks to the ongoing joint effort to defend North American airspace from a possible Soviet attack, assisting its American partners in their initial efforts to dominate space seemed an inevitable follow-on task for the air force. Yet despite the RCAF's desire to sustain this additional relationship and continue its natural evolution over the long term, the financial burden and scale of effort needed to leverage policy, technology, people, and processes in the pursuit of new missile, rocketry, and space capabilities proved to be far greater than what the air force could commit to such an endeavour, as national priorities and programs shifted to other interests.

Though the genesis of Canada's Cold War era rocketry and space capabilities may be traced to early postwar work led by the Defence Research Board (DRB), its continued engagement was contested by the RCAF which, after two key events in 1957, came to see itself as the rightful office of primary interest for everything concerned with Canada's defence of the upper atmosphere and beyond. The first of these events was the ratification of the NORAD agreement that made the RCAF a central actor in the emerging fields of missile and space technologies. The second, the Soviet launch of the world's first satellite, known as *Sputnik*, stoked deep fears among Western allies with respect to Soviet ballistic missile technology and prompted immediate calls for military readiness to meet the new threat. Both incidents served to set the short-term priorities for the RCAF in its attempt to militarize and weaponize space, beginning with a renewed focus on the development of North America's missile defence capabilities.

Missile Defence

Within just two years of the end of the Second World War, the Soviet Union had successfully reverse-engineered its captured German V-2 missile technology into a new, equally capable design known as the R-1. When *Sputnik* was launched a decade later in 1957, it travelled into orbit atop a modified R-7 design capable of more than 30 times the range of the R-1 and easily earning the title of the world's first fully operational Intercontinental Ballistic Missile (ICBM). Such a weapon delivery system, carrying either a conventional or nuclear warhead, could reach North American targets. Canadian defence planners recognized the threat and wasted little time cooperating with their American partners to rapidly develop early warning radar and anti-ballistic missile systems, as well as the space and ground control systems needed to coordinate these technologies into a comprehensive and layered defence.

Binational efforts towards ballistic missile defence grew out of earlier efforts to respond to Soviet air power threats. Anticipating that the first line of defence against a Soviet bombing attack or incursion over the North Pole would need to be deployed far forward in Canada's Arctic, early projects focused on the effects of extreme environments on surface-to-air missiles (SAM) such as the American designed Nike-Ajax and Nike-Hercules. Interestingly, during the initial phase of this testing and evaluation, the army rather than the air force managed Canada's partnership.

The RCAF only took on a more prominent role from 1960 onwards. At the centre of its research program were ballistic missile re-entry characteristics, and the USAF soon requested and supported Canadian expertise to advance its own development. A joint research endeavour heavily funded by the US Advanced Research Projects Agency (ARPA) was initiated in 1960 under the code name Project Defender. The main Canadian contribution to the project came from the RCAF's Central Experimental and Proving Establishment (CEPE), though at various times the DRB and one of its sub-organizations, the Canadian Armament Research and Development Establishment (CARDE), were also involved.

While many aspects of the project remain classified, two RCAF operations received considerable public attention and thus are better known. The first of these, Operation LOOKOUT, ran from January 1960 to September 1963 and involved the deployment of CEPE CF-100 Canuck interceptors, along with DRB scientists and RCAF personnel, to places such as Ascension Island and the Grand Bahamas, from which tracing missions were flown using aircraft fitted with scientific payloads that allowed capture of data on missile re-entry characteristics.[1] Crews were required to intercept and photograph the inbound supersonic warheads before they landed in the ocean, a task demanding considerable skill of pilots unfamiliar with chasing

RCAF transport aircraft load personnel and material in support of a joint Air Force/Defence Research Board undertaking in early 1960 for the long trip to Ascension Island in the South Atlantic. Part of Operation LOOKOUT, the team were to measure infrared radiation characteristics from ballistic missiles launched from Cape Canaveral, Florida.

such quick targets.[2] It was later estimated after the conclusion of the first series of flights that 90 per cent of the data recorded proved valuable to further defence research.[3] The Chief of the Air Staff (CAS), Air Marshal (A/M) Hugh Campbell, congratulated his crews on a job well done.[4] Even the chairman of the DRB, Dr. A.H. Zimmerman, was impressed, noting, "the flying and navigation skills exhibited by the personnel concerned should be a matter of pride to all in the RCAF."[5]

Similarly, the year-long Operation BLIND TWINKLER, commenced June 1962, sought to establish the feasibility of detecting ballistic missiles in mid-course using various reflected sunlight techniques. Led by Flight Lieutenant (F/L) J.F. Dyer, RCAF crews and civilian defence scientists were dispatched to Thule Air Base in Greenland, where they carried out at least 40 high altitude flights to capture scientific data on ICBM re-entry characteristics.[6]

One of two Central Experimental and Proving Establishment CF-100 Canucks deployed to Ascension Island in the South Atlantic at RCAF Station Rockcliffe, ON, 1960. Equipped with special wing-mounted sensor pods, these aircraft gathered information on a wide range of missile tests as part of Operation LOOKOUT.

Space Indoctrination

Senior air officers on the RCAF's Air Council were briefed on the military potential of outer space in April 1959. Anticipating increased RCAF involvement, the Air Council moved quickly to initiate plans for increasing the base level of space knowledge among all ranks of the RCAF.[7] Direction was given to explore the feasibility of establishing space oriented professional military education (PME) programs and to seek to embed select RCAF personnel within USAF missile and space programs at all levels. The PME programs were to include nuclear warfare briefings for all air force officers of the rank of group captain and above, as it was expected that both current ICBMs, and future spacecraft, would carry such warheads.[8]

Air Force HQ developed its first Space Indoctrination Course (SIC) over the course of the summer and it included a series of lectures covering the physics of the solar system, characteristics of rockets, ballistic missiles, and space vehicles, the potential uses of space vehicles, and a review of Canadian work to date in the various fields covered in the course. The first SICs were conducted in 1960 at several headquarters: Air Force Headquarters (AFHQ), Air Materiel Command (AMC), Air Defence Command (ADC), Training Command, and 1 Air Division. While the various commands gave the course only to its headquarters personnel, 1 Air Division presented it to all its wings and to both officers and non-commissioned officers.[9]

Concurrent with the introduction of the SICs, the RCAF's chief of operational readiness and his director of systems evaluation, K.J. Radford, collaborated to evaluate emerging US space initiatives and their potential application to Canadian defence problems. Known as the Advanced Technology Evaluation Program, this initiative examined American developments in space surveillance, ballistic missile defence (in particular the Missile Detection Alarm System), satellite communications systems, and the potential of space-based navigation aids. From 1960 onwards there was also an expressed interest – albeit a limited one – in the American man in space program and the desire to potentially add one or two RCAF officers to the pool of candidates if possible.[10] These studies and evaluations led to a series of detailed research reports that provided the basis for determining future RCAF requirements and increasing the general level of understanding of the broader impacts resulting from achieving access to space.[11]

RCAF Personnel in American Space Programs

In the late 1950s, the RCAF initiated plans for further collaboration with evolving American missile and space organizations. The RCAF air liaison officer in Washington, DC, verified the potential opportunity for integrating select personnel directly into various US missile and space programs. Progress was slow as the US was heavily engaged in many overt and covert programs and was not sure of the benefit of including foreign officers. However, General Curtis Lemay, USAF chief of staff, took a personal interest in the Canadian offer, especially with regard to bringing in RCAF officers with science and engineering backgrounds. With his support, the USAF identified several potential exchange assignments before the end of the year. By December 1959, formal negotiations were in motion for the addition of Canadian officers into selected American programs.[12]

What became known as the Space Indoctrination Program (SIP) got underway in 1961, and 12 officers with science and engineering backgrounds were embedded in a variety of US rocket and spaceflight program offices of interest to Canada.[13] Regardless of their actual posting, attached officers typically fell under the command of the USAF Headquarters Space Systems Division (SSD) in Los Angeles, California.[14] Tasked with the planning, programming, procurement, development, and management of dozens of US space projects and systems, the SSD became the primary point of contact and administration for the SIP cadre.

Among the initial SIP members were Squadron Leaders (S/Ls) Jack Henry, Allan Pickering, John Webster, and Robert White, as well as F/Ls T.M. Harris, J.H. Lathey and Andy Thoma. Of these, Pickering and Webster were assigned first to the Mariner and then later to Atlas-Agena Program Offices, while Thoma was posted to the Engineering Division of the Standard Launch Vehicle II Directorate.[15] Henry and Lathey, meanwhile, were assigned to work in the Aeronautical Systems Division at Wright Paterson Air Force Base, where the latter was heavily engaged on the X-20 Dyna-Soar Program. Prior to being cancelled in 1963, it was considered one of the most advanced spaceflight programs in the world.[16] Similarly, F/Ls Harris and Lathey made a name for themselves as a result of their contributions at the USAF Flight Dynamics Laboratory. Harris worked on spacecraft re-entry problems while Lathey tackled the problems of the fly-by-wire systems for the X-20 Dyna-Soar.[17]

Working in both the Mercury and Gemini Launch Vehicle Directorates, S/L "Bud" White found himself at the very heart of the American space race. He later recalled, "I spent most of my first year seconded to the Mercury Program Office, travelling with the program director, accepting launch vehicles at General Dynamics Astronautics, San Diego, and participating in the final two launches of the Mercury Program at Cape Canaveral. My basic task had been to bring the lessons learned on Mercury back to Gemini."[18] With the expansion of the Gemini program, White soon found himself participant to even more significant events. "As the GLV [Gemini Launch Vehicle] Pilot Safety Operations Officer, I became responsible for all acceptance and flight safety and pre-launch review board operations, and also for propellants, loading, and engine operations at Cape Canaveral."[19] It was a considerable degree of authority, responsibility, and trust given to a young officer who made his National Aeronautics and Space Administration (NASA) colleagues look twice the first day he arrived at work wearing an RCAF uniform.

For others still, assignments would take them to the USAF Space and Missile Systems Organization Headquarters, El Segundo, California, or even more sensitive projects such as the 496L System Program Office, dealing with space object detection and tracking. By 1968, at least 30 RCAF officers had served on exchange under the SIP, though it is estimated that the actual number of RCAF personnel within American programs at this time, not counting NORAD or other related exchanges, was higher.[20]

Space-Based Surveillance and Reconnaissance

Pursued in secrecy from the very start of the space age, much of Canada's early role in ground and space-based surveillance and reconnaissance remains classified, making it still difficult to present a complete picture. However, what information has been released hints at a program that, while not large, was sophisticated and well-integrated within larger US programs.

Shortly after the launch of *Sputnik*, the USAF Cambridge Research Laboratories, located at Hanscom Air Force Base in Bedford, Massachusetts, initiated an in-house project to collect orbital element information on Russian spacecraft. At first the project resembled little more than a quasi-scientific effort, scrounging data from a diverse range of telemetry sources, scientific radars, and even amateur astronomers. However, when it became obvious that there was a serious national security requirement to start tracking the growing number of Soviet satellites and spacecraft, if for no other reason than to determine the potential threat to the US, steps were taken to develop a robust space detection and tracking system under the aegis of the recently created NORAD.[21]

Early efforts to design such a system began in 1959 with the activation of an inconspicuous organization at Hanscom, known simply as the 496L System Program Office (SPO).[22] Resources and support were limited; however, in June 1961, the nascent satellite tracking and data processing centre at Hanscom was transferred to Cheyenne Mountain at Colorado Springs. Briefly, US Air Defense Command assumed responsibility for the capability and renamed it "Spacetrack," but it was integrated into another more complex space detection and tracking system (SPADATS) controlled through the newly created Space Defense Center (SDC), also located within the Cheyenne Mountain complex. Canada formally joined the American data collection effort in late 1960 with the contribution of air force personnel and equipment both in Canada and the US, creating its own Satellite Identification Tracking Unit (SITU) at RCAF Station Cold Lake, Alberta, and sending liaison officers to the 496L SPO at Hanscom in late 1961.[23]

The SITU at Cold Lake was tasked with tracking designated space targets, employing a Baker-Nunn optical satellite-tracking camera system. Roughly the size of compact car, the mounted and stabilized camera followed its orbiting target by taking advantage of sunlight that reflected off of the spacecraft. However, the sensor could only operate in darkness while the target was in daylight and a suitable

Canada's Eye on the Sky. The three-ton Baker-Nunn Satellite Tracking Camera at RCAF's Primrose Lake evaluation range 40 kilometres from RCAF Station Cold Lake, Alberta, is made ready for the night's operation by Sergeant Bob Young. The electronically controlled camera, one of fourteen located around the world, is maintained and manned by twelve technicians of the RCAF.

angle of reflection existed between the two, known as the "look-angle." The RCAF SITU camera crews were given points of reference from the SDC, which were then used to take a series of high-resolution photographs of the orbiting satellite against a dark sky background. Individual frames were taken from the developed film and superimposed against a star atlas transparency marked with a grid reference system. Once oriented to the transparency, it was possible to record the right ascension and declination for any object shown on the film, thus identifying its position in the sky. For high earth and geosynchronous orbit satellites, this method was particularly effective, allowing for accuracy to 30/3600ths of a degree or just 30 seconds of arc. It was later claimed that the whole process could be further refined if needed, bringing the accuracy of the observation down to just two or three seconds of arc.[24]

General view of Baker-Nunn camera and building with roof in open position.

The Baker-Nunn camera itself was an impressive piece of technology for its time. The camera had a five-degree by thirty-degree field of view and the length of film exposure was optional, allowing its RCAF operators some flexibility in tracking and photographing both stationary and fast-moving targets. Once the film was processed and reduced, the satellite position dataset was sent back to the SDC where it was further processed by a computer and entered in a satellite catalogue, and that catalogue grew as more and more satellites were launched.

Within SPADATS, the technical analysis of tracked space objects required substantial computational power, an undeveloped commodity in Canada. Some accounts suggest that there were only four computers in all of Canada in 1960: a British-made FERUT at the University of Toronto, an American-made Computer Research Corporation CRC102A computer at Royal Canadian Air Force Base Cold Lake, an American-built ALWAC III computer at CARDE, Valcartier, Quebec; and

Baker-Nunn Satellite Tracking: Photographer Corporal Ray Tomblin examines camera film after processing. The film is specially prepared panoramic 55mm wide with an ASA rating of 600 frame size, 305 mm long by 55 mm wide. Processing is carried out in a T246 Processor.

the newly designed Defence Research and Telecommunications Establishment (DRTE) computer, nicknamed "Girtie", in Ottawa. The Cold Lake-based CRC102A computer and Baker-Nunn camera constituted the Canadian military's main contribution to SPADATS during much of the 1960s.[25]

The Co-Orbital Satellite Intercept Evaluation (COSINE) Project

The development of capabilities to defend against a Soviet ballistic missile attack focused much of the early efforts of RCAF missile and space research. Data collected through the SPADATS program suggested to defence planners that Soviet strategic reconnaissance of North America was increasing each year and, as early ballistic missile defence studies showed, it would be difficult to defeat adversary

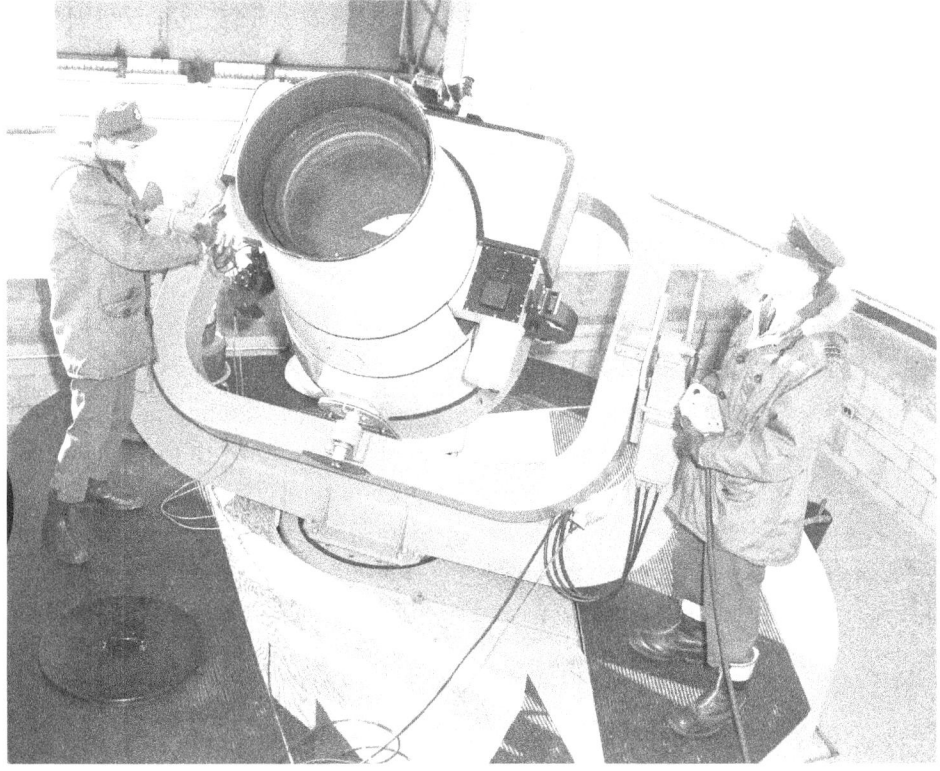

Another view of the Baker-Nunn camera. Flight Lieutenants Don Bamford and Bernard Kadonoff ready the camera for night satellite tracking operations.

weapons during their re-entry phase.[26] Accordingly, in early 1959 the RCAF proposed to complement their satellite tracking expertise with an anti-satellite intercept capability designed to defeat those systems needed to support ballistic missile attacks against Canada.

The RCAF Directorate of Systems Evaluation, at AFHQ Ottawa, led the initial series of studies and computer simulations examining problems involved in the rendezvous of one space vehicle with another in orbit.[27] The COSINE project, as it was known in the RCAF, focused on co-orbital rendezvous problems as these were considered a critical piece of the space operations puzzle affecting everything from launch to anti-satellite weapons, missile defence, and potentially landing humans on the moon. The project sought to determine the most feasible means of proceeding from initial launch to the target vehicle, developing the guidance and telemetry procedures necessary for closing the gap between the two vehicles to some pre-determined distance. Additionally, estimates of the overall probability of success, taking ground environment, launch vehicle, and potential rendezvous system vehicle errors into account, were also examined.[28]

The DRB scientists assigned to the project assumed that the target would not suddenly alter its orbit, or orientation, if another object approached. Therefore, they concluded, the RCAF could feasibly launch ground-based interceptors mounting an automated terminal homing guidance sensor and achieve the desired rendezvous conditions. Preliminary reports on the COSINE project sent to the CAS, A/M C. R. Dunlap, were very favourably received. In June 1963, he ordered the RCAF Directorate of Advanced Engineering and Development (DAED) at AFHQ to expand the COSINE project into a full research and development program with suitable funding. Interestingly, records indicate that at this point the CAS never considered the project's evolution to be a DRB responsibility; however, both DAED and other RCAF planners knew that engagement with DRB offices would still be necessary. Though the decision was easily made, there remained much work ahead of the RCAF to secure the materials and resources needed to bring the COSINE project to a physical testing stage.

The RCAF Space Defence Program

Impressed with the results of the COSINE project, in June 1963 the Air Council approved, in principle, a follow-on study, budgeting another $2.2 million to further develop co-orbital rendezvous techniques within a much larger RCAF omnibus military space program.[29] Specifically, the funds were to be committed to furthering the research and development of terminal homing guidance sensors for satellite interceptors. The interceptor vehicles themselves would be the focus of a separate project. With tentative Treasury Board approval in July 1963, the DAED was tasked the following month to initiate a formal RCAF Space Defence Program (SDP) that would oversee the satellite interceptor design through its hardware and flight test stages.[30] By December, the scope of the program had been further expanded to include the development of various inspection sensors as well as non-nuclear negation and kill capabilities.

The SDP received considerable praise from the senior RCAF leadership. Beyond the capability and prestige it offered, the SDP was exactly the sort of leverage that bought the air force further influence within the USAF. And while it was later learned that the US had undertaken concurrent investigations into similar technologies, the US Department of Defense continued to publicly express its support of, and interest in, the Canadian studies, tests, and field evaluations. When RCAF senior personnel met with their American counterparts at the US Directorate of

Defense Research and Engineering (DDR&E) at the Pentagon in March 1964, discussions concerning options for further cooperation and collaboration led Dr. Harold Brown, Director of the DDR&E, to recommend before the US Senate Committee on Aeronautical and Space Sciences support for Canadian research into co-orbital rendezvous techniques.[31]

By early 1964, the US had yet to conduct a successful rendezvous in orbit, an essential objective that had to be met if its own military and civilian space programs were to continue. The RCAF study was a critical piece of the military problem – the intercept of a potentially non-cooperative target.[32] During the RCAF visit to DDR&E in 1964, the Americans admitted to their Canadian counterparts that they had not yet initiated any serious study into non-cooperative orbital interception, but they were clearly interested in supporting and cooperating with Canadian efforts in this field.[33] Thus, rather than simply being adjunct to a larger American project, on this particular issue the Pentagon had suggested that Canada might lead the way for the time being. As of 1964, the US had limited ballistic intercept capabilities, consisting primarily of short-range proximity intercept missile defence systems such as the Nike-Zeus and Thor-Agena, both of which could carry nuclear warheads. However, although the Nike-Zeus could operate from launch sites in the far Canadian north, the Thor-Agena missile could not. As such the Pentagon was clearly interested in other options, regardless of their origin.

By mid-1964, the RCAF SDP started to take on considerable importance. The next step in the program was to identify the primary agencies that would execute each portion of the program. Unlike the US, where the responsibility for defence research had largely been left within the realms of each of the services, the RCAF Air Council knew that it required support from the DRB.

The Canadian government's tabling of a new *White Paper on Defence* in March 1964 created a new sense of urgency for the RCAF's space community. Earlier indications that the government sought to permanently integrate and unify the armed forces into a new single service were confirmed, and it was uncertain how exactly this restructuring would impact the air force's organization, administration, and budget. Space Defence Program planners met at the Ottawa offices of the DRB on 14 May 1964, to discuss the implications of the pending integration and to lay out a way ahead for its program. The RCAF planning team consisted of S/Ls N.B. Flavin, J.C. Uhthoff and Mr. J.H. Crysdale whose goal was, if possible, to obtain authorization for the proposal and get the Canadian Forces writ large officially involved in the business of military space. The focus of the RCAF program remained centred on the development of space-borne equipment for potential future satellite interceptor capabilities, which itself was divided into three smaller projects.[34]

The first of these focused on terminal homing guidance technologies. Assuming that very small miss distances were allowable in order to achieve close inspection, or a non-nuclear "hit" on the target, the project sought to investigate the employment of a guidance sub-system based on either passive or active spectral (e.g., radar or optical) sensor techniques.[35] The second project pursued the design of inspection sensors and techniques to determine satellite characteristics and functions, critical to the successful identification of a satellite or spacecraft. This project would focus on technologies that would complement, not duplicate, the capabilities of other friendly ground and space-based satellite data gathering platforms. The last project sought to examine non-nuclear kill mechanisms and negation techniques. Several kinetic methods, such as explosive warheads or shaped charges, were proposed, as if the whole enterprise differed little from engaging and destroying an enemy ground target. Little detail was provided on negation methods. However, the proposal did include seeking a means of upsetting the position, spin, or attitude of the target, disrupting its orbit, or even corrupting its heat balance, almost all of which would still result in the physical destruction of the satellite. Still, there was clearly less enthusiasm in the report for pursuing a complex non-lethal option to render the target useless, when a simpler, and likely cheaper, kinetic solution would do. The program was purposely divided such that should any one of the three initiatives fail to realize its objective, it would not result in the demise of the entire effort.

In addition to their meeting with the DRB on 14 May, the RCAF socialized their plans with other key stakeholders, including both the DRTE and CARDE, essential partners in the development phases. Finally, a plan of organization was investigated and a recommendation as to where the work should be done was made.[36]

Initial DRB reception of the SDP was less enthusiastic than anticipated, with senior defence scientists expressing a general opinion that the program would be very expensive in both budget and manpower. There was also some doubt as to whether the requisite technical capabilities and hardware existed within Canadian defence and industry. For example, by 1964 the DRB generally felt that it no longer maintained a leading edge in guidance and control R&D; this was made painfully evident in its ongoing troubles with the early DRB Black Brant III and IV series sounding rocket trials. Likewise, the DRTE was uncertain that it was able to make a substantive contribution to the SDP, and archival records also suggest that the DRTE senior leadership in general had little desire to undermine in any way its already substantial commitment to the Alouette-ISIS topside sounder satellite program already underway.[37]

The DRB also raised concerns that the success of the SDP was largely dependent on the current priorities of US space strategy and policy. If the end products

A fanciful image by Warrant Officer First Class Roy Tracy for an issue of the RCAF *Roundel* magazine.

of the Canadian program would consist of only components and sub-systems for American spacecraft rather than complete Canadian military interceptors or space vehicles, there were obviously huge risks involved in determining whether or not America would actually employ such an interceptor against unknown or potentially hostile satellites to warrant significant Canadian expenditure. Potential scientific prestige to be garnered from the SPD was also a point of contention with the RCAF team, noting that scientific and technological prestige was not a required by-product of a military hardware development program proposal.[38]

With little enthusiasm for the proposal, there was general reluctance from the DRB senior leadership to commit high calibre staff to the SDP working groups without specific instructions from a higher authority such as the chief of the DRB or the chairman of the chiefs of staff. They also expressed the opinion that any initial study undertaken should not be restricted to the proposed SDP, but instead be broadened to include other possible defence programs as well. This may have simply been a DRB attempt to steer the priorities of defence space program writ large towards its own agenda.[39]

Flavin, Uhthoff, and Dr. Crysdale noted in their reports to the CAS that any further attempt to resolve the ideological differences between the RCAF and the DRB at lower levels would be fruitless. The RCAF then recommended the establishment of a steering committee, composed of both senior DRB and RCAF personnel, to provide executive-level decision and guidance over the future of Canadian military space operations. The committee would investigate relevant facets of American programs; survey the state of the art in emerging space programs; evaluate possible programs in terms of expenditure, assess the requirement for available technical capability, and their impact on other Canadian organizations and industry; determine contributions to mutual defence agreements; and ensure compatibility of all defence programs with overall Canadian foreign policy and objectives. The attempt here was clearly, in the absence of clear direction from above, to ensure an oversight committee was in place so that when a definitive national, or defence space policy, was issued, DND would be prepared to enact it immediately. A growing sense of frustration was evident in comments by a senior air force officer when he wrote, "The trepidation of recommending the formation of any committee at this point in time [was] overcome by the frustration of getting nothing done in the way of RCAF space activity in the last four years …"[40] After so much staff effort by so many dedicated people, personalities were now threatening to unravel all that was accomplished. Some RCAF officers, at least, could see the writing on the wall.

On 20 July 1964, the RCAF-DRB working groups completed their report and recommendations and sent them up the chain of command. The subsequent lack of any response to the recommendations drew further RCAF criticism. One officer later noted with disgust, "If we are to opt out of future military technology let it be done by conscious decision rather than by default."[41] These and other similar observations were forwarded through the RCAF Comptroller, Air Vice Marshal (A/V/M) Victor Millard to the CAS.

Unfortunately, the RCAF's space advocates were too late. The integration of the three separate armed services began in August 1964, and A/M C.L. Annis, newly appointed Canadian Forces Chief – Logistics and Engineering, returned both the report and the recommendations back down the chain of command noting that, in view of the statements of the roles of the CF as outlined in the government's 1964 *White Paper on Defence*, and the changes in DND organization, the recommendations made for the RCAF's role in space and the previous funding allocations were no longer considered valid. The 1964 white paper had devoted a small section to the issue of missile defence, but there was no mention of militarizing space beyond a single sentence congratulating the DRB for its launch of the first Alouette satellite.

Annis considered that an *ab initio* submission would be absolutely necessary in gaining authority to embark on any sort of large-scale DND-sponsored space program. Therefore, on 30 September 1964, he directed that such a submission be prepared for consideration by the newly created Development and Associated Research Policy Group (DARPG), which had been assigned to consider such issues.[42] Annis also wrote to Millard of his desire to bring more attention to the issue. In a memo at the end of September 1964 he stated, "I am willing, even anxious, to see a fresh consideration of a DND space program" and commented further that he felt that the new organization's decision-making machinery would facilitate future direction rather than hinder it.[43]

Despite a new report being hastily prepared and submitted to Annis by the end of the year, all such initiatives were being overtaken by events. Further changes in the organization and structure of the new Canadian Forces Headquarters (CFHQ) resulted in the revised report being returned to the DRB-RCAF working group without further ascent. This time, the incoming officer succeeding A/V/M Millard noted that he personally would not be responsible for this type of work in his new organization, and suggested that a more appropriate channel to A/M Annis be found. Such bureaucratic obstruction was frustrating. Yet another report was prepared, but this time the resubmission passed through several deputies, a hallmark of the ever-increasing defence bureaucracy emerging in Ottawa. In the end, A/M Annis was only supportive of the recommendations made that clearly defined an actual space program, not those associated with the approval of the three technical projects laid out in the 1964–6 air force estimates. After nearly seven months of staff effort, Canada's military space program had still not yet taken a single official step towards implementation.

In January 1965, the latest revisions to the plan were submitted to the DARPG. This group determined that it was still inadequate, which then prompted the DRB's leading space development organizations, DRTE and CARDE, to initiate their own alternate detailed national level assessment of Canada's space activities to date. This separate effort, led by DRTE scientist John Chapman, led to the publication of a report that would influence Canada's space agenda for years to come. Meanwhile the extant DRB-RCAF material, along with other recommendations and interviews from various parties involved in space activity, finally culminated in the publication of a report with the non-descript title "DARPG Paper 12/65."

Final Effort: DARPG Paper 12/65

The DARPG distributed its report on the SDP in May 1965, providing a frank assessment of the challenges and successes to date.[44] In addition to a summary of Canada's military space activities, the report highlighted the generally disorganized defence approach towards national space development, and in particular the increased acrimony between the DRB and RCAF over future space priorities since the air force's first involvement in ballistic missile defence and space tracking in 1958.

Since the earliest days of the Cold War the DRB had acted as the primary advocate for the development of a Canadian presence in space. In addition to bringing together and organizing the various agencies within DND that dealt with missiles and space, the DRB was largely responsible for early launcher development in Canada as well as detailed ICBM research and analysis. In 1957, the DRB initiated discussions with NASA on the possibilities of launching a satellite so that by 1959 the DRB was already at the centre of Canada's fledgling outer space program, devoting its energy and resources towards its two primary projects – the Black Brant series of sounding rockets and the Alouette-ISIS experimental satellite project.

The DARPG report noted that despite a general interest in space affairs, up to 1965 Canada's three armed services had only limited direct involvement in the R&D surrounding defence space systems. While technically correct, the report overlooked the fact that all three services had largely divested their extant programs and agendas to the DRB when it was created in 1947. Still, the military was involved in operational matters such as space tracking at RCAF Station Cold Lake and the Prince Albert Radar Laboratory, then serving as a DRTE research site studying the effects of the Aurora Borealis on long-range radio propagation and radar. Otherwise, it was largely regulated to the development of an air-transportable satellite communications terminal and a series of analytical studies on space rendezvous and space surveillance. In addition to these operational projects, the military supplied the DRB with most of its test personnel, logistics support, and equipment such as specially modified jets for tracking incoming missile warheads.

The DRB was essentially free to set its own research agenda and priorities, and as the report correctly points out, by 1965 there were clearly differences of opinion as to what should be the main focus of effort for Canada's national space program. While the armed services were clearly seeking military applications from investments in the space program, the DRB, acting as the country's de facto space agency since the days of Sputnik, felt that it should continue to focus on more fundamental scientific research rather than military applications. There is little doubt from the

DARPG report that the RCAF's growing interest in shaping Canada's defence space program upset some senior DRB officials.[45]

The reluctance to incorporate the RCAF space priorities was perceived by some to be payback for earlier attempts by the RCAF to curb DRB efforts when previously it had had greater control over the defence research agenda. There was also an element of protectionism of the resources needed to pursue the Alouette-ISIS project, knowing that the government could not support more than one program at a time. Whatever the case, the irony that the military's primary scientific research organization appeared to have little or no interest in making defence research its primary objective cannot be understated. Undoubtedly, the Black Brant and Alouette-ISIS projects supported national interests, but the DRB's mandate and raison d'être had not changed. This point was also highlighted in the same report, noting:

> Having regard for the basic responsibilities of this department [DND], there seems to be a strong case for a well-conceived research and development program oriented towards military satellites and space vehicles, rather than devoting the major part of our effort to a cooperative program with the non-military American space agency. This is not to degrade the value of the latter, but rather to bring into question whether it should be allowed to override the military need when funded out of the defence budget.[46]

The report highlighted the fact that without an officially ratified civilian or defence-oriented government space policy, further department-level discussions on the proper direction of Canada's space research and development were purely academic. What was needed more than anything, DARPG advised, was definitive guidance from government. Interestingly, prior to the release of the DARPG report in May 1965, a memorandum issued in April 1965 by J.C. Arnell, who had served as science advisor to the CAS, essentially made the same point. As the senior non-DRB defence official involved in formulating Canada's space program at the time, he wrote, "…on reflection, I consider that until the basic policy decision is made, any detailed proposals for a program only tend to divert attention away from the basic problem."[47]

Perhaps the most important recommendation to appear out of the DARPG paper was the identification of the requirement for senior-level ministerial policy and direction on Canada's future role in space. While the DARPG report clearly favoured the idea that Canada's defence space program should be driven by military priorities, it did not answer the question of who, instead of the DRB, should assume responsibility for Canada's civilian and scientific space priorities.

Uncertain Future

The DARPG findings signalled the grim state of the organization and direction of Canadian military space activities and caused DND's space advocates to re-evaluate their goals and priorities. Missile and space defence programs were becoming more complex, and DND found itself increasingly challenged to maintain a degree of saliency in such activities as its resources shrunk. Worse, the piecemeal approach to military space planning and operations only highlighted the lack of organization and direction over such efforts at CFHQ. If not quickly and seriously addressed, the air power advocates within DND were in danger of losing their remaining space capabilities altogether.

At the end of September 1965, the Science Director for Chief of Technical Services called Lieutenant-Colonel (LCol) D.B.D. Warner, Acting Director of Advanced Concepts and Systems (DACS), to his office "to discuss a number of items relating to Canadian military space activities, or rather the lack of them."[48] The conversation highlighted the fact that within the massive reorganization of the Canadian services as they moved towards unification, the military space agenda was unravelling. The director asked Warner to prepare yet another discussion paper outlining ideas that would serve as the impetus for defining requirements on Canadian military space activities. Warner responded with a report a month later, after having conducted a series of interviews and investigations with each of the three services and several related agencies.

Warner's new report, submitted on 28 October 1965, reflected what many within the RCAF already knew – all military space programs were in trouble. Interviews with various combat development staffs reconfirmed earlier conclusions that very little thought was being devoted to future military space requirements. There were many reasons for this, not the least of which was the departmental disruption caused by bureaucratic integration. What may have been the mandate of an RCAF office one week was suddenly another's responsibility the next. Little was being accomplished.

It was also increasingly apparent that no one was anxious to become a military champion for outer space. Even the RCAF, the primary advocate and proponent of military space programs for many years, began to withdraw its usually high level of support. "The general attitude toward military space activities must be summarized for the time being," the A/DACS later wrote, "as disinterested."[49] He then concluded, "In this environment it is unlikely that much support would be given to space proposals of a long-range nature, and particularly not to proposals that suggest new roles for the Canadian Forces. It is much more likely that proposals directed towards the enhancement of existing and anticipated roles will survive. This is a case of first things first and suggestions probably should be confined to this area if there is to be much hope at this time of meaningful VCDS [Vice Chief of Defence Staff] support."[50]

As the RCAF headed towards unification, its missile and space program, like so many other technologically advanced capabilities, atrophied. There was little, if any, political direction, and the generals seemed unwilling to stake their own interests in high-risk programs that might never come to fruition. Plans for steering existing scientific and technological capability in the direction of future military requirements had yet to materialize. Similarly, efforts to transfer those technology from defence into civilian industry fizzled, challenging the long-believed assertion that military establishments played an important role in shaping technological and economic change by linking national defence with national welfare.[51]

The RCAF's diminishing technology edge served to further divide political interests within the defence community as the DRB scrambled to protect its much-loved Alouette-ISIS satellite program at the expense of all other military efforts. Further agitated by a dynamic shift in Canadian foreign policy and the reorganization then taking place within the defence and scientific communities, RCAF attention and support for missile and defence space endeavours evaporated as it focused simply on survival. Seen as costly and increasingly technologically impossible to develop and sustain, the RCAF ultimately withdrew almost all its investments in these programs to save others. By the end of the 1960s, the RCAF's missile and space programs were all but terminated as its military assets were transferred to civilian government sectors and much needed resources and funds were devoted elsewhere.

NOTES

1 Flight Lieutenant (F/L) L.C Morrison, "South Atlantic Lookout: Canada Assists U.S. Missile Research Program with Infrared Detection Team on Ascension Island," *The Roundel*, (April 1960): 2–3.

2 Anon. "Missile Monitors," *The Roundel*, (May 1962): 15. RCAF crews even conducted measurements on the American Atlas booster used to hoist Astronaut John Glenn on his way to being the first American to orbit the Earth.

3 Anon. "The Cameras Saw Red," *The Roundel*, (March 1961): 13–14.

4 DRB "Resume of Major Research Activities," June 8, 1962, LAC. RG 24, Acc. 83-84/167 Vol.7407 173-1 pt. 1.

5 Op. cit. "The Cameras Saw Red," 14.

6 DRB a Resume…, 4, LAC. RG 24, Acc. 83-84/167 Vol.7407 173-1 pt. 1.

7 Correspondence from A/M Hugh Campbell, Chief of Air Staff to A/M C.R. Slemon, Deputy Commander in Chief of NORAD, dated March 28, 1961, 1, LAC. RG 24, Vol.17829, File 840-105 001.8.

8 Development and Associated Research Policy Group Paper 12/65 – A Canadian Forces Space Development Program dated May 12, 1965. 2, LAC. RG 24, Vol. 17973 File 925-121-3. L1150-4110/D8 (Secret).
9 Op. cit., 2, LAC. RG 24, Vol.17829, File 840-105-001.8.
10 Ibid. 4. While not directly entering the US astronaut corps, RCAF officers did work within the National Aeronautics and Space Administration (NASA).
11 Ibid., 3.
12 Op. cit., 3, LAC, RG 24, Vol.17829, File 840-105-001.8.
13 For the only known published Canadian source on the SIP see Anon. "Canadian Missile Men," *Sentinel*, (September 1969), 32–3. Interviews with RCAF officers in the SIP revealed that they were never informed that their "loan" to the United States fell under any organized plan, though official documentation and the above-mentioned article reference the SIP.
14 Reports and Returns – RCAF Personnel on Exchange Duties – USAF – HQS Air Force Space Systems Division – Los Angeles – Calif. 1963–1965, LAC, RG 24, File 813-89/3-42.
15 Exchange Officer Report Flight Lieutenant A. Thoma, Headquarters Air Force Space Systems Division, Los Angeles, California, March 15, 1963, LAC, RG 24, File 813-89/3-42.
16 D.R. Jenkins, *Space Shuttle: The History of the National Space Transportation System*, 30–1.
17 RCAF Exchange Officer Report – F/L T.M. Harris and F/L J.H. Lathey, 28 February 1965, LAC RG 24, File 813-89/3-42.
18 Email interview with S/L (retd) Robert "Bud" White, March 20, 2003.
19 Ibid.
20 Canadian Military Space Group First Report dated January 31, 1968, Annex 1 – A Note on the SIP, LAC RG 24, Acc 83-84/232 Vol.46 File 1150-110/ M16 pt.2 (confidential). In 1967, 17 officers had completed their SIP, and there were a further 12 RCAF officers on exchange as follows: boosters (4), environmental testing (3), flight dynamics (2), satellite communications (1), space surveillance (1), and Project START (1).
21 Even four decades later, activities surrounding Canadian-American cooperation in the surveillance of space remain classified. Most of the material available on this section was derived from LAC. RG24, Vol.17996, file 947-103-6. Telecommunication Services – Data Processing – Ground Environment – Space Detection and Tracking System (SPADATS) obtained via access to information (ATI) request.
22 Annex A to 947-3-6 (DRDP), November 26, 1964 – A Report on Exchange Duty with the USAF 496L System Program Office, 2, LAC RG 24, Vol.17996, file 947-103-6.
23 Major K. Rodzinyak, "Like a Sapphire in the Sky: Canada's Surveillance of Space Project," (Kingston: Unpublished paper, War Studies Program, Royal Military College of Canada, 2002).
24 Lieutenant Colonels B. Wooding and T.A. Spruston, "The Canadian Armed Forces and the Space Mission", *Canadian Defence Quarterly*, vol. 5, no. 2 (winter 1975): 17.
25 John Vardalas, *The Computer Revolution in Canada*, (Cambridge, Massachusetts: Massachusetts Institute of Technology (MIT) Press, 2001), 95–8.
26 Some unclassified Canadian assessments may be found in later period defence literature; for example, see S.L. Bennett. *Strategic Command, Control, and Communications: Capabilities, Doctrine, and Vulnerability.* (Ottawa: Operational Research and Analysis Establishment, September 1983).
27 An unclassified overview of this study program was published in Canadian literature. See K.J. Radford, "Studies of Orbital Rendezvous," *Canadian Aeronautics and Space Journal*, (May 1962), 105–11. These studies may have been made employing either the CRC102A computer or the recently developed DRTE computer.

28 Advanced Engineering Space Systems Counter Satellite, LAC RG24, Vol.17973 File 925-121-3.
29 Appendix A to S925-121-3 (Secret) Recommendations for Future Action on the RCAF Proposal for a Canadian Defence Space Program, July 20, 1964, LAC RG 24, Vol.17829, File 840-105-001.8.
30 Ibid., 6.
31 Ibid., 6–8.
32 Supplement to RCAF proposal to the DARPG. (Secret) A Canadian Forces Space Development Program, December 21, 1964, Annex B, 4 LAC RG 24, Vol.17973, File 925-121-3.
33 Ibid., 3.
34 Advanced Engineering Space Systems Counter-Satellite 1964–1965. (Secret) Appendix B – Summary of the Proposed Space Defence Program (undated), 8, LAC RG 24. Vol.17973, File 925-121-3.
35 Ibid., 9.
36 Memorandum S925-121-3 (DAED) Canadian Space Defence Program – Recommendations for Further Action, July 20, 1964, 1–2, LAC RG 24. Vol.17973, File 925-121-3.
37 Ibid., 3.
38 Ibid., 4. After 1962, the DRB's main objective was to focus on satellite communications and ionospheric studies.
39 Ibid., 4.
40 Minute sheet from Group Captain P.F. Peter (DAED) to A/AMTS, July 21, 1964, LAC RG 24. S925-121-3 (Secret).
41 Ibid.
42 Memorandum from Group Captain (G/C) A.A. Buchanan, Acting Director General Development to Chief – Logistic and Engineering Directorate (CLED) on DARPG submission, April 15, 1965, LAC RG 24. S925-121-3 (Secret).
43 Ibid. Memo A/M C.L. Annis to A/V/M V.S.J. Millard, September 30, 1964.
44 Temporary Docket 4248 – L1150-4110/DB DARPG Paper 12/65, May 12, 1965, LAC RG 24. S925-121-3 (Secret).
45 Ibid., 3–5.
46 Ibid., 5.
47 Memorandum from J.C. Arnell to Mr. Wilkinson, G/C Peter, and S/L Flavin, April 5, 1965 calling for a unanimous decision on future DND space priorities, LAC RG 24, S925-121-3 TD 4248 (ScD/CLED/ED).
48 Advanced Engineering Space Systems Generally. Memorandum from LCol. D.B.D. Warner (DACS) to A/CTS, October 28, 1965, LAC RG 24, File 925-121-2.
49 Ibid., 3.
50 Ibid., 3, paragraph 7.
51 Merritt Roe Smith, ed. *Military Enterprise and Technological Change*. (Cambridge, Massachusetts: MIT Press, 1987).

CHAPTER TWELVE

THE SEARCH FOR RESCUE LEADERSHIP

JAMES PIEROTTI

Once upon a time, famed First World War ace and interwar bush pilot Wilfred Reid "Wop" May crashed in the remote northern wilderness of Canada. The crash fractured the propeller of his aircraft. The story goes that "he shot a moose; boiled its hooves to make glue; used its sinews for wrappings" and flew back home.[1] It is an amazing story, but he had to do whatever it took. In those days, he would have died in the back country if he could not save himself, because in the 1930s Canada had no search and rescue (SAR) organization and could not effectively respond to searches for missing aircraft or maritime vessels in a coordinated or consistent way.[2]

That situation changed dramatically during the Second World War. Following the German, and then British, examples of rescue organizations set up to recover downed pilots from the English Channel and return them to the war, the RCAF established a similar rescue organization in 1942 for its pilots flying from the east and west coasts of Canada.[3] As the Battle of the Atlantic waned in late 1943, there was decreasing operational rescue work for this organization, and RCAF rescue squadrons turned to work with the local Royal Canadian Mounted Police (RCMP) units, assisting the police when civilian vessels or aircraft went missing. Not only did this save Canadian lives, but it allowed the air force flyers to practise their skills; this cooperation with the Mounties developed into a mutually beneficial arrangement for the police and the air force.[4]

Another major advance during the war was the development of a parachute rescue capability, initiated by Wop May in Edmonton in 1944. This capability was embraced and spread to composite units conducting rescue in Canada in early 1945.[5] By the end of the war, the RCAF had developed a robust SAR capability in Canada

For many years, search and rescue units were equipped with surplus wartime aircraft. A Douglas Dakota, deHavilland Otter, and Consolidated Canso belonging to 103 Rescue Unit on the ramp at RCAF Station Greenwood, NS, June 1958.

for the rescue of its own personnel. And, as a bonus to the Canadian public, the air force often assisted in domestic rescues.[6]

With the end of the war, a reorganization of the RCAF resulted in a renewed emphasis on domestic roles and, due to its previous activities and accomplishments, the air force had inadvertently set itself up as a premier rescue organization; it should come as no surprise that the RCAF was selected for this role. This chapter explores the evolution of national SAR after the Second World War, as the government of Canada shifted to a domestic focus and initiated a search for an organization to conduct aircraft rescue in Canada. The story shows how, in the 1950s, despite being allocated the responsibility for maritime rescue, Cold War defence priorities pushed SAR firmly into the background of military tasks. Finally, after a decade of trial and error, the RCAF's SAR organization matured in the 1960s, permitting it to weather the unification of the Canadian Armed Forces in 1967.

The development of RCAF rescue from the 1950s and early 1960s established a firm foundation for the SAR organization that remains firmly in place today. It may seem curious, but the RCAF did not initially want the responsibility for domestic SAR, and it took a long time for the air force to accept this task.

The Search for a SAR Organization

At the end of the Second World War, military forces all over the world were downsizing, and people were eager, after years of conflict, for a peace dividend. As quality of life improved and nations learned to work together under the auspices of the United Nations (UN), there was an expected boom in commercial aviation and international travel.[7] In order to facilitate a safe postwar expansion the International Civil Aviation Organization (ICAO) was provisionally created in 1944, and the following year it became a specialized agency of the UN. Relatively quickly, ICAO demanded that a search and rescue service be established by signatory nations.[8] The RCAF and RCMP had some forewarning that this new UN requirement was coming, and at the end of the war they arranged, together with the Royal Canadian Navy (RCN), for military forces to hand over rescue boats and aircraft to the police so that the Mounties could establish a rescue capability. Philosophically this transfer worked well for both organizations: the RCAF had no desire to take on a civil role in Canada while the RCMP was fully prepared to undertake a wider range of civil responsibilities in the postwar world.[9] There was general agreement on this plan as it would see the creation of a far more robust rescue organization than anything that had yet existed in Canada.

The RCMP planned for an increase of 1,066 personnel, of which 366 would have provided the air-rescue component, while 700 personnel would have been involved in the marine-rescue component.[10] Together the RCAF and RCN agreed to provide 38 aircraft and 44 vessels from leftover wartime resources; these were to be based at 16 main police locations across the country to respond to aviation and maritime emergencies anywhere in Canada. The RCMP proposal assumed legislative support from the Canadian government for the yet-to-be-mandated marine portion of rescue, which, in addition to the ICAO requirements, would justify the $5,859,370 expense of the RCMP proposal for SAR.[11] The proposal was brought forward by the minister of justice, Louis St-Laurent.

However, Cabinet was particularly concerned about finances, and the proposed cost was quite high. The minister of finance, James Lorimer Ilsley, was particularly concerned about funds needed for new social security and social welfare activities, so he was not supportive of the expensive police proposal.[12] Cabinet was similarly

Flight Lieutenant R.H. Hammond, Senior Flying Control Officer with the Halifax Rescue Co-ordination Centre, looks out from his glass-panelled office overlooking the operations floor of the Search and Rescue Centre.

disinclined to support the police proposal. On 28 December 1945, St-Laurent, who had led the effort to use the RCMP for the SAR organization, was the first to bow to pressure from other ministers; he asked if a SAR capability sufficient to meet ICAO requirements "might be carried on adequately and with less expense under the auspices of the Navy and/or the Air Force."[13] Interestingly, this one Cabinet meeting was not the whole story behind the selection of the RCAF to manage Canadian SAR.

Other members of the government wanted a military that visibly supported the civilian populace during times of peace as well as war.[14] Clerk of the Privy Council and Secretary to the Cabinet A.D.P. Heeney made it clear that a domestic rescue role was part of the expectation of Canada's military when he wrote that "there is considerable goodwill to be maintained by co-operating closely with civil departments in such matters."[15] Military services were expected to take on a civil role to support the postwar society it served, and for the RCAF, SAR was that role. The clear bonus to the government was a SAR organization to meet international requirements that ended up costing nearly $4 million less than the RCMP proposal.[16]

On 9 April 1947, the Cabinet Defence Committee ordered the RCAF to take immediate responsibility for SAR in Canada, in anticipation that Cabinet would agree.[17] This time, Cabinet approved the proposal and the RCAF became responsible for all aeronautical SAR in Canada on 18 June 1947.[18] As the Air Force leadership knew this direction was coming, SAR organizations became immediately operational on the coasts while additional units were rapidly activated throughout the country as the RCAF shouldered this new responsibility. The first Rescue Coordination Centre (RCC) had already been established in Halifax on 1 January 1947, to coordinate SAR activities in the eastern region of the country, and other RCCs followed shortly thereafter.[19] However, at the time, the RCAF did not appreciate the depth and complexity of the SAR task, and there would be significant challenges to overcome in the hard times ahead.

Hard Times

The largely unwanted SAR task aside, the latter half of the decade had been challenging for the RCAF for three principal reasons. First, the 1948 Berlin airlift underscored the increased international tensions between the communist and non-communist nations, and the Korean War heightened the possibility of another global war. Although the Korean conflict was limited in scale, the rising communist threat destabilized the global community and took the air force's focus away from domestic concerns – there would be no return of the RCAF to the bush-flying adventures of the interwar period! Second, there was no maritime rescue capability in Canada, and the rising standards of living in Canada meant that many people started enjoying the pleasures of recreational boating, which meant more boaters were getting into trouble. The rapidly increasing workload in the maritime environment profoundly strained the new SAR organization, which had been created specifically for aviation rescue. Third, when it came to influencing RCAF leadership, the SAR community had a weak voice at the table and found itself unable to successfully advocate for the resources it needed. For these three reasons, the years 1949 to 1959 were tremendously troublesome for the RCAF's fledgling SAR organization.

The escalating friction between Western and Communist nations did not initially require a huge operational commitment from the RCAF, but it did have a large effect on the planning of the personnel establishment. All personnel increases from the postwar low of 14,000 RCAF personnel were aimed at increasing operational fighter, tactical aviation, and transport capabilities; SAR requirements were not even mentioned as a priority.[20] This focus on the possibility of combat operations came about because the Chief of the Air Staff (CAS), Air Marshal (A/M) Wilfred Curtis, focused on the limited political opportunities for RCAF expansion in areas where future war efforts would be most needed.[21] For the SAR community the result – a lack of personnel and new equipment – would be a recurring theme throughout the 1950s.

The addition of maritime rescue to the SAR mandate was a surprise, but one that the RCAF let happen. Under the auspices of the UN, an Intergovernmental Maritime Consultative Organization was formed in 1948 and one of its primary goals was to increase maritime shipping, this partly through agreed-upon safety standards, which in turn involved adding a maritime rescue requirement to signatory nations.[22] With little air force objection, Cabinet added maritime SAR to RCAF responsibilities on 26 June 1950, as a cost-effective solution to the new requirement.[23] Coincidentally, but not unimportantly this decision was made the day after the North Koreans invaded South Korea.

Immediately afterwards, the RCAF developed an internal counter plan, arguing that SAR and other "non-operational commitments" be removed as an air force responsibility in order to focus on combat, or operational, capabilities.[24] The RCAF had maintained a marine auxiliary capability during and after the war, but by 1951 the Air Staff was in the process of significantly reducing the size of the RCAF marine footprint in favour of helicopters for conducting any tasks over water.[25] This shift away from a surface vessel organization and towards air capabilities was all part of an RCAF plan to argue that the Canadian Coast Guard (CCG) take over the consolidated SAR role.[26] The proposal came to naught as it would have involved additional government spending: increasing the Coast Guard personnel and equipment resources would have been an anathema to a government determined to minimize public expenditures. Consequently, the RCAF would struggle with the combined aeronautical and maritime SAR mandate alone for the rest of the decade.

As the 1950s progressed, RCAF SAR equipment became older, procedures remained haphazard, and personnel shortages became very problematic. The RCAF explored a number of creative approaches to mitigate these shortfalls, in many cases using trial and error to determine the best way forward with the combined SAR mandate. One approach was to use any aircraft and crew for SAR missions so that there was no need to maintain a large standing SAR footprint, even though this meant that the crews typically lacked expertise. The plus side to this approach was that it allowed RCCs to request support from any available RCAF asset for a SAR mission. Furthermore, this first available resource approach allowed the RCCs

A Mark X Avro Lancaster belonging to 107 Rescue Unit, Torbay, NL, preparing to depart on a training flight.

to also request RCMP, RCN, and even Canadian Army assistance.[27] How to ask for these resources and how supportive these organizations were prepared to be was not standardized, and over the decade the SAR community learned as it went.

Another approach to bolstering the SAR parachute rescue personnel numbers was to use personnel normally used for other duties to augment the relatively small number of dedicated SAR specialists. These individuals would land by parachute at the site of an emergency and stabilize the situation until additional help could arrive. Military doctors, in many cases RCAF flight surgeons, were utilized to supplement the parachute rescue technicians. There was logic to this as medical expertise was often required, especially during rescues from remote locations where it would take some time for additional assistance to arrive.[28] Although these medical professionals had been part of the SAR program since its inception, they were mainly employed after the rescue had occurred to provide care to patients on the way back to safety.[29] Now, in 1951, the employment of doctors in a more direct role

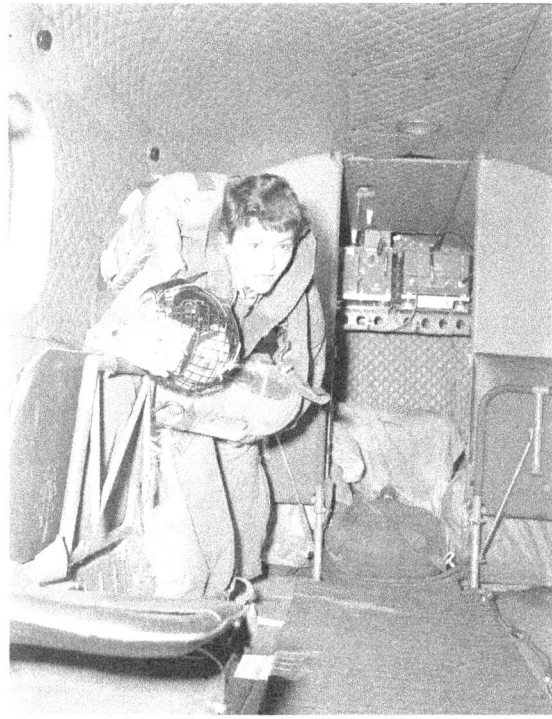

Flying Officer M. Fera, a nursing sister at RCAF Station, Namao, AB. Nursing sisters were an integral part of the rescue team, jumping into crash sites and providing medical support to casualties.

was formalized, and jump training was provided so that they could parachute into a crash site. However, this trial put highly trained and relatively scarce doctors at considerable risk, so the program was discontinued in 1956.[30]

Arguably, the most noteworthy attempt to mitigate the rescue technician shortage involved a trial based on the use of RCAF female nurses within the RCAF. Women were not permitted to enter the Canadian military services after the Second World War, but that changed after the Korean War with the rapid expansion of all three services.[31] In the RCAF, women who enlisted as nursing sisters were immediately offered the opportunity to join the SAR community, learning parachuting and bush skills in the process.[32] Although the trial was successful and showcased the abilities of women in a predominantly male RCAF, they could not remain in military service once married.[33] Flying Officer Marion Macdonald, one of the most photographed people in the RCAF at that time, combined grace and operational effectiveness in one of the harshest non-combat roles in Canada: this woman and her peers were fascinating to Canadians.[34] Unfortunately, the seven women known as "Para-belles" left the service in 1956, mostly to marriage, and the training was deemed too expensive, given the likelihood that women would not remain in the role for sufficiently long periods.

Because SAR was not a significant priority for the RCAF, senior leaders advocating for the SAR community and the associated resources were rare. One outstanding advocate was Group Captain Z. Lewis Leigh. A highly decorated officer and aviation pioneer, he had been responsible for taking Wop May's parachute-rescue technician idea and incorporating it into the RCAF during the Second World War.[35] As well, in 1948, he managed a brilliant mission from Winnipeg that saved five lives: Operation ATTACHÉ involved the successful search for a missing United States Navy aircraft and rescue of four American naval personnel, including the naval attaché to Canada, and an accompanying British naval officer.[36] However, Leigh never made it to Air rank (general officer) and thus his influence was always limited. Still, his retirement in 1957 was a loss to the SAR organization.

Leadership was important because the combined aeronautical and maritime SAR mandate grew rapidly. In 1949, SAR missions doubled from the year prior to 213 operations requiring 3,600 flying hours.[37] As more and more missions took place, units found themselves struggling to balance operational demands against limited resources. Sadly, on 20 April 1953, a Lancaster aircraft on a rescue mission from Greenwood, Nova Scotia, crashed killing six RCAF aircrew.[38] Nevertheless, the pace continued to increase. The average effort between 1956 and 1958 was 388 operations involving 7,971 flying hours annually.[39] With aging aircraft, limited personnel, and little high-level attention, the effort needed to meet these growing demands was often intense.

One of the most difficult missions during this hectic time was the crash of Trans-Canada Airlines (TCA) Flight 810 on 9 December 1956, during a period of horrible weather on the west coast of Canada. Squadron Leader George Sheahan, the commanding officer of No. 121 Composite Flight, located at RCAF Station Vancouver, overnight organized 50 aircraft from military and civilian resources to take part in the search for the 62 missing people on board – one of the worst airline disasters of the era.[40] There were 14 military aircraft involved, almost all of the available RCAF aircraft on the west coast, and the searchers braved fog and rain to scour the mountains for signs of the missing aircraft, but to no avail.[41] It was later discovered that the plane had impacted the side of Mount Slesse near Chilliwack, British Columbia; sadly, all on board the aircraft perished.

Goose Bay Para-Rescue Training, 13 November 1950: Corporals R.E. Braidner and R.W. Crebo preparing to jump. Note the modified helmets and face-cage to protect the jumper when entering foliage.

Initially, SAR requirements were met by posting full-time rescue personnel to composite flying units. These units were normally located at major RCAF stations and equipped with a variety of aircraft, primarily of wartime vintage, to conduct light transport, training and communication (i.e., personnel transport) duties. When necessary, the responsible RCC would notify the appropriate composite unit of an emergency situation and then the commander would launch the necessary resources.[42] The system allowed the RCC to task almost any RCAF resource from nine different locations across the country, including Canada's far north.[43] However, this system could be abused at times. Just before he retired, even long-time SAR champion Lewis Leigh complained that RCCs had so much authority and so little oversight that other missions were put at risk.[44] At the same time, SAR units were crying out for more personnel to meet rescue mission demands, especially in the maritime environment where the RCAF was decidedly out of its element.

Piasecki H-21 Vertol helicopter used by 103 Rescue Unit, RCAF Station Greenwood, NS.

The sorry state of the SAR organization's maritime rescue abilities achieved national attention in 1955. The deputy minister of transport, J. R. Baldwin, concluded that there was a need for additional helicopters and rescue vessels to meet the rapidly growing demand.[45] However, it was not just a matter of more rescue conveyances. A 1958 RCAF report determined that to address the government's goal, especially without support from the Coast Guard, the air force would need 100 new personnel to bolster SAR organizations across the country.[46]

And yet growth of the SAR community was not an RCAF priority. Senior air force leadership was firmly focused on support to NATO in the form of 1 Air Division, and countering the Soviet nuclear threat through the provision of air defence assets to NORAD.[47] With this philosophy foremost, the CAS determined that the rescue operations for mariners and marine vessels was only a by-product of the original RCAF mandate for aeronautical SAR, and he refused to add the extra personnel. Instead, he directed the use of limited SAR launch times in order to reduce the expectations on the overworked rescue personnel.[48] With limited resources, overworked personnel, increasing expectations from the government, and air force leadership focused on other priorities, there was little doubt that by the end of the 1950s the RCAF SAR organization was itself in desperate need to be rescued.

The Rescue

Fortunately, assistance would quickly arrive to save the SAR organization. In short order, marine coordinators and military radar capabilities began to be integrated into the RCCs to provide maritime expertise and in-flight location support. The CCG, long sought after to conduct rescues at sea, would finally come into being. And long-suffering air force SAR personnel would finally receive new aircraft to replace the Avro Lancasters and the Consolidated Cansos left over from the Second World War. Canada became serious about its SAR system and, between 1959 and 1964, made wholesale changes that would serve the Canadian public for future decades.

However, the RCAF made one last attempt to ditch the SAR mandate. During a meeting with the Department of Transport (DoT) in February of 1959, and aware that the department was developing a coast guard organization, the RCAF wanted to know if Transport could take over the whole SAR mandate associated organization.[49] The short answer was no: Transport believed that the RCAF was doing a great job with the SAR role, and they were simply going to support the air force's existing system with personnel and equipment.[50] It is clear from the archival sources that this definitive answer was really a turning point for the RCAF: with help coming in the form of a CCG to conduct maritime rescues and a government insistent on the military maintaining a domestic presence, it was time for the RCAF to accept its role and fix the SAR organization.

As a direct result of the aforementioned meeting, experienced mariners were hired in late 1959 by the Department of Transport to work within the RCAF RCCs as maritime rescue coordinators. These experts reported on SAR matters to the officer in charge at each RCC and significantly improved the conduct of searches and rescues in and on the water.[51] This was not the only major improvement to SAR coordination at the RCCs. Air Defence Command, which had established an extensive array of search radars throughout the country, contributed radar information

Piasecki H-21 in the middle of hoisting search and rescue personnel down to a waiting whaler in order to treat a critically ill member of the ship's crew, 11 May 1960.

to the SAR system starting in 1959: Air Defence Command radars could vector lost aircraft to safe locations and in the case of fighter aircraft pinpoint ejection locations.[52] This assistance would immediately prove to be very effective in finding aircraft that failed to arrive at their destination. The RCCs, now manned by RCAF officers familiar with, and able to access, air defence radar information, assisted by mariners able to provide maritime expertise, became highly effective organizations that developed outstanding rescue coordination proficiency.

During the same years, the RCAF began to upgrade the aircraft assigned to SAR duties. The Canso, an amphibious aircraft initially acquired during the Second World War, had been a main SAR platform due to its ability to land on water. However, it was aging and becoming difficult to maintain.[53] In order to improve its amphibious SAR capability, the RCAF included in its 1959 acquisition plan the purchase of 10 SA-16B Albatross amphibious seaplanes, which, like the Cansos, they would replace had excellent long-range capability.[54] In one of the most rapid procurement processes ever for the RCAF, the CSR-110 Grumman Albatross entered service in

How the compartment of a CSR-110 Grumman Albatross was configured to carry patients.

November of 1960. Significantly, these 10 airframes were the first aircraft purchased specifically for the SAR mandate.[55]

The 1959 plan also included the procurement of six CH-113 Labrador helicopters that were to be used solely for SAR purposes, and these were ordered to specifically enhance rescue capability over land and sea.[56] Manufactured by Boeing, the Labrador would spend its entire RCAF service life as a SAR asset. It greatly enhanced the RCAF's short-range SAR capability and provided an excellent platform for operating in the mountainous terrain of Canada's west coast. Together, these new aircraft were excellent additions to replace the aging Cansos and Lancasters.

At the end of the 1950s, there were four RCCs and five air stations controlling a total of 25 fixed-wing aircraft and helicopters. However, vessels operated by the RCAF marine component were no longer capable of conducting SAR missions at any appreciable distance from the stations to which they belonged.[57] The need for permanent or semi-permanent northern SAR stations, once deemed important due

Jump training from the back of a Douglas Dakota, RCAF Station, Trenton, ON.

to the construction of northern radar systems, were no longer required as the arctic radar sites shifted their focus to the detection of intercontinental missiles.[58] Other minor improvements moved the RCAF SAR organization away from a trial-and-error approach towards an operational philosophy that concentrated on established procedures and forging partnerships with other organizations. Even better news was that government resistance to a coast guard was fading fast, and the overall system that was developing was becoming ever more effective.

Reviewing the SAR philosophy in October 1961 the Air Council agreed "that both civil and military SAR requirements in Canada and the seaward approaches should continue to be met by a single SAR organization [and] that the RCAF SAR organization [was] to be retained at its present level of establishment to meet Canadian SAR requirements."[59] This was an important change in attitude by the air force's most senior body, mired as they had been in their earlier determination to

Gradually, wartime aircraft were replaced by newer equipment. A CSR-110 Albatross and Piasecki H-21 in the waters off Comox, BC. Note that both aircraft belong to Air Transport Command, the entity responsible for search and rescue.

rid the RCAF of what they considered to be a purely civilian mandate. It was finally recognized that the government requirement for the military to remain involved in civilian matters was not going to go away. The last needed change was greater improvement in maritime rescue.

The Progressive Conservatives had been elected in 1957, and one of their platform promises had been the formation of a coast guard. Progress towards that goal was immediately apparent: several SAR surface vessels had been ordered by the Department of Transport in 1958 to provide an expanded rescue fleet on both coasts.[60] The increasing importance of maritime rescue to successive Canadian governments was almost certainly spurred on by the opening of the St. Lawrence Seaway on 29 April 1959, which opened the Great Lakes to oceanic vessels and greatly increased commercial vessels operating in Canadian waters.[61] The need for a robust marine SAR capability had become very apparent as a larger strategy to enhance the growth potential of Canadian business abroad.

By 1960, plans were in place to augment rescue resources on both coasts and on the Great Lakes with new SAR cutters.[62] Complementing these new marine craft, the Canada Shipping Act was amended in 1961 "to empower the Minister of Transport to designate marine coordinators [in three RCCs] to organize search and rescue work on the high seas and on the coast of Canada."[63] This amendment simply captured changes already in place at local levels, but it re-enforced the importance of the DoT maritime and RCAF partnership within the RCCs. Then, on 26 January 1962, the Honourable Léon Balcer, the minister of transport within Prime Minister John Diefenbaker's government, "rose in the House of Commons and announced that the government had decided that the Department of Transport fleet of ships would, in the future, be known as the Canadian Coast Guard."[64] The formal creation of the CCG alleviated the much of the pressure on the RCAF regarding the provision of vessels earmarked for maritime rescue, and was a vast improvement over the haphazard approach from the 1950s. All the pieces were falling into place for an effective SAR system, and the RCAF immediately commissioned a report to evaluate the newly modified system.

The Centre for Operational Research and Analysis (CORA) released their report in February 1964: "An Evaluation of the Future RCAF Search and Rescue Requirement."[65] What was important about this report was not the myriad of changes it recommended but the fact that all changes were minor in nature and reinforced the basic structure of RCAF and CCG cooperation that had now developed. The report concluded that the RCAF had developed an admirable system that emphasized cooperation with other government departments to meet all international SAR requirements and let Canadians rest easy that someone would come when they were in trouble, whether on the water or involved in an aircraft crash.

The Future

As the sixties advanced, the air force continued to refine its approach to SAR. Although there were now dedicated SAR aircraft – the Albatross and Labrador – staffs looked for additional ways to improve both the efficiency and effectiveness of the overall organization. The RCAF accepted its leadership of the SAR responsibility but worked in a clear partnership with many organizations to ensure the best possible response to aeronautical and maritime emergencies throughout this vast country. It was only through close collaboration that a complex organization like SAR could be maintained.

The first Labrador helicopters arrived at SAR squadrons in November 1964, and the vast improvement in range, speed, and carrying capacity made it a rescue platform that was so effective that the aircraft served into the new millennium.[66] The 1964 CORA report had noted that the Albatross fleet had only one water landing operation in 1962, a statistic which seriously questioned the necessity of amphibious aircraft when the new Labrador helicopter was clearly showing itself as the better platform for rescue.[67] But the mighty Albatross continued to serve Canada well, as demonstrated on 16 March 1966, when a crew worked with the CCG ship *Alexander* to rescue 24 men from a sinking sailing vessel, the *Eric Neilson*.[68] Although relatively slow, it was a modern aircraft with significant range, but its time in SAR was short, and it was removed from active service in 1971.

The concept of using seaplanes for SAR was waning all over the world and the RCAF felt that greater speed and carrying capacity was likely a much better fit for the vast majority of operations compared to the ability to land on water. To meet these changing realities, 15 CC-115 Buffalo aircraft were purchased in 1967. Their acquisition not only added to the available aircraft for SAR and the medium-range airlift capacity to the RCAF, but also provided valuable work for a Canadian aerospace firm, De Havilland Canada.[69] It is difficult not to oversell the importance of the Buffalo; together, these two aircraft would provide outstanding coverage, solidifying the SAR model still in use today. The Buffalo, as a fixed wing aircraft with retractable gear, was able to travel at faster speeds than any previous aircraft used for SAR and was also able to transport SAR technicians and a great deal of equipment to emergency locations. This aircraft could deliver SAR technicians by parachute to stabilize a situation and await rescue by the Labrador. Thus, fixed wing aircraft developed to become search assets with an on-board rescue capability, while the rotary wing aircraft could then pull everyone to safety. The CCG resources complemented these aircraft; the vessels were able to handle the harshest weather at sea and provide rescue capabilities called for by the RCCs.

The trial and error of the 1950s was solidified with integration and unification of the different services into the Canadian Armed Force in 1968 to produce a model for SAR delivery that has remained effective ever since. Today, the RCCs include maritime and aeronautical experts who are connected to a range of organizations, giving the centres access to modern radar and communications. At specific locations across the country, modern fixed wing aircraft, manned by SAR-trained aircrew, are able to deliver SAR technicians when and where required, and modern rotary wing aircraft are available to retrieve and transport casualties to safety. The CCG provides an amazing depth of rescue capability at sea. The people who work within this system are proud to be a part of the SAR organization that has proven so successful for Canada over the decades. Since the 1960s, the RCAF has led an outstanding and effective system which, with the participation of CCG and other partners, has saved lives nearly every day. The search for rescue leadership found an RCAF filled with dedicated people who ensure that, no matter the weather or circumstances, help is not far away.

NOTES

1. The Para Rescue Association of Canada, *That Others May Live: 50 Years of Para Rescue in Canada* (Astra: The Para Rescue Association of Canada, 1994), 11.
2. James Pierotti, *Becoming a No-Fail Mission: The Origins of Search and Rescue in Canada* (n.p.: Lulu Publishing, 2018), 6–7.
3. George Galdorisi and Tom Phillips, *Leave No Man Behind: The Saga of Combat Search and Rescue* (Minneapolis: Zenith Press, 2008), 31 and 32; DHH, 96/24, Air Force Headquarters fonds, Box 6, File 1, Air Council Meetings.
4. Hugh A. Halliday, "The Role of the Boats: Air Force Part 46," *Legion Magazine*, 30 August 2011.
5. Air/Sea Rescue Services – Parachute Rescue Personnel and Equipment Policy, LAC, RG24-E-1-b, Vol. 3411, File Part 1-3, 466-1-5 Vol. 1.
6. Pierotti, *Becoming a No-Fail Mission*, 79.
7. David MacKenzie, *Canada and International Civil Aviation 1932–1948* (Toronto: University of Toronto Press, 1989), 125–6.
8. ICAO, *Convention on International Civil Aviation* (Chicago: 7 December 1944), 11.
9. James Pierotti, "Reluctant to Rescue: The RCAF and the Search and Rescue Mandate, 1939–1959" (MA diss., Royal Military College of Canada, 2016), 45.
10. "Meeting Four, Rescue," LAC, RG2-B-2, Vol. 103, File T-30-1, November 30, 1945.
11. Ibid.
12. Colin Campbell, "J.L. Ilsley and the Transition to the Post-war Tax System: 1943–1946," *Canadian Tax Journal* (2015): 13.
13. "Cabinet Defence Committee Minutes for 10 January 1946," 2, Canadian Joint Operations Command (CJOC) Historical Files, Ottawa.
14. W.A.B. Douglas, *The Official History of the Royal Canadian Air Force*, vol. 2, *The Creation of a National Air Force* (Canada: University of Toronto Press, 1980), 117.
15. Territorial Waters and Districts – Official – Air Search Rescue, Canadian Coast Guard, Privy Council Office – Air Search Rescue, 8 January 1946, "Cabinet Document D-30," LAC, RG2-B-2, Vol. 103, File T-30-1.
16. LAC, "Meeting Four, Rescue."
17. Memorandum to Distribution List from CAS, signed by S/L R. B. Inglis, April 9, 1947, "Air Force: SAR Arrangements." DND, DHH, R. L. Raymont fonds 73/1223.
18. "National Defence – Air Search and Rescue Service." Cabinet Conclusions, June 18, 1947, LAC RG-2, Privy Council Office, Series A-5-a, Vol. 2640, No. 5435.
19. Search and Rescue – Policy, File 976-1, Letter to CAS from AOC #10 Group, A/C F. G. Wait, June 26, 1947, "SAR Coordination Centre." LAC, RG24-E-1-c, Vol. 18113.

20 (Cabinet Committees During War), Brooke Claxton (1946–54), LAC, MG32 B5 R3306-0-1-E, Vol. 94.
21 Ray Stouffer, *Swords, Clunks, and Widowmakers: The Tumultuous Life of the RCAF's Original 1 Canadian Air division* (Canada: Department of National Defence, 2015), 16.
22 "United Nations Maritime Conference," January 22, 1948, LAC, RG2, Cabinet Documents Vol. 66, Doc. No. 593.
23 "Search and Rescue Service," June 26, 1950, LAC, Cabinet Conclusions, Vol. 2645, No. 9983.
24 RCAF Plan G, September 1, 1950, Revision, 3, DHH, 96/24, Air Force Headquarters fonds, Box 9.
25 Search and Rescue - Operations - Marine and aircraft Cases, "Memo on Marine Craft Policy, 8 September 1960." LAC, RG24-E-1-C, Vol. 18,116.
26 Pierotti, *Becoming a No-Fail Mission*, 134.
27 Search and Rescue – Policy, "RCC Trenton Overview of Communications, 14 July 1954" LAC, RG24-E-1-C, Vol. 18,113; and Report of Interdepartmental Committee on Air Sea Rescue, Policy, letter to CA formations from CGS, LGen Foulkes, 5 July 1949, "Search and Rescue – Army Participation," DHH, 112-32M2 (D340).
28 The Para Rescue Association of Canada, *That Others May Live*, 44.
29 Search and Rescue – Crash Rescue Assistance by Others, "Meeting on Standardization of Procedures between USAF, RAF, and RCAF, 3 June 1952." LAC, RG24-E-1-C, Vol. 18,128, File No. 978-7-3.
30 The Para Rescue Association of Canada, *That Others May Live*, 67.
31 National Defence and the Canadian Armed Forces, "Women in the Canadian Armed Forces," Government of Canada. Accessed, June 14, 2021, http://www.forces.gc.ca/en/news/article.page?doc=women-in-the-canadian-armed-forces/izkjqzeu.
32 Veterans Affairs Canada, "The Nursing Sisters of Canada." Accessed, June 21, 2021, https://www.veterans.gc.ca/eng/remembrance/those-who-served/women-veterans/nursing-sisters.
33 Jill St. Marseille, "An Air Force Pioneer: Grace MacEachern, Para-belle," last modified July 6, 2018, http://www.rcaf-arc.forces.gc.ca/en/article-template-standard.page?doc=an-air-force-pioneer-grace-maceachern-para-belle/izkjr5ic.
34 June Callwood, "The Blonde Who Leaps from the Clouds," *Maclean's*, April 30, 1955, 19–21.
35 Letter to DDFC from AMAS/D of ATC, G/C Leigh, April 4, 1944, "Air Rescue Development," Search and Rescue – Policy, File 976-1, LAC, RG24-E-1-c, Vol. 18113.
36 Z. Lewis Leigh, *And I Shall Fly: The Flying Memoirs of Z. Lewis Leigh* (Toronto: Canav Books, 1985), 185.
37 RCAF Search and Rescue Operations 1947–1970, DIS File 3, SAR Ops 1949, File 2, DHH 31, DHH, 79/631.
38 G.Y. Smith, *Seek and Save: The History of 103 Rescue Unit* (Erin, ON: The Boston Mills Press, 1990), 48.
39 "DOT-RCAF Meeting, 10 Feb 1959" Search and Rescue Policy, 976-2. LAC, RG24-E-1-C, Vol. 18,114.
40 Betty O'Keefe and Ian Macdonald, *Disaster on Mount Slesse: The Story of Western Canada's Worst Air Crash* (Halfmoon Bey, BC: Caitlin Press, 2006), 15.
41 Ibid., 58 and 64.
42 DHH, 81/224, CAP 342, *Orders for Aircraft Control and Services for the RCAF*, April 1956, 17.
43 Ibid., 9.
44 Letter to CAS from AOC TC G/C Z. L. Leigh, 9 October 1959, "SAR Aircraft - 111KU Winnipeg, Utilization on Other than SAR Missions." SAR - Policy, 976-2, LAC, RG24-E-1-C, Vol. 18, 114.
45 Charles D. Maginley, *The Canadian Coast Guard 1962–2002* (St. Catherines, Ontario: Vanwell Publishing Ltd., 2003), 29.

46 "SAR – Standby Policy." 28 May 1958; LAC, RG24-E-1-c, Vol. 18114.
47 Randall Wakelam, *Cold War Fighters: Canadian Aircraft Procurement 1945–54* (Vancouver, BC: UBC Press, 2012), 131.
48 Letter to MAC [Maritime Air Command], ATC [Air Transport Command], TAC [Tactical Air Command], and ADC [Air Defence Command] from CAS, signed by W/C [Wing Commander] J.G. Showler, June 11, 1958, "SAR – Standby Commitment." SAR – Policy, File 976-1 Vol. 5, LAC, RG24-E-1-C, Vol. 18,114.
49 "DoT – RCAF Meeting on SAR Operations in Canada." 10 February 1959, LAC RG24-E-1-c, Vol. 18114.
50 Ibid.
51 "Report from Marine Coordinators." July 13, 1960, LAC RG24-E-1-c, Vol. 18114.
52 Smith, *Seek and Save*, 63.
53 "Procurement of SA16B Aircraft, 26 January 1959." LAC Cabinet Document 39-59, RG2 Vol. 2742.
54 RCAF Programme of Activities, 1963–1968 with Amendments, page numbers N/A, DHH, 181.004 (D23). See also STOL Transport/SAR 1959–1961, November 24, 1959, "Standard of Preparation – Vertol 107 Model II-1 Helicopter"; and "Operational Characteristics for a Short Range, STOL, Transport/SAR Aircraft" 24 July 1959, LAC, RG24-E-1-c, Vol. 18149.
55 The Para Rescue Association of Canada, *That Others May Live*, 77.
56 "Standard of Preparation – Vertol 107 Model II-1 Helicopter." DHH, 181.004 (D23).
57 E.D. Bryson and N.D. Bray, "An Evaluation of the Future RCAF Search and Rescue Requirement," Department of National Defence, Chief of Operational Requirements, DRDC CORA (Ottawa: February 1964).
58 Walter J. Boyne, "The Rise of Air Defense," *Air Force Magazine*, last modified December 1, 1999, https://www.airforcemag.com/article/1299airdefense/.
59 "Air Council Meeting: Review of the SAR Organization." October 4, 1961, LAC, RG24-E-1-c, Vol. 18117.
60 "SAR Vessel for British Columbia 1957–1965" LAC, RG12, Vol 8906-81; and "SAR Vessel for East Coast 1957–1964" LAC, RG12, Vol 8906-78.
61 Maginley, *Canadian Coast Guard*, 35.
62 Proposed Patrol Cutter for SAR 1960–1967, LAC, RG12, Vol 8906-109.
63 Thomas Appleton, *Usque Ad Mare: A History of the Canadian Coast Guard and Marine Services* (Ottawa: DoT, 1968), section on Search and Rescue.
64 Maginley, *Canadian Coast Guard*, 12.
65 E.D. Bryson and N.D. Bray, "An Evaluation of the Future RCAF Search and Rescue Requirement," Department of National Defence, Chief of Operational Requirements, DRDC, CORA (Ottawa: February 1964).
66 Smith, *Seek and Save*, 89.
67 Bryson and Bray, "An Evaluation of the Future."
68 Smith, *Seek and Save*, 94.
69 Clinton Mowbray, "Lessons Forgotten? A Historical Examination of the RCAF Search and Rescue Organization" (directed research project, Canadian Forces College, Toronto, Ontario, 2014), 65.

CHAPTER THIRTEEN

ON WINGS OF HOPE AND PEACE: THE RCAF AND HUMANITARIAN AND PEACEKEEPING OPERATIONS, 1946–1967

WILLIAM MARCH

The sight of Royal Canadian Air Force aircraft carrying relief supplies to a foreign land ravaged by disaster or operating under a United Nations (UN) mandate in a troubled corner of the world today seems commonplace. However, utilizing Canadian military aircraft for missions that would come to be labelled as "humanitarian" or "peacekeeping" was a post-Second World War development. These international undertakings were never envisaged by a Canadian government determined instead to reap the "peace dividend" expected after six years of war. Mackenzie King, Canada's long-serving prime minister, was as resolute in 1946 as he had been in the years prior to the war to avoid external commitments – a difficult task given the internationalist outlook of the Foreign Affairs department, led by future prime ministers Louis St. Laurent and Lester B. Pearson.[1] Indeed, King's government participated in the drafting of the Charter of the United Nations which would have a profound impact on Canada's international engagement. As one of the founding signatories, the Charter would, eventually, become a key document in shaping the nation's foreign policy.[2] For the RCAF, and indeed the Canada's military forces writ large, as Canada's role within the UN evolved over the next two-decades, it opened doors to unanticipated secondary, or ancillary, humanitarian, and peacekeeping missions.

Not all secondary tasks are deemed to be of equal importance: the Charter contains a single "humanitarian" reference, while "peace" is mentioned 42 times.[3] Both are highlighted as basic UN principles. Article 1 points to the desirability of achieving "international cooperation in solving international problems of an economic, social, cultural, or humanitarian character," but there is no doubt that

Participation in a United Nations mission could last years. The RCAF's 115 Air Transport Unit had this crest approved after more than five years in support of the United Nations Emergency Force. Courtesy of the March collection.

the Charter places its emphasis on maintaining "international peace and security, and to that end: to take effective collective measures for the prevention and removal of threats to the peace, and for the suppression of acts of aggression or other breaches of the peace."[4] Perhaps there was a pervasive belief that the elimination of conflict, a collective inter-state responsibility, would alleviate the root cause of many of the humanitarian problems, viewed more as a non-state area of action.

During and immediately after the war, the government of Canada (GC) had been heavily engaged in humanitarian efforts such as the UN Relief and Rehabilitation Administration (UNRRA).[5] However, the Canadian government viewed its participation in relief efforts as part of the war effort and, as such, gradually scaled back its direct participation. To a large extent this policy was followed by most

Western nations, and the humanitarian "void" was filled by a variety of non-governmental organizations (NGOs). The growth in these agencies was phenomenal, and an estimated 200 humanitarian NGOs were established throughout the West between 1945 and 1950.[6] In Canada, wartime inspired NGOs such as the United Polish Relief Fund (UPRF) flourished, but it would be long-standing agencies such as the Canadian Red Cross (CRC) that held the most sway with the government in power.

Officially founded in 1896, the CRC focused on helping Canadians at home and, in times of war, doing what it could through volunteer work wherever Canadian forces were engaged. This changed after the Second World War as a new sense of internationalism meant that peacetime humanitarianism need not be limited to within Canada's national boundaries.[7] The government saw the value in CRC engagement in the world and as early as 1947 encouraged the agency's involvement in such undertakings as the provision of aid to the newly independent India and an emerging Pakistan. Employing humanitarian aid as an element of Canadian foreign policy and diplomacy was a trend that blossomed after the war.[8]

This practical strategy underpinned Canada's approach to peacekeeping in these formative years. Although meeting its overt security needs through participation in postwar alliances such as NATO and NORAD, Canada's overarching safety was predicated on global order and stability.[9] Thus, the postwar RCAF was specialized in its outlook and committed to a short, nuclear war strategy.[10] But at the same time, dreading a general nuclear war, Canadian foreign policy strove to "keep a lid on things" while remaining a strong defence partner.

Support for the UN meshed well with these themes, and Canadian participation in the various UN missions throughout the 1950s and 1960s should be examined in the context of Cold War (east-west) politics and Canada's national interests.[11] When Canada advocated the formation of a force to be positioned between the belligerent forces of Egypt, Israel, France, and England during the 1956 Suez Crisis, a proposal that would earn the Canadian minister of external affairs and future prime minister Lester B. Pearson a Nobel Peace Prize, it did so in an international atmosphere wherein the Soviets were threatening direct intervention in the Middle East while crushing opposition in Hungary, and the United States was demonstrably furious with France and England for their aggressive actions. Canada's offer to provide land and air elements to the United Nations Emergency Force (UNEF), the first of many such peacekeeping forces, was consistent with a foreign policy that concentrated on defusing situations that divided NATO members and threatened to bring the Soviet Union and US into

A lineup of United Nations aircraft at El Arish, Egypt. The Otters and Dakota aircraft were operated by the RCAF's 115 Air Transport Unit.

direct conflict.[12] The speed by which Canadian military personnel arrived in the Middle East as part of the UNEF was due, largely, to a robust RCAF air transport capability that had evolved to support Alliance commitments. The Canadian contribution to the UNEF had as much, if not more, to do with the being a staunch member of NATO, experience in overseas operations stemming from two world wars, and sophisticated technical capabilities as it did with seeing peacekeeping as a unique Canadian role.[13]

Canada's ability and willingness to participate in UN peacekeeping operations were soon put to the test. Indeed, the late 1950s and early 1960s was a volatile period in international relations with regional wars, the emergence of post-colonial

RCAF's 116 Air Transport Unit amphibious Otter on floats next to a United States Air Force Helicopter. Both aircraft operate in support of the United Nations Security Force, West New Guinea. Courtesy of the UN.

nations, and more direct confrontations between east and west, such as in Vietnam. Successive Canadian governments came to view the UN's primary purpose as the prevention of conflict in general.[14]

Not surprisingly, support for UN operations was elevated during this period to become a primary defence concern. When Paul Hellyer, minister of national defence (MND) under Pearson, released the *White Paper on Defence* in March 1964, peacekeeping was added to the list of departmental priorities.[15] The same document, in accordance with the need for mobile, air transportable forces to meet Canadian defence requirements, including support to the UN, spoke to the augmentation of RCAF airlift. However, the white paper made it clear that the "air truck" component would be available for the "United Nations and other requirements" in that order.[16] For the first time in the postwar period, RCAF air transport was, at least in the eyes of the government, placed on par with the combat functions of the air force. This status was visibly demonstrated with the

The RCAF's Approach to Ancillary Missions

Regardless of the ebb and flow of the RCAF's fortunes in the decades following the Second World War, government defence policy remained consistent. As part of the Canada's military forces, the RCAF was committed to defending the nation, assisting civil authorities in the maintenance of law and order, and collaborating with friendly nations, perhaps under the UN umbrella, on undertakings deemed to be in Canada's interest.[18] The Cold War, and Canada's participation in collective military organizations, skewed how the services fulfilled their commitments. This meant that Canadian forces evolved during these years to serve the needs of collective defence rather than being postured strictly to provide security along its land and ocean borders.[19] The RCAF met its collective defence obligations by concentrating on air defence and fighter aircraft. Therefore, anything not directly supporting collective defence requirements was viewed as an ancillary mission that, important as they might be such as search and rescue, risked diverting limited defence resources. Peacekeeping, much like humanitarian assistance, was "something the [RCAF] was expected to do," but not what "it must do."[20]

Happily for humanitarian and peacekeeping undertakings, the breadth and scope of the RCAF's commitments, as well as those of the other services, required a robust air transport organization. This need was reflected with the creation of Air Transport Command (ATC) in 1948 and the equipping of 426 Squadron with the long-range Canadair North Star transport aircraft and the eventual provision of two squadrons of Fairchild C-119 Flying Boxcars. Both these aircraft served the needs of the RCAF as it met domestic and alliance commitments. By the end of the 1940s, air force plans noted that all regular force squadrons would be "liable for duty under NATO or UNO [UN operations]."[21]

By the mid-1950s, the RCAF's Long Range Strategic Plan, looking at the period from 1956 to 1966, emphasized forces-in-being capable of participating in general East versus West global war that would involve atomic weapons.[22] In this context, support for the UN was viewed as a means to limiting smaller conflicts that might escalate into a confrontation between the major powers. As a result, the same planning document recognized the UN's role as a deterrent to limited war, noting that member states needed to "possess forces capable of rapid deployment," and for Canada "this requires strategic mobility of forces that can best be achieved by the use of air transport."[23] While it is likely that RCAF planners envisaged another Korean War scenario, the advent of peacekeeping as a Canadian military mission fit well with existing operational and strategic concepts. Employing RCAF airlift in this fashion would not be dissimilar to tasks undertaken domestically or in support of NATO.[24]

This period also saw an unprecedented growth in defence spending and the size of the Canadian military. In 1955, the government authorized a ceiling for the air force of 51,000, which meant, for the first time, the Canadian air force outnumbered the Canadian army.[25] While the growth was due primarily to alliance commitments, the increase in resources permitted the RCAF to maintain several auxiliary and composite flying units and increase the strength of regular squadrons. The ability to support humanitarian and peacekeeping operations benefited from this growth. Many of the composite units, equipped with light transport aircraft such as the Douglas DC-3 Dakota and de Havilland Canada Otter, provided personnel and equipment to UN missions, while 426 Squadron, whose North Star aircraft were key to Canadian international engagement, grew to become, by 1957, the RCAF's largest flying squadron with 440 personnel. In many ways, Cold War rearmament allowed the nation to play a larger peacekeeping role.[26]

By the early 1960s, the venerable North Star was inadequate to meet ATC's air transport requirements. Planning for a suitable replacement by the RCAF had begun as early as 1956, and the RCAF supported the acquisition of the Lockheed Hercules transport due to its impressive range and cargo capacity, but internal politics intervened, and the Canadair CC-106 Yukon was purchased instead. Although newer, larger, and faster, it retained the same problems as the North Star with respect to cargo capacity.[27] Four C-130B Hercules were acquired in 1960, and the Air Staff recommended the purchase of additional aircraft, but reductions in the defence budget placed the buy in jeopardy. The Liberal victory in the 1963 federal election did not reverse the downward trend in defence spending, but it did bring Hellyer in as the new MND. Hellyer's vision of a unified Canadian Armed Forces (CAF) included air mobile forces supported by a robust air transport capability. This led to the acquisition of additional Hercules and several short takeoff and landing (STOL) de Havilland Canada CC-115 Buffalo aircraft. And although Hellyer claimed that the purchase of these platforms was undertaken in opposition to the wishes of senior air force staff, historian Richard Mayne has pointed out that the RCAF was very much in favour of increasing ATC's resources.[28]

Regardless of who led the charge to purchase additional capable aircraft, ATC found itself utilizing these new assets within months of their arrival. The Buffalos proved the efficacy of specialized tactical STOL aircraft in UN operations in India and Pakistan, while the Hercules allowed Canada to deploy troops to Cyprus in

1964 with minimal external assistance. The Yukons proved their worth conducting humanitarian flights to Europe, Asia, and South America. Between 1960 and 1965, the increase in transport capacity brought about by the additional aircraft allowed the RCAF to more than double its passenger kilometres, from 193.4 to 427.3 million and to increase its cargo tonne miles from 14.7 to 59.7 million.[29] Much of the increase was attributable to Canadian participation in numerous humanitarian and peacekeeping operations as the RCAF's ancillary tasks grew in importance.

RCAF and Humanitarian Operations

The RCAF undertook its first postwar humanitarian foray in the fall of 1945. The RCAF's 168 (Heavy Transport) Squadron, utilizing converted B-17 Flying Fortress and B-24 Liberator bombers, delivered penicillin to war-ravaged Poland. Between 16 October 1945 and 25 January 1946, approximately 4.5 tonnes of penicillin and medical supplies were dispatched to Poland, albeit at the cost of one aircraft and five RCAF crew members killed when their B-17 crashed near Halle, Germany, on 19 October.[30] The utilization of a small number of RCAF aircraft, often diverted for a short period of time from their primary duties, became the hallmark of Canada's official humanitarian efforts.

Even if RCAF resources were available, their commitment often involved coordinating with several departments of the Canadian government, perseverance by the requesting agency, and the occasional nudge highlighting national, or political, interests. In 1945, the United Polish Relief Fund routed its request through Canadian Senator Thomas Vien, who in turn contracted the MND for Air, Colin Gibson. Gibson approved RCAF participation, but External Affairs (EA) assistance was required to gain Soviet flight clearance, as Poland was within their sphere of influence. When it appeared as if EA was too slow to respond, the United Polish Relief Fund wrote the undersecretary of state at EA, Hume Wrong, on 12 October, enclosing a newspaper clipping from a Canadian newspaper, the *Ottawa Journal*, titled "Declare Disease in Poland Slowly Exterminating Nation." The article, which described the horrendous health conditions, reminded EA that this was an issue of national, as well as international, concern. In short order, arrangements were put in place and the RCAF's first postwar humanitarian flight departed Canada on 19 October.[31]

In a pinch, suitably large aircraft could be re-rolled in the short-term to undertake a transport function, but the overseas movement of relatively large amounts of humanitarian supplies from Canada necessitated the use of dedicated RCAF

426 (Transport) Squadron North Star being loaded with humanitarian relief supplies for the Congo as part of Canada's contribution to the Opération des Nations unies au Congo (ONUC). Note the United Nations emblem on the tail.

long-range transport aircraft. Unfortunately, by June 1946, 168 Squadron had been disbanded, and a suitable air force transport aircraft would not become available until North Star entered service in 1947. Over the next decade and half, as the RCAF's sole strategic transport aircraft, it would be the mainstay of the RCAF's participation in humanitarian missions until gradually replaced by the Canadair CC-106 Yukon and CC-130 Lockheed Hercules in the early 1960s.

Canadian involvement in any humanitarian operation was discretionary as there were no international agreements binding a nation to contribute. Although, as shown in table 13.1, Canada did take part in a several humanitarian undertakings, the level of contribution was minimal, often amounting to what cargo could be carried in a single North Star flight. In most cases, relief supplies carried by RCAF transport aircraft were provided by external agencies, primarily the CRC, that often solicited the government for assistance in moving their supplies to the crisis area.

At times participation by the RCAF in a humanitarian mission was expedited by the presence of Canadian politicians. During the catastrophic flooding of Italy's Po Valley in 1951 Canada's secretary of state for EA, Lester B. Pearson, was scheduled to preside over a North Atlantic Council meeting in Rome on 24 November. His subsequent request to Cabinet for aid generated intense discussion, influenced by the need to support efforts to deal with floods in western Canada, but Cabinet was reluctant to intervene lest a precedent be set whereby future requests of this nature would be "difficult to resist ... particularly if they originated in one of the NATO countries."[32] However, Cabinet noted, if an international relief scheme was put in place under the auspices of a NATO member or the UN, Canada would consider the request. Fortunately for the residents of the Po Valley, and for Pearson in Rome, the CRC stepped forward with relief supplies and two North Star aircraft were made available to ferry the humanitarian cargo to Europe.[33] This particular mission highlighted recurring themes in Canadian government humanitarian efforts: a reluctance to go it alone, a desire and willingness to be part of an international effort, and the preference to provide a means for the dispatch of NGO-provided aid rather than providing relief supplies directly from government. For the RCAF this meant that Canada's response to a given event could be dealt with using only a limited number of flights.

These themes remained generally consistent regardless of the severity of the disaster or whether the impacted nation was a member of NATO, the Commonwealth, or unaligned. When substantial parts of the Netherlands were inundated by flood waters in the winter of 1953, the government was quick, on the behalf of Canadians, to express its concern, but it would take weeks before the first of four RCAF aircraft shuttled CRC aid to Europe.[34]

India and Pakistan, two Commonwealth nations, were particularly hard hit by flooding in late 1955. Despite an urgent request from the undersecretary of state for EA, almost two weeks would pass before the RCAF could rearrange its schedules to dispatch aircraft.[35] Early in December, two 426 Squadron North Stars departed with CRC supplies and diplomatic mail and, as was often the case with these missions, maximum benefit was gained by merging the task with ATC training requirements. Many stops were made along the way both for logistical reasons and to provide exposure of aircrew to foreign airfields and procedures.[36] Behind this approach were the realities of the limited long-range transport capacity of the RCAF, and the need to balance unexpected demands with maintaining maximum support for air force operations in Canada and overseas. Therefore, taking the time to ensure that critical support tasks could be accommodated, while capitalizing on the training benefits of international taskings, was prudent policy. Until the 1960s,

Table 13.1. List of RCAF participation in humanitarian operations, 1946–1966

Date	Country / Focus / Operational NAME (if assigned)	Primary Contributor – Relief Supplies	RCAF Contribution
Oct 16, '45–Jan 25, '46	Poland – Medical	Canadian Red Cross	168 Squadron 5 x B-17 / B-24 flights
Oct 14–Nov 14, '47	India – Pakistan – Medical	Canadian Red Cross	Squadron unknown 1 x Dakota flight
Aug 24–6, '51	Jamaica – Hurricane	Canadian Red Cross	426 Squadron 2 x North Star flights
Oct 27–8, '51	Italy – Flood	Canadian Red Cross	426 Squadron 2 x North Star flights
Feb 3–22, '53	Netherlands – Flood Operation WET FOOT	Canadian Red Cross	426 Squadron 4 x North Star flights
Aug 27–30, '54	India – Flood	Canadian Red Cross	426 Squadron 1 x North Star flight
Dec 5–16, '55	India – Flood	Canadian Red Cross	426 Squadron 1 x North Star flight
Dec 7–17, '55	Pakistan – Flood	Canadian Red Cross	426 Squadron 1 x North Star flight
Jul 6–25, '56	India - Pakistan – Flood Relief	Canadian Red Cross	426 Squadron 3 x North Star flights
Apr 24–May 3, '56	Lebanon – Earthquake	Canadian Red Cross	426 Squadron 1 x North Star flight
Jul 25–8, '56	Greece – Earthquake	Canadian Red Cross	426 Squadron 1 x North Star flight
Oct 29–Nov 4, '56	Austria – Hungarian refugees	Hungarian-Canadian Community	426 Squadron 1 x North Star flight
Dec 29, '57 –Jan 16, '58	Ceylon – Flood Relief	Canadian Red Cross	426 Squadron 2 x North Star flights
Dec 21, '59–Apr 2, '60	Morocco – Medical	Canadian Red Cross	1 x RCAF Flight Surgeon
Mar 5–7, '60	Morocco – Earthquake	Canadian Red Cross	426 Squadron 1 North Star flight
May 26–Jun 12, '60	Chile – Earthquake	GC / Various Agencies	426 Squadron 5 x North Star flights North Star Detachment in Chile
Jul 19 –Aug 17, '60	Congo – Civil Unrest	GC	426 Squadron 4 x North Star flights
Nov 8–12, '61	Belize – Hurricane	Canadian Red Cross	426 Squadron 1 x North Star flight
Sep 4–7, '62	Iran – Earthquake	Canadian Red Cross	437 Squadron 1 x Yukon flight
Jun '63	East Pakistan – Cyclone	Unknown	437 Squadron 1 x Yukon flight
Sep 21, '63	Brazil – Forest Fire	Canadian Red Cross	437 Squadron 1 x Yukon flight

(*continued*)

Table 13.1. List of RCAF participation in humanitarian operations, 1946–1966 (*continued*)

Date	Country / Focus / Operational NAME (if assigned)	Primary Contributor – Relief Supplies	RCAF Contribution
Nov 20, '64	Yugoslavia – Flood	Canadian Red Cross	No. 4 (Transport) Operational Training Unit (OTU) 1 x North Star flight
Dec 22, '65 –Apr 30, '66	Zambia – Fuel Blockade Operation NIMBLE	GC – Request from United Kingdom	435, 436 Squadrons Hercules Detachment (2 Hercules from each squadron)
Aug '66	Turkey – Earthquake	Humanitarian Supplies	No. 4 (Transport) OTU 1 x Yukon flight

transport support to humanitarian efforts never strained RCAF resources as they were usually limited to a single, or a small number, of flights that could be blended into the overall flying schedule.

On 22 May 1960, Chile experienced the most powerful earthquake in recorded history, a magnitude 9.5, and the resulting devastation and loss of life made worldwide headlines. Canada's response to the catastrophe, this time under the auspices of the Conservative government of John Diefenbaker, followed the traditional pattern of waiting for the CRC to assess the situation and request government assistance to transport relief supplies.[37] As part of an international effort, 426 Squadron commenced flights to Chile on 28 May, transporting CRC cargo as well as a Canadian army field hospital and medical personnel. In total, seven crews, five aircraft, and 20 maintenance personnel were tasked to support the non-officially named Operation AMIGO, and the aircraft were to return to Canada once they had delivered their supplies.[38]

The initial "in-out" tasking changed in early June. Diefenbaker's minister of EA, Howard Green, had been on a tour of South America when the earthquake struck, and he pushed to increase Canadian efforts. At the same time, US military aircraft were withdrawn from the area due to heightened tensions with the Soviets who had shot down a US Air Force U-2 surveillance aircraft on 1 May. Green authorized the retention of RCAF aircraft in Chile, placing them at the disposal of the Chilean Disaster Committee in Santiago to help offset the departing Americans by airlifting supplies and personnel, as well as evacuating casualties, within Chile. The short-term commitment of RCAF resources became an in-situ detachment that did not return to Canada until 12 June.[39] Utilizing what amounted to almost one-quarter of 426 Squadron on a single operation, even if for a relatively short period of time, placed increasing strain on the unit to carry out its regular tasks.

Leading Aircraftman J.R. Conlin, centre, accepts responsibility for a shipment of Red Cross relief supplies from Miss Olga Pollock, left, Red Cross Volunteer driver, and Mrs. Marguerite Wilson. The food and medicine was loaded aboard an Air Transport Command North Star aircraft of 426 Squadron at Dorval, QC, for delivery to flood victims in Ceylon.

In 1965, Canada established another airlift detachment, this time in support of a Commonwealth-led operation in Africa. Criticism of the white minority government of Rhodesia (now Zimbabwe) resulted in a unilateral declaration of independence on 11 November, and the resulting international economic sanctions led Rhodesia to impose an embargo on the shipment of petroleum products to neighbouring Zambia. Canada joined an international coalition, led by Britain, providing two CC-130 Hercules aircraft from 435 and 436 Squadrons respectively to operate under the direction of the Royal Air Force.[40]

The aircraft were to ferry fuel and petroleum products from Ndjili airport, Congo, into various locations in Zambia. Commencing on 22 December, Operation NIMBLE, the RCAF commitment, was anticipated to last for four weeks. However, the government decided to extend the mission until the end of April the following year. At its peak, Operation NIMBLE involved 150 air and ground crew as well as a significant portion of the RCAF's air truck capability.[41] NIMBLE took place during a Yukon commitment to the Congo and a major northern training exercise resulting in the suspension of all routine flights that involved either the Yukon or Hercules aircraft.[42] This would be the last major humanitarian operation undertaken by the RCAF until its dissolution as part of unification.

Peacekeeping Operations

Like humanitarian missions, undertaking a UN task was and is determined by the prime minister and Cabinet as informed by foreign affairs; it is not a DND decision.[43] Few of the peacekeeping operations embarked upon by Canada were undertaken without the active participation of the RCAF, this normally in the form of transport to and from the theatre of operations. However, at various times it also included the provision of small, integral flying units and / or specialist personnel. The support provided to peacekeeping operations never seriously strained air force resources, although in the realm of air transport certain missions, such as the Korean War and the UNEF, could, if for a short period, impact on routine operations.[44]

Between 1945 and 1956, with the exception of the UN mandated Korean conflict, RCAF participation in UN operations was minimal except for the deployment of a small number of personnel and the occasional transport flight. When conflict flared between India and Pakistan over the Kashmir region in 1948, the original Canadian contingent, reluctantly offered by Canada to help defuse a situation potentially damaging to the Commonwealth, contained two RCAF intelligence officers.[45] Several years later, as the French government sought to extricate itself from its colonial quagmire in Indochina, an International Commission for Supervision and Control (ICSC) was formed under UN auspices to monitor an agreement reached in Geneva that divided the former French region into Laos, Cambodia, communist North Vietnam, and western South Vietnam. Canadian participation consisted of a delegation staffed by a mix of military and civilian personnel, including several RCAF officers. In August and September 1954, 426 Squadron crews set a gruelling pace as they transported Canadian ICSC members between Canada, Switzerland, and Indochina.[46] Afterwards, support became a matter of the occasional flight to reposition or exchange personnel.

During the Korean conflict, Canadian military personnel from all three services were committed. Involvement by the RCAF, concurrently engaged in a significant

Canadian Army Signal Corps personnel strapped in with Mae Wests on in preparation for takeoff on a 426 (Transport) Squadron North Star as part of Canada's contribution to Opération des Nations unies au Congo (ONUC).

expansion focused on NATO and Europe, was limited. Although the commitment of a handful of fighter pilots, 22 in all, often garnered the lion's share of press, it was RCAF's air transport capability that was most effective and explicitly requested by the US. Between July 1950 and May 1954, North Star aircraft from 426 Squadron logged 34,000 hours in the air while transporting three million kilograms of freight and approximately 13,000 Canadian and UN personnel to and from the Korean theatre of operations.[47] Dubbed Operation HAWK, the use of air transport resources in this manner was not indicative of UN support as a unique mission; instead, it demonstrated the utility of long-range transport aircraft as a core element of RCAF planning. A little more than two years later, ATC would again be strained to meet its regular commitments as it was tasked to support the UNEF.

An aerial view of Abu Suweir airfield in the Sinai showing part of the runway and bombed out hangars centre foreground with the RCAF hangars opposite. This would be the main airfield for the United Nations Emergency Force until it was relocated to El Arish, Sinai, later in 1957.

Much has been written about Canada's role in the establishment of UN peacekeeping and the first deployment of "peacekeeping" forces, and it is beyond the scope of this chapter to delve into the intricacies of the international negotiations that led to awarding of the Nobel Peace Prize to Canada's Lester B. Pearson.[48] Still, as noted by historian J.L. Granatstein, Canada's agreement to participate in the UNEF was given reluctantly. And its acceptance as a contributing nation to the mission had more to do with its status as a reliable NATO ally, experienced in overseas operations, and with sophisticated technical capabilities, such as long-range transport, as it did from any inherent belief in Canadian neutrality.[49]

Born of the 1956 Suez Crisis, wherein Britain and France sought to ensure their respective aims by colluding with Israel in an attack on Egypt, Canadian support for the UNEF placed inordinate demands on ATC. All three of the RCAF's transport squadrons, 426 with its North Stars, as well as 435 and 436 equipped with C-119s, were engaged in airlifting the Canadian contingent to the Middle East. Operation RAPID STEP involved the gathering of military personnel from across the country, transporting them and their equipment to an air or sea point of embarkation, and permitting the onward movement of the contingent into the theatre of operations.[50]

Undertaken between 6 November 1956 and 31 March 1957, RAPID STEP highlighted ATC's ability to respond quickly as directed by the government. From a UN perspective it would be repeated for the Opération des Nations Unies au Congo (ONUC, 1960–4), and the UN Peacekeeping Force in Cyprus (UNFICYP, 1964–ongoing). In both cases, ATC resources proved sufficient for the initial deployment of elements of the respective Canadian contributions to the Congo (Operation MALLARD, 28 July–31 August 1960) and Cyprus (Operation SNOWGOOSE, 15–22 March 1964).[51] At the same time, however, routine commitments, such as service flights within Canada and to Europe, as well as some training functions, were reprioritized during the intense period of initial airlift.

Limitations in the cargo capacity, range, and numbers of ATC crews meant that the RCAF required assistance for transporting large cargo, aircraft logistical support, and administrative matters.[52] For both UNEF and UNFICYP, the Royal Canadian Navy's sole aircraft carrier, HMCS *Magnificent* was withdrawn from NATO duties and pressed into service as a cargo vessel. For all three missions, the USAF played a major supporting role, providing logistical support when required and in the case of ONUC, assisting in deploying heavy equipment to Africa.[53] From 9 to 30 August 1960, 13 C-124 USAF Globemaster aircraft carried heavy vehicles and equipment from Canada to the UN theatre of operations. It was evident, in this last pre-Unification surge, that Canada's aging fleet of transport aircraft were not capable of transporting the forces deemed necessary to meet peacekeeping requirements.

Canadian air support to peacekeeping operations also involved the provision of small, self-contained Air Transport Units (ATUs). By the very nature of their employment, which usually revolved around light transport, liaison, and reconnaissance, the units were ad hoc. Equipped with aircraft and personnel mainly found within the plethora of communication and composite flights scattered across RCAF stations in Canada, they were not a significant drain on RCAF resources.[54] The RCAF provided ATUs for the UNEF, the United Nations Yemen Observer Mission (UNYOM), the United Nations Security Force (UNSF) in West New Guinea, and for UN operations in both India and Pakistan.[55] Flying from primitive landing strips, often from makeshift facilities and with little or no formal procedures to follow, these units were almost a return to the bush-flying days of the inter-war period.

In support of the United Nations Emergency Force (UNEF), HMCS *Magnificent* transported three RCAF Otter aircraft to Egypt in 1957. Here is an image of one of the Otters leaving the *Maggie* – the only time RCAF fixed-wing aircraft took off from an aircraft carrier.

The ATUs proved to be remarkably effective. Two of these units, 114 and 115, supported the UNEF and were initially equipped with wartime vintage Dakotas and DHC's unique Otters. They proved adequate to ferry supplies and personnel between various locations as well as a modicum of aerial surveillance using the "mark-one eyeball." The largest of the two units was 115, which, at its peak, numbered approximately 100 air and ground crew with six aircraft; it operated for over a decade.[56] However, the aircraft employed lacked cargo capacity and performance that would have made support operations more efficient; and the Dakotas were well worn. Maintenance of these aging aircraft, difficult and expensive at the best of times, was more difficult due to the primitive conditions and harsh environment.

Similar problems were encountered within the UNYOM and UNSF ATUs. The 56 personnel deployed to Yemen with 134 ATU were dispatched before adequate

An RCAF amphibious Otter being loaded into the back of a Hercules aircraft at RCAF Station Trenton, ON, enroute to operate with the United Nation Security Force, West New Guinea.

support and operational preparations were in place. Living and maintenance facilities were practically non-existent. As part of a report provided to ATC HQ, the resident RCAF medical officer noted that "... there is a feeling in United Nations circles that Canadians are an easy touch and much more malleable than other nationalities ... we seem to them to be capable of existing on promises and ... we begin operations with less than adequate United Nation provided facilities and equipments [sic]. The worst example of this is Yemen where living conditions of R.C.A.F. personnel are simply described as atrocious."[57] Unfortunately, there was little improvement to be had in with the deployment of 134 ATU to West New Guinea.

RCAF 134 Air Transport Unit de Havilland Caribou aircraft serving as part of the United Nations Yemen Observer Mission (UNYOM). The aircraft and personnel were "borrowed" from the United National Emergency Force.

Deployments of specialist air force personnel also took place. Normally, this involved a senior air advisor, usually from within ATC, and a small staff to look after "air matters" for the UN force commander. During ONUC, Wing Commander William (Bill) Carr, who would go on to lead Air Command in 1975, was dispatched to "command all UN forces in the Congo," and assisting him was a small contingent, including air traffic control and communication specialists. They were responsible for airlift both external and internal to ONUC, coordinating aircraft and personnel from 11 different countries whose participants spoke six different languages.[58] Underpinning Canada's contribution, and to a certain extent the UN operation as a whole, was 426 Squadron whose round-trip flights to the Congo involved 70 flight hours and the use of extra crews. Carr credited the unit with being critical to the initial UN response and buildup of peacekeeping forces, as well as providing four years of twice-weekly regular support flights.[59]

The 1964 white paper not only elevated the importance of peacekeeping, it also provided impetuous for Canada to address perceived weaknesses within the UN when it came to these types of operations. To this end, EA undertook to hold a Peacekeeping Conference in Ottawa from 2–6 November. Initially, the event was to be limited to only those countries that had provided substantial peacekeeping forces, but it proved politically impossible to restrict participation and eventually 27 nations attended. As outlined by Paul Martin, the secretary of state for EA, to the House of Commons on 26 October, the conference sought to improve the UN's peacekeeping capacity by addressing practical issues including composition, command and control, logistical support, and legal problems. He anticipated that majority of the participants would be military and emphasized that the exchange of views would be "informal, confidential, and without commitment."[60]

The RCAF was represented at the conference by Group Captain H.A. Morrison, the ATC chief of staff, operations. While several issues highlighted by Martin were examined in Ottawa, the main point of discussion was the establishment of a standby airlift element for use by the UN, with the aircraft provided by the US, while crews were contributed by suitable nations.[61] The RCAF outlined its position on the matter in June 1964, finding it more practical to provide both aircraft and crews. The training benefit to participation in UN operations was acknowledged and, provided the request could be accommodated within the yearly flying rate, it was recommended that airlift be provided free of charge to the UN. The RCAF also noted that while Canada could express a willingness to support the UN in principle, it could reserve the right to assess each request on its own merits.[62] Morrison advanced this position at the conference, but after four days of talks, it appears that little or no concrete action was taken by the UN.

Prior to the conference, negative reports from UNYOM and UNSF were discussed at ATC headquarters. Summarized in a letter to AFHQ were a range of shortcomings: lack of UN advance planning, provision of rations and quarters, lack of a logical allowance policy, absence of safe operating conditions due to lack of knowledge of terrain, a scarcity of navigational aids, and problematic health standards. The letter was followed by a document entitled "Planning Guide for Air Transport Command Participation in U.N. Operations" with the recommendation that a similar guide be adopted at the headquarters level. In addition, it was proposed that responsibility for the items listed in the letter remain with Canada rather than the UN.[63] Eventually, ATC would publish a small handbook for use by UN-deployed crews.

Prior to the handbook's publication, the UNEF deployment that brought peacekeeping to the world ended abruptly on 16 May 1967, when Egypt's president Gamal Abdel Nasser revoked his country's permission for UN forces to be stationed on his country's soil. This unprecedented demand spawned debate and confusion on both the legitimacy of the demand as well as its practical implementation in the UN and, in Canadian Forces Headquarters in Ottawa, concern for the Canadian contingent.[64] Existing Canadian plans had called for an orderly withdrawal by sea, but these were dashed when, on 27 May, Nasser, believing that Canada was biased towards Israel, ordered the Canadian contingent be withdrawn within 48 hours. Within hours ATC went into action and

> ...in the space of approximately 55 hours, between 29 and 31 May, 702 Canadian soldiers and airmen, along with almost all of their equipment, were safely evacuated from Egypt. Operating up to six flights per day, the Hercules aircraft made 18 trips between El Arish [Egypt] and Pisa [Italy], three from El Arish to Nicosia, Cyprus (heavy cargo) and 12 flights to move individuals and material from Pisa to Canada (these 33 flights totaled 530 hours and 45 minutes of flight time). The Yukons were busy as well, making six trips from Pisa to Canada (112 hours and 40 minutes of flight time). The three 115 ATU [aircraft] "self-deployed" back to Canada, arriving on 6 June 1967 – the last of the Canadian contingent with UNEF to return home.[65]

Canada's first foray into peacekeeping ended as it began, with a massive RCAF airlift.

Conclusion

Humanitarian and peacekeeping operations were a product of Canada's postwar internationalism and undertaken at the discretion of the government. Evolving during the Cold War period, Canadian participation in both these endeavours should be viewed through the dual lens of East–West politics and the prevention of global conflict. Although the RCAF, especially ATC, played a key practical role in these missions, they were viewed as ancillary, or secondary, tasks fulfilled by air force aircraft and personnel focused on supporting alliance defence commitments. The provision of deployed flying units and specialist personnel was common, especially on peacekeeping missions, but the bulk of support was provided by long-range, strategic air transport deploying, sustaining, and redeploying Canadian contributions. Occasionally, a humanitarian or peacekeeping operation might disrupt routine ATC activity for a short period of time, but the RCAF never shifted its focus away from NATO and NORAD. And while RCAF humanitarian and peacekeeping operations were undertaken with dedication and professionalism, they were never viewed as a primary function of Canada's air force.

NOTES

1 For an overview of the viewpoints of King and Foreign Affairs see Donald Creighton, *The Forked Road, Canada 1939–1947* (Toronto: McClelland and Stewart, 1976), 140–70.
2 Canada's role in drafting the Charter is well documented in John W. Holmes, *The Shaping of Peace: Canada and the Sear for World Order,* Vol. 1, (Toronto: University of Toronto Press, 1979), 229–68.
3 United Nations (UN), *Charter of the United Nations and Statute of the International Court of Justice*, San Francisco, 1945, accessed June 20, 2020, https://treaties.un.org/doc/Publication/CTC/uncharter-all-lang.pdf.
4 Ibid., 3.
5 For details on Canada's participation in this UN organization see Susan Armstrong-Reid and David Murray, *Armies of Peace, Canada and the UNRRA Years* (Toronto: University of Toronto Press, 2008).
6 Eleanor Davey, John Borton, and Matthew Foley, "A History of the Humanitarian System: Western Origins and Foundations," *Humanitarian Policy Group Working Paper*, (London: Overseas Development Institute, 2013), 10.
7 Sarah Glassford, *Mobilizing Mercy: A History of the Canadian Red Cross* (Kingston, Ontario: McGill-Queen's University Press, 2017), 243.
8 Ibid., 245.
9 D.W. Middlemiss and J.J. Sokolsky, *Canadian Defence, Decisions and Determinants* (Toronto: Harcourt Brace Jovanovich, 1989), 24.
10 Douglas L. Bland, "Controlling the Defense [sic] Policy Process in Canada: White Papers on Defense and Bureaucratic Politics in the Department of National Defence." *Defense Analysis* vol. 5, no. 1 (1989): 5–6.
11 Sean M. Maloney, *Canada and UN Peacekeeping: Cold War by Other Means, 1945–1970* (St Catharines, ON: Vanwell Publishing, 2002), 6–8.
12 John Hilliker and Donald Barry, "Choice and Strategy in Canadian Foreign Policy: Lessons from the Postwar Years, 1946–1968." *Canadian Foreign Policy Journal* vol 3, no. 2 (1995): 73–4.
13 J.L. Granatstein, "Peacekeeping: Did Canada Make a Difference? And What Difference Did Peacekeeping Make to Canada," in *Canada's Foreign Policy in a Changing World Order*, eds. John English and Norman Hillmer (Toronto: Lester Publishing, 1992), 231.
14 John Hilliker and Donald Barry, "Choice and Strategy in Canadian Foreign Policy: Lessons from the Postwar Years, 1946–1968." *Canadian Foreign Policy Journal* vol 3, no. 2 (1995): 78.
15 Government of Canada (GC), *White Paper on Defence* (Ottawa: Queen's Printer, March 1964), 24.
16 Ibid., 23.
17 Established between 1965 and 1967, the other functional commands of a unified Canadian Armed Forces were Mobile Command, Maritime Command, Material Command, Training Command and NATO – Europe. For an overview of the impact of unification on the air force

see Allan English and John Westrop, *Canadian Air Force Leadership and Command: The Human Dimension of Expeditionary Air Force Operations* (Trenton, ON: Department of National Defence (DND), 2007), 31–54.

18 James Eayrs, *In Defence of Canada: Peacemaking and Deterrence* (Toronto: University of Toronto Press, 1972), 95.

19 D.W. Middlemiss and J.L. Sokolsky, *Canadian Defence, Decisions and Determinants* (Toronto: Harcourt, Brace and Jovanovich, 1989), 9.

20 Ibid., 173–4.

21 GC, DND, Directorate of History and Heritage (DHH), File 181.004(D48), Folder 36, "Plan 'G' for the Royal Canadian Air Force, 1 Sept 1950 – Revision" 2.

22 DHH, File 181.004(D48), Folder 39, "Long Range Plan for the Royal Canadian Air Force, 1956–1966," September 5, 1956, 18–19.

23 Ibid., 19.

24 J.L. Granatstein and D. Bercuson, "Peacekeeping: The Mid-East and Indochina," in *Canadian Military History: Selected Readings*, ed. Marc Milner (Toronto: Copp Clark Pitman, Ltd., 1993), 339.

25 John Griffin and Samuel Kostenuk, *RCAF Squadron Histories and Aircraft: 1924 – 1968* (Toronto: Hakkert and Company, 1977), 144. The ceiling for the Canadian army was authorized at 49,000.

26 Granatstein et al., "Peacekeeping: The Mid-East and Indo-China," 332.

27 Richard Mayne, "Flying 'Truck Drivers' or 'Captains of the Clouds': Paul Hellyer and the RCAF's Acquisitions of the CC130 Hercules," in *Sic Itur Ad Astra: Canadian Aerospace Power Studies*, Volume 6, *From Hot War to Cold War*, eds. Mike Bechthold and William March (Trenton, ON: Department of National Defence, 2017), 71.

28 Mayne, "Flying 'Truck Drivers'" 72–4.

29 GC, Standing Committee on National Defence, *Minutes of Proceedings and Evidence*, No. 9, Queen's Printer, June 16, 1966, 215.

30 DHH, "Details / Information for Canadian Forces (CF) Operation Poland 1945," accessed October 10, 2021, http://www.cmp-cpm.forces.gc.ca/dhh-dhp/od-bdo/di-ri-eng.asp?IntlOpId=229&CdnOpId=271. Although notionally called "Operation Poland," the mission was never assigned an official operational name.

31 Hugh Halliday, "Penicillin for Poland: A Tale of Two Plaques," accessed September 5, 2021, *Legion Magazine*, https://legionmagazine.com/en/2011/12/penicillin-for-poland-a-tale-of-two-plaques-air-force-part-48/.

32 GC, Foreign Affairs and International Trade, Documents on Canadian External Relations, Vol 17, 895, Extract from Cabinet Conclusions, December 22, 1951. Accessed December 27, 2021, https://epe.lac-bac.gc.ca/100/206/301/faitc-aecic/history/2013-05-03/www.international.gc.ca/department/history-histoire/dcer/details-en.asp@intRefId=6275.

33 Ibid., Vol 17, 896, Extract from Cabinet Conclusions, December 22, 1951. Accessed December 27, 2021, https://epe.lac-bac.gc.ca/100/206/301/faitc-aecic/history/2013-05-03/www.international.gc.ca/department/history-histoire/dcer/details-en.asp@intRefId=6276.

34 GC, House of Commons *Debates*, Seventh Session, 25th Parliament, Vol II, 1952–53 (Ottawa: Queen's Printer, 1953), 2517.

35 Bill Rawling, "No Task Fit for a Soldier? Canadian Forces Medical Personnel and Humanitarian Relief Missions since the Second World War" *Scientia Canadensis*, Vol 26, (2002), 83.

36 Laurence Motiuk, *Thunderbirds for Peace: Diary of a Transport Squadron* (Ottawa: Larmot Associates, 2004), 464.
37 GC, *Debates*, 3rd Session, 24th Parliament, Vol. 4, May 26, 1960, 4249.
38 Motiuk, 596.
39 Ibid., 596–600.
40 DHH, "Past Operations – Operation NIMBLE." Accessed January 12, 2022, https://www.canada.ca/en/department-national-defence/services/military-history/history-heritage/past-operations/africa/nimble.html.
41 Ibid.
42 GC, Standing Committee on National Defence, *Minutes of Proceedings and Evidence*, No. 9, Queen's Printer, June 16, 1966, 225.
43 Middlemiss et al., *Decisions and Determinants*, 17.
44 William March, "The Royal Canadian Air Force and Peacekeeping," Proceedings of the 21st Colloquium of the International Commission of Military History, August 20–26, 1995, *Peacekeeping, 1815 to Today* (Ottawa: DND, 1995), 471.
45 Maloney, 24–8.
46 Motiuk, 422–3.
47 Stephen J. Harris, *Canada and the Korean War* (Montreal: Art Global, 2002), 129.
48 For a detailed examination of the Suez Crisis and Canada's involvement see Michael K. Carroll, *Pearson's Peacekeepers: Canada and the United Nations Emergency Force, 1956–67* (Vancouver: University of British Columbia Press, 2009).
49 J.L. Granatstein, "Peacekeeping: Did Canada Make a Difference? And What Difference Did Peacekeeping Make to Canada," in *Canada's Foreign Policy in a Changing World Order*, eds. John English and Norman Hillmer (Toronto: Lester Publishing, 1992), 225–31.
50 William March, "A Most Abrupt Departure: The Royal Canadian Air Force and the United Nations Emergency Force," *From Hot War to Cold War*, 57–9.
51 For details see DHH, Operations Data Base, accessed December 5, 2021, http://www.cmp-cpm.forces.gc.ca/dhh-dhp/od-bdo/europe/GREYBEARD1-SNOWGOOSE-eng.asp.
52 Jon B. McLin, *Canada's Changing Defense Policy, 1957–1963*, (Baltimore: Johns Hopkins Press, 1967), 195.
53 David Cox, "Peacekeeping: The Canadian Experience," Alastair Taylor, David Cox, and J.L. Granatstein eds., *Peacekeeping International Challenges and Canadian Response* (Toronto: Canadian Institute of International Affairs, 1968), 52–3.
54 There are 18 miscellaneous and composite flying units scattered through the country during this period. Kestrel Publications, "RCAF Post-war Misc / Composite Units." Accessed December 2, 2021, https://static1.squarespace.com/static/5ce2eac378733900016331b2/t/5cf14057afdab3000196b197/1559314520165/RCAF+Post-War+Misc+%3A+Composite+Units.pdf.
55 These operations were the United Nations Military Observer Group in India and Pakistan (UNMOGIP) and the United Nations India-Pakistan Observer Mission (UNIPOM).
56 DHH, Unit Annual Historical Reports for 115 Air Transport Unit, 1956–1967.
57 DHH, Historical Report No. 13, "Canada and Peace-Keeping Operations Yemen," 33.
58 William K. Carr, "Planning, Organizing, and Commanding the Air Operation in the Congo, 1960," in *Air Power in UN Operations*, ed. A. Walter Dorn (Farnham, UK: Ashgate Publishing, 2014), 6–9.
59 Ibid., 14.

60 GC, *Debates*, Second Session, 26th Parliament, Vol. IX, 1964–65 (Ottawa: Queen's Printer, 1953), 9402–3.
61 Library and Archives Canada (LAC), RG 24, Vol. 20714, Chiefs of Staff Committee documents, Part II, File CSC 2.4.1.2.1. Extract from brief prepared for the Canada-US Ministerial Committee on Joint Defence, June 1964.
62 Ibid.
63 DHH, Historical Report No. 13, 34–5.
64 March, "A Most Abrupt Departure," 64–5.
65 Ibid., 65.

CHAPTER FOURTEEN

MARITIME AIR

ERNEST CABLE

Shortly after the end of the Second World War, Soviet expansionism in eastern Europe and the arms buildup in the Soviet Union and its Eastern European satellites raised security concerns among some Western European nations. In response, Belgium, France, Luxembourg, the Netherlands, and the United Kingdom signed the Treaty of Brussels on 17 March 1948, pledging mutual cooperation in a number of areas including defence. In mid-1949, the original pact was enlarged to include Denmark, Iceland, Italy, Norway, Portugal, the United States and Canada. The newly signed North Atlantic Treaty resulted in the formation of the North Atlantic Treaty Organization (NATO), which bound all signatories to the mutual defence of any member who might be attacked. A cornerstone of the agreement was to establish and maintain security throughout the North Atlantic area.[1]

Although initially seen through the lens of land forces, albeit with a nuclear element, NATO was very much a maritime alliance from the beginning. Russian expansion of its submarine fleet was concerning as the Allies had experienced the near severing of the crucial sea lines of communication between North America and Europe by German U-boats less than a decade earlier. Fortuitously, maritime collaboration between the US, UK, and Canada did not cease at the end of the Second World War, and with the establishment of NATO, maritime cooperation now expanded to include new member nations. In 1952, the various maritime forces were integrated into Allied Command Atlantic (ACLANT), the alliance's command and control structure under the direction of a Supreme Allied Commander Atlantic (SACLANT).[2]

404 (Maritime Reconnaissance) Squadron Lancaster flying over Lands End, Cornwall, England.

Naval forces were not permanently assigned to NATO. Instead, member nations agreed to contribute specified ships and aircraft to the Alliance in the event of a crisis or war. ACLANT admirals were usually "dual hatted" and commanded national fleets in addition to their NATO responsibilities. While undertaking their national roles, Allied navies at the same time cooperated by sharing information on Soviet naval and air movements in areas for which they accepted responsibility under ACLANT.[3]

With the creation of ACLANT, Canada committed specific naval and air force anti-submarine warfare (ASW) forces to NATO during times of increased tension. Additionally, Canada accepted surveillance responsibilities for the Canadian Atlantic Area (CANLANT), an ACLANT sub-area stretching from the east coast of Canada to approximately the mid-Atlantic (40° W longitude) and south of Nova Scotia to 40° N latitude. In 1952, Admiral Bidwell, the Royal Canadian Navy's

(RCN) Flag Officer Atlantic Coast was the first to command the CANLANT area. Although NATO naval cooperation did not extend to the Pacific, Canada assumed responsibility for a large area adjacent to its west coast under a bilateral arrangement with the US.[4]

National postwar plans assigned the main responsibility for Canadian coastal defence to the navy. The RCN recognized that the massive expansion of the modern Soviet submarine fleet rendered its wartime anti-submarine close escort role, where warships would accompany merchant ships, obsolete and that it needed to adopt an offensive open ocean ASW doctrine.[5] New doctrine was one thing, but postwar downsizing left the RCN with a small cadre of wartime ships until such time as a fleet of modern anti-submarine destroyer-escorts could be built. Naval rebuilding efforts were now heavily influenced by the successes of carrier-borne aircraft that had worked with surface ships in ASW actions during the Second World War. The RCN believed a modern navy required an air component to complement its new destroyer-escorts. The RCAF took a contrary stance; it strongly opposed an air component for the RCN, believing that all air resources should be controlled by the air force. The Cabinet resolved the impasse when it authorized the formation of the Naval Air Branch, giving the RCN responsibility for carrier based naval aviation while the RCAF remained responsible for land based maritime aviation.[6] The RCN's first aircraft carrier, HMCS *Warrior*, made its maiden voyage to Halifax in March 1946, with 21 Fairey Firefly FR 1 strike-reconnaissance fighters and 32 Supermarine Seafires embarked; these resources constituted the nucleus of the RCN's embryonic Naval Aviation Branch.[7]

Not designed for North Atlantic winters, the RCN replaced *Warrior* with HMCS *Magnificent* in 1948. Early the following year, the *Magnificent*, or "*Maggie*" as she was affectionately called, departed the UK with 18 ASW configured Firefly AS 5s embarked to replace the Firefly FR 1s, and the first batch of Hawker Sea Furies, Britain's newest naval fighter, to replace the Seafires.[8] Unfortunately, the difficult-to-maintain Firefly AS 5 was not an all-weather aircraft, and they were replaced in 1950 by 75 ex-US Navy (USN) Grumman Avengers modified by Fairey Canada for all-weather ASW duties.[9] Having embarked on a new ship-building program, and having created a Naval Air Branch, the RCN would soon be well equipped to assume responsibility for the CANLANT sub-area.

Rebirth of RCAF Maritime Air Capability

Postwar coastal defence plans did not include RCAF squadrons. Following demobilization after the Second World War, AFHQ disbanded the massive Eastern

Maritime Air Command Lancaster during an anti-submarine warfare (ASW) exercise with Royal Navy submarine HMS *Andrew*.

Air Command (EAC), which had been responsible for the air defence of eastern Canada and RCAF ASW operations in the Atlantic. With the demise of EAC, the RCAF's interests in maritime operations on the east coast were relegated to Central Air Command's No.10 Group, established on 1 March 1947, and headquartered in Halifax, Nova Scotia. Two squadrons, one on each coast and both under the direction of 10 Group, were deemed adequate to fulfill both bomber and reconnaissance roles with a secondary responsibility for search and rescue. Establishing these two units was of secondary importance as the Air Force adjusted to peacetime demands, strategic uncertainty, and parsimonious budgets. As with other air force functions the use of wartime aircraft saved money, and the two squadrons were thus to be equipped from existing aircraft resources, in this case Mark-X Lancaster bombers.[10] A credible air force maritime presence would not be established until the start of the next decade.

Reflecting the increasing polarization between the Soviet Bloc and the West, the RCAF's 1949 Plan "F," recognized that "another serious threat to this country stems for the Russian Submarine Fleet. Increases in the number of submarines and in their performance is such as to require greater emphasis on Maritime Squadrons in the RCAF for co-operation with the Navy."[11] The Chief of the Air Staff (CAS), Air Marshal (A/M) W.A. Curtis, emphasized the requirement for "a Maritime Force capable of immediate operations."[12] Accordingly, despite the continued pre-eminence of air defence, the establishment of a peacetime maritime organization to include a group headquarters (to operate cooperatively with the RCN), three maritime squadrons, and appropriate stations were given priority. Each squadron was to be equipped with 12 suitable aircraft and were to be stood up by 1954.[13]

The RCAF reorganized its structure, and on 1 April 1949, No.10 Group was redesignated Maritime Group under the command of Air Commodore (A/C) G.F. Wait who was tasked with recreating the RCAF's anti-submarine capability. Maritime Group became autonomous on 15 January 1951, as the increasing size and complexity of the Group's role prompted its elevation to Maritime Air Command on 1 June 1953.[14] A/C A.D. Ross was appointed Air-Officer-Commanding (AOC) Maritime Air Command and was double-hatted as the deputy commander and air commander of the CANLANT area.[15]

The RCAF's four-year absence from ASW operations and peacetime demobilization of the late 1940s left a dearth of experienced personnel to mentor new aircrews. Consequently, with Wait's arrival Maritime Group announced that its highest priority was training new aircrew and reactivating RCAF Station Greenwood, NS, from its postwar caretaker status to house a newly established maritime operational training unit. In the summer of 1949, Squadron Leader (S/L) Marshall, officer commanding (OC) the new No. 2 (Maritime) Operational Training Unit (2 (M) OTU), and his staff of two travelled to Halifax to observe how the RCN conducted ASW training for its surface ships and naval air arm. Similarly, Marshall renewed operational ties with the RAF's Coastal Command. which had worked closely with the RCAF during the Battle of the Atlantic and had remained operational after the war. During a visit to Coastal Command, Marshall and a group of 10 RCAF officers learned about current ASW equipment, tactics and procedures, and training methods. This small cadre of RCAF personnel became the nucleus of the instructor cadre at 2 (M) OTU.[16]

During Canada's haste to demobilize after the Second World War, the RCAF had disposed of most of its aircraft through the government's War Assets Corporation (WAC). Among the resources was a fleet of very-long-range (VLR) B-24 Liberators that had proven so vital in the Battle of the Atlantic.[17] In the process of reinstituting the RCAF's anti-submarine capability, AFHQ searched for a long-range aircraft similar in capability to those used by EAC and was delighted to learn that WAC had not yet disposed of surplus Lancaster bombers, the mainstay of the RCAF's wartime No. 6 Bomber Group. Fortunately, many of the Mark X Lancasters were stored in vacant wartime hangars across Canada, allowing AFHQ to immediately reclaim them. Avro Canada and De Havilland Canada restored a small number of Lancasters to their wartime bomber configuration, which were transferred to the OTU and to the newly formed maritime reconnaissance squadrons for training purposes. Following the initial restoration, Avro concentrated on modifying the remaining 70–75 Lancasters to their new Maritime Reconnaissance (MR) configuration.[18]

On 1 November 1949, No. 2 (M) OTU officially formed at Greenwood and conducted training on the wartime Mark X Lancasters until the modified MR versions arrived.[19] The MR Lancaster had a crew of seven: two pilots, one flight engineer, two navigators, and two radio officers. The "routine" navigator guided the aircraft to and from the area of operations while the tactical navigator directed the aircraft through the search and attack phases. The two navigators alternated on consecutive trips with one always acting as a second navigator to the other. The radio officers rotated duties in-flight, alternating between operating the long-range communication radios and the various ASW sensors.

During conversion, the MR Lancasters were fitted with an obsolescent suite of wartime ASW sensors; however, the human "Mark 1 eyeball" remained the most effective method for detecting the telltale wake, or feather, created by a submarine periscope or snorkel mast protruding above the ocean surface. Between 1949 and 1951, more capable sensors were incrementally installed to improve ASW effectiveness. The APS-33 radar replaced the wartime H2S radar and was adequate against large surface targets but not very good at detecting periscopes. Other additions included electronic counter measures (ECM) receivers to detect submarine radars, exhaust trail indicators (ETI) that detected diesel exhaust from snorkelling submarines, and a 1943-era CRT-1 sonobuoy system.[20]

The first Lancaster-equipped unit, 405 MR (Eagle) Squadron, was formed at RCAF Station Greenwood on 31 March 1950, under the command of Wing Commander (W/C) D.T. French. French and his first three crews had graduated from the OTU a scant two-weeks before. The squadron was directed to

1. Train in all aspects of air operations including
    a Offensive maritime air operations including reconnaissance, search, shadowing, illuminating, radio counter measures, and strike against submarine and surface vessels at sea and in harbour;
    b Defensive maritime operations including escort of surface vessels, defensive reconnaissance, and airborne counter measures;

Lancaster from 404 (MR) Squadron dropping a torpedo at the training range, St. Margaret's Bay, Nova Scotia.

    c Meteorological and ice reconnaissance;
2. Cooperate with RCN and other forces in operational exercises;
3. Conduct long-range search and rescue duties; and
4. Undertake any other air operations as may, from time to time, be directed.[21]

Just a few months later, in July 1950, the squadron was tasked to fly ice reconnaissance missions in support of Operation NANOOK, the US Navy's annual resupply of the Arctic weather stations at Resolute Bay, Alert, and Eureka. During a supply paradrop at Alert, W/C French and six members of his crew, along with two civilian scientists, were killed when their aircraft crashed. Bad weather and ice conditions prevented the bodies being evacuated, so they were interred at Alert where a cairn was erected to mark the site of 405 Squadron's first postwar fatalities.[22]

By the end of its first year of operations 405 Squadron proved that it could carry out most of its roles under extremely hazardous and difficult conditions. Having set the standard for future maritime squadrons, 405 took on the responsibility of documenting new procedures and recommending new equipment, including modifications for the MR Lancaster, which were forwarded to Avro. In February1951, the squadron conducted trials on the new APS-33 radar, and later an aircraft was sent to US Naval Air Station Quonset Point, Rhode Island, to test loading and dropping of American torpedoes from the Lancaster's bomb bay.[23]

On 27 April 1951, No. 404 MR (Buffalo) Squadron reformed at RCAF Station Greenwood, under the command of the temporary S/L S.S. Mitchell and joined 405 Squadron in the maritime reconnaissance role. A year later the squadron had completed most of its training and was ready to participate in two major exercises in July 1952. Exercise Microwex involved air strikes on a convoy while Exercise Convex III had the unit join 405 Squadron in Florida to form the RCAF's first deployed Maritime Wing. The wing commanded by 404 Squadron's new commanding officer, W/C D.E. Galloway, who reported to the commanding officer of US Naval Air Station Key West.

With increased Soviet naval activity in the Pacific, the RCAF reactivated No. 407 MR (Demon) Squadron in July 1952 at RCAF Station Comox, on Vancouver Island, under the command of W/C C.W. McNeill. Initially, the squadron was assigned to 12 Air Defence Group in Vancouver for administration and support, but it answered to Maritime Group in Halifax for operations and training. Under a Canada-US bilateral defence agreement the squadron was responsible for patrolling a large area of the eastern Pacific adjoining the BC coast; nationally, it was also responsible for surveillance of the Yukon and the western half of the Northwest Territories. Because of delayed deliveries only seven Lancasters arrived during its first year; however, activity picked up in early 1953 with Operation SEA SPRING, a west-coast convoy escort exercise, which gave 407 Squadron the opportunity to work with 405 and 404 Squadrons as well as RAF, RCN and USN forces.[24]

Modernization of the RCAF's Maritime Capability

In 1954, NATO's Military Committee issued document MC-48, "The Most Effective Pattern of NATO Military Strength for the Next Few Years."[25] This document envisaged a two-phase conflict with the Soviet Union where the initial phase, lasting up to 30 days, would see the use of atomic weapons and involve intensive military operations. Although combat operations might continue during a prolonged second phase, this would principally be a period of readjustment and follow-up, the nature of which would be dependent on the outcome

Lineup of Lancaster aircraft at RCAF Station Greenwood.

of the initial phase.[26] From an RCAF perspective, MC-48 reinforced the need for forces-in-being and the primacy of air defence. Therefore, as underscored in the RCAF's Long Range Plan, issued in September 1956, and intended to steer plans and capabilities for the following decade, the Service's priority would be the air defence of Europe and North America with the intention being to minimize damage from Soviet strategic air attack and protect the US and NATO atomic retaliatory capabilities.[27]

With this primary focus, maritime air forces were of secondary priority. Their purpose would be to deal with atomic threats from the sea, a necessary requirement with the introduction of sea-launched missiles equipped with atomic warheads. Thus they would act as an additional layer of protection for the North American continental air defence system. In terms of ASW activity, during the initial phase of a global war, the RCAF deemed that the submarine would "present only a minor threat to dispersed shipping" …as convoys were "not envisaged during this phase."[28] This outlook led to a shift away from direct cooperation with the RCN towards more of an independent ASW role for the RCAF.

In 1956, the RCN and RCAF undertook discussions concerning a joint concept of maritime warfare. Occurring within various bodies ranging from the Chiefs of Staff Committee (COSC) to a bi-service Air/Sea Warfare Committee, the discussions were driven by the adoption of MC-48 as a planning guide for Canadian defence priorities, as well as a "turf war" over the operation of ASW helicopters. The ASW helicopter issue was resolved by the following year with the acceptance of the Air/Sea Warfare Committee's recommendation that the RCN be responsible for these aircraft where they operated from naval vessels, but that any shore-based ASW helicopters would be operated by the RCAF.[29] However, the Air/Sea Warfare Committee also endorsed the concept of a "denial zone" extending from the coast to approximately 175 nautical miles seaward, an "inner combat zone" that extended from the boundary of the denial zone to the maximum effective range of underwater sensors, and an "outer combat zone" that extended a further 85 nautical miles. Canadian naval ASW assets would focus on operations within the inner combat zone, while the RCAF ASW aircraft would extend the nation's ASW capability to the outer combat zone and beyond.[30] The need to push ASW operations ever further out to sea was soon apparent, this the result of evolving submarine and missile technology, which in turn drove the need for more capable aircraft.

The postwar MR Lancasters had quickly become obsolete and were proving difficult to maintain. Predictably, the Lancaster could no longer deal with the more sophisticated latest generation submarines as effectively as the newer British Avro Shackleton or the American Lockheed P2V Neptune. As early as 1949, the RCAF had issued a preliminary operational requirement for a Lancaster replacement that would lead to the production of CP-107 Argus. However, the design, testing and production of this aircraft was years away. In 1951, the CAS explained to Cabinet that the Lancaster would be viable until only 1955 and was given authority to procure the Lockheed P2V-6 Neptune, as reflected in RCAF planning documents, to fill the gap created by the Lancaster's acknowledged shortcomings and the entry of a planned Canadian manufactured maritime aircraft into service.[31] In late 1954, with the support of the RCN, the RCAF placed an order for 25 P2V-7 Neptune aircraft directly off the Lockheed production line for the USN.[32]

All 25 Neptunes were delivered in less than six months and arrived in Canada in the USN's midnight blue paint scheme with RCAF roundels and white identification letters and fuselage markings.[33] Unlike the Lancaster phase-in, which had been done one squadron at a time, Neptunes alternately equipped 404 and 405

Three 405 (MR) Squadron Neptunes in formation. The aircraft are sporting the original United States Navy paint scheme.

Squadrons at Greenwood as they were delivered: odd serial numbers to 405 and even numbers to 404. In early January 1955, a small number of pilots, flight engineers, and ground crew from both squadrons travelled to Lockheed's plant at Burbank, California, for training; these later provided the nucleus for the Neptune Conversion Unit at Greenwood that trained the remaining air and ground crews on the Neptune. Navigators and radio officers from Greenwood joined the first graduated pilots and flight engineers in Burbank to deliver the first Neptune, arriving in Greenwood on 30 March 1955, where Air Commodore M. Costello, AOC Maritime Air Command, was on hand to officially welcome the new aircraft.

The Neptunes were powered by two Wright R-3350 reciprocating engines; however, the RCAF found that single engine performance was marginal and, like the USN, retrofitted a Westinghouse J34 podded jet engine under each wing. Since the RCAF Neptunes came from the USN production line, the instruments, throttles, electrical controls, and fuel system were already installed, making the retrofit relatively simple. However, the aircraft could not be safely flown on the jet engines alone and these were used during takeoff or when dash speed was required to close on a "datum." When not in use the jet intakes were shuttered to reduce drag. For submarine detection the Neptune was equipped with up-to-date ECM and ETI sensors, as well as a more powerful APS-20 air search radar with a very long detection range. A magnetic anomaly detector (MAD) mounted in a distinctive stinger-like boom extended from the tail of the aircraft. The MAD sensed anomalies in the earth's magnetic field caused by large ferrous objects such as a submerged submarine. Explosive Echo Ranging (EER) recorders were also used for submarine hunting: radio officers would measure the time delay between the detonation of an explosive charge dropped beside a sonobuoy and the return echo to determine the range of the submarine from the sonobuoy. Intersecting range circles from two or more sonobuoys plotted on the tactical navigator's chart fixed the submarine's position.[34] Also, a steerable 70 million candlepower searchlight, mounted in the nose of the starboard tip tank, replaced the Lancaster's parachute flares for illuminating contacts at night. In addition to torpedoes and depth charges carried in the bomb bay, the Neptune was armed with under-wing mounted rockets to attack surface vessels or surfaced submarines.[35]

Initially, the Neptune was manned with a crew of nine: two pilots, one flight engineer, two navigators, and four radio officers. The Neptune was a pilot's airplane; the wide comfortable cockpit with modern instrumentation and controls accommodated the two pilots and the flight engineer. The small cramped tactical compartment behind the cockpit accommodated two radio officers who operated the radar, MAD, ETI, EER and ECM, and one navigator who performed both the routine and tactical navigation. The second navigator manned the lookout position in the nose and alternated with the navigator in the tactical compartment. Two radio officers manned the radio and aft lookout positions in the relatively roomy expendable stores compartment aft of the main spar.

In April3 1956, following the last course at the interim Neptune Conversion Unit, the first Neptune was delivered to 2 (M) OTU in Summerside. The four-month OTU course taught new crew members the fundamentals of anti-submarine warfare, ship recognition, maritime communications, and navigation procedures. At the same time crews learned to function as a team within the aircraft and how to work with other allied forces. Although the Neptune had shorter legs than the Lancaster, it could still participate in international exercises around the North Atlantic perimeter, including USN air stations and NATO bases in Bermuda, Azores, Gibraltar, Northern Ireland, and Iceland. The Neptune remained in service until

Gleaming with a new paint job, an RCAF Neptune is shown here at the Fairey Aviation Plant prior to acceptance by the Air Force: the bright colours replace the former navy blue shade. This Neptune will take its place at RCAF Station Summerside, guarding Canada's East Coast from submarine threats.

1968, but it had always been intended as an interim aircraft to be replaced by the Canadair CP-107 Argus. The Argus was the first and only maritime patrol aircraft designed and built in Canada to meet unique Canadian requirements. It was admired by Canada's allies on both sides of the Atlantic and regarded as one of NATO's premier maritime patrol aircraft in the 1950s and 1960s. The success of the Argus procurement can be attributed to A/M Curtis's political rapport with the highest levels of government. In 1949, the RCAF issued a preliminary operational requirement for a maritime reconnaissance landplane; the document served as a baseline for a Lancaster replacement. Curtis briefed Cabinet that an aircraft with greater range and endurance than any aircraft currently flying or in production was required to close the mid-Atlantic gap between Iceland and Newfoundland and that after a number of studies by Canadair Ltd., the RCAF favoured a design based on the Bristol 175 Britannia airliner.[36] Curtis steered the maritime aircraft program through the government approval process and advised the Minister of National Defence that construction of the maritime version of the Bristol 175 had the added advantage of using the same airframe intended to replace the North Star transport aircraft in service with the RCAF and Trans-Canada Air Lines. Increased production numbers could justify tooling and manufacture in Canada. At a June 1952 meeting of RCAF, Department of Defence Production, Bristol, and Canadair officials on how to convert the Bristol 175 to maritime aircraft, it was decided that Bristol would manufacture those parts common to both the Bristol 175 and the maritime version – wings, empennage, rudder, undercarriage, and so on, while Canadair would manufacture the fuselage and perform the final aircraft assembly.

In late 1953, Cabinet was presented with a Cabinet document requesting funds ($11,131,000) to build a prototype maritime version of the Bristol 175.[37] The RCN supported the request for funds with the proviso that the expenditure be limited to producing a flying prototype; and that a scientific evaluation of future Canadian ASW policy, both surface and air, be undertaken before funds were committed for the production of the operational Bristol 175 ASW aircraft.

The study confirmed the requirement for a maritime surveillance aircraft, clearing the government to award Canadair a contract on 23 February 1954, to build 13 maritime patrol/ASW aircraft, designated the CL-28, based on the Bristol 175. The CL-28 prototype rolled off the production line two years later, in December 1956. In the spirit of the CL-28's all-seeing surveillance role, the RCAF named the aircraft "Argus," after the Greek mythological monster with 100 eyes, only two of which would close at any one time. Before construction was completed on the first batch of 13 Argus aircraft, Canadair received a contract for 20 additional Mark 2 Argus. The Mark 2 differed from the Mark 1 in that the American APS-20 air search radar was replaced with the British air-to-surface-vessel (ASV) 21 maritime radar. On completion of Mark 2 Argus production the RCAF had a total of 58 maritime patrol aircraft, 33 Argus and 25 Neptunes.

Since the first six Arguses off the production line were dedicated to flight-testing, the first operational Argus was not officially turned over to Maritime Air Command until 17 May 1958 at RCAF Station Greenwood. Maritime air crews continued to receive their initial ASW training on the Neptune OTU in Summerside; those OTU graduates destined for Argus squadrons underwent a short conversion course at the newly formed Argus Conversion Unit at Greenwood, with conversion training commencing in June 1958. Almost a year later, in April 1959, 404 Squadron accepted its first Argus. With no sign of the Cold War abating 415 (Swordfish) Squadron was reactivated at Summerside in June 1961 to form a third

Neptune over surfaced submarine – 405 (MR) Squadron.

Argus squadron. In Comox, 407 Squadron continued to fly the Neptune until its retirement in May 1968 when the unit converted to the Argus. The aircraft's long range allowed an expansion of 407's areas of operation to Australia, Fiji, and the Philippines. With the retirement of the Neptune there was no longer a requirement for 2 (M) OTU, and on 24 June 1968, the Argus Conversion Unit became 449 (Unicorn) Squadron and the OTU for Argus crews.

As planned, the Argus retained the Britannia's wings, empennage, and flight control system, while Canadair designed and manufactured a completely new fuselage with two massive 18-foot weapons bays that could accommodate 3,600 kilograms of torpedoes, bombs, depth charges, or mines. The fuselage also incorporated a transparent nose observer's position, a bulbous chin-mounted radome for the APS-20 radar antenna and the addition of a tail boom measuring just over 18 feet to isolate the sensitive MAD sensor from the aircraft's magnetism. The most critical change from the Britannia was the replacement of the four Proteus turboprop engines with

Argus tactical compartment.

Wright R-3350-32W turbo-compound reciprocating engines for more efficient fuel consumption at low altitude.

The redesigned cockpit accommodated two pilots and a flight engineer with the routine navigator and radio operator positions located immediately behind the flight deck. To facilitate the interchange of tactical information, five sensor operators and the tactical navigator were grouped in a spacious tactical compartment in mid-fuselage. The tactical navigator plotted sensor information on his chart to depict the tactical situation and directed the crew through submarine localization tactics to the final attack.

In July 1961, an Argus set an endurance record of 30 hours 20 minutes; however, the length of typical patrols varied between 14 and 18 hours. The Argus' remarkable endurance required a crew of 15 to rotate through the 11 positions in the aircraft, allowing the four off-duty crewmembers to prepare hot meals in a well-equipped galley and sleep in the four bunks.

Lineup of 15 Canadair Argus aircraft from 405 and 404 (MR) Squadrons. This display was laid on for the final visit of the Chief of the Air Staff to RCAF Station Greenwood.

The Canadian designed and built air navigation and tactical control (ANTAC) system was the heart of the Argus and was regarded as the most technically sophisticated navigation system in NATO. The ANTAC's analogue computer continuously computed the aircraft's latitude and longitude, which the routine navigator periodically updated with LORAN A or celestial observations.[38] In the tactical compartment the ANTAC computer projected a moving light symbol onto the tactical navigator's chart to indicate the aircraft's current position in relation to the tactical symbols plotted on the chart – for example, sonobuoy positions and radar contacts. By manually slewing the light symbol, the tactical navigator could determine the range and bearing to any point on his chart and transfer the corresponding course and distance steering commands to the cockpit instruments.

In addition to the MAD, ECM, ETI, and EER sensors inherited from the Neptune, the Argus' highly classified "Jezebel" system proved to be its most effective sensor, which exploited low frequency noise emitted by submarine machinery, propellers, diesel engines or nuclear reactor turbines. Argus crews would deploy sonobuoys that transmitted the noises to the Jezebel system, which transformed them into a family of frequencies that were unique to each class of submarine. In its correlated detection and recording (CODAR) mode Jezebel determined bearings from closely spaced pairs of sonobuoys to the submarine.[39] As well as the system worked, scientists continually improved sonobuoy hydrophone and suspension cable technology to increase Jezebel's ability to detect ever-quieter submarines at longer ranges.

Jezebel enabled the Argus to passively search a large area without alerting the submarine to the aircraft's presence. The search started with Jezebel detecting a submarine from sonobuoy(s) dropped in a search pattern and then localizing its position with two intersecting CODAR bearings. The position was further refined using EER and MAD tactics before finally attacking the resulting datum, using four Mark 43 homing torpedoes to straddle the submarine.[40] With its sophisticated avionics, long range, and endurance the Argus was NATO's most effective submarine hunter in the late 1950s and 1960s. It would be many years before any ASW aircraft would challenge its capabilities.

The speed, range, loiter time, and advanced sensor systems made the Argus a formidable ASW platform, especially when partnered with cueing provided by the US-developed underwater sound surveillance system (SOSUS). Soviet submarines posed the double threat: interdicting the sea lines of communication with NATO forces in Europe, but also launching submarine launched ballistic missiles (SLBM) against strategic targets in North America.[41] To counter the threat the US Navy established a shore-based SOSUS system to provide long-range detections of Soviet submarines approaching the coasts of North America. Relying on the presence of a deep-water sound channel that trapped and focused low frequency sound waves that could be detected over thousands of kilometres, the SOSUS system was top secret, and details were restricted strictly to those with a need to know.[42] The USN was keen on Canadian participation in the SOSUS system because the great circle route from Soviet naval bases on the Russian Kola Peninsula to the American eastern seaboard passed through the CANLANT area. Operating on the same principles as Jezebel, SOSUS consisted of arrays of hydrophones mounted on the ocean floor that were connected by underwater cables to shore stations that were jointly manned by American and Canadian personnel.

The Argus-SOSUS team was Canada's most effective ASW asset. Upon detecting a submarine, the SOSUS shore station generated a submarine probability area (SPA) that was transmitted to an Argus standby crew. With its range and endurance the Argus could arrive over the SOSUS SPA with minimum delay and conduct a Jezebel search of the SPA for longer "on-station" time than any other aircraft. The mission was considered successful when the Jezebel system detected the same submarine frequencies within the SPA as those reported by the SOSUS station. The submarine was then covertly tracked according to the rules of engagement, allowing significant intelligence gathering of both technical and tactical information.

RCAF Maritime Air and the Cuban Crisis

On 14 October 1962, when American intelligence assets photographed the construction of missile sites in Cuba, US President John F. Kennedy ordered an immediate naval blockade to bar the passage of the missile-laden ships in transit from the Soviet Union. In a televised address on 22 October, Kennedy informed the world of the crisis and threatened additional military action if the missiles in situ were not removed and those on route were not turned back. Canada, along with most of America's allies, was informed just prior to the broadcast. Under the auspices of the North American Air Defence Command (NORAD) and NATO agreements, the US requested that Canada raise the alert status of its military forces to Defence Condition (DEFCON) 3. Skeptical of US and Soviet intentions Prime Minister Diefenbaker hesitated, seeking to obtain additional information upon which to base such a decision. The Minister of National Defence, Douglas Harkness, realized the world was on the precipice of a third world war and quietly and unobtrusively advised the chairman of the chiefs of staff, A/C/M F.R. Miller, on the evening of the 22nd to discretely increase readiness levels, thereby allowing operational commanders to honour their continental defence commitments. Although Harkness kept the prime minister posted on the escalating events, Diefenbaker refused to call Cabinet to authorize the increase in military readiness. Therefore, national authority for the blockade and the equivalent maritime DEFCON 3 rules of engagement were never promulgated.[43] Nevertheless, RCN and RCAF maritime forces were now prepared to take part in the blockade.[44]

Under the guise of "training," naval and air operational commanders ingeniously advanced by one month a previously planned "sub-air barrier" exercise across the Greenland-Iceland-UK gap.[45] With USN concurrence, Canadian planners adjusted the sub-air barrier approximately 550 nautical miles southeast to extend from Cape Race, Newfoundland, to a point just under 300 nautical miles from the Portuguese Azores. For the first two weeks of the "exercise," 24 Argus from Greenwood were

405 (MR) Squadron Argus over a Royal Canadian Navy "O-boat" submarine.

divided between surveillance and barrier patrols to locate and track Soviet ships and submarines. Eight more Argus later joined from Summerside.

The Argus, with its very long range, was the key player from the start.[46] It was the only aircraft able to cover the far southeast end of the barrier, over 850 nautical miles from Greenwood. Three Argus were continuously present, with each aircraft conducting six-hour transits to the patrol area, remaining eight hours on station and then flying six hours back home – 20 hours per flight. They carried full war loads of torpedoes and depth charges but had no national authority to release weapons. Hundreds of sonobuoys were dropped, and when sonobuoy stocks ran low the USN flew an additional 500 to Greenwood at no cost![47]

Bowing to American pressure, the Soviets ordered their ships to turn around on 28 October; however, Canadian participation in the blockade was not officially recognized in Washington because there was no political authority to do so. Privately, the RCN and Maritime Air Command prided themselves on their effective response to the crisis and the smooth implementation of existing North American and NATO defence plans. In contrast, the Canadian government and even some of the senior military leaders seemed paralyzed by the crisis.[48] The government's response to the Cuban missile crisis highlighted shortcomings in the Canadian concept of civilian control of the military caused by systemic coordination problems between various levels of the command structure along with Diefenbaker's autocratic style of management and his distrust of the military.[49] In the absence of leadership from politicians and support from military staffs in Ottawa, the operational naval and air commanders, who had been granted a high degree of autonomy, did what they believed was in the best interests of their continental defence commitments to their American allies. USN Vice Admiral Edmund Taylor, commander of the Atlantic anti-submarine forces, privately and sincerely thanked his Canadian counterparts; a public expression of USN gratitude would have divulged Canada's role in the blockade and caused heads to roll.[50] Maritime Air Command's finest hour, in which it played a key role in defusing a crisis that had brought the world to the brink of war, passed unheralded.[51] Had the effort been known it would have underscored the years of hard work to develop technology, organization, and tactics that were cutting-edge in the early 1960s.

RCAF Maritime Aviation and Coastal Surveillance

Maritime Air Command had always played a role in the surveillance of Canada's coasts and territorial waters but was often limited by the range and capability of its aircraft. The advent of the Argus increased the RCAF's utility in safeguarding Canadian sovereignty. It was the first RCAF aircraft with sufficient range to patrol any segment of Canada's coastline, including the Arctic Archipelago, from any airfield in Canada. Similarly, the aircraft's exceptional endurance enabled it to conduct surveillance of Canada's east coast continental shelf, the world's largest and richest in terms of natural resources, in a single mission. True to its name, the Argus became the nation's eyes that gathered unprecedented amounts of intelligence on coastal activities, including drug smuggling, illegal immigration, shipping, and fishery violations that were reported to other government departments responsible for regulating and enforcing sovereignty in Canadian waters.

The International Commission for the Northwest Atlantic Fisheries Organization was particularly concerned about the very large number of domestic and foreign fishing vessels, including those of the Soviet Union, that were overfishing the Canadian Grand Banks and depleting long-established fish stocks.[52] The extent of domestic and foreign fishing activity gathered by the Argus provided compelling substantiation for the creation of the Canadian Exclusive Economic Zone which gave Canada the legal authority to enforce environmental regulations 200 nautical miles from its coast in order to conserve its natural resources.

The large Soviet fishing fleet off Canada's coast was also a national security concern and the focus of regular surveillance. The Argus kept regular tabs on these fleets spotting Soviet submarines replenishing from fish factory ships, monitoring fishing location and size of catches, and also noting that Russian fishing vessels often masked submarine movements, visually, electronically, and acoustically. Also a concern were Soviet electronic intelligence vessels, disguised as fishing trawlers surreptitiously extracted intelligence from the full radio spectrum-ranging from marine and military communications to data links and microwave services.[53] Since these fleets were centrally controlled from the Soviet Union, changes in their disposition often signified Soviet intentions. In the event of East-West relations deteriorating, accurate and timely intelligence about the latent enemy off the Canadian coast would be critical to national decision makers, and this intelligence could be garnered effectively by Maritime Air Command's aircraft.

RCAF Maritime Aviation: A National Asset

From the beginning of the Cold War the RCAF was resolved to regain its ASW expertise by incrementally rebuilding its maritime patrol squadrons that were fundamental to NATO maintaining the balance of power in the North Atlantic. The RCAF's little discussed partnership in the Argus-SOSUS team and its major, if unheralded, involvement in the Cuban missile blockade proved Canada to be a trusted and reliable ally in the maritime defence of North America. The success of many of the RCAF's ASW operations relied on covertness and therefore received none of the visibility or publicity afforded NORAD fighter interceptions of Soviet aircraft. Although out of the public's eye, maritime aircraft surveillance of Canada's adjacent oceans provided an important deterrence against Soviet probes during the first decades of the Cold War. Domestically, the RCAF shared maritime intelligence with other government departments, establishing maritime aircraft as one of the principal guardians of Canadian coastal sovereignty and a vital national asset.

NOTES

1 NATO *The North Atlantic Treaty*, April 4, 1949, accessed October 21, 2021, https://www.nato.int/cps/en/natohq/official_texts_17120.htm.
2 J.J. Sokolsky, "A One Ocean Fleet: The Atlantic and Canadian Naval Policy," *Cahiers de géographie du Québec* 34, no. 93 (1990): 302.
3 Ibid., 303.
4 Ibid., 303.

5 Mark Milner, *Canada's Navy, The First Century* (Toronto: University of Toronto Press, 1999), 176.
6 Ibid., 162.
7 Patrick Martin and John Pettipas, *Royal Canadian Navy Aircraft Finish and Markings 1944–1968*, (Self-Published 2007), 231.
8 Ibid., 234.
9 J.D.F. Kealy and E.C. Russell, *Naval Aviation, 1918–1962* (Ottawa: Queen's Printer, 1967), 52.
10 Canada, Department of National Defence (DND), Directorate of History and Heritage (DHH), File 181.004 (D44) "'Plan B' – Post War Plan for the Royal Canadian Air Force, April 1946.
11 DHH, File 180.004 (D46), "Summary of Requirements for RCAF Plan 'F', 1950–51," 1.
12 Ibid.
13 Ibid., 2, Tab 1.
14 S. Kostenuk and J. Griffin, *RCAF Squadrons and Aircraft* (Toronto: Samuel Stevens Hakkert & Company, 1977), 209.
15 Tony German, *The Sea Is at Our Gates: A History of the Canadian Navy* (Toronto: McClelland & Stewart, 1990), 247.
16 Anonymous, *The History of CFB Greenwood 1942–1992* (Winnipeg, Manitoba: Craig Kelman & Associates Ltd, 1992), 48.
17 Alex Souchen, "Peace Dividend: The War Assets Corporation and the Disposal of Canada's Munitions and Supplies, 1943–1948" (PhD diss., University of Western Ontario, 2016), 300, 300n12.
18 Terry Higgins, "Canada's Postwar Lancasters," *Canadian Historical Society Journal* 57, no. 2 (Summer 2019): 75.
19 Squadron Historical Committee, *405 Squadron History* (Winnipeg, Manitoba: Craig Kelman & Associates Ltd, 1986), 71.
20 Roger A. Holler, "The Evolution of the Sonobuoy from World War II to the Cold War," *US Navy Journal of Underwater Acoustics*, January 2014, 328, accessed October 29, 2021, https://apps.dtic.mil/sti/pdfs/ADA597432.pdf.
21 *405 Squadron History*, 70.
22 Ibid., 72.
23 Ibid., 75.
24 Larry Milberry, *Canada's Air Force at War and Peace*, Volume 3 (Toronto: CANAV Books, 2001), 406.
25 NATO, North Atlantic Military Committee Decision on M.C. 48, "The Most Effective Pattern of NATO Military Strength for the New Few Years." Accessed 2 December 2021, https://www.nato.int/docu/stratdoc/eng/a541122a.pdf.
26 Ibid., 4.
27 DHH, File 181.004(D50), "Long Range Plan for the Royal Canadian Air Force, 1956–1966".
28 Ibid., 24.
29 Shawn Cafferky, *Uncharted Waters: A History of the Canadian Helicopter-Carrying Destroyer* (Halifax: Dalhousie University Centre for Foreign Policy Studies, 2005), 234. For additional detail on the RCN / RCAF ASW helicopter debated see chapter seven of this reference: "Troubled Waters: The Navy's Fight for Naval Aviation," 215–46.
30 Ibid., 233.
31 DHH, File 181.004 (D48), "RCAF Plan 'H' for the RCAF, 1 Apr 51 Edition, Tab 3.
32 The P2V Neptune was designed as an ASW aircraft for the US Navy in 1945. The P2V-6 was an improved version with a larger bomb bay, the P2V-7 was the latest version with more powerful reciprocating engines, two jet engines and an improved radar.

33   Milberry, 413.
34   MAD anomalies, ETI exhaust detections and EER range measurements were recorded by pen deflections on paper trace recorders.
35   Milberry, 411.
36   Ron Pickler and Larry Milberry, *Canadair: The First Fifty Years* (Toronto: CANAV Books, 1995), 120.
37   Cabinet Defence Committee Document D 50/53 dated November 26, 1953.
38   LORAN, an abbreviation for long-range aid to navigation was a land-based radio navigation fixing aid.
39   Roger A. Holler, "The Evolution of the Sonobuoy from World War II to the Cold War," *United States Navy Journal of Underwater Acoustics* (January 2014), accessed December 2, 2021, http://www.navairdevcen.org/PDF/THE%20EVOLUTION%20OF%20THE%20SONOBUOY.pdf.
40   The Argus later converted to the more advanced Mark 44 torpedo requiring only two torpedoes for an attack.
41   Peter T. Haydon, "Canadian Involvement in the Cuban Missile Crisis Re-Reconsidered," *The Northern Mariner* 17, no. 2 (April 2007): 46–7. Early ranges for Soviet SLBMs were approximately 600–900 kilometres.
42   John Howard, "Fixed Sonar Systems: The History and Future of the Underwater Sentinel," *The Submarine Review* (April 2011), 3–4. Accessed December 2, 2021, https://nps.edu/documents/103449515/0/HOWARDAPR2011.pdf/1219db41-a727-4940-ab0b-b953c54f6e01.
43   For additional detail on this complex civil-military issue see Brad Gladman and Peter Archambault, "Advice and Indecision: Canada and the Cuban Missile Crisis," *Canadian Military History* 23, no. 1 (Winter, 2014) 11–32.
44   Tony German, *The Sea Is at Our Gates, the History of the Canadian Navy* (Toronto: McClelland & Stewart, Toronto, 1990), 265.
45   German, 266. A sub-air barrier consisted of submarines and aircraft establishing a barrier to detect enemy forces.
46   Ibid., 268.
47   Ibid.
48   Milner, 235.
49   Peter Haydon, *The 1962 Missile Crisis: Canadian Involvement Reconsidered*, Canadian Institute of Strategic Studies, 1993, 210.
50   German, 23.
51   Ibid., 272.
52   Ibid., 311
53   Ibid.

CHAPTER FIFTEEN

FROM ARMY CO-OPERATION TO ARMY CO-OPTATION: CANADA'S STRUGGLES WITH AVIATION SUPPORT TO THE LAND FORCES

DEAN BLACK

Introduction and Context

In this chapter we delve into the cultures of two competing organizations: the RCAF and the Canadian Army. By culture we mean the accumulated shared learning of the group, as "it solves its problems of external adaptation and internal integration."[1] Change brings problems; adapting to and integrating external forces and internal mandates, respectively, helps to bring solutions. Our exploration of culture, therefore, explores how these organizations adapt to changing (external) threats, respond to the need for internal integration, and in doing so rewrite doctrine for the path forward. Adaptation and integration are made necessary by a desire to innovate. Quite often such a desire does not materialize.

The chapter will focus on the organizations and some of the people – the agents – who had the power to render decisions and make policy about tactical aircraft in support of the land forces. In the present chapter, there are many agents, not just the RCAF. In the Canadian Army there are at least four other agents representing the combat arms and combat support arms (Infantry, Artillery, Armour, and Service Corps), each with its own culture.

Individuals play important roles too, and in this chapter one of the central actors is Albert Karl "Bert" Casselman, a young pilot who, after being demobilized from the RCAF in late 1945, subsequently rejoined the military, electing to serve in the Royal Canadian Armoured Corps (RCAC). Several years passed when one day Bert was invited to hop into a Harvard at the Canadian Joint Air Training Centre (CJATC) in Rivers, Manitoba. That flight would mark the beginning of a sterling

An Auster "Air Observation Post" aircraft used by the Canadian Army in the immediate post-war period.

postwar tactical aviation career, with little to no reference to his Second World War RCAF experiences flying Thunderbolts. It would be Bert Casselman's vision for a tactical air force organic to the Canadian Army, encompassing the roles of observation, medium and heavy utility transport, and anti-tank/armed helicopter operations, all enflamed by his passion for innovation and the helicopter, that would have a substantive impact on efforts to shape Canada's RCAF for decades to come. Casselman was not alone; all during these years there would be a number of officers with RCAF experience who subsequently flew for the Army.

RCAF Army Co-operation Gives Way to Canadian Army Aviation

From the earliest days of the Second World War, RAF and RCAF references to the role and terminology of "army co-operation" dominated the discourse.[2] It would be inaccurate, however, to portray army co-operation in 1939 as something new. Much of what aviation did from earliest days of the First World War directly supported the land forces.

A.K. "Bert" Casselman in the dress uniform of the Royal Canadian Dragoons with his spouse, Kathleen Georgina. Courtesy of the Black collection.

One year into the Second World War, Canadian Colonel E.L.M. Burns informed the chief of the general staff (CGS) about an idea shared by a First World War veteran and colleague, W.J. Sanderson. A new type of light aircraft described as "Cavalry of the Air" was under consideration by British authorities. It was to be used "to attack enemy columns and concentrations using aircraft flown by army personnel [because] the army has been pressing for this kind of co-operation, and the R.A.F. does not seem disposed to do much about it."[3]

In early 1941, Lieutenant-General Andrew McNaughton, senior Canadian Army commander in Britain, wrote that it was "very desirable for each armoured division to be closely associated with an army co-operation squadron."[4] Close association was described in terms of "intimate personal contacts, mutual understanding and liaison." From Ottawa the Vice-CGS Brigadier Kenneth Stuart responded saying, "… the Chief of the Air Staff (CAS) would not play as no new squadrons will be formed in Canada at the present time,"[5] since much of the RCAF attention was focused on pilots and crews for fighters and bombers. Meanwhile, efforts in the UK and the US did lead to the creation of small units to provide direct assistance to field forces.[6]

The RCAF's army co-operation efforts during this period can be traced to creation of 101 Wing, consisting of three squadrons (2, 110 and 112) of Lysander aircraft.[7] These RCAF assets were assigned under RAF Army Co-operation Command, which eventually would consist of two groups (No. 70 and No. 71). At the time, however, affected pilots were unenthusiastic. The requirement for them to acquire "a thorough knowledge of army organization and training in army tactics" exposed them to "one of the duller subjects ... at a time when such tactics were obsolete (in their minds)."[8]

On 1 June 1943, Army Co-operation Command itself was disbanded, as part of a reorganization of tactical air forces, in advance of D-Day. No. 110 Squadron, renumbered 400 Squadron in 1941, was joined by Nos. 414 and 430 Squadron, under command of 39 (Army Co-operation) Wing of 83 Group of the 2nd Tactical Air Force. In late 1943, Lieutenant-General McNaughton was succeeded by Lieutenant-General H.D.G. Crerar, who supported the push to create three Air Observation Post (AOP) squadrons (664, 665, and 666) "under Canadian Army control."[9] These AOP units would provide spotting and fire direction for the artillery regiments of affiliated army units. Some months later they were redesignated as "Canadian Army Component – 664, 665, and 666 (AOP) Squadrons, Royal Canadian Air Force."[10] From the Army's point of view a change from RAF-controlled and piloted Lysander aircraft to lighter two-place Taylorcraft aircraft, provided and maintained by the RCAF but flown by artillery officers in Army-controlled AOP squadrons, was "a proven example of army/air cooperation."[11]

Meanwhile, proposals and counterproposals for a postwar RCAF had begun, as described earlier in this volume. Despite being held to a mere handful of regular and auxiliary squadrons, throughout all these machinations the RCAF acknowledged as part of its role continuing cooperation with and support to the army and navy.

At the end of the war army cooperation seemed heavily focused on AOP, but the postwar army had other evolving needs, including troop transport where wartime surplus gliders were used. The formation of No. 1 Airborne Research and Development Centre, located at Camp Shilo, Manitoba, signalled early postwar army/air collaboration. By April 1947, the unit was renamed the Joint Air School (JAS) and was moved to Rivers, Manitoba, where various RCAF units were stationed: 417 Fighter Reconnaissance Squadron was operating with Mustang aircraft, No. 112 Flight was

RCAF Station Rivers, Manitoba, with hangars and airfield used by the Canadian Joint Air Training Centre.

co-operating with gliders, and No. 444 (AOP) Squadron was forming with light aircraft. The purpose of the JAS "was to meet all requirements of training and development for the Canadian forces in tactical support of land and airborne operations."[12] An organizational change in March 1949 created a tri-service air training centre out of the elements of the JAS. In 1948, the Canadian Army took possession of its first helicopters, three Bell 47s issued to what had become the Canadian Joint Air Training Centre (CJATC).[13]

In the US, the role of the helicopter in aerial support to the field army was advancing. At the sixth annual forum of the American Helicopter Society, keynote speaker USAF Major-General Robert M. Lee insisted "control of air forces must be centralized." Lee further explained "tactical air power must be capable of close, direct support of surface forces in the immediate zone of combat." Lee shared that light helicopters were being put to many tasks, and a heavy lift helicopter requirement was not in dispute. He said the helicopter was not a weapon, but a vehicle. He marvelled at the pace of helicopter development, from the four-place version fielded in 1945, to the 10-place helicopter due out the following year. Lee and his USAF colleague Lieutenant-General Nathan Twining were witnesses to a binational air and ground exercise in the Canadian north, Exercise SWEETBRIAR, and both had commented in an article in the *Canadian Army Journal* how helpful helicopters would be in those environs.[14] In the wake of Lee's observations, the first US Army helicopter transport company took shape at Fort Sill, Oklahoma, on 1 November 1950, organic to the Transportation Corps.[15] But where the Americans had acquired a helicopter capability by the close of the 1940s and before the Korean War erupted, Canadian Army Aviation was limited to AOP and glider-equipped transport as its primary functions.

Clarence Henry "Harry" Reid and the Flying Truck

After the war, Canadian Army aviation took shape within the Mobile Striking Force, which was conceived as an airborne/air portable force. At first, the available transport aircraft were wartime Dakotas and gliders. The Army bought a number of US CG4A Waco gliders for this purpose. A number of NCOs were sent to the CJATC to be trained as glider pilots; this followed the wartime practice of the British Glider Pilot Regiment but was looked upon with concern by the RCAF and its commissioned flying ranks. Aviation technology and equipment was changing rapidly, and the introduction of helicopters and larger transport aircraft (C-119s) capable of transporting and dropping large loads would soon obviate the requirement for gliders. That left Army glider pilots with two choices: cease active flying and return to their units; or remain as active pilots, convert to new aircraft types, and seek a commission. The first RCAC transport helicopter pilots came from that group, as did some of the Royal Canadian Armoured Corps (RCAC) reconnaissance (recce) pilots in addition to some infantry officer pilots.[16]

One of these coverts was Clarence Henry "Harry" Reid, whose service was synonymous with the rise of the helicopter transport capability in the Canadian Army. Unlike Casselman, Reid had served in the war, but as an airborne soldier. In 1948, Harry was commissioned shortly after successfully completing the glider pilot training course at Rivers. He eventually accumulated over 5,000 hours on dozens of different fixed-wing and rotary-wing (helicopter) aircraft from Canada and the US and was the first Canadian Army Captain to pass promotion exams in both the infantry and the service corps. He served as chief flying instructor at the newly

Canadian Army pilots C.H. "Harry" Reid and G.C. Walker discuss the day's activities.
Courtesy of the Black collection.

formed Army Aviation Training School in Rivers, Manitoba, in 1960. Thereafter, he was the first to command No. 1 Transport Helicopter Platoon, RCASC, the first such unit in the Canadian military. The utility of helicopters in such a role would take years of experimentation and practice before units like Harry Reid's "1 Thump" were declared operational.

American experiences in Korea reinforced the idea that placing tactical aviation under operational control of the Army would be key to enhancing overall battlefield effectiveness. "The command most capable of controlling [aviation in direct support of the land forces] adequately and effectively is the artillery," one officer proclaimed, emphasizing how experiences in Korea demonstrated the important need for close support aviation organic to the army.[17] Korean experience also showed replacing jeeps and trucks was inevitable, but that such a transformation was taking far too long, in part because those opposed to the innovation tended to exaggerate the helicopter's problems.[18] For example, one officer offered up, "[the

Cessna L-19 "Bird Dog" Canadian Army light observation aircraft: the mainstay of army aviation until they were replaced by helicopters.

helicopter is just] another mode of transport, with severe limitations, and does not replace the work horse of the Army, the 2 and ½ ton truck ... noise and dust clouds made clear the helicopter is a slow vehicle with no place to go but down ... they are sitting ducks ... one high or low-speed aircraft could have crippled the whole battalion." [19] By September 1954, however, helicopters began to show promise on reconnaissance missions, with properly trained "aerial observers."[20]

While these debates continued in the American forces the Canadian Army seems to have adopted the term "Canadian Army Aviation," implying organizational ownership which somewhat contrasted the RCAF's undeniably proprietary, but more functionalist, terminology of "army co-operation." What had survived during the Second World War as army co-operation now seemed poised for co-optation primarily because all too often when army units needed the support it was not readily available: "air-land cooperation was an unpopular pastime for participating soldiers and airmen."[21] The structure of the immediate postwar RCAF offered little reassurance to the army. Prime Minister Louis St-Laurent's "Big Air Force," while exhibiting some balance, specialized in alliance roles resulting in the buildup of a large fighter force, owing to the nature of combat in the Korean theatre and other developments elsewhere. Soviet developments in atomic weapons, for example, effectively encouraged a preoccupation in the West with air power's primary role as "final arbiter in the event of global nuclear war."[22] Armies struggling to thrive in the international security environment of the early 1950s likely shared the sentiment "that the [air force] had 'flown away' from the Army, having become strongly preoccupied with the new super firepower afforded by atomic fission and with the new means of propulsion – the jet engine."[23]

Those same atomic weapons and the experiences of Korea caused the Army under the CGS Lieutenant-General Guy Simonds to initiate the Gold Rush studies in early 1955 which led to an acceptance that in the near and mid-term future the army would need both transport helicopters and a fixed wing transport aircraft to support army formations on either conventional or highly dispersed nuclear battlefields.[24] Work during that year led to a late December "Report of the Ad Hoc Committee on Service Requirements for Helicopters," which included recommendations to the Chiefs of Staff Committee (COSC) that the Army needed two types of helicopters: a light machine for command and liaison work and a larger transport helicopter capable of casualty evacuation. Specific aircraft were suggested, the Bell 47 and the Sikorsky S-58 respectively. Perhaps more importantly the report recommended coordination between the Services so that helicopter requirements could be coordinated for ease of logistics.[25] And finally the report noted the activities that had already been taking place at Rivers. Indeed, six RCASC officers had reported for flying training at the Brandon Flying Club in May.

The Army was interested in equipping an experimental helicopter unit to investigate replacing first-line transport vehicles with helicopters. By July, while the Gold Rush study was still underway, Simonds concluded a Canadian Army unit would require seven helicopters.[26] The Land/Air Warfare committee reported on the military characteristics of aircraft for logistical supply within the army field forces. Fixed-wing aircraft would lift supplies forward to the Division Maintenance Area and forward movement from there to fighting units would be done by vehicles and/or cargo helicopters. The S-58 helicopter was recommended, along with a proposed establishment for the unit. It was also determined the unit should reside at CJATC Rivers. In a report released in early November 1955,[27] an evaluation of light helicopters (H-21s) and medium helicopters (S-58s), along with fixed wing C-119s and Otters, recommended the use of medium or large helicopters as

Bert Reid (on step) and two other Canadian Army aviation officers are instructed on the H-34 helicopter by a member of the US Army, October 1955. Courtesy of the Black collection.

transport for the assault force on future Mobile Strike Force (MSF) operations and exercises. The RCAF now weighed in on the subject of "... the Control and Operation of Helicopters in the Canadian Services," distinguishing between air force air transport for special missions in support of the army and the army's need for any transport system, which formed a part of its day-to-day existence in the field and upon which the army must depend for essential supplies. These latter requirements the RCAF identified as an integral part of the army supply system, to be manned by army personnel and maintained to a certain degree by army facilities.[28]

By December 1955, the report of the Ad Hoc Committee on Service Requirements for Helicopters informed the COSC that the army had an immediate requirement for a helicopter for both training and utility tasks, including integral liaison between units and logistic support for casualty evacuation (CASEVAC). It was also noted that helicopter training for the Canadian Army and the RCAF was being offered at the Light Aircraft School (LAS) CJATC Rivers, using aircraft and instructors from both services.[29] A few weeks later, the RCAF commented on the report, defending the merits of "retaining design, development, procurement, operation and maintenance of all helicopters used by any of the services."[30] However, both the navy and the army members "considered it essential that they operate and maintain their own helicopters." The committee recommended that the army be made responsible for their own operation and maintenance of their own helicopters, and that the application for the experimental helicopter unit for the Army be approved. Centralizing all helicopter flight training in Rivers was not recommended, however.[31]

More studies followed throughout 1956 with the Army exploring the creation of its own fixed wing transport capability or, if not, having access to air force assets. Alternatively, obtaining heavy transport helicopters for a variety of logistics and battlefield mobility functions was a better option – better because it dispensed with the need for impractical airfields within the combat zone. These studies also identified virtually the full range of modern army helicopter functions and pointed to a sophisticated, but perhaps not solely Canadian vision of army helicopter capabilities. Indeed, Canadians serving with US and United Kingdom (UK) armies were exposed to many forward-thinking notions.[32]

In February 1958, the CGS, Lieutenant-General H.D. Graham, recommended activating one aviation company consisting of three light fixed-wing aircraft, 12 light observation and reconnaissance helicopters – for artillery work, liaison, and reconnaissance – and 12 light cargo helicopters – for transporting of personnel, casualties, and urgent supplies. In May, a paper on army aircraft requirements submitted to the COSC proposed roles for the Canadian Army air support. "The Vice Chief of the General Staff (VCGS) pointed out that to perform these tasks properly there was a need for an aviation service organic to Army formations so that the air vehicles would be under the control of, and readily available to the commander concerned. This concept of having air vehicles organic to the army had been accepted as a sound principle, as reflected by the fact that the British, French, Americans, and Russians all have air components within their Armies."[33]

In early 1959, the CAS made a number of recommendations: that one light helicopter type (Bell 47) would meet the training requirements of all services and is suitable as a light utility helicopter as well; two medium heavy helicopter types (Sikorsky S63 or Kaman HU2K and Vertol 107) are required, the first primarily to meet naval requirements and the second primarily to meet Army requirements (of the two types, the RCAF requirement was best met by the Vertol 107.[34] In response, approval was sought for the procurement by the Army of ten reconnaissance helicopters, four cargo helicopters and four Beavers (L-20) with associated spares.[35]

While coordinated procurement had been a feature of the ad hoc committee recommendations of late 1955, the responsibility for training had not been ironed out. Basic flight training on the Chipmunk was now needed for 24 Army trainees annually.[36] When combined with the needs of the Navy, these changes proved to be a strain on the RCAF's diminishing resources. The RCAF Comptroller, Air Vice Marshal I.C. Cornblat, stated: "I am accepting as a matter of principle that we cannot give up to the Army or to the Navy control of functions vital to our roles." "Any activity in which we are engaged," explained Cornblat, "which does not directly contribute to the 'M Day" (Mobilization Day) capability must automatically be of lower priority."[37] Among the activities deemed not essential to immediate M-Day Capability were Army co-operation and the human resource complement at a number of stations including (CJATC) Rivers.

Finances being tight, procurement and provision of common items by the RCAF were to be done on a cost-recovery basis, and the RCAF was to be responsible for training land force pilots to the "Army Wings standard," but assigning RCAF pilots to these tasks was ruled out, and the integration of RCAF units into the field army was deemed "uneconomical and unsatisfactory."[38] The Army consented to RCAF flight training for its pilots and instructors but insisted that operational flying training would be left to the Army, and it reserved the right to seek such operational training outside the RCAF, if it so desired. The Army also claimed responsibility for first- and second-line maintenance of aircraft.

In May of the same year the RCAF received the nod from Treasury Board for the purchase of 25 H-13 helicopters.[39] Later that summer, the COSC encouraged the Canadian Army to agree on only two types of helicopters, one light and one heavy.[40] Correspondence presented during their September meeting confirmed the Canadian Army's requirements for specific helicopter types, as well as for the procurement of four Beaver aircraft at a cost of $292 million.[41] The Chief of the Air Staff (CAS), Air Marshal (AM) Campbell, suggested the term "Army Aircraft" was more acceptable than the Army's use of the term "Air Vehicles." As the meeting continued concerns were raised with having 26 aircraft consisting of four different types: General Foulkes and the deputy minister initiated a debate on the possible elimination of the Beavers in favour of making more use of the light helicopters, but AM Campbell favoured the Beaver. A limited purchase of four aircraft was supported, during the upcoming fiscal year, but the greater urgency of acquiring support for the Brigade in Europe occupied the conversation. At the 19 November COSC meeting the number of helicopters required was specified as three light and six heavy.[42]

Despite the apparent importance of an aviation capability, progress towards fielding that capability was dragging.

The year 1960 was the first in which helicopters deploying from Rivers to army training concentrations (in Wainwright and Gagetown) were manned entirely by army personnel.[43] This was a promising development, for it served as an impetus to the armoured corps to take steps to form its own aviation capability as part of the reconnaissance squadrons of its armoured regiments. The first pair of pilots assigned to this capability reported to the CJATC in 1961 and, after training, proceeded to Germany to join the Fort Garry Horse armoured regiment to fly the CH-112.[44] In 1961, seven RCAC pilots reported to CJATC to form the nucleus of the RCAC Helicopter Reconnaissance Troop.[45] Bruce Muelaner was among them, and his leadership ten years later as part of a multinational attack helicopter trial in Europe would have international consequences for the field of army aviation from that time on. By November, 12 RCAC sergeants were also being assessed to determine their suitability as air observers, and seven of the 12 eventually qualified. The last remaining Bell H-13 was despatched for disposal in September, following the arrival in Rivers, just weeks before, of the first CH-112 Raven, tail number 10264.[46] Twenty more would arrive before the end of the year, with an additional three going not to the Army but to the RCAF. In a significant development, but one which followed the protocol established in 1955, the Air Council approved the plan to procure more Hiller H-12E light helicopters along with sixteen Vertol 107 heavy helicopters for auxiliary squadrons, these to be procured on a 1962–3 timeline.[47]

Nine CH-112s were shipped to northwest Europe via C-130 Hercules, in May 1962.[48] These light reconnaissance helicopters were some of those authorized for purchase specifically for use by the RCAC reconnaissance squadron then serving as part of the 4 Canadian Infantry Brigade Group (CIBG). Each armoured reconnaissance squadron, in Europe and in Canada, was to consist of six Raven helicopters and eighteen tracked Lynx vehicles.[49] Military historian Brereton Greenhous seems to characterize the Canadian Army's implementation of the helicopter in the reconnaissance role as somewhat slow, given that its utility in that role had been quite clear a decade earlier in Korea. However, Greenhous does sing the helicopter's praises later, explaining how use of the helicopter enable reconnaissance tasks to be done up to four times faster. Perhaps the most interesting observation Greenhous makes is the impact on the individual armoured regiments if they rotated for operational duty in Germany with insufficient pilots. In such a case, another armoured regiment with sufficient pilots, or another combat arm entirely, even the RCASC, would fulfill the reconnaissance helicopter tasks, these soldiers serving in the shorthanded regiment but without rebadging. It is clear from Greenhous'

CH-112 Helicopter – Two Hiller Helicopters, from the aerial observation flight of the 4th Canadian Infantry Brigade serving NATO in Germany, hover near a Scout car of a Canadian reconnaissance unit.

account these "bubble-troop" pilots felt somewhat like outcasts, but "it added some colour to the mess life."[50]

Meanwhile, the RCASC had initiated a project called "The Flying Truck," the outcome of which was to be an aircraft capable of matching the capacity of the Canadian Army's "deuce and a half" (2 ½ - ton) truck but able to cover the increased distances on the nuclear battlefield. The two-engine de Havilland Caribou was examined as the company offered retractable landing gear and full instrumentation for instrument flying rules (IFR) operations, with no effect on the cost nor contract. The Canadian Army accepted the added capabilities, and the aircraft was selected. But the RCAF did not see a "Flying Truck," nor did they see an "Air Vehicle." Instead, the Caribou was an aircraft and one presumably belonging to the air force. The RCASC was denied the aircraft that it had sponsored – and funded – and in

1960 the RCAF took delivery of nine aircraft it had never ordered. Perhaps not surprisingly the Caribou caught the attention of other armies and met a United States Army requirement; 159 were bought, and deliveries began in December 1962.[51] Subsequently, the Australian Army purchased several more.

Soon it was possible to reflect on the use of helicopters and their impact on army culture and capabilities. In his Army Aviation Newsletter editorial for the winter of 1962,[52] Casselman paraphrased an idea presented by David N. Solomon, writing, "a modern army is above all a dynamic institution, seeking to adapt to rapidly changing conditions largely outside its control. It constantly exhibits an amazing flexibility and versatility."[53] Casselman used the opportunity to emphasize, yet again, the dual responsibility to maintain proficiency in both the corps and in Army Aviation subjects. The armoured corps experiment had early growing pains, however. Control of the helicopter assets deployed to summer concentrations, and, under the reconnaissance troop leader, was proving ineffective. Recommendations to place the helicopters under command of the reconnaissance squadron headquarters and give them specific missions from the command post was anticipated to be more effective.[54] The artillery, on the other hand, was pleased with the local air support. In Gagetown, for example, summer concentrations had been relying on aircraft deployed from afar since 1954, but during the 1962 concentration aircraft resident in Gagetown were available to them for the first time.[55]

Following the US Lead

Many of the original Army helicopter cadre were trained in the US and would have been witness to US defence policy and the impacts on US Army doctrine and culture first-hand. And while aviation decisions and events were unfolding in Canada, to the south the US government and services were dealing with their own challenges surrounding the use of nuclear weapons. Unlike Eisenhower, Kennedy and Secretary of Defence McNamara found first use a restrictive if not disturbing doctrine. Kennedy pushed for other solutions, and the doctrine of "Massive Retaliation" gave way to the Kennedy-McNamara era's "Flexible Response." If McNamara's mission was to shake army generals out of their overly conservative-minded tree, Major-General Hamilton Howze was brought in to cut the tree down. McNamara stood up the Howze Board, which worked on the massive introduction of helicopters and aircraft from May through August 1962.[56] Howze Army Tactical Mobility Requirements Board recommended the creation of multiple air assault divisions, air cavalry combat brigades (complete with anti-tank helicopters), and air transport brigades. The central "assumption was that aircraft, and helicopters in particular, were capable of fulfilling the army's five combat functions – reconnaissance, manoeuvre, firepower, command and control, and logistics."[57] Howze's recommendations meant culture change and effectively served to corral leaders who would go on to champion the creative employment of helicopters in direct support of the land forces. Everywhere he turned, Howze confronted someone who stood to lose if helicopters succeeded. This was especially true when it came to talking about arming the helicopter for anti-tank and close air support missions. The armoured corps saw the armed helicopter as a replacement for the tank.

Despite many challenges, Howze was able to forge a path that promoted the further development of helicopters in support of the army. Part of the success derived from a decision to integrate the helicopter into each of the more critical branches (artillery, armoured and service corps). Canadian Army officials shared these ideas, having acknowledged the previous year the importance of: concentration; firepower; manoeuvrability; protection; spirit; and, training. Logistics organizations saw an end to army trucks. Howze's ideas were captured in a reprinted 1958 article in the *Canadian Army Journal*.[58] By 1961 a document specifically pertaining to the role of aviation in such matters (CDY 60-15-1 "Air Support to a Canadian Field Force") was nearing completion.[59] Some thought was also being directed towards combining RCAF/Army helicopter squadrons.[60]

In Search of a Champion

A program to promote aviation had been initiated in the US Army some years earlier, and was proving successful.[61] With aviation champions in the right offices, they would be in position to argue in favour of whatever procurement or program or operational decisions might be required, thereby contributing to the success of innovations pursued later.

The Canadian Army seemed to understand this strategem and set about creating champions – leaders who would create, bolster, and honestly assess their "Army Aviation" vision, as the Cold War unfolded. The process would involve training the army's most senior officers to a level of skill that earned them the coveted army flying badge. Doing so was expected to serve "as a contributing factor in selling the concept of aircraft being operated by and for the army."[62] Training these very senior officers how to fly was about providing them some aviation knowledge that might help inform future discussions and strategic military capability decisions. When former "Vandoo" General Jean Victor Allard, Chief of Defence Staff between 1966 and 1969, pondered the meaning of the wings on his chest, he claimed they bestowed upon him the status as "F.I.N.K – or flying infanteer with naval knowledge."[63] Having men like Allard, and later J-A Dextraze (who washed out unfortunately) at the table in future discussions was far more important than not. Pinning wings on their chest might actually have meant that they might not be at the table at all.

Canadian army aviation became a mix of helicopter and fixed-wing aircraft. Here three CH-112 Hillers, three L-19s, and one L-182 are on the hangar line at the newly christened Canadian Forces Base Rivers, Manitoba.

The Rise of Army Aviation

The Cold War Canadian Army espoused no pan-institution organizational culture that would have nurtured an air power capability with a mission and vision pertaining to the Canadian Army as a whole. Instead, the various components of the army in need of an aviation capability were able to pursue and develop whatever capabilities that suited their comparatively fragmented needs, and problems arose when vision and limited resources did not align, but the vision persisted. The realization of this important aviation capability for Canada would eventually come with the re-establishment of an air force element, in the form of Air Command, in 1975, which also included a formation (10 Tactical Air Group) that could more properly be referred to as an air power capability primarily dedicated to the mission of providing direct air support to Canada's land forces. By exploring the evolution of army aviation in Canada, against the backdrop of elements of organizational culture, this chapter hopefully illuminated two competing organizations, highlighting their actions, some of which may have contributed to the successful deployment of operational aviation forces in support of Canada's army.

The RCAF operating concept seems to have viewed its mission through a lens informed not by the nation's evolving strategic interests per se, but by the recent strategic capabilities forged under the conditions of Total War.[64] For as long as those capabilities had viable application under the changing postwar security environment, they warranted continuing emphasis and priority funding. The Canadian Army's operating concept seems to have viewed a more diverse mission for an air force, through a lens informed not entirely by the past, with the exception of artillery spotting, but more so by the implications of an evolving security environment featuring atomic weapons, and the concomitant need for innovation to find purpose for an army as the Cold War unfolded. Each of the two services deemed a certain form of air power essential to their success, but each was marred by their own idiosyncrasy. While the RCAF remained beholden to the most decisive (read strategic) capabilities, the Canadian Army retained a vested if segmented interest in the element of air power relevant to their tactical needs within each of the various arms. The RCAF leadership held their ground, essentially promoting strategic applications of air power over all others, thereby opening the door for the Canadian Army to pursue its own much-needed more tactical air power capability interests. The Canadian Army leadership pursued an integral air power capability but was somewhat beholden to a form of occupationalism within a stovepipe organizational structure made up of the various combat arms (infantry, artillery, armoured, and service corps).[65] Army aviators were selected for their corps knowledge, and their careers were linked primarily to their original corps, not their aviation duties. As Peter Dudley concludes, "there was no quantum leap into a unique concept [of operations] other than a practical adaptation of a machine [the helicopter] that could be used as a force multiplier for the existing units and formations of the Canadian Army."[66]

Casselman and other Canadian Army aviation leaders raised a professional corps of pilots, technicians, observers, and other crewmen some of whose exploits would reverberate throughout the armies of our allies as well as our own. Men like Murray Macdonald affiliated with the most respected founding aviators in the US

Army Aviation Tactical Training School, No. 5 Hangar, at the Canadian Joint Air Training Centre, Rivers, MB.

and the UK, including Major-General Hamilton Howze, while on exchange postings to those allied countries. In a similar fashion, Bruce Muelaner earned the accolades of US and German aviators for his professionalism and leadership that had a profound impact on the path of the AH-64 Apache armed helicopter for decades to come. Today, in 1 Wing, a substantial award for innovation bearing Muelaner's name is presented to a suitable individual. Nick Mulikow established himself as a respected F-86 Sabre pilot with 413 Squadron (RCAF), before serving in the artillery thereafter and, eventually, as an army aviator flight instructor responsible for training army generals how to fly, thus enabling them to serve as credible champions for Canadian Army aviation. Their legacy and that of countless others, exists today in the form of 1 Wing, a professional formation dedicated to providing qualified aviation forces to the Canadian Land Forces, the RCAF and to Canada, at home and abroad.

NOTES

1. Edgar Schein, *Organizational Culture and Leadership*. (Hoboken, NJ: Wiley & Sons, 2017), 6.
2. Colonel Peter Simpson. "The Third Dimension in Land Force Operations: The Present and the Future from an Australian Perspective," in *From Past to Future: The Australian Experience of Land/Air Operations, Proceedings of the 1995 Australian Army History Conference*. Jeffrey Grey and Peter Dennis, eds. (University of New South Wales, 1995), 126. Simpson attributes the term "army co-operation" to Air Vice Marshal Sir Arthur Coningham.
3. DND Memorandum H.Q.S. 15-1-238, Ottawa, September 4, 1940. Sanderson was identified as Director of Aircraft Production of the Department of Munitions and Supply.
4. Canadian Military Headquarters Great Britain Telegram to NDHQ Ottawa, February 25, 1941 G.S. 301.
5. H.Q.S. 8122-3 May 10, 1941.
6. Darrell Knight. *Artillery Flyers at War: A History of the 664, 665, and 666 'Air Observation Post' Squadrons of the Royal Canadian Air Force* (Bennington, Vermont: Meriam Press, 2010), 47. Frederic A. Bergerson. *The Army Gets an Air Force: Tactics of Insurgent Bureaucratic Politics* (Baltimore: Johns Hopkins University Press, 1980), 29.
7. Samuel Kostenuk and J. Griffins. *R.C.A.F. Squadron Histories and Aircraft, 1924–1968* (Ottawa: A.M. Hakkert Ltd and Samuel Stevens & Co., 1977), 75.
8. Department of National Defence (Air), *The R.C.A.F. Overseas: The First Four Years* (Toronto: University of Toronto Press, 1944), 9.
9. Knight. 67. Knight is citing General Order 493/44 of May 4, 1944.
10. Ibid., General Order 159/46 effective December 9, 1944.
11. E-mail from Peter Dudley to the author.
12. Squadron Leader C.L. Heide, "Stations of the RCAF: CJATC Rivers," *The Roundel* vol. 13, no. 8 (October 1961).
13. See https://canadianarmyaviation.ca/service_corps_the_army_in_the_air_alpha_to_omega.html, accessed April 12, 2021. See also Elke C. Weal et al., *Combat Aircraft of World War Two*. (Fakenham, England: Cox & Wiley Ltd., 1977), 209.
14. Major Robert M. Lee, USAF, "The Helicopter's Role in Tactical Air Power," *Canadian Army Journal* vol. 4 no. 9, (February 1951): 41–9. Exercise SWEETBRIAR (February 13–24, 1950) was a joint Canadian-United States defence exercise involving 5,200 personnel, close to 1,000 vehicles and more than 100 aircraft including RCAF Vampires operating in an Arctic environ for the first time.
15. "Air Transport (Reprinted from *Officers' Call (US), Part 2*," *Canadian Army Journal* vol. 5, no. 1 (April 1951): 39.
16. E-mail Louis E. Grimshaw to the author, May 24, 2005.
17. Colonel W.W. Ford, "Direct Support Aviation," in *US Army Combat Forces Journal* vol. 1, no. 8 (March 1951).
18. Major Bert Decker, "Copter Cavalry," *Combat Forces Journal*, April 1954.
19. Major James S. Douglas, "Exercise LIFT," *The Army Combat Forces Journal* vol. 5, no. 4 (November 1954): 20–3.
20. Major George H. Reid, "Helicopter Patrol," *The Army Combat Forces Journal* vol. 5, no. 2 (September 1954).
21. Raymond Stouffer, "Military Culture and the Mobile Striking Force," in Canadian Aerospace Power Studies Vol 4, 42–54.
22. Bertram C. Frandsen, "The Rise and Fall of Canada's Cold War Air Force, 1948–1968" (2015). *Theses and Dissertations (Comprehensive)*. 1754, 1. See http://scholars.wlu.ca/etd/1754.

23 Hamilton H. Howze. *A Cavalryman's Story: Memoirs of a Twentieth-Century Army General.* (Washington: Smithsonian Institution Press, 1996), 184.
24 Randall Wakelam, "Creating an Air Arm for the Army: Lessons from the Past," *The Canadian Army Journal* vol. 15, no. 2 (Autumn 2013): 69.
25 Wakelam, "Creating an Air Arm," 70–1.
26 Canada. Canadian Army, Letter "Determination of Minimum Unit Required," HQS 5800–3 (DSD) July 1955. See also Minutes of the 581st meeting of the Chiefs of Staff (COS) Committee. Author's collection.
27 Canada. DND. Report HQS 6016-1 (MT 6A) "Review of Report 'An Appreciation of the Possible Use of Helicopters on Mobile Striking Force Operations.'" November 7, 1955. Author's collection.
28 Canada. DND. TS 1038-200 "A Paper on the Control and Operation of Helicopters in the Canadian Services." November 17, 1955. Author's collection.
29 Dec 21, 1955 CSC 10-9 (TD 3) DND Author's collection.
30 Canada. DND. HQS 6101-Helicopters TD 5322 (DCGS) "Report of the Ad hoc committee on service requirements for helicopters." January 4, 1956. Author's collection.
31 February 28, 1956, 590th Meeting COS Committee HQS 6101-Helicopter (MT 6A)
32 Wakelam, "Creating an Air Arm," 71. See also March 1956 – *The British Army Review*, no. 2 – "The Vertical Patrol," by Captain John C. Buchanan, 80–5. Colonel P Arkwright, "Sky Cavalry," *British Army Review* no. 6 (March 1958).
33 Canada DND, Chiefs of Staff Committee "Army Aviation Requirements" CSC:10.9 May 13, 1958, and October 6, 1958. The VCGS described the army plan for an army aviation battalion with four aviation companies, one for each of four brigades; three light fixed-wing aircraft, 12 light helicopters and 12 light cargo helicopters and 332 persons in each company, with only one company to be activated now, and the others later (future years).
34 Canada, DND, Report S 1038-Helicopters (CAS), dated January 27, 1959, Attachment "Tri-Service Committee on Service Requirements for Helicopters."
35 Canada, DND, Minutes of the 628th Meeting of the COS Committee, January 29, 1959, Agenda Item "Tri-Service Helicopter Requirements."
36 Canada, DND, Vice Chief of the Air Staff (VCAS) Briefing to the Air Officers' Conference – Army commitments, March 17, 1959.
37 March 18, 1959, Distribution of Resources 1959–1964 Air Officers Conference 1959 address by AVM I.C. Cornblat, Comptroller.
38 Canada, DND H.Q.S. 6001-Aircraft (DCD/AVN) Letter to the Minister of National Defence, "Provision of Army Air Vehicles," dated April 28, 1959. The letter seeks 31 recce helicopters, 31 cargo helicopters, six beavers and five L-23 or similar type (aircraft). The operational roles were specified in a paper on Army Aircraft Requirements submitted to the COS Committee on May 13, 1958.
39 632nd meeting May 22, 1959, COS Committee Author's collection.
40 16 Jul 1959 COS Committee Author's collection.
41 September 24, 1959, COS Committee (Foulkes, Campbell, Clark, Tisdall and Zimmerman) – Item IV Army Aircraft (COSC:10.9 TD:14 of 22 Sep 59) HQS 6001-Aircraft (DCD/AVN) 11 Sep 59 and Memo "Provision of Army Air Vehicles" dated 16 Sep 59.
42 Canada, DND, Minutes of the 649th Meeting of the COSC, November 19, 1959.
43 Canada, DND, Annual Historical Report File 71-00-501 (Comdt) CJATC Rivers Camp, February 14, 1961, 29.
44 G.T. Service and Captain J.K. Marteinson, eds. *The Gate: A History of the Fort Garry Horse.* (Calgary, 1971).

45 Lieutenant G.P. March, "8th Canadian Hussars Reconnaissance Squadron Helicopter Troop Organization and Move to Germany," *Army Aviation News* vol. 3, no 14 (Sep 5, 1961). Only 45 RCAC officers qualified for the Canadian Army Flying Badge.
46 Canada, DND, Canadian Joint Air Training Centre Historical Narrative, Appendix 2, January 1 to December 31, 1961, 11.
47 Canada, DND, Minutes of the 35th Air Council Meeting, September 6, 1961.
48 Canada, DND, Canadian Joint Air Training Centre Historical Narrative, January 1 to December 31, 1962, 8.
49 Brereton Greenhous. *Dragoon: The Centennial History of the Royal Canadian Dragoons: 1883–1983.* (Ottawa: The Guild of the Royal Canadian Dragoons, 1983), 470.
50 Ibid., 471.
51 Lorne Rodenbush, "The Corps in the Air," in *The Last Waggon: The Final Story of the Royal Canadian Army Service Corps,* ed. Colonel J.D. Murray (RCASC Foundation Fund, 2001).
52 Major A.K. "Bert" Casselman, Officer Commanding Army Aviation Tactical Training School (AATTS) CJATC Rivers, *Army Aviation Newsletter* vol 4, no. 15 (Winter 1962).
53 David N. Solomon. "Sociological Research in a Military Organization," in *The Canadian Journal of Economics and Political Science.* Vol 20, No. 4 (Nov. 1954), 531–41.
54 Captain C.A. Sangster, RCD and Lt J.K. Marteinson, FGH, "CJATC Helicopter Troop – Gagetown 1962," *Army Aviation Newsletter* vol. 4, no 15 (Winter 1962).
55 Captain H.D. Saxen, RCA, "AOP Troop 1 RCHA – Gagetown 1962," *Army Aviation Newsletter* vol. 4, no. 15 (Winter 1962).
56 Hamilton H. Howze, *A Cavalryman's Story: Memoirs of a Twentieth Century Army General.* (Washington: Smithsonian Institution Press, 1996). See also Christopher C.S. Cheng, *Air Mobility: The Development of a Doctrine.* (London: Praeger, 1994).
57 Matthew Allen, *Military Helicopter Doctrines of the Major Powers, 1945–1992* (Westport, Connecticut: Greenwood Press, 1993), 6–9.
58 Major-General Hamilton Howze, "Helicopters in the Army," *Canadian Army Journal* vol. 12, no. 2 (April 1958): 48–58 (reproduced with permission from the January–February 1958 issue of *ORDNANCE Magazine*).
59 Canada, DND, August 8, 1961 – "The Canadian Army 1966–70 Tactical and Logistic Concept Summary of Amendments to Second Draft" – Annex A to HQS 2100-2-1 (DCD) Author's collection.
60 Sep 6, 1961 – Minutes of the 35th Air Council Meeting. Author's collection.
61 See Frederic A. Bergerson, *The Army Gets an Air Force: Tactics of Insurgent Bureaucratic Politics.* (London: The Johns Hopkins University Press, 1978), 102.
62 Rodenbush, 503.
63 General Jean V. Allard and Serge Bernier, *The Memoirs of General Jean V. Allard.* (Vancouver: The University of British Columbia Press, 1988).
64 See Hans J. Morgenthau, *Politics among Nations: The Struggle for Power and Peace,* 5th ed. (New York: Alfred A. Knopf, 1973), 238. Among the four respects making Morgenthau inclined to apply the adjective "total" on war of the 20th century was the fraction of the population engaged in activities essential for the conduct of war, which seemed to help justify treating the civilian population as a strategic target, the demoralization or destruction of which was essential for victory.
65 See Carl Builder, *The Icarus Syndrome: The Role of Air Power Theory in the Evolution and Fate of the U.S. Air Force.* (London: Transaction Publishers, 1994).
66 Major (retd) Peter Dudley to the author.

CHAPTER SIXTEEN

AIR TRANSPORT COMMAND: VERSATILE AND READY IN COLD WAR AND HOT WAR

BERTRAM FRANDSEN

Introduction

During the post-1945 period, the RCAF developed, expanded, and frequently upgraded its air transport component, a process that continued beyond 1968 and up to the present day. The senior RCAF leadership consistently viewed the maintenance of the air transport role as essential to meet RCAF capabilities that would in turn satisfy RCAF and broader defence requirements for movement of personnel and equipment. This chapter will examine the development, organization, equipment, and operation of air transport in the RCAF during the period between 1945 and 1968. Topics examined include the establishment of Air Transport Command (ATC), the impact of the Korean War, the defence buildup of the early 1950s, and the increased emphasis placed on air transport that emerged from the 1964 *Defence White Paper*. The chapter also discusses the postwar development of RCAF logistics and Air Materiel Command (AMC); indeed, the maintenance of an effective and responsive air transport organization was closely linked to a successful RCAF logistics system.

Wartime Legacy and Peacetime Re-establishment

Throughout the Second World War, greater emphasis was placed on the provision of fighter, bomber, and bomber-reconnaissance squadrons rather than air transport. While the RCAF Home War Establishment included six transport and communications squadrons based across the country, out of 48 overseas RCAF squadrons

435 Squadron C-119 Flying Boxcars at RCAF Station, Namao, Alberta, prepare to board personnel from the Princess Patricia's Canadian Light Infantry in preparation for an airborne exercise.

only three were established as transport squadrons.[1] Rather than establishing additional bomber squadrons as stipulated to meet its Article XV commitments, three transport squadrons flying Douglas Dakota aircraft were formed in 1944.[2] Of the two squadrons allocated to South East Asia, No. 436 Squadron was formed on 20 August 1944, in India whilst a second squadron, No. 435, was established in India on 1 November.[3] These squadrons flew "the Hump" into Burma to re-supply the 14th British Army. No. 437 Squadron, the sole European-based unit, was formed on 14 September 1944, just in time to participate in the large-scale Allied Arnhem airborne operation.[4] Soon after the conclusion of hostilities in the Pacific theatre, all three of the RCAF's Dakota transport squadrons were consolidated in Europe. They were grouped into 120 (Transport) Wing, part of the RAF's Transport Command, and flew missions in support of occupation forces in Germany. The three units, along with the Canada-based No. 168 Squadron, equipped with long-range Liberator aircraft, constituted the RCAF's transport capability in the immediate

426 (Transport) Squadron North Star aircraft in flight. The North Star was the RCAF's strategic transport aircraft until the early 1960s.

postwar period. However, by June 1946, all of these squadrons had been disbanded as the RCAF reorganized to meet peacetime requirements and manpower limits.[5]

Postwar planning began in 1943 with the completion of the "Brief on Post-War Planning for the Royal Canadian Air Force" by Air Commodore (A/C) K.M Guthrie, the deputy air member (plans).[6] One of the study's four guiding principles was the requirement for the RCAF to be highly mobile, capable of deploying and fighting in either North America or overseas. Guthrie proposed a balanced air force consisting of 16 regular force squadrons of which two were to be equipped for long-range transport and one for troop transport.[7] However, the size and shape of Canada's military was in a state of flux as service plans came up against financial retrenchment.[8] The roles envisaged for the RCAF were determined by October 1945, when Colin Gibson, minister of national defence (air), stated that a mix of regular, auxiliary, and reserve units would be prepared to fulfill bomber, fighter, transport, and photo-reconnaissance roles. Given the speed of technological advancement experienced during the war, Gibson determined that all the roles assigned to the RCAF, except for transport, would be conducted with aircraft currently within the RCAF's inventory. Postwar transport squadrons, when feasible, would be re-equipped with American C-54 Skymasters, the military derivative of the four-engine Douglas DC-4.[9]

During the war domestic RCAF air transport requirements and taskings were handled by an Air Transport Directorate established at Air Force Headquarters (AFHQ) in August 1943. With the end of the war in sight, the Directorate became No. 9 (Transport) Group on 5 February 1945, headquartered at Rockcliffe, Ontario. In the immediate postwar period there were five squadrons, as well as a myriad of smaller units, under the Group's direct, or operational, command. Aerial photography became the responsibility of 413 and 414 Squadrons, while transport was undertaken by 426 and 435 Squadrons. Finally, a communication role, mainly light cargo and personnel transport, was fulfilled by 412 Squadron.[10]

In 1948, the RCAF underwent a major reorganization, moving away from regional to functional commands. Gone were geographic designations such as Eastern or Western Air Commands, replaced with titles that reflected the primary role of the command organization, such as Air Defence or Training Commands.[11] ATC was the first of the functional flying commands to be established on 1 April 1948, with its headquarters at Lachine, (Montreal), Quebec. The formation of ATC recognized the importance of air transport to defence planning. The Canadian Army, under the auspices of the 1946 Canada – US Basic Defence Plan, was committed to providing an airborne/air transportable Mobile Strike Force (MSF) as Canada's contribution to continental defence. This force was dependent on air transport for three main tasks: to bring together various MSF components from across Canada; deploy the force when and where required; and support the force once it was in the field.[12]

Included in the new RCAF structure was Air Materiel Command (AMC). First formed in 1945 as Maintenance Command, the title changed to AMC in 1949 to better reflect the complexity of its responsibilities in the new age of air power. AMC was a key organization in allowing the RCAF to implement its tremendous expansion in the early 1950s with the command serving as the conduit for the expenditure of the bulk of the RCAF's capital procurement and construction budget. Headquartered at Rockcliffe, Ottawa, it exercised normal command and control functions of its field units, but also included the necessary staff to provide logistics support for the entire RCAF.[13]

Although plans to establish several Air Materiel Bases (AMBs) ran afoul of budget restraints, a positive change in the new postwar logistics concept was to concentrate aircraft spares, supporting parts, and components at the two main supply depots at Downsview, Ontario, and Namao, Alberta, where AMBs were to have been located.[14] This was a major step forward compared to the previous distribution method where these items were scattered across the country at regional supply depots; however, this concept was reliant upon, and drove an increased requirement for, air transport to meet internal RCAF needs.

The increasing use of airlift to deliver high priority supply items across the country was achievable with the co-location of No. 435 Squadron at Namao and No. 436 Squadron at Downsview, both equipped with Flying Boxcar transports. No. 426 Squadron's North Star aircraft (these were a follow-on from the C-54 concept) were also available to undertake long-range strategic airlift to deliver high priority cargo, particularly to No. 1 Air Division in Western Europe.

The Berlin Airlift

The Communist Party coup d'état in Czechoslovakia in February 1948, coupled with a Soviet blockade of Berlin from June of that year until May 1949, heightened international tensions. Though the RCAF was short on combat air power in the spring of 1948, it did possess a reasonable number of transport aircraft and crews in its three transport squadrons. These units were not to participate in the airlift, that decision being a political one. Although the minister of national defence, Brooke Claxton, raised several military uncertainties likely put forward by the military staff,[15] he advised Cabinet on 25 September 1948, that a squadron of 10 Dakota aircraft with 90 aircrew and 219 ground crew was immediately available. Cabinet, however, declined to make a Canadian contribution.[16]

Regardless of this inaction, concern over the potential for European conflict caused the government to reconsider its defence priorities. It announced on 28 December 1948, that changing circumstances required an expanded defence program for 1949, including various improvements for the RCAF. The establishment of the North Atlantic Treaty Organization (NATO) in April 1949 and the detonation of a Soviet atomic bomb in August 1949 provided an added impetus for limited Canadian re-armament.

Still, the RCAF was primarily focused on its North American defence commitments, and in early 1950, RCAF transport aircraft were engaged in support to Exercise SWEET BRIAR.[17] This was a joint exercise involving some 5,000 personnel from the Canadian and United States (US) armies and air forces operating in Alaska and the Yukon, along the length of the Alaskan Highway.[18] The airlift role involved North Star and Dakota aircraft, with the latter also conducting paratroop drops. The participation of RCAF transport aircraft in any overseas role at this time was not envisioned, except in the event of global conflict. However, ATC had demonstrated its long-range capability in January 1950 with its first around-the-world flight that carried External Affairs Minister Lester Pearson to the Commonwealth meeting in Colombo, Ceylon (now Sri Lanka).

The Korean War and Operation HAWK

The outbreak of the Korean War on 25 June 1950, caught the West off guard. The only immediate response involved the dispatch of ill-prepared US ground forces, supported by air units, both coming from their occupation troops in Japan; these forces were to bolster the lightly armed army of the Republic of Korea. An initially precarious situation, with the distinct possibility of North Korean victory, was stabilized through the use of overwhelming air and sea power; however, United Nation (UN) forces, now found themselves engaged in a protracted ground war. Canada, as part of the UN coalition, pledged military support, but its initial contribution came from its "forces in being," comprising naval and air units.[19]

In the case of the RCAF, 426 Squadron undertook preparations in advance of its likely participation. Less than a month after the conflict erupted, on 12 July, the Chief of the Air Staff (CAS) wrote to the Air Officers Commanding (AOC) of ATC and AMC to explain that since the USAF did not have sufficient airlift, RCAF participation would be welcomed.[20] Cabinet approval was granted on 19 July, and the CAS issued direction for the integration of 426 Squadron into the USAF Military Air Transport Service (MATS), placing the Canadian unit under MATS' operational control, and bringing the squadron's unit establishment to its wartime level of 12 North Star aircraft. At the same time, however, the CAS directed that RCAF aircraft were not to operate in Korea.[21] On 25 July, the initial six aircraft departed from Dorval for McChord Air Force Base, Washington, to commence operations.

During the course of its participation in Operation HAWK, from 27 July 1950, until 9 June 1954, the squadron flew 599 sorties between McChord and Haneda Air Base in Japan.[22] No. 426 Squadron flew 9.7 million kilometres, logging 34,000 flying hours and carrying 13,000 personnel and almost 3.2 million kilograms of freight.[23] Flights were flown on two routes: the North Pacific route: McChord – Elmendorf (Anchorage, Alaska) – Shemya (Aleutians) – Misawa Air Base or Matsushima (Japan) – Haneda (Tokyo, Japan), and the Mid-Pacific route, via McChord – Travis (San Francisco, CA) – Hickam (Honolulu, HI) – Wake Island – Haneda.[24] The round trip to Japan took 45 flying hours over 3½ days, covering a distance of 16,000 kilometres, or 8,600 nautical miles.[25] Flights on the North Pacific route involved serious challenges due to the weather conditions and

426 (Transport) Squadron North Star on the ramp, Haneda Air Base, Japan, as part of Operation HAWK during the Korean War.

also required vigilance when nearing the Kuril Islands due to Soviet electronic interference.[26] The fact that there were no fatalities, though some near misses, during the four years of operations was testimony to the excellent skills and professionalism of RCAF aircrew and groundcrew.

RCAF Expansion and Re-equipment

The outbreak of the Korean War was the catalyst for the massive RCAF expansion, and though slow to commence, Claxton announced a three-year $5 billion rearmament program on 5 February 1951. The program was to see the RCAF built up to a strength of 41 regular and reserve flying squadrons with 3,000 aircraft, along with a radar system that, with the fighters, provided for the air defence of Canada, an air division with NATO in Europe, and the establishment of a large training organization, all supported by a robust aircraft industry.[27] The expansion included an increase

A Fairchild C-119 Flying Boxcar – the backbone of the RCAF tactical transport capability during the 1950s.

in the operational strength of ATC from three to four squadrons with the establishment of 436 Squadron at Dorval on 1 April 1953.[28] More importantly, both 435 and 436 Squadrons were re-equipped with the C-119G Flying Boxcar transport.[29]

The Flying Boxcar was an important addition to ATC, with 35 aircraft in service from 1952 to 1965. Training on this aircraft commenced at 4 (Transport) Operational Training Unit (OTU) in March 1952, allowing 435 Squadron to begin Boxcar operations in September, followed by 436 Squadron in April 1953. By December 1954, the RCAF had reached its peacetime expansion goals, and despite being a "second tier" command, ATC had re-equipped with modern transport aircraft and was making its presence felt in support of home defence, while also developing a strategic worldwide transport capability in support of NATO and the UN.[30]

As discussed above, equipped with the North Star, 426 Squadron had gained substantial experience with long-range strategic transport during the Korean War.[31] This capability was relatively rare, as only a few air forces at this time, principally the USAF and Royal Air Force (RAF), operated strategic transport aircraft on global routes. With the completion of its Korean War airlift role in 1954, the squadron remained busy with several tasks including Northern re-supply flights supporting in the construction of the Mid-Canada Line series of radar sites, domestic scheduled flights, and logistics support to Canada's European-based 1 Air Division that included thrice-weekly regular scheduled flights between Dorval and the United Kingdom.[32] New international tasks commenced in 1954 and included annual deployment flights to the former Indo-China these needed to move Canadian personnel assigned to the International Control and Supervisory Commission. In addition, the North Stars supported Operations RANDOM and NIMBLE BAT involving the flyover of Sabre and CF-100 fighters to 1 Air Division. In order to perform its long-range transport role, 426 Squadron was to become the largest flying squadron in the RCAF, numbering 440 personnel in 1957.[33]

In the fall of 1956, 426 Squadron was involved in Operation RAPID STEP, the airlift supporting the deployment of a UN Emergency Force (UNEF) to Egypt in the aftermath of the Suez crisis.[34] This operation permanently amplified the importance of ATC within the RCAF and the broader Canadian defence establishment; it also resulted in a public call for increased RCAF transport capabilities to enable the rapid deployment of troops.[35] In recognition of the critical importance of airlift, in August 1956, the Cabinet Defence Committee approved the procurement of a new strategic transport aircraft, the Canadair CC-106 Yukon (based on the Bristol Britannia design) powered with four turboprop engines, to replace the remaining 18 North Star transports. The initial order was for eight Yukons, although the intent was to eventually replace the North Star on a one-for-one basis for a total of 24 aircraft.[36] The Yukon was a significant improvement over the North Star in terms of cargo and personnel capacity, speed, range, and operational capability.[37] Designed and manufactured in Canada, the Yukon also represented a boost for the Canadian aircraft industry. Ultimately, the air force would operate 12 Yukons until the end of the 1960s.

Air Transport Command also included 412 Squadron, which had roles in light cargo and Very Important Personnel (VIP) transport. It was equipped at various times with North Star four-engine transports and two de Havilland Comet jet transports, as well as wartime vintage Dakota, Mitchell, and Expeditor transport aircraft. In 1953, the RCAF became the first military service in the world to operate jet transports with its Comets. The two Comets had been procured on the premise that four additional North Star transports were required by the RCAF but could not be provided by Canadair.[38]

The Canadair CL-44 served in the RCAF as the CC-106 Yukon long-range transport aircraft.

The two workhorse squadrons in ATC were 435 and 436 Squadrons. Originally equipped with Dakota twin-engine aircraft, 435 Squadron supported tactical transport operations in Western Canada, including support to the MSF. In 1952, the squadron began partial replacement of the Dakota with 12 Boxcar transports, though four Dakotas remained in service as well. The same aircraft establishment was applied to 436 Squadron. In comparison to the Dakota, the Boxcar represented a significant increase in airlift not only in matters of range, speed, and carrying capability. Importantly, it provided considerable improvement for parachute operations both for dropping troops and for aerial re-supply. Indeed, when the Boxcar entered in 1952, it was considered to be the best available tactical transport aircraft then in production.[39]

As mentioned, the squadrons were also tasked for the rapid delivery of high priority cargo from the two RCAF supply depots located at Edmonton and Downsview (436 Squadron had moved from Dorval to Downsview in 1956). Equipped with the Boxcars, the two squadrons also assumed much of the Arctic re-supply tasks from No. 426 Squadron.[40] The squadrons were also expected to support maritime reconnaissance squadrons during wartime, a role that

De Havilland Canada Comet – the RCAF's first jet transport.

Air Transport Command made good use of wartime vintage transport aircraft, such as these Douglas Dakota, for activities in Canada's Arctic. Their ruggedness and ability to operate from austere airfields, often with short or non-existent runways, made them ideal.

Bristol Freighter with 137 Transport Flight, Europe.

anticipated them operating from bases other than their home stations. It became problematic for these aircraft and their crews to undertake such wide-ranging roles.

The acquisition of the 35 Boxcars filled the gap in cargo capability between the Dakota and the North Star but now also provided an overall greater lift capability as typically only a dozen North Stars were available at any given time.[41] Support to the MSF was an important factor in the decision to acquire the Boxcar, especially with respect to aerial delivery, but the Canadian Army's interest in the MSF and large-scale parachute operations gradually waned by the late 1950s. Subsequently, the Boxcars were employed on more RCAF-centric transport tasks. Essential as these aircraft were, and despite original procurement plans for the acquisition of 48 aircraft, the RCAF decided that 35 aircraft would be sufficient to meet its requirements.[42] However, international commitments, such as the need to provide 12 aircraft as part of 114 Communications Flight, operating out of Capodichino air base near Naples, Italy, in support of the UNEF, added additional stress on the personnel and equipment resources of 435 and 436 Squadrons.[43]

Apart from ATC, numerous small detachments, referred to as "K Flights" (Composite Flights), based throughout the RCAF fulfilled light transport (communication) duties in support of headquarters staff of the other commands and these aircraft could also be used for SAR tasks. The flights were controlled by their respective commands and were outside the purview of ATC. For example, 1 Air Division operated 137 Transport Flight with five Bristol Freighter aircraft; similarly, the Transport Support Flight at the Canadian Joint Air Training Centre at Rivers, Manitoba, included three Boxcar and six Dakota transport aircraft. Approximately 80 aircraft operated outside of ATC on transport, communications, and rescue duties – a considerable number in comparison to the 103 aircraft controlled by the Command.

Into the Sixties: New Equipment, Smaller Fleets

By the late 1950s, ATC was in transition, as plans for major aircraft re-equipment were impacted by the nation's adverse economic situation that called for significant budget reductions. These affected force structure, acquisition, and modernization programs. Tactical Air Command was disbanded on 1 January 1959, resulting in the absorption of most of its units and bases into ATC.[44] The Auxiliary squadrons relinquished their combat aircraft in 1958, and by 1961, 11 squadrons had been re-equipped with Expeditor light transports. In the case of the Yukon strategic transport, the original procurement envisaged eight aircraft being delivered by February 1961, with another 16 to follow by September 1963 in order to completely replace the North Star. However, due to fiscal restraints, Yukon procurement ended with the delivery of only 12 aircraft. The RCAF did, however, receive its full order of 10 Canadair CC-109 Cosmopolitan passenger transports at a cost of $23 million; this contract helped Canadair offset the reductions in other government contracts.[45] The Cosmopolitan, a turboprop version of the Convair 440 airliner, replaced the Dakota aircraft in No. 412 Squadron in 1960.

Throughout the late 1950s, the RCAF has been in search of a transport aircraft capable of airlifting heavy bulk cargo. Detailed investigation led the Air Staff to conclude that the Lockheed C-130B Hercules aircraft was the best choice. As a complement to the Yukon fleet, which would continue to airlift personnel and light cargo, Hercules aircraft could do the heavy lifting, an attractive capability for supporting NATO and the UN.[46] The RCAF received its first four Lockheed C-130B Hercules four-engine turboprop transports in 1960 at a cost of $14 million. And while the Air Staff made a solid case concerning the new aircraft's utility, it was

412 (Transport) Squadron, CC-109 Cosmopolitan utilized as a VIP aircraft.

ultimately the attractive price of the mass-produced US aircraft that enabled the procurement of the Hercules.[47]

The initial four of eight de Havilland Canada CC-108 Caribou tactical transports entered service that same year. The aircraft had been designed with the US Army's transport needs in mind, but in 1958 the Canadian Army expressed interest and was willing to provide the funding for 11 aircraft to conduct trials using both the Caribou and helicopters for battlefield re-supply, particularly on the nuclear battlefield. The RCAF balked at the idea of the army operating large aircraft, but, eventually, the Air Council agreed to cooperate with army so that the trials could go ahead.[48] Ultimately, no trials were conducted as the Army re-focused away from nuclear battlefield operations, and it was agreed that only the RCAF would operate aircraft the size of the Caribou. The program might have died there, but the need to provide additional tactical transport support to the UN resulted in the air force placing an order for four aircraft.[49] The Caribou replaced the Dakota transports serving with Canada's 115 Air Transport Unit in Egypt with UNEF.[50] Ultimately, the RCAF acquired only nine Caribou, and most were used only on UN operations; it was evident that there was little interest in acquiring this type of aircraft.

To operate the Yukons, 437 (Transport) Squadron was formed at Trenton in the fall of 1961. While new, the aircraft and its procurement were not universally welcomed. The view was that the Yukon was a turboprop aircraft that had just been purchased when jet transports were about to enter production. One RCAF transport pilot who later served as the commanding officer of 437 Squadron, subsequently wrote:

> The air staff view was that since we were already operating the Comet jet transport and Boeing and Douglas were about to launch the 707 and DC-8 respectively, the obvious course for a new logistics transport should be a fast, high capacity, jet-powered aircraft.... A political decision had been made that another version of the Bristol Britannia ... would be built at Canadair, thus solving the political and aerospace industries problem while relegating the military to making do with an aircraft that was destined to be obsolete before the first aircraft rolled off the production line.[51]

There were additional reservations. Given the operational requirement to operate transports from austere airfields, pure airliner types such as the Cosmopolitan and Yukon were considered to be the wrong aircraft for ATC.[52] These airliners required well-prepared airfields with hard-surfaced runways, and as side-loaders with cabin floors well off the ground, they required specialized cargo handling equipment often only available at established airports. In contrast, the Hercules with its low floor, rear ramp, and rough-field capability meant greater ease in loading and unloading and provided a greater flexibility for air transport capability.

In February 1961, the Air Council authorized the establishment of the Special Studies Group on Long Range Objectives for the RCAF with the aim of developing strategic guidance for the air force of the 1970s and beyond. A/C Fred Carpenter, who had held the appointment of AOC of ATC since 1956, was appointed chief of special studies in June 1961, with his mandate coming directly from the CAS, A/M Hugh Campbell. The Special Studies Group report was submitted to the CAS on 29 June 1962, where it was promptly filed away in a classified filing cabinet.[53] The report identified the Soviet Union as being the main military threat, but at the same time the possibility of total war with the Soviet Union was considered the least likely scenario. In contrast, the threat of so-called "brushfire," or small, unexpected conflicts seemed more likely. Response to these required highly flexible and mobile conventional armed forces, including air forces, capable of a full spectrum of operations to include monitoring truce agreements, counterinsurgency operations, and participation in limited warfare. To meet these smaller conflicts, a revised RCAF force structure was proposed, which focused on conventionally armed, multi-role combat aircraft and a tremendous increase in tactical and strategic transport capabilities. The proposed future structure included a Tactical Air Command with eight tactical transport squadrons, along with a greatly expanded ATC operating five heavy transport squadrons and an inflight refuelling squadron.[54] The rationale for the remarkable increase in air transport forces was the need to move and support large army formations, and the associated tactical air forces, required for these smaller conflicts. The Carpenter Report could not have come at a worse time. Campbell retired in September, replaced by A/M C.R. "Larry" Dunlap. The new CAS was busy enough running an air force and contending with the ongoing calamities that had engulfed the Diefenbaker government including the nuclear weapons issue and the Cuban missile crisis. Dunlap had no time to reconsider RCAF force structure.

A new Liberal government, elected in April 1963 and led by Lester Pearson, quickly initiated a defence review to bring in fresh thinking. By this time the US, under the Kennedy administration, had recognized the need for larger and better-equipped conventional armed forces to deal with limited wars. Flexible response required a massive expansion in airlift capabilities to quickly move troops to contend with incidents of rising tensions. Although these ideas had attracted little support in the Air Staff, they were in tune with approaches favoured by Paul Hellyer, the Liberal defence minister. Hellyer preferred spending limited defence capital resources on an increased number of transport aircraft and a simple ground attack aircraft, the Freedom Fighter, suitable for operations in Third World conflicts rather than more sophisticated and expensive material for fighting in the NATO European Central Region.[55]

The Liberal government published its *Defence White Paper* in March 1964, placing emphasis on the creation of a mobile force including both land and tactical air forces.[56] The mobile force was to be supported by a significant enhancement of air transport capabilities "in order to have the flexibility in circumstances where improved air strips are not available ... a considerable augmentation of the 'air truck' component of the air transport fleet is being undertaken."[57] The rationale for expanding air transport capabilities, apart from the lift required for the mobile force, had come from the lessons learned in recent UN peacekeeping experience in Suez in 1956 and the Congo in 1960, when scarce air transport had been a serious

Two of the RCAF's new Lockheed C-130B Hercules transport aircraft at Thule Air Force Base, Greenland, in the process of their first Operation BOXTOP – the resupply of Alert.

limitation. As well, both these peacekeeping operations demonstrated the importance in having air and ground crews fully prepared to deploy on short notice. It was also apparent that Canada, as one of the few troop-contributing nations with a robust air transport capability, could reasonably expect future UN requests for air transport.[58] Even as the white paper was being released, the Yukon and Hercules aircraft of ATC enabled the rapid deployment of a Canadian contingent to the new UN force being established in Cyprus.

An early result of the white paper's call to improve airlift capabilities was the December 1964 announcement to procure 24 Lockheed C-130E Hercules long-range transport and 15 de Havilland Canada CC-115 Buffalo tactical transport aircraft.[59] These improved Hercules aircraft entered service in 1965 with 436 Squadron and in 1966 with 435 Squadron, replacing the Boxcar. The need to replace the Boxcar was, however, somewhat controversial. According to Hellyer, RCAF senior leadership had been content to simply refurbish the C-119s, but upon seeing for himself the extensive corrosion of an aircraft undergoing maintenance at the De Havilland Canada plant in Toronto, Hellyer decided that this type required replacement.[60] Intriguingly, subsequent research refuted Hellyer's allegation that the RCAF was content with the Boxcars with clear proof that the Air Staff, during the tenure of A/Ms Campbell and Dunlap, actively sought the replacement of the C-119s with the Hercules.[61]

The C-130E Hercules acquisition provided a tremendous increase in RCAF air transport capability, representing more than mere numbers of aircraft. The 24 C-130E and the 12 Yukon transports greatly expanded both tonnage and passenger capacity of ATC, enabling the deployment of an air transportable battalion-size force, albeit lightly equipped, of 1,200 or more troops as part of a NATO or UN operation. However, this was still a far cry from the estimated 50 Hercules aircraft required to airlift a light brigade (about 5,000 soldiers) from Canada to Europe over a four-week period.[62] If the numbers needed to be proven, ATC's new-found ability was made clear with the emergency withdrawal of the Canadian contingent of the UNEF in May 1967. Egyptian President Nasser's demand that the Canadians withdraw from UNEF in 48 hours resulted in the evacuation of 700 personnel and 100,000 kilograms of equipment, carried on 18 flights, in less than 24 hours[63]

Conclusion

The utility of RCAF nascent air transport operations during the Second World War grew more essential to the application of air power throughout first decades of the Cold War. Air force postwar planning recognized the requirement for a robust transport capability in meeting Canadian domestic and international defence commitments, including the MSF, NATO, and UN operations, added to which were RCAF materiel requirements. Tied to these growing responsibilities, the acquisition of more capable aircraft served issues of national security and helped maintain key players in the aerospace sector of the economy.

For the first two decades of the Cold War, the RCAF was one of just a handful of air forces, including the USAF and RAF, that possessed sizable strategic airlift resources. Ably demonstrated during the Korean War, the benefit of air transport for the Canadian government grew as Ottawa's evolving defence and foreign policy continued to place greater emphasis on alliance and UN support. From the mid-1950s and into the early 1960s, an increasing number of UN operations ascribed even greater importance to air transport capabilities, and this was reflected in government support for new aircraft such as the Yukon and Hercules long-range transports, Caribou tactical transports, and Cosmopolitan personnel transports.

The 1964 *Defence White Paper* clearly signalled the importance of air transport as a cornerstone of Canada's defence. The ability to move personnel and cargo globally, often on short notice, provided the government with additional options when addressing UN or alliance concerns. Equally important, as amply demonstrated with the evacuation of the Canadian UNEF contingent in 1967, was the role that a robust ATC could play in ensuring the safety of Canadian personnel abroad.

Although often thought of as a "second tier" command, ATC's vital support role was recognized when it became one of only two RCAF operational-level organizations, the other being Air Defence Command, that remained intact after unification in 1968. Its fleet of tactical and strategic transport aircraft would sport a new paint scheme, and the traditional RCAF identifiers would be replaced with CAF, representative of the integrated Canadian Armed Forces; however, ATC would continue to live up to its motto, "Versatile and Ready."

NOTES

1 Samuel Kostenuk and John Griffin, *RCAF Squadron Histories and Aircraft 1924-1968*, (Toronto: Samuel Stevens Hakkert & Company, 1977), 75.
2 Brereton Greenhous, et al., *The Crucible of War 1939-1945, The Official History of the Royal Canadian Air Force – Volume III*, (Toronto: University of Toronto Press, 1994), 875.
3 Kostenuk and Griffin, 132-3.
4 Greenhous, 881-2.
5 Kostenuk and Griffin, 78.
6 James Eayrs, *In Defence of Canada – Volume 3: Peacemaking and Deterrence*, (Toronto: University of Toronto Press, 197), 79.
7 Alexander Babcock, "The Making of the Cold War Air Force: Planning and Professionalism in the Postwar Royal Canadian Air Force, 1944-1950" (PhD diss., Carleton University, 2009), 44.
8 For an overview of the issues surrounding planning for Canada's postwar military see James Eayrs, *Peacemaking and Deterrence* (Toronto: University of Toronto Press, 1972), 75-136.
9 Ibid., 86.
10 Ibid., 144.
11 Ibid. By 1952, the RCAF command structure was organized as Air Defence Command, No. 1 Tactical Air Command, Maritime Air Command, Air Transport Command, Training Command, Air Materiel Command and No. 1 Air Division (Europe). A.R. Durston, "Organization of the R.C.A.F.," *The Roundel* 5, no. 9, (October 1953): 20-8.
12 J.L. Granatstein, *Canada's Army: Waging War and Keeping the Peace* (Toronto: University of Toronto Press, 2002), 106-7.
13 "The RCAF Air Materiel Command," *Canadian Aviation*, 26, no. 12, (December 1953).
14 "Plan 'H' for the RCAF," August 1, 1952. Canada. Department of National Defence. Directorate of History and Heritage. (DHH) 96/24, Box 4, File 9.

15 Leigh E. Sarty, "The Limits of Internationalism: Canada and the Soviet Blockade of Berlin, 1948-1949," in *Nearly Neighbours – Canada and the Soviet Union: From Cold War to Détente and Beyond*, eds. J.L. Black and Norman Hilmer (Kingston: Ronald P. Frye & Company, 1988), 56.
16 Cabinet's decision not to participate stemmed more from concern about perceptions of having come "late to the party" or, in the case of providing only aircrew to serve with the RAF, as a revival of Canada's colonial status. For a complete overview see James Eayrs, *In Defence of Canada, Volume 4 – Growing Up Allied*, (Toronto: University of Toronto Press, 1980), 38–50.
17 O.M. Solandt, "Exercise Sweetbriar," Address to Empire Club of Canada, Toronto, March 30, 1950.
18 Ibid.
19 Stephen J. Harris, *Canada and the Korean War* (Montreal: Art Global, 2002), 19–20.
20 Ibid., 180.
21 Ibid., 182–3.
22 Ray Jacobson, *426 Squadron History*, (Astra, ON: The Squadron, 1988), 86.
23 Ibid., 86.
24 Motiuk, 196.
25 Jacobson, 76.
26 Motiuk, 209–13.
27 Canadian Press (CP) "15 Point Arms Program," and Warren Baldwin, "Build RCAF to 40 Sqdns [sic], 11 for Europe," *The Globe and Mail*, February 6, 1951, 1.
28 Kostenuk and Griffin, 192.
29 Alwyn T. Lloyd, *Fairchild C-82 Packet and C-119 Flying Boxcar*, (Hinckley: Midland Publishing, 2005), 134.
30 RCAF operational flying commands consisted of 1st and 2nd tier command hierarchy. The 1st tier consisted of No. 1 Air Division and Air Defence Command. The 2nd tier consisted of Maritime Air Command, Air Transport Command and Tactical Air Command. For the most part, priority for new equipment and personnel was assigned to the 1st tier commands.
31 Larry Milberry, *The Canadair North Star*, (Toronto: CANAV Books, 1982).
32 H.C. Langille, "Royal Canadian Air Force Air Transport Command," *Air Power*, 1, (October 1953).
33 Motiuk, 513.
34 Ibid., 500.
35 "'Air Power' Means Transport Too," (Editorial), *Canadian Aviation*, 29, no. 12, (December 1956) and "Not to Be Underestimated," (Editorial), *Aircraft*, 18, no. 10, (October 1956).
36 Memorandum (Draft) MND to Cabinet Defence Committee, June 7, 1956, and Memorandum, MND to Cabinet Defence Committee, June 28, 1956. DHH 73/1223, Series 1, File 128.
37 Larry Milberry, *Canada's Air Force at War and Peace – Volume 3*, (Toronto: CANAV Books, 2001), 370.
38 Memorandum, Deputy Minister of National Defence to Chief of the Air Staff, October 22, 1951, DHH 73/1223, File 1325; and T.G. Coughlin, "Jet Travel – A.T.C. Style," *The Roundel*, 11, no. 4, (May 1959).
39 H.G. Maxwell, "The Fairchild C-119 in the RCAF," *CAHS Journal*, 32, no. 1, (Spring 1994).
40 J.D. Harvey, "Spring Re-supply in the Arctic," *The Roundel*, 7, no. 8, (September 1955).
41 Milberry, *Canada's Air Force at War and Peace – Volume 3*, 360.
42 Air Council #2, Minutes of the 156th Meeting of Air Members, May 28, 1952, DHH 73/1223, Series 3, Sub-series 13. See also Richard Mayne, "Keep Them Flying: The C-119 Flying Boxcar, Its Replacement and the Development of the RCAF's Air Transport Capability (Part 1)," *CAHS Journal* 54, no. 1, (Spring 2016), 18–22.

43 Michael K. Carroll, *Pearson's Peacekeepers: Canada and the United Nations Emergency Force, 1956-67*, (Vancouver: UBC Press, 2009), 123–4. The fifth flying squadron in ATC was the Arctic surveillance unit, 408 Squadron, which flew the Lancaster from Rockcliffe until 1964.
44 "Taps for T.A.C.," *The Roundel*, 11, no. 2, (March 1959).
45 Ron Pickler and Larry Milberry, *Canadair the First 50 Years* (Toronto: CANAV Books, 1995), 156–8. Argus procurement was reduced from 50 to 33 aircraft, and the Yukon from 24 to 12 aircraft.
46 Richard Mayne, "Flying 'Truck Drivers' or 'Captains of the Clouds': Paul Hellyer and the RCAF's Acquisition of the CC130 Hercules," in *Sic Itur Ad Astra: Canadian Aerospace Power Studies, Volume 6, From Hot War to Cold War*, eds. Mike Bechthold and William March (Trenton, Ontario: Department of National Defence, 2017), 71.
47 Richard Mayne, "Keep Them Flying," 23.
48 Minutes of Air Council Meeting March 12, 1958, and Minutes of Air Council Meeting 19 March 1958. DHH 73/1223 File 1828.
49 Fred W. Hotson, *The De Havilland Canada Story* (Toronto: CANAV Books, 1983), 150.
50 T.G. Coughlin, "Our Men in the Desert," *The Roundel*, vol. 14, no. 8 (October 1962).
51 Lieutenant General David R. Adamson (retd), "The Yukon Saga," *Air Force Magazine*, 33, no. 3, (Fall 2009).
52 Ibid.
53 "Royal Canadian Air Force Report of the Special Studies Group on Long Range Objectives for the RCAF," June 1962, DHH 73/1223, Series 3, Subseries 13, Box 90, File 1819. See also Colonel Fred Carpenter (retd), "The RCAF Report That Wasn't," *Canadian Military Journal* vol. 3, no. 2 (Summer 2002).
54 "Report of the Special Studies Group on Long Range Objectives for the RCAF," 25–8.
55 Paul Hellyer, *Damn the Torpedoes: My Fight to Unify Canada's Armed Forces*, (Toronto: McClelland and Stewart, Inc., 1990), 109–10.
56 Government of Canada, *White Paper on Defence* (Ottawa: Queen's Printer, 1964).
57 Ibid., 23.
58 D.J. Goodspeed, *Canada and Peacekeeping Operations*, Report No. 4, Directorate of History, Canadian Forces Headquarters, October 22, 1965; and J.L. Granatstein, *Canada and Peacekeeping Operations: The Congo 1960-1964*, Report No. 8, Directorate of History, Canadian Forces Headquarters, June 16, 1966.
59 Jon B. McLin, *Canada's Changing Defense Policy, 1957–1963: The Problem of a Middle Power in Alliance*, (Baltimore: Johns Hopkins Press, 1967), 200–1. The C-130B Hercules aircraft were withdrawn from service in 1967.
60 Hellyer, 73–5.
61 Mayne, "Flying 'Truck Drivers,'" 74.
62 McLin, 201.
63 Carroll, 176.

ANNEX A: BUDGET, PERSONNEL, AND ORGANIZATION

Budget

Depending on perceived national requirements, the budget for the Department of National Defence, and the RCAF's portion thereof, varied from year to year. The low point occurred in 1947, which was to be expected as the nation adjusted to peacetime. However, as domestic operational requirements solidified, the departmental

Defence Expenditure and the RCAF Portion (Millions of dollars)

Year	Total Defence Budget[1]	RCAF Portion[2]
1945	2,942	1,260
1946	388	99
1947	196	60
1948	269	90
1949	387	136
1950	787	231
1951	1,447	651
1952	1,959	913
1953	1,891	913
1954	1,762	915
1955	1,838	815
1956	1,830	799
1957	1,712	864
1958	1,654	814
1959	1,537	797
1960	1,538	743
1961	1,652	755
1962	1,606	788
1963	1,730	715
1964	1,582	685
1965	1,555	656

and individual-service funding allocations grew albeit slowly. The hardening of an East-West rivalry, exacerbated by the Korean conflict caused the government to drastically increase defence spending. The need to meet a potential Soviet threat, both in Europe and in the skies of North America, resulted in dramatic increases in the RCAF's portion of the defence budget, and for most of the 1950s more than half of defence monies were allocated to the air force. By the 1960s, governmental focus on domestic social programs, coupled with changing defence requirements brought on by improved technology and Western military doctrine, resulted in decreased defence spending and a corresponding fall in the allocation of funds to the RCAF. A separate budget for the RCAF ceased to be part of the defence estimates in 1966.

Personnel

The personnel strength of the Regular component of the RCAF underwent a steady growth from its post-Second World War nadir in 1948, reaching its maximum strength in 1962. Interestingly, from 1955 until personnel data for separate services ceased to be recorded in 1969, the size of the RCAF exceeded that of the Canadian Army. Air force reserves began to be actively recruited in 1948 and slowly grew in number until they reached their peak in 1956, after which point the number of reserve personnel began to slowly drop. Unfortunately, data on RCAF reserve numbers is not available for the years 1959–70.[3]

RCAF Regular and Reserve Personnel Numbers

Year	Regular Force[4]	Reserves
1945	174,254	0 (All personnel were considered to be on active service)
1946	35,523	0 (All personnel were considered to be on active service)
1947	12,627	408
1948	12,017	744
1949	12,552	1,427
1950	17,274	2,369
1951	22.359	3,207
1952	32,611	4,810
1953	40,423	5,874
1954	45,596	5,440
1955	49,461	5,774
1956	49,989	5,600
1957	50,070	5,259
1958	51,698	4,740
1959	51,627	
1960	51,737	
1961	51,349	
1962	53,119	
1963	52,458	
1964	51,411	
1965	48,114	

Organization

The RCAF went through a number of organizational changes between 1945 and 1964 – far too many to be depicted in a single volume. The diagrams on the following pages show how various senior elements and headquarters were organized in 1958, arguably the heyday of the postwar RCAF. Hopefully, they will provide the reader with a more complete understanding of how complicated the day-to-day activities were for an air force with worldwide responsibilities. The majority of the diagrams (1–8, 10, 10a, and 13) were taken from the RCAF's *General Service Knowledge: Qualifying Examinations (Study Material).*[5] This text was used to introduced new RCAF personnel to a wide range of subjects, including various organizational structures. Diagrams 9 and 12 were created using information found in *RCAF Squadrons and Aircraft*,[6] while diagram 11 was adapted from a 1957 diagram titled "Chain of Operational Control to an Air Division Squadron," located at the Military Communications and Electronics Museum, Kington, Ontario.[7]

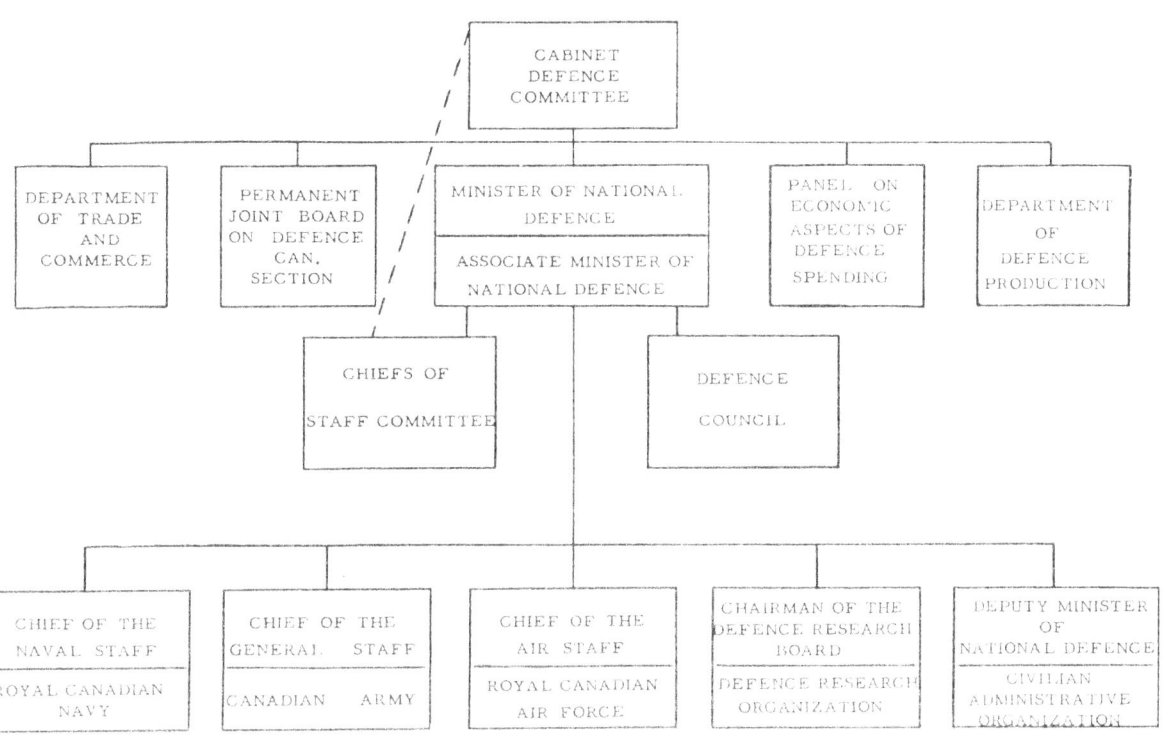

Department of National Defence

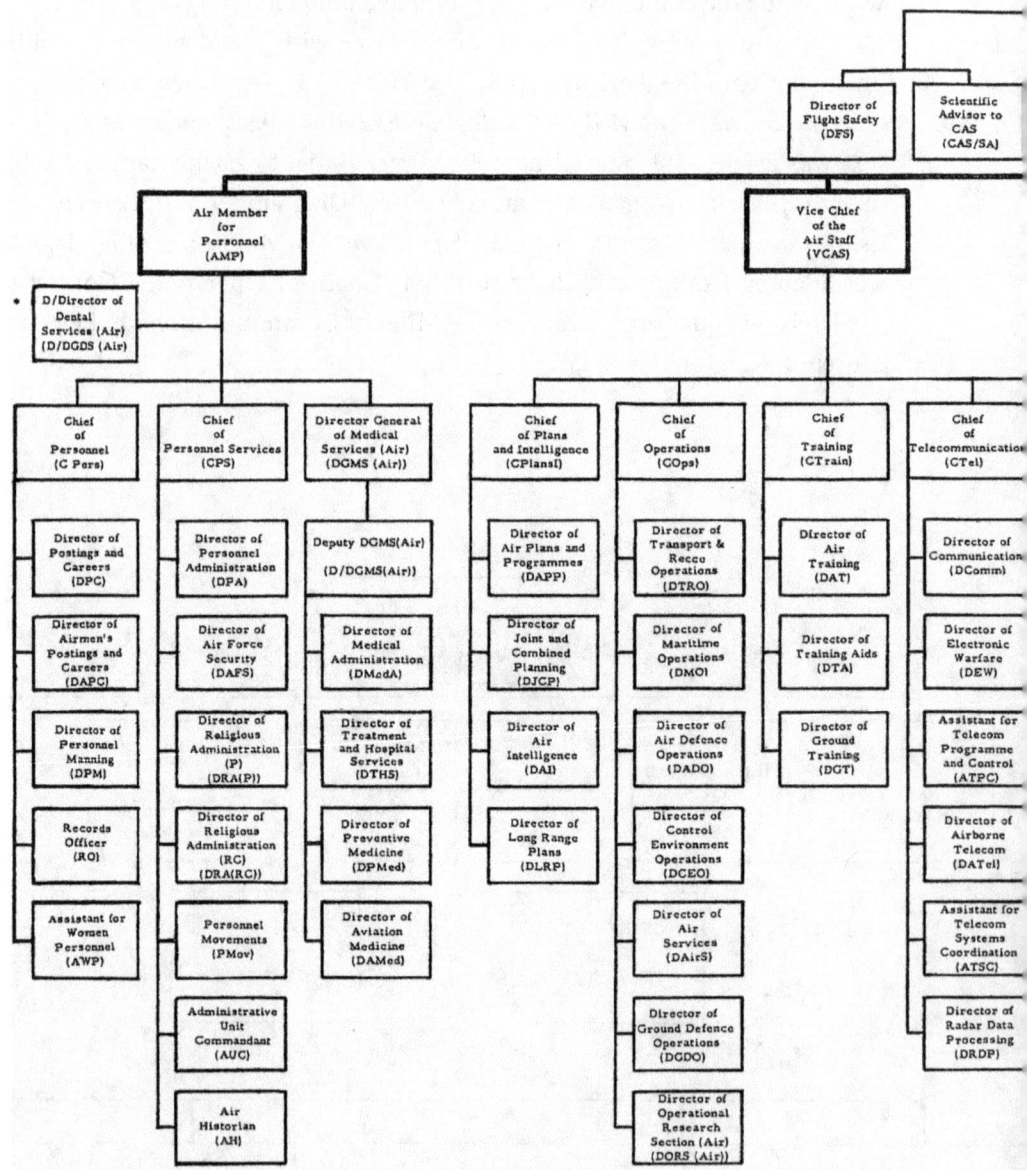

Air Force Headquarters

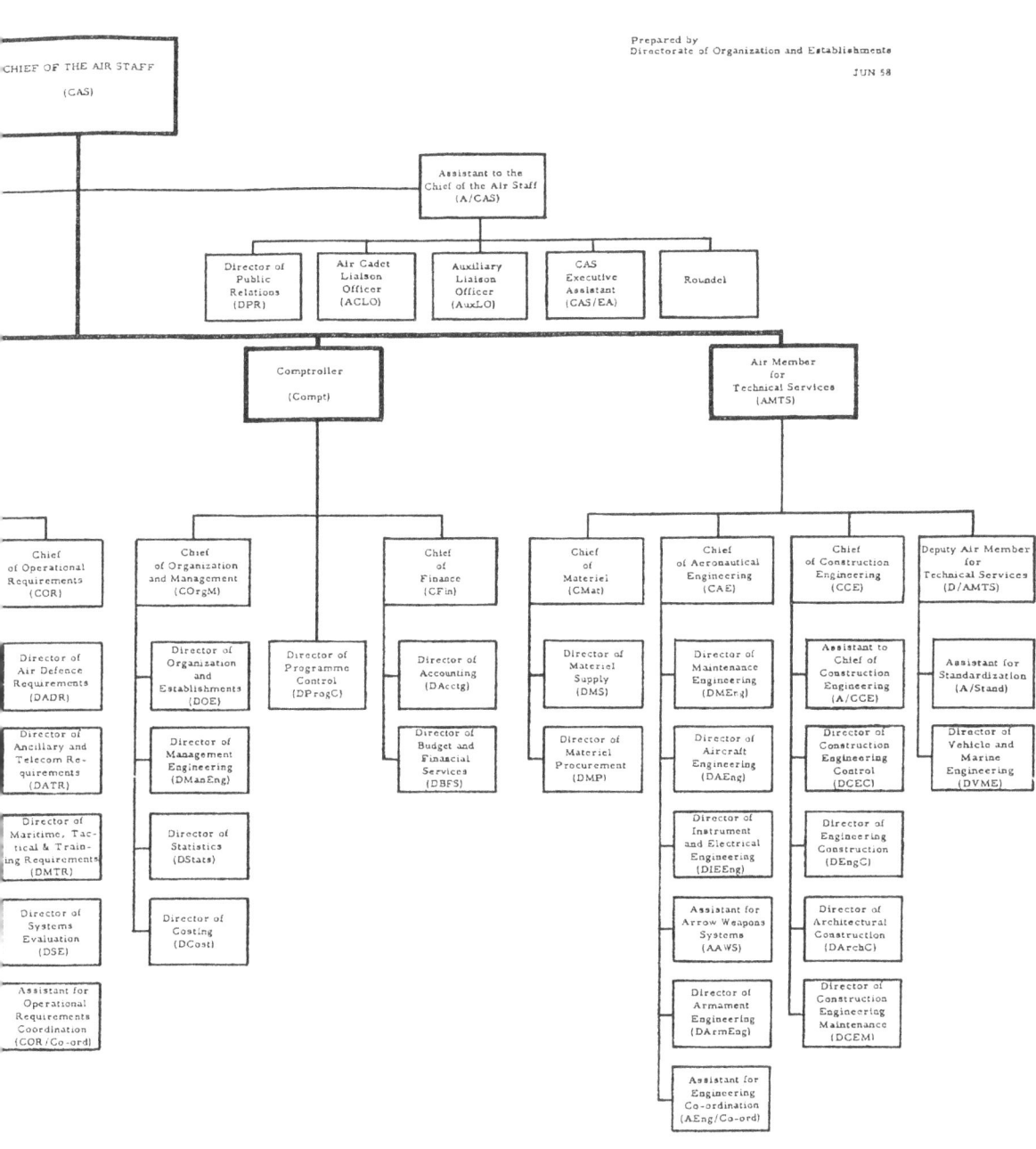

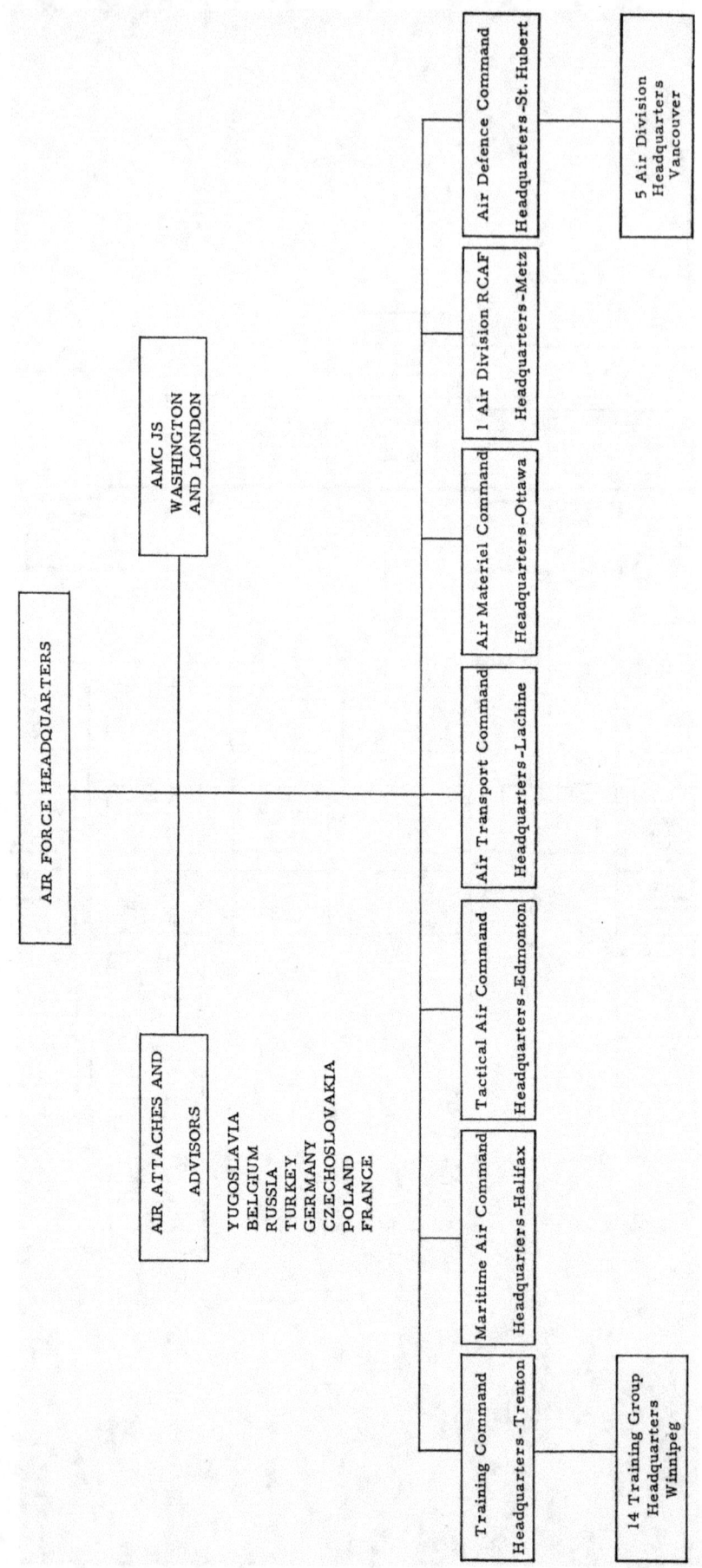

RCAF Major Components

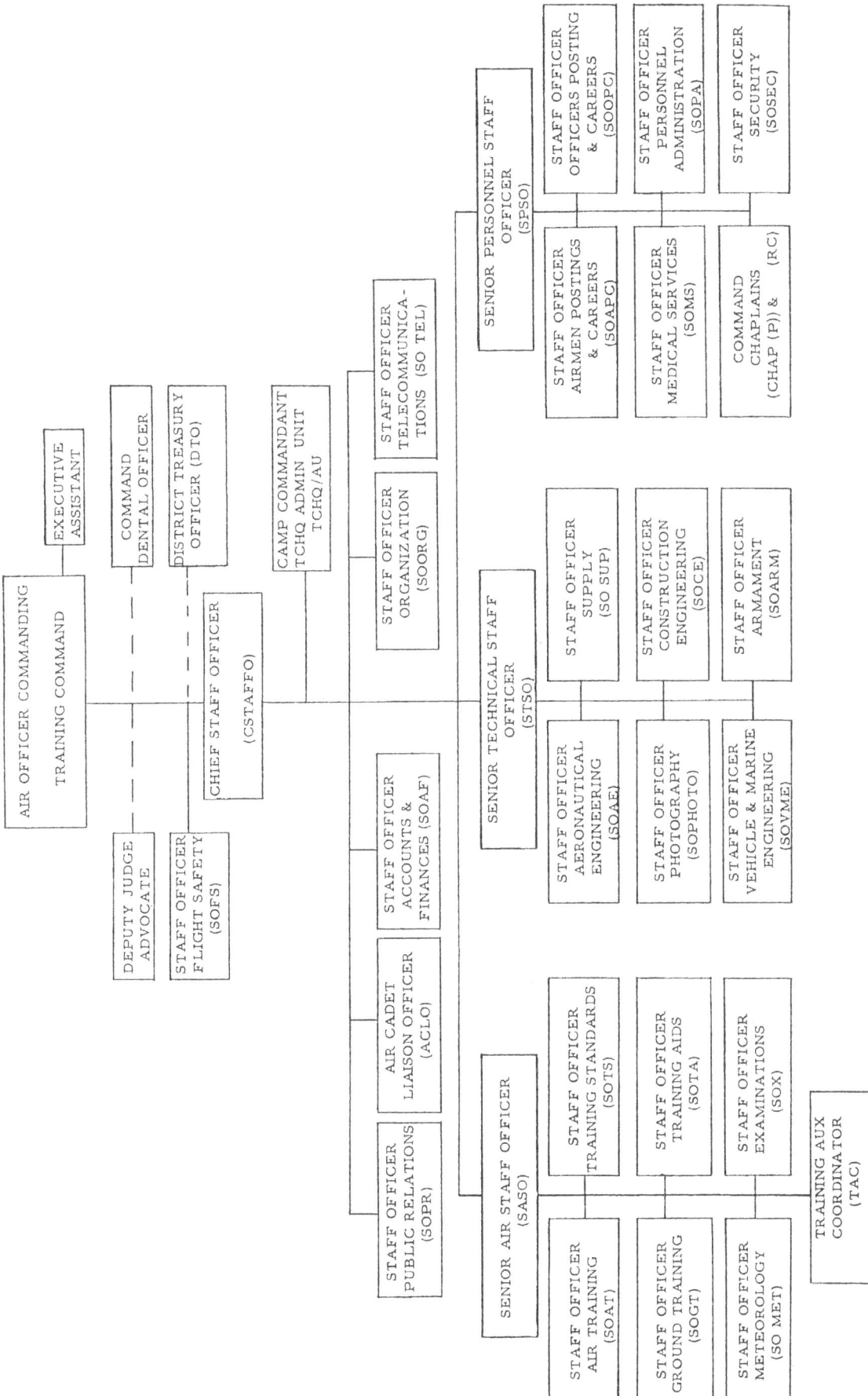

Training Command Headquarters

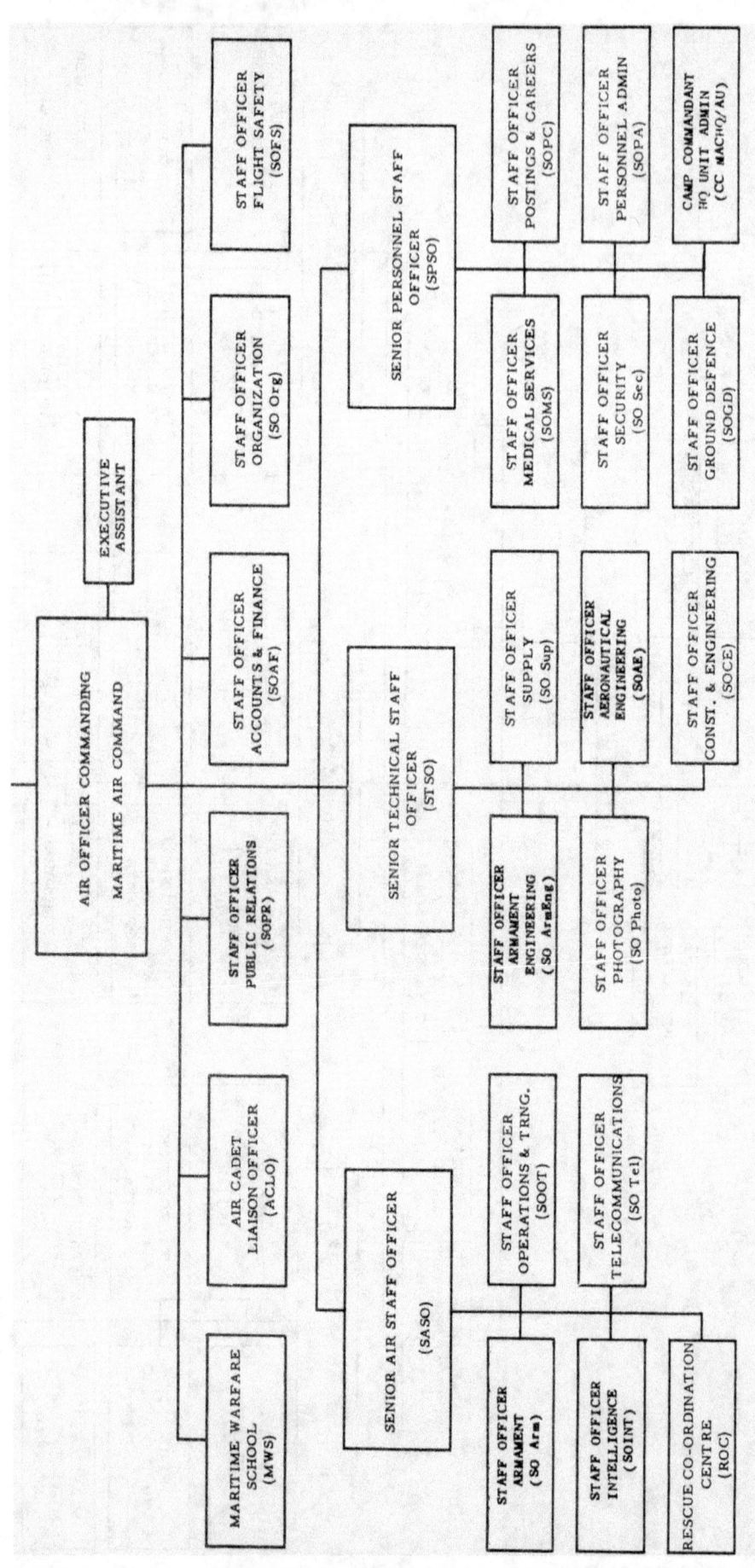

Maritime Command Headquarters

TACTICAL AIR COMMAND HEADQUARTERS

- Air Officer Commanding Tactical Air Command (AOC)
  - Chief Staff Officer (CStaffO)
    - Staff Officer Accounts & Finance (SOAF)
    - Staff Officer Organization (SOOrg)
    - Staff Officer Public Relations (SOPR)
    - Staff Officer Flight Safety (SOFS)
    - Air Cadet Liaison Officer (ACLO)
    - Senior Technical Staff Officer (STSO)
      - Staff Officer Supply (SO Sup)
      - Staff Officer Armament (SO Arm)
      - Staff Officer Aeronautical Engineering (SOAE)
      - Staff Officer Construction Engineering (SOCE)
      - Staff Officer Vehicle & Marine Engineering (SOVME)
      - Staff Officer Photo (SO PHOTO)
      - Staff Officer Telecommunication (SO Tel)
    - Senior Personnel Staff Officer (SPSO)
      - Staff Officer Postings & Careers (SOPC)
      - Staff Officer Security (SO Sec)
      - Staff Officer Religious Admin (SORA) Prot
      - Staff Officer Personnel Admin (SOPA)
      - Staff Officer Medical Services (SOMS)
      - Staff Officer Religious Admin (SORA) RC
    - Senior Air Staff Officer (SASO)
      - Staff Officer Intelligence (SO Int)
      - Staff Officer Ground Defence (SOGD)
      - Staff Officer Operations & Plans (SOOP)
      - Staff Officer Air Training (SOAT)
      - Staff Officer Ground Training (SOGT)

Tactical Air Command Headquarters

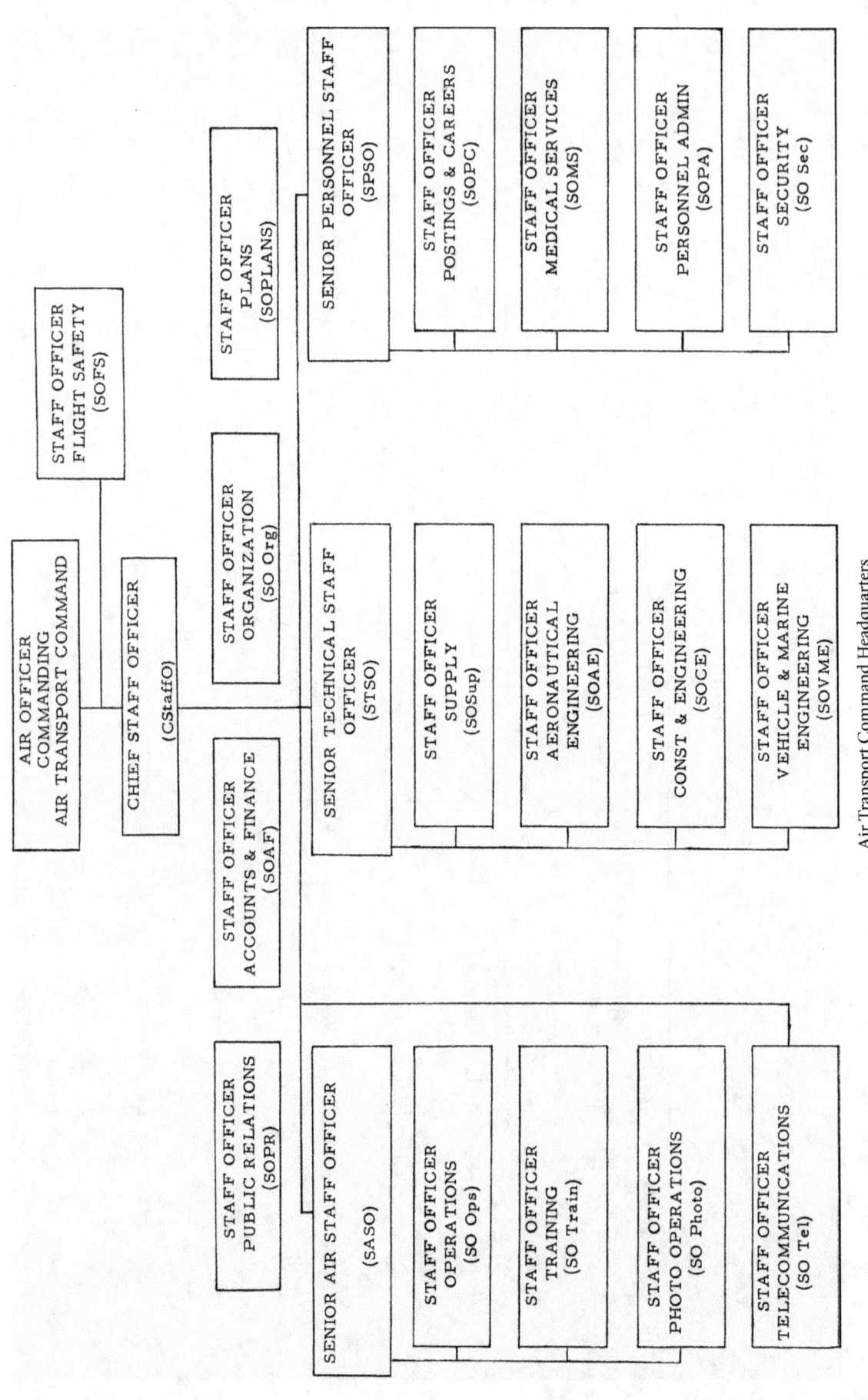

Air Transport Command Headquarters

Air Material Command Headquarters

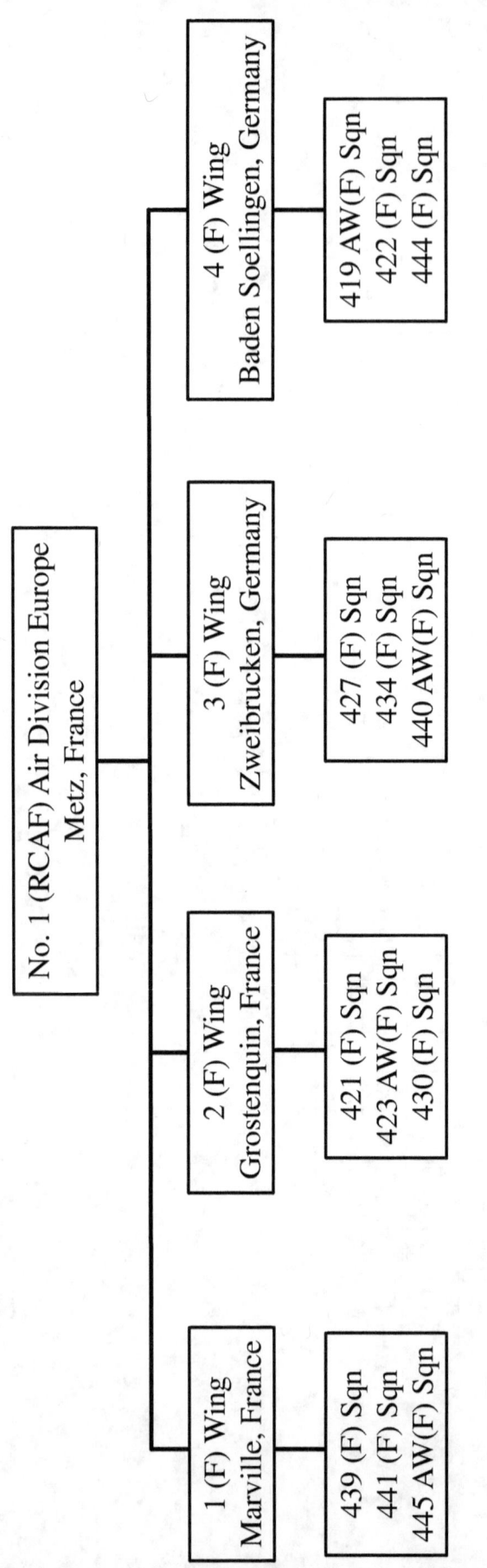

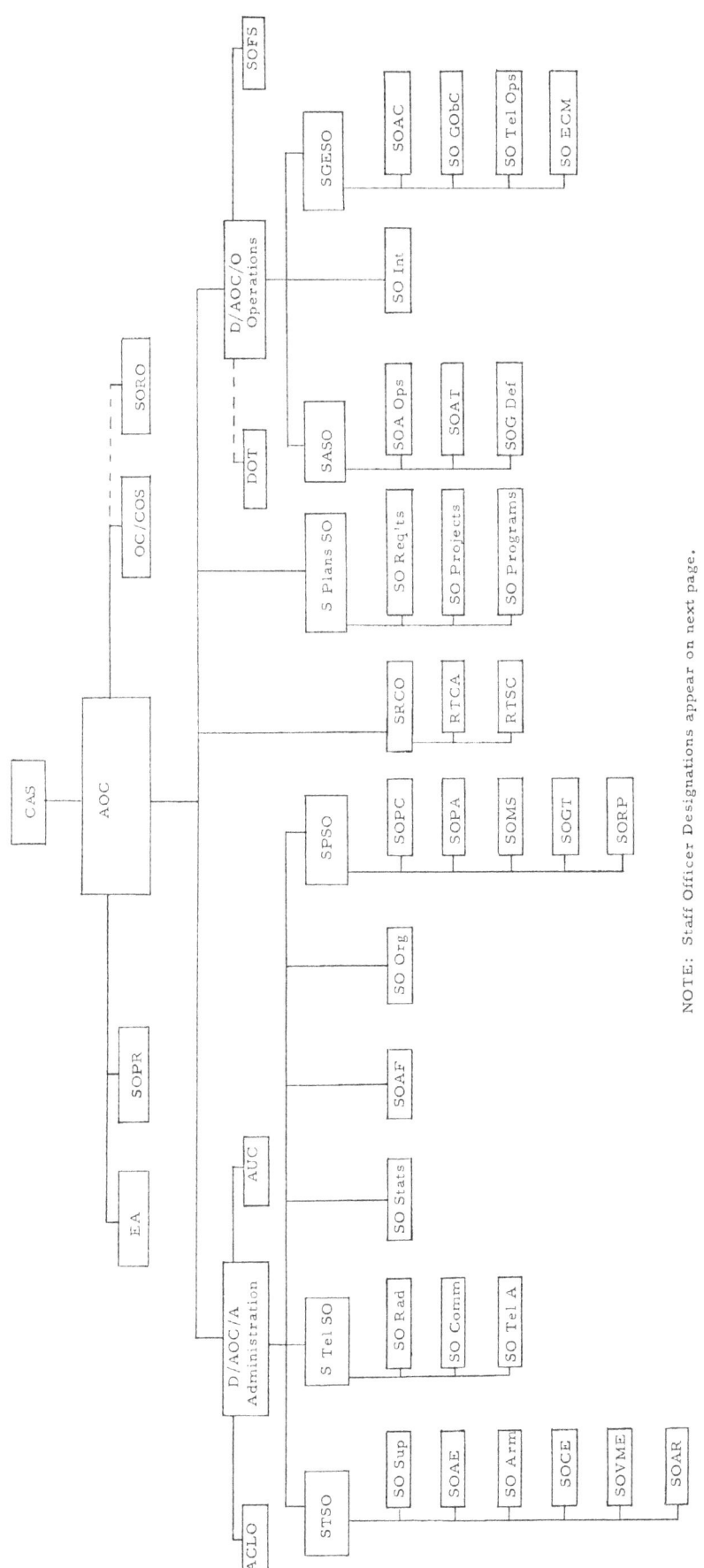

NOTE: Staff Officer Designations appear on next page.

Air Defence Command Headquarters

ADCHQ STAFF OFFICER DESIGNATIONS

DESIGNATION	ABBREVIATION
Air Officer Commanding	(AOC)
OC Combat Operations Center	(OC/COC)
Staff Officer Public Relations	(SOPR)
Deputy/Air Officer Commanding	(DEP/AOC)
Air Cadet Liaison Officer	(ACLO)
Camp Commandant	(CC)
<u>Senior Technical Staff Officer</u>	(STSO)
Staff Officer Supply	(SOSup)
Staff Officer Aero Engineering	(SOAE)
Staff Officer Vehicle Mobile Equipment	(SOVME)
Staff Officer Armament	(SOArm)
Staff Officer Construction Engineering	(SOCE)
Staff Officer Accommodation Requirements	(SOAR)
Staff Officer Accounts & Finance	(SOAF)
Senior Telecommunications Staff Officer	(STelSO)
Staff Officer Radar	(SORad)
Staff Officer Communications	(SOCom)
Staff Officer Telecom (Airborne)	(SOTel(A)
Staff Officer Organization	(SOOrg)
<u>Senior Personnel Staff Officer</u>	(SPSO)
Staff Officer Postings & Careers	(SOPC)
Staff Officer Personnel Administration	(SOPA)
Staff Officer Medical Services	(SOMS)
Staff Officer Ground Training	(SOGT)
Senior Plans Staff Officer	(SPlansSO)
Staff Officer Projects	(SOProjects)
Staff Officer Programs	(SOPrgms)
Staff Officer Requirements	(SOReq'ts)
Senior Operational Research Officer	(SORO)
Senior Reserve Coordinator	(SRCO)
Deputy for Operations	(D/OPS)
Dept of Transport Liaison Officer	(DOT)
Staff Officer Flight Safety	(SOFS)
<u>Senior Air Staff Officer</u>	(SASO)
Staff Officer Air Operations	(SOAOps)
Staff Officer Air Training	(SOAT)
Staff Officer Ground Defence	(SOGDef)
Staff Officer Intelligence	(SOInt)
Senior Ground Environment Staff Officer	(SGESO)
Staff Officer Aircraft Control	(SOAC)
Staff Officer Ground Observer Corps	(SOGObC)
Staff Officer Telecom Operations	(SOTelOps)
Staff Officer Electronic Counter Measures	(SOECM)

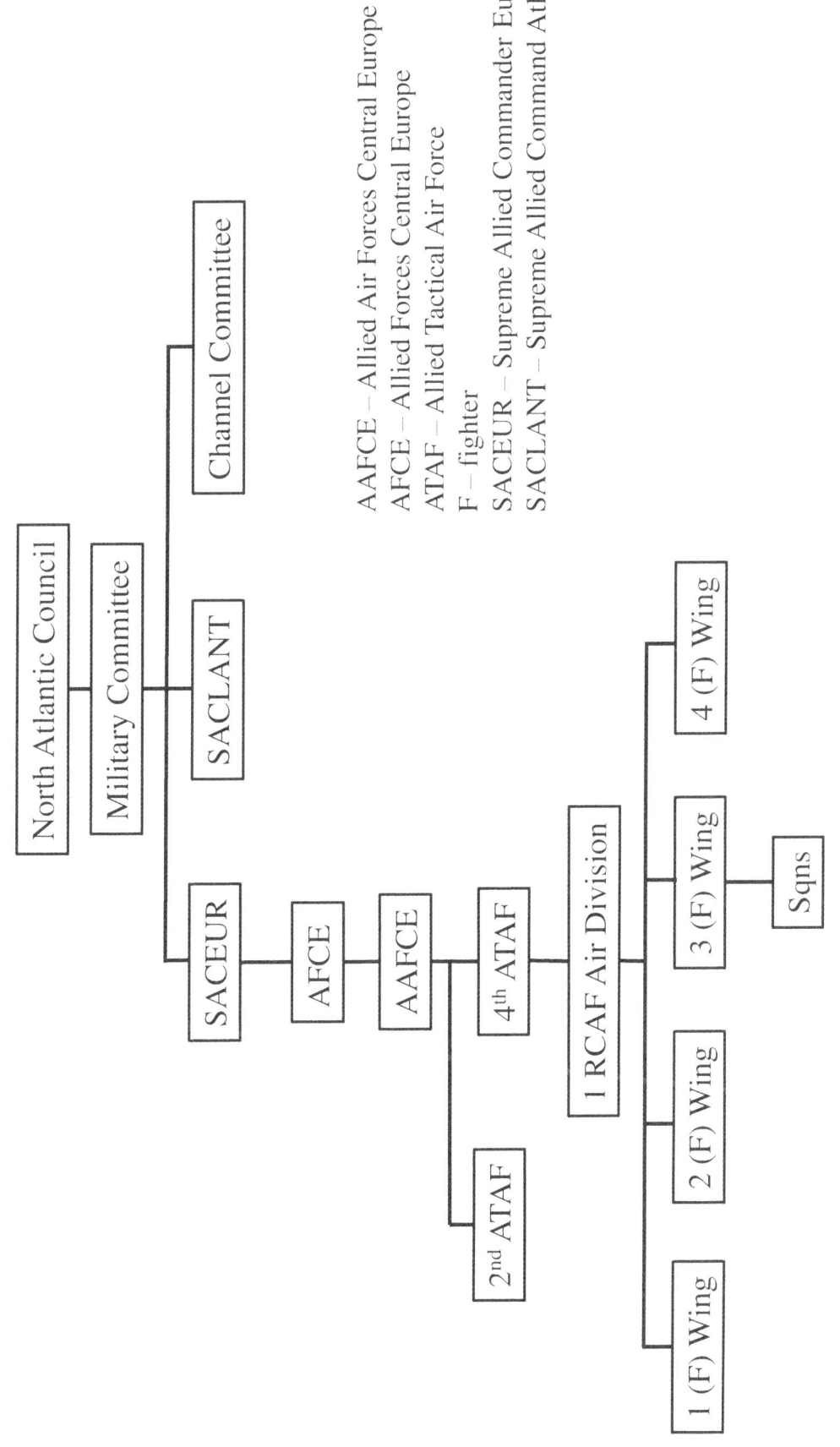

NATO Air Force Chain of Command

Training Command
Trenton, ON

402 Sqn (Aux) – Winnipeg, MB
403 Sqn (Aux) – Calgary, AB

Aux – auxiliary
AW – all weather
F – fighter
M – maritime
MR – maritime reconnaissance
OTU – operational training nit
R – reconnaissance
T – transport

Air Defence Command
St Hubert, Quebec

No. 1 (F) OTU – Chatham, NB
No. 3 AW(F) OTU – Cold Lake, AB
400 (F) Sqn (Aux) – Downsview, ON
401 (F) Sqn (Aux) – St Hubert, QC
409 AW(F) Sqn – Comox, BC
410 AW(F) Sqn – Uplands, ON
411 (F) Sqn (Aux) – Downsview, ON
413 AW(F) Sqn – Bagotville, QC
414 AW(F) Sqn – North Bay, ON
416 AW(F) Sqn – St Hubert, QC
424 Sqn (Aux) – Mont Hope, ON
425 AW(F) Sqn – St Hubert, QC
428 AW(F) Sqn – Uplands, ON
432 AW(F) Sqn – Bagotville, QC
433 AW(F) Sqn – North Bay, ON
438 (F) Sqn – St Hubert, QC
442 (F) Sqn (Aux) – Comox, BC
443 (F) Sqn (Aux) – Comox, BC

Air Transport Command
Lachine, Quebec

No. 4 OTU – Trenton, ON
408 (R) Sqn – Rockcliffe, ON
412 (T) Sqn – Uplands, ON
426 (T) Sqn – Dorval, QC
435 (T) Sqn – Namao, AB
436 (T) Sqn – Downsview, ON

Maritime Air Command
Halifax, Nova Scotia

No. 2 (M) OTU – Summerside, PE
404 (MR) Sqn – Greenwood, NS
405 (MR) Sqn – Greenwood, NS
407 (MR) Sqn – Comox, BC

Tactical Air Command
Edmonton, Alberta

416 Sqn (Aux) – Saskatoon, SK
418 Sqn (Aux) – Namao, AB

1 April 1958

Squadron Allocation by Command

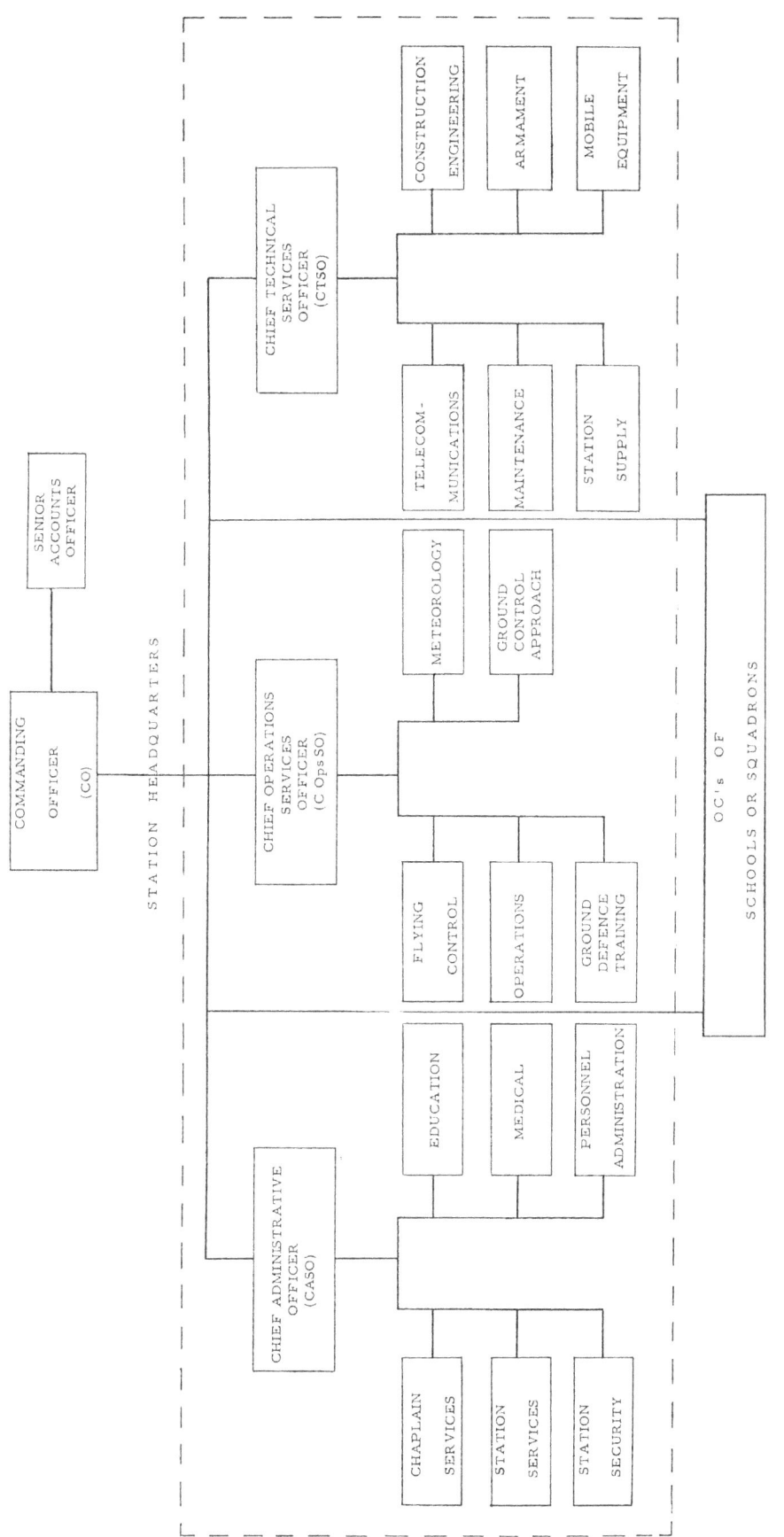

Organization – RCAF Station Headquarters

NOTES

1. Government of Canada, Statistics Canada, Richard M. Bird, University of Toronto, *Historical Statistics of Canada*, "Section H: Government Finance." Accessed June 22, 2022, https://www150.statcan.gc.ca/n1/pub/11-516-x/sectionh/4057752-eng.htm.
2. Bertram C. Frandsen, "The Rise and Fall of Canada's Cold War Air Force, 1948–1968" (PhD diss., Wilfred Laurier University, 2015). The information is taken from Table 3-3, 109; Table 5-6, 220; and Table 6-1, 225.
3. Government of Canada, *Defence 1980* (Ottawa: Queen's Printer, 1980), 14–17.
4. Government of Canada, Statistics Canada, Richard M. Bird, University of Toronto, *Historical Statistics of Canada*, "Section H: Government Finance." Accessed June 22, 2022, https://www150.statcan.gc.ca/n1/pub/11-516-x/sectionh/4057752-eng.htm.
5. Government of Canada, Canadian Air Publication (CAP) 488, *General Service Knowledge: Qualifying Examinations (Study Materia)*, (Ottawa: Queen's Printer, 1959).
6. S. Kostenuk and J. Griffin, *RCAF Squadrons and Aircraft* (Toronto: A.M. Hakkert, Ltd, 1977), 239.
7. Miliary Communications and Electronics Museum, Kingston, website, accessed July 12, 2022, http://www.c-and-e-museum.org/Pinetreeline/metz/otherm1/otherm1-17.html.

ANNEX B: CHIEFS OF THE AIR STAFF, 1944–1964

Air Marshal Robert Leckie, CB, DSO, DSC, DFC, CD, 1944–7

Born in Glasgow, Scotland, on 16 April 1890, the only CAS not to be Canadian-born, Robert Leckie immigrated to Canada in 1907, and worked for his uncle in

Toronto. With the advent of the First World War, he took advantage of the proximity of the Curtiss Aviation School and, upon completion of his flight training, found himself in England by the end of 1915, a provisional sub-lieutenant. Flying missions over the North Sea and coastal Europe he engaged enemy aircraft, ships, submarines and took part in the downing of a German Zeppelin. By the end of the war, Leckie had risen to the rank of major (acting) in the newly formed RAF when he transferred to the fledgling Canadian Air Force (CAF) in 1919 with the rank of lieutenant colonel. However, given the uncertainly of employment with the CAF, he transferred back to the RAF with the rank of squadron leader in August.[1]

As fate would have it, the followed year he was seconded to Canada to serve on the Dominion's Air Board tasked with developing procedures and policies with respect to aviation. Returning to England in 1922, he would serve in a variety of staff and command positions including a tour on the aircraft carriers HMS *Hermes* (1926) and HMS *Courageous* (1928). In 1936, by now Group Captain Leckie, was appointed director of training at the Air Ministry in London, a post he held until 1938. Just prior to the start of the Second World War, Air Commodore Leckie became the Air Officer Commanding (AOC) of RAF Mediterranean, based on the island of Malta.[2]

The need for large numbers of trained aircrew led Canada, Britain, Australia, and New Zealand to create a centralized training organization – the British Commonwealth Air Training Plan (BCATP). The largest part of the organization would be in Canada, and in response the minister of national defence for air, C.G. Powers, reorganized AFHQ in Ottawa, creating a new position, air member for training (AMT), specifically to oversee the BCATP. Air Commodore Leckie, on secondment from the RAF, with his wealth of knowledge and training experience, was personally selected to fill the position.[3] Although his position and seniority might have caused some angst among the Canadian officers, Powers came to hold him in high regard, noting that Leckie was

> widely read beyond his technical and professional knowledge, and had a thorough, strictly non-partisan understanding of politics and politicians. He was quiet and unassuming, and his counsel was certain to be the result of deliberation and sound thinking [and] he was popular with the members of the force..."[4]

It is difficult to summarize the myriad issues and challenges that Leckie faced during his time as AMT, but historian James Eayrs suggested that Leckie's administrative task as akin to "organizing D-Day itself."[5] Not only was it necessary to build, organize, equip, and man the numerous schools and stations throughout the country, there were also the inherent problems in dealing with the various nations and air forces participating in the BCATP. Then there was the Americans. They too, had a vested interest in coordinating, as far as possible, training activities between the allied nations. Leckie's ability professionalism, ability, and quiet confidence proved invaluable in keeping the BCATP running as well as could be expected.

Leckie's administrative skills and his record as AMT made him a sound choice to replace Air Marshal Lloyd Breadner as CAS when the latter was chosen to take command of RCAF Overseas Headquarters in early 1944. However, what may have been equally important to Powers was that Leckie had demonstrated an apolitical approach to his work and would be more likely to follow government direction with respect to the future of the RCAF. Regardless of the underlying rationale, Leckie transferred to the RCAF and became its last wartime CAS in January 1944.

As CAS, Leckie's responsibilities include not only the administration of the RCAF writ large, but he was also responsible for operations conducted from within Canada via the Home War Establishment (HWE). While the war still raged in Europe, the German submarine threat had been contained if not eliminated, and any possibility of Japanese activity on the West Coast was deemed virtually impossible. Therefore, he did not hesitate to reduce the HWE to free up personnel, resources, and funds.[6] Not only did this allow him to ensure that overseas units were fully supported, the reduction in the RCAF's budget endeared him to a government always concerned with the bottom line.

Despite spending virtually his entire career with the RAF, Leckie understood the desire for the RCAF to maintain its independence. During discussions with the Air Ministry on the RCAF's contribution to the war in the Pacific and occupation forces in Europe, Leckie disagreed with RAF approach for an Imperial formation. He recommended to the government that RCAF units be provided as a national entity, serving with, but separate from the RAF. Thus, the Tiger Force, as Canada's proposed heavy bomber contribution to defeating Japan was called, was to be entirely Canadian.[7]

During the closing months of the war, and during the years leading up to his retirement in 1947, Leckie was primarily focused on restructuring the RCAF to a peacetime footing. Government pressure to reduce overall military spending meant that the postwar RCAF would be limited in personnel, units, and equipment. Leckie placed increased reliance on a reserve organization that would cost the government little but that could be mobilized in time of crises.[8] With this in mind, his choice of a reserve officer to replace him as CAS made perfect sense.

Air Marshal Wilfred Austin Curtis, OC, CB, CBE, DSC & Bar, ED, CD, 1947–53

The last of the CAS with First World War experience, "Wilf" Curtis was born on 21 August 1893, in Havelock, Ontario. After completing a two-year business course at the Central Training School, Toronto, he found work as a clerk with a local branch of the Royal Bank of Canada. However, in 1915, as so many other of his contemporaries were doing, he enlisted with the Canadian Expeditionary Force (CEF) and proceeded overseas. His stay in Europe was short-lived as he was accepted provisionally by the Royal Naval Air Service (RNAS) as a pilot, provided he successfully completed flight training, at his own expense, at the Curtiss Aviation School back in Toronto. He graduated from the Curtiss facility on 11 August 1916, and found himself back in England as an RNAS fighter (scout) pilot.

He served with No. 6 and No 10 (Naval) Squadrons flying the Sopwith Camel and with the RAF when it was created in 1918. Credited with 13 aerial victories, Curtis was twice awarded the Distinguished Service Cross (DSC) for "continuous courage as a fighting pilot."[9] Removed from operational flying due to exhaustion, he resigned from the RAF in June of 1919 due to ill health.

Returning to Toronto after the war, Curtis embarked on a very successful career in the insurance industry. In 1920, his health had improved, allowing him to undertake refresher flight training at Canadian Air Force Station Camp Borden, Ontario. While at Borden, Curtis befriended another veteran flyer, Harold "Gus" Edwards, who would have a pivotal influence on Curtis's RCAF career.[10]

Relinquishing his air force commission in 1924 to concentrate on his business, Curtis maintained his connection with the Canadian military establishment. Initially as an officer with the Toronto Scottish militia regiment and then in 1933 as a member of the Non-Permanent Active Air Force (NPAAF) reserve element of the RCAF. In that capacity he helped form No. 110 (Army Cooperation) Squadron in Toronto. Two years later Squadron Leader Curtis was appointed the squadron's commanding officer, a position he still held when Canada entered the Second World War on 10 September 1939.[11]

On active duty as of 1 September, Curtis initially served as the senior air staff officer, Training Command Headquarters, Toronto, as a wing commander. However, this posting was brief as newly promoted Group Captain Curtis found himself on his way to AFHQ, Ottawa, as the director of postings and careers on 21 January 1940. Apparently his "his astute business skills translated well to air force administration."[12]

Following a short period in command of No. 2 Service Flying Training School (SFTS) Uplands, Ontario, in the summer of 1941, Curtis returns to AFHQ as an air commodore. The reasons for his abrupt departure from Uplands soon become readily apparent. Air Vice Marshal Gus Edwards was heading to England as the Air Officer Commanding (AOC) RCAF Overseas Headquarters and insisted on taking Curtis along as his deputy. Perhaps the greatest challenge to face Edwards and Curtis while in London was fulfilling the Canadian government's desire to quickly form RCAF squadrons overseas and fill them with Canadians. Labelled "Canadianization," this goal was not well received by Britain and the RAF. As noted in official history of the RCAF, Curtis's "sound reasoning and considered approach to Air Ministry liaison would prove a restraining influence on the more emotional Edwards. With his chief frequently rendered *hors de combat* by ill-health throughout their two years in London, Curtis's role at Overseas Headquarters was destined to be a large one."[13]

Curtis returned to AFHQ in January 1944 as an air vice marshal, filling the position of air member for air staff primarily dealing with operations and plans. In this role, he oversaw the organization of the RCAF's abortive contribution to the Pacific War Tiger Force, sat as the senior Canadian officer on the Canada-US Permanent Joint Board on Defence, and contributed to the Canadian government's Working Committee on Post-Hostilities Problems.

These responsibilities were not assigned at random; they reflect a conscious decision by the CAS Air Marshal Leckie to groom his successor. In a letter written in 1950 to Brooke Claxton, the minister of national defence (MND) reflecting on Curtis, Leckie wrote:

> For some time prior to my retirement on pension, I had given earnest thought to whom I should recommend to you as my successor as Chief of the Air Staff. Having regard to the fact that the post-war Air Force would consist very largely of non-regular squadrons, it seemed to me appropriate that the senior post in the R.C.A.F. should be filled by an auxiliary officer, if one with suitable qualifications were available. Soon after Air Vice Marshal Curtis's appointment to Headquarters in the capacity of Air Member of Air Council for Air Staff, it became apparent to me that he might be my nomination. For fully two years he was under close observation and at least a year before I retired I had decided to recommend him for the post and steadily groomed him for the job. However, since I was quite uncertain how you would regard the departure from normal practice in recommending a non-regular officer for appointment as Chief of the Air Staff, and since I could scarcely discuss it with you so long before my own retirement, it was necessary to allow Air Vice Marshal Curtis to assume he would return to civil life along with other non-regular officers. This he did until such time as you yourself informed him of his pending appointment.[14]

With Leckie's full support, Curtis was transferred to the regular RCAF on 1 September 1947, with the rank of air marshal to assume the duties of the CAS.

Curtis took over the direction of the RCAF as it transitioned from a period of retrenchment following the Second World War to one of steady growth with the onset of the Cold War. It was also a period where Canada's military focus returned once again to Europe with the establishment of NATO. Equipping the RCAF to meet these postwar responsibilities was a major undertaking for the CAS who remembered the difficulties inherent with acquiring aircraft during the war. Strongly supporting a robust Canadian aircraft industry, Curtis did not neglect both his connections with the USAF and RAF – both major contributors of material to the RCAF. Historian James Eayrs credits Curtis's relationships with senior US aviation figures, such as General H.S. Vandenberg (USAF chief of staff as of April 1948) and J.H. Kindelberger (president of North American Aviation), as well as former RAF comrades-in-arms Marshals Arthur Tedder and John Slessor in helping to ameliorate some of the RCAF's supply and acquisition problems.[15] Indeed, Eayrs wrote that it was Curtis who nudged Slessor during a meeting of the NATO Military Standing Group to suggest that Canada be asked for a contribution to the air defence of Western Europe – a suggestion that led to the formation of 1 Air Division.[16]

Curtis stood down as CAS in 1953 after approximately six years, a relatively long period. According to Claxton, Curtis stayed on so that his preferred successor, Air Vice-Marshal Roy Slemon, could gain valuable experience in varied posts.[17] There was no doubt that Curtis's efforts left Slemon with a service that was well positioned to make a valuable contribution to the defence of Canada and support of our major allies.

Air Marshal Charles Roy Slemon, CB, CBE, CD, 1953-7

Hailing from Winnipeg, Manitoba, Slemon was born on 7 November 1904, and spent most of his early years in that city. While studying engineering at the University of Manitoba, he enlisted in the Canadian Officer Training Corps in preparation to becoming a military army officer. However, he jumped at the chance to take flight training and was accepted in the Pilot Officer (Provisional) program instituted by the Canadian Air Force.

He was one of nine students who undertook the first post-First World War basic flight instruction course at Air Board Station Borden, in May 1923. Returning to continue their training the following year, Slemon and three other candidates were offered, and accepted, the opportunity to continue their instruction past the end of the summer rather than returning to university. Awarded his pilot wings on 23 December 1924, he was commissioned as a pilot officer in the permanent RCAF.[18]

While continuing his training at Borden, Slemon came to the attention of wing Commander Stanley Scott, the director of the RCAF. Scott saw potential in the young officer but thought that he needed to complete his education. Arrangements were made for Slemon to have a two-year leave without pay to finish his engineering degree. Keeping an eye on Slemon's performance, that at the beginning was less than stellar, Scott forcefully informed Slemon that he could expect little advancement in the RCAF without completing his education.[19] Slemon got the message loud and clear, buckled down and graduated with a Bachelor of Science degree in 1927.

For the next four years, Slemon participated in a variety of Civil Government Air Operations throughout the country, building his skills as a pilot and leader. Between 1932 and 1938 he spent time as an instructor at Borden, a staff officer at RCAF headquarters in Ottawa, and a short period of time as the commanding officer of the Ottawa photographic detachment.[20] It was during his time in Ottawa, that he renewed his acquaintance with one of his instructors from Borden, George Eric Brookes. In assessing Slemon, Brookes wrote that he had excellent character and outstanding professional knowledge, tact, common sense, and good judgment.[21]

After successfully completing the RAF Staff Course at Andover, England, in 1938, he was promoted to wing commander, and filled various senior RCAF senior positions as the country transitioned from peace to war. In 1942, as part of RAF Bomber Command, the RCAF was establishing its own formation, 6 Group, with Brookes as its first commander. He lost no time in securing Slemon to become his deputy – a job that he excelled at.[22] He completed his wartime service as the deputy air officer commander-in-chief of RCAF Overseas Headquarters before proceeding back to Canada, with the substantive rank of air vice marshal, to command the RCAF's proposed contribution to the Pacific war.

Between 1945 and 1953, Slemon was posted to various staff and command positions throughout the RCAF as he was groomed to become a future CAS. Finally, the moment arrived, and on 31 January 1953, he was promoted to air marshal and took over the reins from Curtis. It was a tumultuous time for the RCAF as it dealt with rapid expansion driven by the Cold War, equipment challenges brought on by the emerging jet and missile age, new warfighting consideration due to the advent of atomic weapons, and the demands of Alliances such as NATO and NORAD.[23]

Part of wider defence considerations, the issues noted above were often discussed at the normally weekly Chiefs of Staff Committee (CoSC) meetings attended by the service chiefs, the deputy minister, and the head of the Defence Research Board. Hardworking, Slemon was "thorough in preparation, [tenacious] in debate, and stubborn as a mule."[24] As noted by author Sandy Babcock, "he would examine the agenda items from every possible angle to see whether there was any impact on the RCAF and would strongly represent his service's interests."[25]

One of his greatest achievements as CAS was shepherding the formation of the bi-lateral air defence agreement between Canada and the United States. When a somewhat lukewarm Liberal government was replaced by a Conservative one under John Diefenbaker in 1957, Slemon's groundwork was more readily supported. On 1 August 1957, the North American Air Defence Command was created in an exchange of diplomatic notes with a US Air Force commander and an RCAF deputy. Its first commander, General E.E. Partridge, credited Slemon in helping to "avoid many pitfalls in dealing with the Canadian government and in our understanding of the best way to proceed in improving the air defense [sic] posture in North America."[26] It was only fitting then, that Slemon would relinquish his position as CAS to become NORAD's first deputy commander-in-chief – a position he would occupy for seven years.

Air Marshal Hugh Lester Campbell, CBE, CD, 1957–62

Born in Salisbury, New Brunswick, on 13 July 1908, Campbell spent most of his formative years in that province. As a student at the University of New Brunswick, where he was studying electrical engineering, he joined the Canadian Officer Training Corps in 1926 both from interest and to earn extra money to help pay for his education. As a member of the NPAAF he spent his summers at RCAF Station Camp Borden, Ontario, under training as a pilot officer (provisional). Awarded his pilot wings on 27 August 1930, Pilot Officer Campbell, commenced his civilian career, accepting a position with the Canadian General Electric Company in Ontario.

Unfortunately, his civilian employment ran afoul of the Great Depression and, perhaps seeing the writing on the wall, Campbell accepted a permanent commission with the RCAF in 1931. The next few years were spent on flying on various CGAO operations interspersed with additional flight and staff training. In 1934, he was posted to AFHQ, Ottawa, as the Assistant Staff Officer Personnel. Two years later, on 31 May 1936, now a squadron leader, he assumed command of No. 11 Detachment, Vancouver, British Columbia.

To progress in rank from pilot officer to squadron leader in such a short period was no mean feat in the peacetime RCAF, but Campbell impressed his superiors with his staff abilities and organizational acumen. In the spring of 1940, he was summoned to AFHQ to work on the RCAF's most pressing concern, the establishment of the BCATP. Placed under Air Commodore Robert Leckie in the newly created Directorate of Training, Campbell assumed the position of director of training plans. Working tirelessly to establish a network of BCATP schools across the country, he earned high praise from Leckie who marked the young officer for higher command.[27]

Campbell's next posting was as the commanding officer of one of the very schools that he had established, Service Flying Training School (SFTS) Claresholm, Alberta. However, Wing Commander Campbell's tour was cut short when he was sent to RCAF Overseas Headquarters, London, England, in March of 1942 as the director of air staff. In London, he worked for another future CAS, Air Commodore Wilf Curtis, who was in the midst of a bureaucratic, administrative, and at all times political fight with the RAF over the Canadianization of RCAF squadrons overseas. The push by the Canadian government to take back administrative and manning control of RCAF personnel and units was a constant struggle, and Curtis came to appreciate Campbell as a hardworking and diligent staff officer.[28] Having returned to AFHQ by the end of 1943, Campbell worked in a number of different positions, ending the war as the air member for personnel (AMP) with the rank of air vice marshal. As AMP, he was intimately involved in shaping the postwar RCAF.

After attending the Imperial Defence College in England in 1947, he was appointed as AOC Northwest Air Command in Edmonton. Barely eight months later, he was sent to Washington DC as the chairman of the Canadian Joint Staff. Talks between Canada and the US over North American air defence integration were taking on increased importance, and Campbell's selection of the senior Canadian military officer on the ground in Washington was deliberate.[29]

After three years in Washington, he was chosen in 1952 to be the first AOC of Canada's No. 1 Air Division within NATO. The equipping of the Air Division with American F-86 Sabres, built under license in Canada, meant an increased reliance on USAF supply chains. His experience and connections within the USAF stood him in good stead as the RCAF was shifting away from the RAF to greater connectivity with the US.[30]

With the signing of the NORAD agreement in 1957, and the selection of Air Marshal Slemon to be its first Canadian deputy commanding officer, the choice of Campbell as his replacement as CAS came as no surprise. He had a good working relationship with the chairman of the Canadian chiefs of staff, General Charles Foulkes, who, as a believer in the importance of air power, was an ally with DND.[31] Such allies were important as Canada's postwar boom was ending, and the resulting economic challenges necessitated hard choices for the RCAF.

Prior to his retirement in 1962, Campbell would deal with some extremely difficult issues, such as the acquisition of new aircraft fleets to replace wartime vintage platforms; a re-focus on nuclear war resulting in a shift away from relying on reserve forces; the continuing evolution of NATO and NORAD; and the Avro Arrow debacle. With respect to the latter, although Campbell did not always agree with Prime Minister Diefenbaker, he did believe that it was cost prohibitive.[32] Nevertheless, when Campbell stepped down as CAS, the RCAF had successfully transitioned to its postwar structure, equipped for the most part with modern aircraft and operationally anchored on NORAD and NATO.

Air Marshal Clarence Rupert Dunlap, CBE, CD, 1962–4[33]

Clarence Dunlap was born in Sydney Mines, Nova Scotia, on 1 January 1908. Educated at the Nova Scotia Technical College and Acadia University, he enlisted with the permanent RCAF on 16 July 1928, as a pilot officer (provisional). Flight training was undertaken at RCAF Station Camp Borden, and he was awarded his pilot wings on 4 April 1929. Soon thereafter, he was dispatched to RCAF Jericho Beach, Vancouver, British Columbia, on a seaplane course. Over the next five years he participated in CGAO throughout Canada.

In 1934, Dunlap was selected for armament training and was posted to the Air Armament and Bombing School in Borden. As the RCAF had no advanced armament training facilities in Canada, he proceeded to England in 1935 to complete the Special Armament Course, and upon his return to Canada he commenced instructional duties. Just prior to the outbreak of the Second World War, Squadron Leader Dunlap was posted to AFHQ as the director of armament, a position he held until January 1942.[34]

Now a wing commander, Dunlap spent the next nine months as the commanding officer of No. 6 Bombing and Gunnery School (BGS), Mountain View, Ontario. This tour was cut short as the RCAF needed experienced senior commanders overseas due to the expansion of No. 6 (RCAF) Group, part of RAF Bomber Command. As additional squadrons were added to 6 Group's order of battle, they were grouped together at various RAF stations that were then turned over to the RCAF. Promoted to group captain, Dunlap arrived in England to take command of RCAF Station Leeming, North Yorkshire.[35] Eventually four RCAF heavy bomber squadrons would call Leeming home.

By now Dunlap had established a reputation as very level-headed, competent leader and manager capable of getting along well with RAF senior personnel. Therefore, it came as no surprise when he plucked from Leeming in May 1943 to take command of No. 331 (Medium) Bomber Wing, consisting of three RCAF squadrons operating Wellington bombers, for duty in the Mediterranean. Operating from Tunisia, 331 Wing successfully supported Allied landings in Sicily and Italy until November 1943 when it was disbanded and the squadrons returned to 6 Group.[36]

Reflecting his experience in Tunisia, upon his return to England Dunlap took command of No. 139 (Medium Bomber) Wing of the RAF. Under his leadership it took part in supporting the D-Day landings and subsequent Normandy campaign. Finally, in January 1945, he returned to the RCAF fold, becoming AOC No. 64 RCAF Base controlling stations at Middleton St. George and Croft, responsible for four squadrons and approximately 80 Lancaster heavy bombers.[37]

With the European war over in May 1945, he turned to AFHQ Ottawa to serve at the deputy air member for air staff under Air Vice-Marshal Curtis. At this point in his career his armament background result in a close association with the USAF and their nuclear weapons program. After having attended the US Bikini Atoll atomic tests, Operation CROSSROADS, during the summer of 1946, Dunlap spent the following year at the US National Defense War College in Washington, DC.[38]

The next seven years were spent in a variety of staff and command positions including a three-year stint as the commandant of the National Defence College, Kingston, Ontario. Modelled after the British Imperial Defence College, its purpose was to allow select senior military and government officials "to study Canadian defence policy in all its multifarious aspects."[39] His time in Kingston also allowed Dunlap to build a number of relationships with senior government and military personnel.

Between 1954 and 1962, Dunlap filled the positions of vice-chief of the air staff at AFHQ and NATO's deputy chief of staff operations at the Supreme Headquarters Allied Powers Europe (SHAPE) in Paris. In both positions he was heavily involved in the transitioning of the RCAF, and the Alliance, from a conventional warfare posture to one incorporating nuclear weapons. Within the RCAF this meant the acquisition of the BOMARC missile and the CF-101 Voodoo, both armed with nuclear warheads for North American defence, decisions he favoured in opposition to the acquisition of the Avro Arrow.[40] As well, within SHAPE, he supported the government's decision for the Air Division in Europe to adopt a nuclear strike with the advent of the CF-104.[41]

On 14 September 1962, Dunlap was appointed as CAS, a position he would hold for a tumultuous 23 months. The only CAS to serve two different governments, he led an RCAF that was dealing with fiscal restraint, a broad range of equipment acquisitions, modernization, and the adoption of a nuclear role. Under Diefenbaker's Conservative government, Dunlap seemed to work well with the MND, Douglas Harkness, but the minister resigned from Cabinet in 1963 in protest to the prime minister's opposition to US nuclear weapons being placed in Canada, and this left Dunlap and the other chiefs of staff in a difficult position – a difficulty that was exacerbated with the election of the Liberals under Lester B. Pearson later that year.

With a new government came a new MND, Paul Hellyer, who as the opposition defence critic had opposed a nuclear equipped RCAF.[42] A defence review submitted to the government in September, the Sutherland Report, advocated a shift from forces solely committed to NATO and NORAD to an airmobile model capable of supporting a broader range of Canadian interests including United Nations operations.[43] This became the backbone for the Liberal government's 1964 *White Paper on Defence*.

Hellyer also sought to reduce duplication and solidify civilian control of the military through reorganization and unification of the various branches of the

Canadian military. Although Dunlap tried to dissuade the MND for this decision, he was unsuccessful.[44] Bill C-90, *An Act to Amend the National Defence Act*, came into effect on 1 August 1964, The act created an integrated Canadian Forces Headquarters, established the chief of the defence staff (CDS) position, and eliminated the chiefs of staff of the three services. A year later, a functional command structure was introduced with six integrated commands: Mobile, Maritime, Air Transport, Training, and Material Commands. The RCAF was no more.

Dunlap, the last of the "old" RCAF CAS, spoke to the future of air power in Canada. Prior to his posting to become the new deputy commander of NORAD, he published a letter in the May issue of the RCAF's *Roundel* magazine, titled "Statement to RCAF Personnel," where he stated that "we are well fitted to play our part in the process of unification. It will be necessary ... to plan these further steps towards unification carefully. Providing this is done, I believe the RCAF and later the air element in a unified service can continue to perform its function efficiently.... The importance of air power has in no way diminished.... I believe that the proposed organization changes and the ultimate unification of the three armed services are sound in principle and will result in maximum military effectiveness."[45] Fitting words from a professional airman.

NOTES

1. Leckie Biographical File, DHH.
2. Ibid.
3. Library and Archives Canada (LAC), Robert Leckie Personnel File, Recommendation for Honours and Awards, Leckie, DSO, DSC, DFC, 2 Apr 43.
4. C.G. Powers and Norman Ward, eds., *The Memoirs of Chubby Power, A Party Politician* (Toronto: Macmillan, 1966), 232.
5. LAC, MG 30, E251, James Eayrs, "The Man Who Said No to Uncle Sam's Generals," newspaper clipping, n.d.
6. W.A.B. Douglas, *The Creation of a National Air Force: The Official History of the Royal Canadian Air Force, Volume II* (Toronto: University of Toronto Press, 1986), 370.
7. Brereton Greenhouse, Stephen J. Harris, William C. Johnston and William G.P. Rawling, *The Crucible of War, 1939–1945: The Official History of the Royal Canadian Air Force, Volume III*, (Toronto: University of Toronto Press, 1994), 114–16.
8. LAC, MG 30, E251, "Place Reliance on Auxiliaries Says Air Chief," Newspaper simply identified as the *Colonist*, October 16, 1946.
9. Curtis biographical file, DHH.
10. Douglas, *The Creation of a National Air Force*, 52.
11. Ibid.
12. Brereton Greenhouse et al, 52.
13. Ibid.

14 Robert Leckie to Brooke Claxton, August 3. 1950, Curtis personnel file, Library and Archives Canada.
15 James Eayrs, *In Defence of Canada: Peacemaking and Deterrence* (Toronto: University of Toronto Press, 1972), 60.
16 Ibid.
17 Brooke Claxton fonds, LAC, MG 32, B5, vol. 222, file "Memoirs – Defence (9)," 1533E.
18 Charles Roy Slemon, Personnel File, LAC.
19 DHH 79/128, Interview of AM C.R. Slemon by W.A.B. Douglas and W.J. McAndrew, October 20, 1978.
20 Slemon Personnel File.
21 Confidential Report – R. Selmon, dated October 9, 1935, Slemon Personnel File.
22 Highly rated by Brookes, even Ari Marshal Sir Arthur Harris, Air Officer Commanding RAF Bomber Command, described Slemon as an "outstanding officer." RAF Confidential Report (Officers), dated 17 August 1944, Personnel File.
23 Sandy Babcock, "Air Marshal Roy Slemon: The RCAF's Original," in *Warrior Chiefs: Perspectives on Canadian Military Leadership,* eds. Bernd Horn and Stephen Harris. (Toronto: Dundurn Press, 2001).
24 Ibid.
25 Ibid.
26 Letter from General E.E. Partridge to George R. Pearkes, July 24, 1959, Slemon Personnel File.
27 H.L. Campbell personnel file, National Defence Record Center, quoted in Brereton Greenhouse et al, *The Crucible of War,* 63.
28 Greenhouse et. al., *The Crucible of War, 1939–1945,* 63.
29 Ray Stouffer, *Swords, Clunks and Widow Makers: The Tumultuous Life of the RCAF's Original 1 Canadian Air Division*, (Trenton, Ontario: DND, 2015), 33.
30 See notes on discussions with General Norstad at SHAPE, October 26, 1954, File 73/1223, Raymont Papers, Box 132, DHH.
31 Joseph Jockel, "From Demobilization to the New Look: Canadian and American Rearmament," Canadian Historical Association paper, 1981, 26.
32 Special Meeting of the Air Council held August 21, 1957, File 73/1223, Raymont Papers, DHH.
33 Post Nominals: Companion of the Order of the Bath (CB), Distinguished Service Order (DSO), Distinguished Service Cross (DSC), Distinguished Flying Cross (DFC), Canadian Forces Decoration (CD), Order of Canada (OC). Commander of the Order of the British Empire (CBE), second award of a decoration (Bar), Efficiency Decoration (ED).
34 Dunlap Biographical File, DHH.
35 Ibid.
36 The story of 331 Wing is chronicled in Greenhouse et al., *The Crucible of War,* 646–55.
37 Dunlap file.
38 Ibid.
39 George Stanley, "Military Education in Canada, 1867–1970," in *The Canadian Military: A Profile*, edited by Hector Massey. (Toronto: The Copp Clark Publishing Company, 1972), 190.
40 *Financial Post*, May 14, 1955, as quoted in Jon B. McLin, *Canada's Changing Defense Policy, 1957–1963: The Problems of a Middle Power in Alliance*, Baltimore: The Johns Hopkins Press, 1967, 32.
41 DHH 73/1223, Series 1, Box 149, File 464, Memorandum "Re-Equipment of the Air Division – SHAPE Planning Guidance 1957," 5 February 1959.

42 Paul Hellyer, *Damn the Torpedoes: My Fight to Unify Canada's Armed Forces* (Toronto: McClelland & Stewart Inc., 1990), 34.
43 "Report of the Ad-Hoc Committee on Defence Policy," September 30, 1963, 11, III.61, vol. 8, 87/253, Lindsey-Sutherland fonds, DHH.
44 K.R. Pennie, "The Impact of Unification on the Air Force," in *The Evolution of Air Power in Canada Volume 1, edited by* William March and Robert Thompson. Papers delivered at the Air Force Historical Convention held at Air Command, Winnipeg, Manitoba, November 1994.
45 C.R. Dunlap, "Statement to All RCAF Personnel," *The Roundel*, Vol. 16, No. 4, (May 1964), 2–3.

NOTES ON CONTRIBUTORS

Dean Black, MA, is a retired Canadian Forces tactical helicopter pilot with extensive experience in command and staff appointments. Since retirement he has become executive director of the RCAF Association and has served on a number of air force-related boards, while also researching and writing on various air force topics.

Ernest Cable served in flying, staff, and command appointments as a Maritime Patrol Navigator in the RCAF. In retirement, he has been a member of the board of directors for the Shearwater Aviation Museum and the museum's historian. He has also advised the Centre for Foreign Policy Studies at Dalhousie University on maritime security issues and has published extensively on matters of maritime security.

Allan English, PhD, flew as a Transport navigator in the Canadian Forces. He also taught leadership and psychology at the Royal Military College. As history professor at Queen's University, he has mentored dozens of serving personnel through their graduate education. As a researcher, he has focused on issues of the human dimension within the military profession.

Bertram Frandsen, PhD, served in the Canadian Armed Forces for 37 years as a logistics officer, strategic analyst and military educator. Since his retirement from the military in 2012, he has been a weekly volunteer at the Canadian War Museum as a researcher and at the Canada Aviation and Space Museum as an interpreter/Cold War subject matter expert.

Andrew Godefroy, PhD, is a serving Army officer and currently head of Professional Military Education at the Canadian Army Staff College. A former Canada-US defence space policy analyst, he has served as an official historian for the Canadian Space Agency, has published short histories of various aspects of the Canadian aerospace industry, and is also a member of the Royal Astronomical Society of Canada.

Richard Goette, PhD, is an air power specialist and member of faculty at the Canadian Forces College. He teaches and lectures for many RCAF education programs and parallel military history courses in academe. In addition to many publications, across the broader air force community, he is a central member of many air and aviation societies in Canada.

Rachel Lea Heide, PhD, is a defence scientist and strategic analyst for the Department of National Defence. Her professional research focuses on a range of contemporary security issues. As an air force historian, she specializes in the period from 1914 to 1959, including such topics as air force organization, training, leadership, morale, professionalization, mutinies, accident investigation, and government policy.

Russell Isinger, MA, is the registrar of the University of Saskatchewan and teaches in the Department of Political Studies. He has published on many political issues in Canada with a focus on aircraft procurement decision, in particular those surrounding the Avro Arrow.

Joseph T. Jockel, PhD, is a long-time researcher and teacher of Canadian-American security and defence issues. Active in various US government organizations over the years, in the '80s he served on exchange at the Canada desk of the US Department of State where he was acting secretary of the Canada US Permanent Joint Board on Defence.

Mathias Joost, MA, served in the CAF from 1986 to 2021; from 2003 to 2021 he worked within the Directorate of History and Heritage, where he answered most of the inquiries on the RCAF and served as head of the war diaries section. He has developed specialties in the Air Reserve and on Asian and Black Canadians in the military. He serves as a consultant and continues to write on these two topics.

Terry Leversedge is a retired senior RCAF officer. His career in military aerospace engineering encompassed a wide number of positions at both field units and within the headquarters of the RCAF, before he retired as a brigadier general after 35 years of service. He is now a widely published Canadian military aviation author and amateur historian.

William March, MA, is a retired Long Range Patrol navigator. He has spent the past three decades working in various RCAF history and heritage appointments. He has also been very active with editorial duties for the Canadian Aviation Historical Society and the RCAF Association.

General (retired) Paul Manson joined the RCAF in 1952. A fighter pilot who served primarily with NATO in Europe during the Cold War, he commanded at all levels of the Air Force, including Air Command from 1983–5. He was appointed as Canada's Chief of the Defence Staff from 1986–9. Notably, he led the New Fighter Aircraft project that resulted in selection of the CF-18 in 1980. After retirement from the service, he was president of a large aerospace company, following which he became active in numerous capacities as a defence and security analyst. Among his many honours and awards are the Order of Canada, the Order of Military Merit, the Vimy Award, and induction as a member of Canada's Aviation Hall of Fame.

James Pierotti, MA, is a retired RCAF Search and Rescue navigator. In addition to flying and command appointments, he has also had several unique staff appointments in innovation-related fields. He has published extensively on SAR history and topical issues.

Peter Rayls, PhD, is a retired U.S. Army personnel officer. Coming to Canada for his PhD at Queen's University, he focused his research on the personal interactions between RCAF and USAF officers working on continental air defence policies and programs in the 1940s, '50s and '60s.

Raymond Stouffer, PhD, was an air movements and logistics officer for many years before joining the faculty of RMC, where he taught history and served as the university's registrar. At RMC he taught a range of courses in Canadian military history with a focus on the RCAF, a topic which is at the centre of his many publications.

Randall Wakelam, PhD, a tactical helicopter pilot in the first half of his military career, subsequently served in teaching and education administration appointments. His research and publications focus on issues of air power, aircraft procurement, military education, and leadership.

INDEX

Note: RCAF Squadrons are listed in **bold** and by number under the heading "Squadron." RCAF Stations are listed in **bold** and by station name under the heading "RCAF Stations."

accidents: B-17 Halle Germany (1945), 306; Lancaster crash (1953), 286; Operation NANOOK (1950), 331; TCA 810 (1956), 286
Ad Hoc Committee on Service Requirements for Helicopters, 358–60
AERE classification. *See* Aerospace engineering classification
aeromedical evacuation, 13, 233, 358
Aerospace Engineering classification, 200–2
Air Command, 31, 202, 318
Air Control and Warning (AC&W) role, 14, 16, 48, 51, 71, 216, 232–3, 235–7, 240, 243–4
Air Council, 131, 133, 137, 143, 239, 244–6, 258, 266–7, 292, 361, 384–6, 416
Air Defence Command (ADC), 10, 16, 20–6, 30, 61–2, 65–8, 70–7, 82, 91, 199, 234, 238, 241, 259, 289–90, 389
Air Defence Group (ADG), 13, 63, 65, 71, 77, 332
Air Division, No. 1: general, 6, 30, 214, 236, 243, 288; established, 7, 15, 20, 41, 416, 421; strike reconnaissance role, 10, 21, 27, 50–5, 423; operational control of, 6, 15, 39, 43, 66; organization, 15, 30, 42, 54; aircraft, 15, 21–4, 49–51, 54, 109, 241; nuclear weapons, 21, 27, 52–6; air defence role, 39, 42–3, 46–8, 50–1; headquarters, 46; logistics, 48–9, 194, 375, 379, 383; conventional attack role, 54–6; closure of bases in France, 54; disbanded, 55–6
Air Force College, 143–6, 148
Air Force College Journal. See *Royal Canadian Air Force Staff College Journal*
Air Materiel Command (AMC), 193–4, 201–2, 259, 371, 374, 376. *See also* Canadian Forces Material Command
air-to-air missiles, 14, 17, 24, 110, 113
Air Transport Command (ATC): role, 20, 26, 29, 383, 386, 389; and peacekeeping, 20, 320; aircraft replacement, 25, 305, 378, 383, 388; post-unification, 30; auxiliary role, 241–2, 245–7, 383–4; established, 304, 371, 374–5; resource challenges, 313–15; proposed standing UN airlift, 319; Korean War, 376–7. *See also* transport planes, United Nations
aircraft maintenance: and Canadian industry, 182; squadron vs centralized, 189–91
aircraft maintenance training: 182; personnel, 183; trades, 183, 187; schools, 183–4, 186–7; impact on BCATP, 183–4;

aircraft maintenance training (*cont.*)
  Royal Canadian Navy, 194–6; Canadian Army, 196–9; impact of unification, 199–202. *See also* Canadian Forces Aircraft Trades School; technical training schools; Technical Aeronautical Engineering School; School of Aeronautical Engineering
Allard, Jean V., 55, 364
Allied Command Atlantic (ACLANT), 325–6
Allied Tactical Air Force, 2 (2 ATAF), 15, 43
Allied Tactical Air Force, 4 (4 ATAF), 15, 43–4, 46, 50–5
Alouette-ISIS satellite, 268, 271–3, 275
AMES II radar, 235–7
Annis, Clare, 12, 22, 28, 30, 68, 270–1
anti-submarine role, 326–30, 333–4, 338, 342–3, 346. *See also* maritime patrol aircraft
APS-33 radar, 330, 332
army co-operation, 349–52, 356
Astra fire control system, 24, 113, 116, 118, 121
A.V. Roe Canada Ltd., 111–12

B-25 Mitchell, 19, 171, 231, 234, 236, 243, 279
Babcock, Sandy, 12, 419
Baker-Nunn camera, 82, 88, 90–1, 261–5
Ball, F.M., 30
ballistic missile defence: impact on NORAD, 29, 86, 90, 99–100; space surveillance, 89–90; Diefenbaker views, 91, 93, 99; Pearson views, 100; Arrow cancellation, 117; RCAF-DRB research, 255–8, 264–5, 272
Bell 47 helicopter, 47, 243–4, 253, 257, 359
Berlin Airlift, 61, 282, 375–6
Black Brant rockets, 269, 272–3
BOMARC, 10, 21, 24, 28, 32, 83–4, 86–7, 93, 100, 116, 118, 120, 123, 423
"Brief on Post-War Planning for the Royal Canadian Air Force," 10–11
Bristol Aerospace Ltd., 338
Bristol Britannica, 104, 379, 385
Bristol Freighter, 48–9, 383
British Commonwealth Air Training Plan (BCATP): aircraft maintenance, 183, 185, 190; and Canadian war aims, 157–8; cost, 160; established, 152, 412–13; and French-Canadians, 135; lessons for post-war training, 175–6; navigator and bomb aimer training, 160; total trained, 3, 161; training schools, 159–60, 420
Brown, Harold, 267
Bundy, McGeorge, 99

C-45 Expeditor, 171–2, 240–1, 245–6, 379
C-47 Dakota, 48–9, 172, 246–7, 305, 315–16, 354, 357, 372, 375, 379–83
C-119 Flying Boxcar, 304, 375, 378–80, 382–3, 388
Cabinet Defence Committee (CDC), 40–1, 108, 112, 116, 162–3, 282
Cadieux, Pierre, 55
Campbell, Hugh, 11–12, 25–6, 46, 50–1, 109, 257, 360, 385–6, 388, 419–21
Campney, Ralph, 240
Canada-US Air Defence Study Group (ADSG), 74–5
Canada-US Basic Security Plan (BSP), 12, 62
Canada-US Military Cooperation Committee (MCC), 12, 61–2
Canadair Ltd., 103–4, 109, 337–9, 379, 383, 385
Canadair North Star (transport plane), 304–10, 315, 338, 375–9, 382–3
Canadian Air Group, No. 1, 55
Canadian Armament Research Development Establishment (CARDE), 256, 263, 268, 271
Canadian Armed Forces: command structure, 199; support to families, 224. *See also* Unification (Canadian Armed Forces)
Canadian Army: RCAF tactical air support, 19, 39, 43, 56, 236, 242; nuclear weapons, 53, 83; air defence role, 65, 74, 243; organic tactical aviation, 350, air observation role, 350, 352; transport role, 350; helicopters, 350, 353; army-air support in the Second World War, 350–1. *See also* aircraft maintenance; Canadian Joint Air Training Centre
Canadian Army Staff College, 68, 132, 138, 147
Canadian Atlantic Area (CANLANT), 326–8, 342
Canadian Aviation Corps, 2
Canadian Chiefs of Staff Committee (COSC), 74–6, 90, 108–18, 121, 162, 239–40, 243–4, 334, 357, 360, 418
Canadian Coast Guard (CCG), 283, 288–9, 292–4, 295–6
Canadian Defence Quarterly, 142

Canadian Forces Aircraft Trades School (CFATS), 201
Canadian Forces Materiel Command, 201–2
Canadian Forces Reorganization Act, 30–1
Canadian Joint Air Training Centre (CJATC), 198–9, 349, 353–6, 359–61, 367, 383
Canadian Red Cross (CRC), 301, 306–10
Carcallen, H.M., 145
Carpenter, Fred, 25–7, 285–6
Carr, William "Bill", 318
Casselman, Karl Albert "Bert," 349–50, 354, 363, 366
CELE classification, 200
Central Air Command, 188, 328
Central Experimental and Proving Establishment (CEPE), 256
CC-106 Yukon, 49, 104, 234, 305–7, 309–10, 312, 320, 379–80, 383, 385, 387–9
CC-108 Caribou, 104, 245–7, 318, 362–3, 384–5, 389
CC-115 Buffalo, 295, 305, 387
CC-130 Hercules, 305, 307, 310–12, 320, 361, 383–5, 387–9
CC-137 Boeing 707, 385
CF-100 Canuck, 13–17, 23–4, 32, 49–51, 55, 71, 82, 91, 103, 109–10, 231, 239, 256, 279
CF-101 Voodoo, 21–2, 25, 28, 32, 82–4, 93, 100, 120, 423
CF-104 Starfighter: strike-reconnaissance role, 10, 21, 26–7, 32, 51–2, 423; procurement, 25, 27, 32, 51–4, 94, 103; and Canadair, 53; accidents, 54; F-5 as replacement, 54
CF-105 Avro Arrow: program, 4, 23,103, 107–10; cancellation, 10, 21, 82, 91–3, 99, 116–23; roles, 21, 24; costs, 24, 91,109–13, 115–19, 123, 141; foreign sales, 24, 91, 118; engines, 109–10, 121; criticism of project, 111–12, 116, 423; flight testing, 113; and Auxiliary, 113
CF-5 Freedom Fighter, 29, 32, 54, 386
CH-113 Labrador, 291, 294–5
Chiefs of Staff Committee (COSC), 11, 42, 74–6, 90, 108–14, 116–18,121,162, 239–40, 243–4, 334, 357, 360, 418
Christie, Loring, 154
Claxton, Brooke, 15–16, 40, 43, 107, 111, 133–4, 163, 167, 375, 377, 416–17
Collège Militaire Royal de St-Jean, 135–6

Communication and Electronics Engineer classification, 200
Consolidated Canso, 289–91
Continental Air Defense Command (CONAD), 74–6, 90, 97, 99
Co-Orbital Satellite Intercept Evaluation (COSINE) Project, 264–6
CP-107 Argus, 18, 104, 334, 337–46
Croil, G.M., 181
Crysdale, J.H., 267, 270
Cuban Missile Crisis 1962, 21, 26, 84–5, 96–9, 343–6, 386
Curtis, Wilfred, 12, 53, 109, 283, 420; RCAF organization, 13; NATO, 42–4, 46; and RAF, 43; on MCC, 62; educating the RCAF, 134; NATO flying training, 162; maritime air, 329, 337–8; biography, 414–17
Curtiss JN4 Canuck, 155
Curtiss School (Toronto), 2, 153, 155, 412, 414

Decimomannu (Sardinia), 47
Defence Research Board (DRB), 14, 90, 108–9, 116, 135, 255–7, 266–75, 418
de Havilland Canada Ltd., 104, 109, 295, 330, 388
de Havilland Comet, 379, 385
deterrence, 9, 123, 142, 347
Development and Associated Research Policy Group (DARPG), 271–4
Dextraze, Jean-A., 364
DH-100 Vampire, 13, 63–4, 71, 231–2, 234, 241
DHC-1 Chipmunk, 172, 174, 200, 360
DHC-2 Beaver, 104, 360
DHC-3 Otter, 29, 104, 243–5, 305, 316, 357
Diefenbaker, John G.: RCAF roles, 6, 10, 20–1, 25; nuclear weapons, 10, 21–2, 51–2, 84, 87, 93–6, 99–100, 386, 423; NORAD, 21, 76, 82–4, 87, 91–2, 96–100, 113–14, 419; Arrow cancellation, 25, 91–3, 117–21, 421; NATO, 50–1, 56; Cuban Missile Crisis, 21, 26, 84, 96–9, 343, 345, 386; Canadian Coast Guard established, 294; humanitarian relief, 310
Distant Early Warning (DEW) Line, 16, 71–3
Dunlap, L.R. "Larry," 12, 22, 28, 62, 66; as CAS, 26, 266, 386, 388, 411, 422–4

Eastern Air Command, 328
Eayrs, James, 88, 107, 141, 413, 416

education: requirement for joint education, 133–4, 147–8; review of RCAF professional education, 142–4; impact of unification, 147–8; space curriculum, 258–60. *See* Air Force College; Canadian Army Staff College; Collège militaire royal de St. Jean; Graduate Assistance Program; Regular Officers Training Plan; Royal Canadian Air Force Staff College; Royal Canadian Air Force Staff School; Royal Military College of Canada; Royal Roads Military College; Subsidization of Serving Airmen Plan; University Reserve Training Plan
Eisenhower, Dwight, 26, 43, 94–5, 363
Evans, E.H., 64
exchange postings, 13, 259–61, 312, 367
Exercise CHECKPOINT, 236–7
Exercise CONVEX III, 332
Exercise EAGLE, 234
Exercise METROPOLIS, 237
Exercise MICROWEX, 332
Exercise SIGNPOST, 235
Exercise SWEETBRIAR, 354, 375
Exercise TAILWIND, 236

F-4 Phantom, 27, 29
F-86 Sabre: procurement, 14, 16, 32, 103; NATO role, 15, 21, 23–4, 38–9, 41–3, 46–51, 55, 109, 379, 421; continental air defence role, 43, 71, 116, 240–2
F-84, 42, 44, 46
Fairey Canada, 327
families, 49, 205, 209, 211, 213–14, 218–24
fighter aircraft. *See* CF-100 Canuck; CF-101 Voodoo; CF-104 Starfighter; CF-105 Arrow; CF-5 Freedom Fighter; DH-100 Vampire; F-86 Sabre; P-51 Mustang
First World War flight training. *See* RFC Canada
Flexible Response strategy, 26–7, 53, 363, 386
Foulkes, Charles, 42–3, 50, 112–13, 360, 421
French Canadians and the RCAF, 135–6

Gellner, John, 142
Genie air-to-air missile, 93, 100
Gerhart, John, 21, 90, 97
Gibson, Colin, 306, 373–4
gliders, 352–3
Godwin, Harold, 43, 50

Gordon, Walter, 30
Graduate Assistance Program (GAP), 144, 146–7
Green, Howard, 22, 95, 97, 310
Ground Observer Corps, 16, 65–6
Gruenther, Alfred, 49–50
Grumman Albatross (CSR-110), 290, 294–5
Grumman Avenger, 327
Guthrie, K.M., 10–11

H2S radar, 330
Harkness, Douglas, 22, 49, 97–9, 136, 343, 423
Harris, Stephen, 31
Harvard trainer, 159, 171–2, 174, 231, 234, 249
Hawker Sea Furies, 327
helicopters: and Canadian Army, 198–9, 350, 353–68, 384; and Royal Canadian Navy, 199, 252, 334; maintenance of, 199–200; and Auxiliary, 240, 244–5; search and rescue role, 240, 283, 288, 291, 295; antisubmarine role, 334; transport role, 357–8; aeromedical role, 358; reconnaissance role, 355–6, 359–61
Hellyer, Paul: nuclear weapons, 27, 423; aircraft procurement, 29, 388; strike reconnaissance role, 54; unification, 54, 56, 305; and Auxiliary, 245; defence policy, 303, 386, 423–4
Hendrick, Max, 22
Higham, Robin, 31
Hillier 12E helicopter, 244, 361
HMCS *Magnificent* (aircraft carrier), 315, 327
HMCS *Royal Roads*. *See* Royal Roads Military College
HMCS *Warrior* (aircraft carrier), 327
Hodson, Keith, 12, 43–4, 46, 68, 77
Howe, C.D., 111, 120
Howze, Hamilton, 363–4, 367
Hughes, Sam, 2, 153–4
humanitarian relief: and Canadian foreign policy, 252, 299–301; RCAF role, 252, 306–12, 320–1

Imperial Defence College, 130, 420, 423
Imperial Munitions Board, 154
International Civil Aviation Organization (ICAO), 280–1

Jackson, J.I., 68
Jezebel system, 342–3
Johnson, Lyndon B., 27, 86, 100

Kennedy, J.F.K., 26–7, 84, 93–7, 343, 363, 386
Korean War, 9, 13, 20, 40, 65, 107, 111, 282, 286, 304–5, 312–13, 354–5, 357, 371, 376–9, 388, 394
Kuter, Lawrence, 89, 93

Lancaster bomber, 18, 286, 289, 291, 328, 330, 332, 334, 336–7, 422
Lane, R.J., 54, 246–7
Lemnitzer, Lyman L., 55–6
Lewis Leigh, Z., 286–7
Long Range Strategic Plan (RCAF), 304, 333
Louden, T.R., 186

MacBrien, W.R., 64–6
Macdonald, Mariam, 285–6
MacKenzie King, William Lyon, 3, 157–8, 299
Maritime Air Command, 18, 25, 329, 335, 338, 344–6
Maritime Group, 329, 332
maritime patrol aircraft. *See* CP-107 Argus, PV7 Neptune
Massey, Vincent, 158
Massive Retaliation strategy, 26, 363
May, Wilfred Reid "WoP," 278, 286
MB-1 Genie. *See* Genie air-to-air missile
McEwen, C.M., 129
McLin, John B., 93, 96, 99
McNair, R.W., 237–9
McNamara, Robert, 100–1, 363
McNaughton, Andrew, 351–2
medical personnel: doctors in SAR role, 284–5; nurses in SAR role, 285–6
Merchant, Livingston, 97
Mid-Canada Line (MCL), 17, 71–3, 82, 100, 240, 379
Military Air Transport Service (MATS), 13, 376
Miller, Frank, 22, 29, 90, 238, 343
Mobile Command, 30, 199, 247
Mobile Strike Force (MSF), 19, 358, 374, 380, 382, 388

NATO. *See* North Atlantic Treaty Organization
NATO Air Training Plan, 152; established, 161–3; observer training, 163; training schools, 163–6; 171–4; and RAF, 162, 166–7; expansion, 167–8; terminated, 168–9; curriculum, 171; number trained, 174–5; lessons learned from BCATP, 176
NATO Flying Training Program in Canada (NFTC), 176
navigator training, 134, 160–1, 163, 166, 169, 171–4
Nike-Ajax surface-to-air missiles, 256
Nike-Hercules surface-to-air missiles, 87, 256
Nike-Zeus missile defence system, 267
NORAD. *See* North American Aerospace Defence Command
Norstad, Lauris, 21, 42–3, 50
North American Air Defence Command: established, 7, 21, 60, 74–6, 256 ; and Diefenbaker government, 21, 83–4, 93, 95, 98–9, 113–14; US views on, 26; and Pearson government, 27–8, 95–6, 98–100; RCAF-USAF shared culture, 66–7; binational command, 76–7, 419; space surveillance role, 82, 88–91, 261; RCAF air defence role, 82–3, 86, 91–3, 100–1, 116, 120; nuclear weapons and Canada, 83–4, 86, 93–6, 98–9; Soviet missile threat, 86; Cuban Missile Crisis, 96–9, 343; in Canadian defence priorities, 288, 301, 418, 423. *See also* BOMARC; SAGE
North Atlantic Treaty Organization (NATO): St. Laurent government, 9, 15, 40–1; Diefenbaker government, 9, 21–2, 52–3, 99, 116; Pearson government, 9, 27–8, 52–3; strategy, 25, 27, 50, 56, 332–3; Trudeau government, 54–5. *See also* Air Division, No. 1; Allied Tactical Air Force; anti-submarine warfare; NATO Air Training Plan; Supreme Commander Allied Forces Europe
North Atlantic Treaty Organization Air Training Plan. *See* NATO Air Training Plan
nuclear weapons and Canada: Diefenbaker government, 10, 21–2, 50, 52, 56, 83–5, 94–100, 116–17; Pearson government, 10, 27, 52–3, 56, 83, 96, 99–100; Soviet threat, 17, 21, 49, 60–1, 69–72, 77, 89, 97, 115–16, 205–6, 243, 252, 256, 288; Trudeau government, 55. *See also* BOMARC; Genie air-to-air missile
nurses, 13, 205, 207, 285–7

Officer Development Board, 148
Operation AMIGO, 310
Operation ARCHITECT, 236
Operation ATTACHÉ, 286
Operation BLIND TWINKLER, 257
Opération des Nations unies au Congo (ONUC), 29, 311–12, 315, 318, 387
Operation HAWK, 313, 376–7
Operation LOCKSTEP, 236
Operation LOOKOUT, 256
Operation MALLARD. *See also* Opération des Nations unies au Congo (ONUC)
Operation METROPOLIS, 234, 237
Operation NANOOK, 331
Operation NIMBLE, 312
Operation NIMBLE BAT, 379
Operation PHOENIX, 236
Operation RANDOM, 379
Operation RAPID STEP, 315. *See also* United Nations Emergency Force (UNEF)
Operation SEA SPRING, 332
Operation SKYHAWK, 84
Operation SNOWGOOSE. *See also* United Nations Peacekeeping Force in Cyprus (UNFICYP)
operational control of RCAF units: and NORAD, 6, 74–6, 87, 97; and NATO, 6, 15; and USAF, 6, 13, 70–1, 376; and RAF, 6, 15, 41
Orenda Engines Ltd., 109–10, 119, 123

P2V Neptune, 18, 334–9, 342
P-51 Mustang, 13–14, 16, 63, 231, 252
Partridge, Earle, 76–7, 92–3, 419
peacekeeping: Canadian views, 301–3, 314–15, 319; RCAF transport role, 4, 20, 27, 29, 252–3, 299, 303–6, 312, 319–21; Canadian Army role, 252. *See also* Air Transport Command; United Nations
Pearkes, George, 22, 87, 97, 113–14, 116–18
Pearson, Lester B., 10, 25–7, 32, 52–3, 56, 84, 95, 99–100, 120, 299, 301, 303, 308, 314, 376, 386, 423
Perley, George, 154
Permanent Joint Board on Defence (PJBD), 12, 415
pilot training: Training Command, 19–20, 165–6; officer cadets, 134; training program, 163–5, 171–7; United Kingdom, 157, 154–5; Malaysia, 174; Netherlands, 169, 174; Norway, 169, 174; Denmark, 169, 174; Turley, 169–70, 174; Germany, 171; Tanzania, 174; RCAF Auxiliary, 230, 236, 239; Canadian Army, 360. *See also* British Commonwealth Air Training Plan; Canadian Joint Air Training Centre; NATO Air Training Plan; NATO Flying Training in Canada; RFC Canada
Pinetree Line, 17, 71–2, 82, 87, 93, 100–1, 109, 236, 240
Planning Guide for Air Transport Command Participation in UN Operations, 319–20
Post-Hostilities Problems Working Committee, 11, 417
Post War Organization Committee, 11
Power, C.G. "Chubby," 131
Prince Albert Radar Laboratory (PARL), 90, 272

Rabat (Morocco), 47–8
Radar and Communications School (R&CS), 200
RAF Canada. *See* RFC Canada
RAF Staff College, 3, 129–30, 133
RAF Station North Luffenham, 15, 41, 46
RCAF Radio School, 187
RCAF Stations: **Aylmer**, 187–9; **Baden-Solingen**, 43, 46, 52, 55–6; **Bagotville**, 71, 100, **Borden**, 2, 155–6, 165, 183, 188–9, 201, 415, 417–18, 420, 422; **Centralia**, 163, 165, 174, 189–200; **Chatham**, 100; Clinton, 163, 165, 187–8, 200; **Cold Lake**, 90, 261, 263–4, 272; **Comox**, 71, 100, 135, 332, 339; **Edgar**, 216–17; **Greenwood**, 286, 329–30, 332, 335, 338, 343–4; **Grostenquin**, 43, 46–8, 52, 54, 207, 218, 220; **Jericho Beach**, 422; **Lac St. Denis**, 211; **London**, 163–4; **Marville**, 43, 46, 49–51, 54; **Moose Jaw**, 163; **Namao** (Edmonton), 194, 278, 374–5, 380, 420; **North Bay**, 71, 87; **Penhold**, 163; **Portage La Prairie**, 163; **Rockcliffe (Ottawa)**, 193; **Saskatoon**, 163, 174; **St. Hubert**, 66, 71, 238; **St. Sylvestre**, 216; **Summerside**, 163, 336, 338, 344; **Trenton**, 49, 165, 183, 192, 385; **Uplands (Ottawa)**, 71, 193, 415; **Vancouver**, 286; **Whitehorse**, 217; **Zweibrücken**, 44, 46, 52, 223

RCAF Technical and Engineering School, 187
Regular Officer Training Plan (ROTP), 136, 166
Reid, Henry Clarence "Harry," 354–5
Report of the Special Studies Group on Long-Range Objectives for the RCAF, 25, 385
Rescue Coordination Centre (RCC), 282–3, 287, 289–93, 295
Reyno, Edwin, 30
RFC Canada, 2, 152, 154–7, 176, 208–9
Robinson, Basil, 95
Rowley, Roger, 148
Royal Air Force: RCAF–RAF relations, 3, 6, 15, 43, 60, 66–7, 413, 416, 420–1; 1 Air Division bases in UK, 13, 41; pilot training, 157–8, 163, 166–7; army co-operation, 351–2. *See also* British Commonwealth Air Training Plan; RAF Staff College; RFC Canada
Royal Canadian Air Force: budget by year, Annex A; organization charts, Annex A; personnel strength, Annex A; Chief of the Air Staff biographies, Annex B
Royal Canadian Air Force Auxiliary: role, 11, 14–16, 63, 66, 105, 110, 228; strength, 228; air defence role, 229, 231, 234–5; tactical aviation role, 229, 234; radar role, 229, 233–4; ground crew recruiting and retention, 231; transport role, 231; support role, 231; Plan G, 231–2; intelligence role, 234; medical role, 234; technical training, 233–4
Royal Canadian Air Force Radio School, 187
Royal Canadian Air Force Staff College: instructors, 68, 142; RAF influence, 129–30, 133; value of, 104; and Canadian Army, 132, 138; curriculum, 137–9; and Air Force College, 144
Royal Canadian Air Force Staff College Journal, 139–41
Royal Canadian Air Force Staff School, 144–6
Royal Canadian Air Force Technical and Engineering School (Aylmer, ON), 187
Royal Canadian Air Force War Staff Course, 130–3
Royal Canadian Armoured Corps (RCAC), 349, 354, 361
Royal Canadian Army Service Corps (RCASC), 354–5, 357, 361–2

Royal Canadian Electrical and Mechanical Engineers (RCEME), 198–200
Royal Canadian Mounted Police (RCMP), 278, 280–2, 284
Royal Canadian Navy, 4; education of officers, 128, 133; aircraft maintenance, 194–6; and NATO, 327
Royal Flying Corps (RFC), 2, 152–7, 161, 165, 175–6, 183, 207–8
Royal Flying Corps (RFC) Canada. *See* RFC Canada
Royal Military College of Canada (RMC), 128–30, 133–6
Royal Naval Air Service, 2, 153, 155, 157, 414
Royal Naval College, 147
Royal Roads Military College, 133–5

SAGE, 82, 86–7, 210, 244
Satellite Identification Tracking Unit (SITU), 260–1
School of Aeronautical Engineering (AE), 186–7
search and rescue, 4, 251, 304 : Auxiliary role, 240, 242–4, 246; RCAF SAR role, 278–82, 289; RCMP proposed role, 278, 280, 282; technicians, 278, 284–6; debate on SAR responsibility, 280–2; maritime SAR role, 283, 293–4; aircraft, 283–4, 289–92, 295, 328, 330, 383; expanding requirements, 287–9; reports on SAR, 294; helicopters, 295. *See also* Canadian Coast Guard
Second World War flight training. *See* British Commonwealth Air Training Plan
Semi-Automatic Ground Environment. *See* SAGE
Sharp, Mitchell, 55
Simonds, Guy, 43, 111, 357
Slemon, Roy, 12, 22, 28, 138; as CAS, 49, 109, 240, 411, 417–19, 421; and NORAD, 50, 76–7, 92–3
Sound Surveillance System (SOSUS), 342–3, 346
Soviet bomber threat, 60, 123, 214
Space Defence Program (SDP), 266–71
Space Defense Center (SDC-US), 261–3
Space Detection and Tracking System (SPADATS), 90, 261, 263–4
Space Indoctrination Course (SIC), 259
Space Indoctrination Program (SIP), 259–60

space surveillance, NORAD role, 82, 88–90, 257, 261–4
Sparrow II air-to-air missile, 113, 116, 118, 121
Special Study Group on Long Range Objectives for the RCAF (Carpenter Report), 25–7, 385
Squadron (RCAF): **2**, 352; **110**. *See* **400**; **112**, 352; **61**, 48, 51; **137**, 48; **168**, 306–7, 372–3; **400**, 231, 241, 352; **401**, 231, 234, 236, 241; **402**, 231, 234, 240; **403**, 231, 236, 240; **404**, 332, 334–5, 338; **405**, 330–2, 334–5; **406**, 231, 236, 243; **407**, 332, 339; **410**, 41; **411**, 231, 236, 241; **412**, 374, 379, 383; **413**, 46, 367, 374; **414**, 46, 352, 374; **415**, 338; **416**, 46, 236; **417**, 352; **418**, 231, 236, 243; **420**, 236, 240; **421**, 46, 51, 54; **422**, 46, 52; **424**, 240; **426**, 13, 305, 307–10, 312–13, 315, 318, 374–80; **427**, 46, 52; **430**, 46, 51, 54, 352; **434**, 46, 52, 311; **435**, 311, 372–5, 378, 380, 382, 388; **436**, 311, 372–3, 375, 378, 380, 382, 387; **437**, 49, 372–3, 385; **438**, 231, 234, 236, 241; **439**, 41, 51, 53; **441**, 41, 51, 53; **442**, 234, 241; **443**, 241; **444**, 46, 52; **449**, 339, 352–3; **664**, 352; **665**, 352; **666**, 352
squadrons: Canadian squadrons, First World War, 2; Canadian squadrons, Second World War, 3; 400 series, 300
Stedman, Ernest W., 134, 185–6
St. Laurent, Louis: and air power, 6, 9–10; RCAF expansion, 13, 25, 32, 107, 357; defence budget, 27, 111; Avro Arrow, 113, 118, 121; NORAD, 113; search and rescue, 280–1; minister of foreign affairs, 289
Strategic Air Command (SAC), 16–17, 60, 64–5, 67–9, 73, 116, 123
Strother, Dean, 44
Subsidization of Serving Airmen Plan, 136–7
Suez Crisis, 20, 29, 301, 314, 379, 388
Supermarine Seafire, 327
Supply Officers School, 189
Supreme Allied Commander Atlantic (SACLANT), 18, 325
Supreme Allied Commander Europe (SACEUR): RCAF assigned to 4ATAF, 43; Canadian command 1 Air Division, 49–50; strike role 1 Air Division, 50–1, 55; air defence role 1 Air Division, 51, 55; NATO Air Training Plan, 169

Tactical Air Command (TAC): role, 18–20, 386; disbanded, 19, 383
Technical Aeronautical Engineering (Tech AE) School, 189
technical training schools (TTS): No. 1 TTS (Trenton), 183; No. 1 TTS (St. Thomas), 183–5, 187; No. 1 TTS (Aylmer), 188–9; No. 2 TTS (Borden), 183, 188–9
Thor-Agena missile defence system, 167
training aircraft. *See* C-45 Expeditor; DHC-1 Chipmunk; Harvard trainer
Training Command (TC), 19, 144–6, 165, 189, 199, 241, 259, 374, 415
transport planes. *See also* Bristol Freighter; C-47 Dakota; C-119 Flying Boxcar; CC-106 Yukon; CC-108 Caribou; CC-115 Buffalo; CC-130 Hercules; CC-137 Boeing 707; Canadair North Star; de Havilland Comet
Trudeau, Pierre, 30, 54–6
Tu-4 bomber, 49, 61

Uhthoff, J.C., 267, 270
Unification (Canadian Armed Forces), 7, 10, 26–7, 30–1, 147–8, 199–202, 206, 247, 251–2, 274–5, 279, 295, 304, 312, 315, 389, 424
United Nations Emergency Force (UNEF), 20, 301–2, 312–16, 320, 379, 382, 384, 388–9
United Nations Peacekeeping Force in Cyprus (UNFICYP), 305, 315, 387
United Nations Relief and Rehabilitation Administration (UNRRA), 300
United Nations Security Force (UNSF) in New Guinea, 315–17, 319
United Nations Yemen Observer Mission (UNYOM), 315–17
United Polish Relief Fund (UPRF), 301, 306
United States Air Force (USAF): and RCAF alignment, 6, 12–13, 15, 43, 46, 66–8, 83, 421; and RCAF space program, 258–61. *See also* North American Air Defence Command; Strategic Air Command
United States Northeast Command (USNEC), 69–71, 74
University Reserve Training Plan, 136–6

Vertol 107 helicopter, 243–5, 359, 361

Wait, George, 129, 131–3, 137–8, 329
Walker, Willa, 209
War Assets Corporation, 329
Western Air Command, 374
White Paper on Defence (1964), 27–9, 100, 267, 270–1, 302–3, 319, 371, 386–9, 423
Whiting, R.B., 30
Why Air Forces Fail, 32
Women's Division, 104, 205, 209
women in the RCAF: general, 104–5; authorized level, 206; retention, 206–7; recruiting, 206–7, 210–11; pay, 209; trades, 209; as Fighter Control Operators, 210–11, 216; documentaries about, 211; and marriage, 214–18; attrition, 216–18

www.ingramcontent.com/pod-product-compliance
Lightning Source LLC
Chambersburg PA
CBHW051358070526
44584CB00023B/3207